Harvard Studies in Cultural Anthropology, 3

General Editors
David Maybury-Lewis
Stanley J. Tambiah
Evon Z. Vogt, Jr.
Nur Yalman

The Harvard Studies in Cultural Anthropology is founded in the belief that answers to general questions about the human condition may be discovered through the intensive study of other cultures. The series will publish books that elucidate and interpret cultural systems in order to contribute to comparative understanding.

IRAN

From Religious Dispute to Revolution

Michael M. J. Fischer

HARVARD UNIVERSITY PRESS
Cambridge, Massachusetts
and London, England
1980

Library of Congress Cataloging in Publication Data

Fischer, Michael M   J   1946-
  Iran: from religious dispute to revolution.

  (Harvard studies in cultural anthropology; 3)
  Bibliography: p.
  Includes index.

  1. Shiites—Iran.   2. Islam and politics—
Iran.   3. Iran—Politics and government—1941-1979.
4. Iran—Religious life and customs.   I. Title.
II. Series.
BP192.7.I68F57   301.5'8   79-24330
ISBN 0-674-46615-2 (cloth)
ISBN 0-674-46617-9 (paper)

To the warm, courageous, and complex people of Iran, and to my parents and our intellectual and religious traditions

Preface

*O*NE OF THE GREAT PUZZLES for anthropologists and philosophers is how and why culture and common sense are differently constituted in different historical times and in different
societies. Today in Iran both culture and common sense are undergoing
change. This book examines that transformation, particularly the part
played by religion. The focus is on religious education, both learned and
popular, and its function in molding character and thereby reinforcing
the common sense. This function is what the Greeks called *paideia*, and
what today we might call the anthropology of education, taking "education" in its broadest sense. Paideia, or the anthropology of education,
should include a series of questions critical to understanding how common sense changes: intellectual questions (about the organization of
culture, the filiation and sponsorship of ideas), sociological questions
(about the interest groups and power relations that cause ideas to succeed
or be popular at one time rather than another; about the recruitment,
training, and employment of culture carriers), and historical questions
(about the reorganization of culture through new goals and new institutions).

The contemporary change in Iran exhibits parallels to and differences
from modern European and American history. The parallels lie in the
challenge of science and technology to religious fundamentalism and in
the changes in social consciousness encouraged by modern education and
a more modern class structure or division of interest groups. The differences result from the suppression of the Constitional Revolution at the
turn of the century and a return, from 1925 to 1978, to an authoritarian,
albeit modernizing, monarchy, as well as from a still very underdevel-
oped industrial economy and a demographic explosion. This last means
an infusion into the national political arena of a very young population

imbued with a popular religious culture and an enthusiastic attitude toward modern technology. The young people coming into the modern labor market from the villages and towns of Iran, literate and with modern education, retain a profound respect for Islamic morals and tradition, if not necessarily for the scholasticism of their religious leaders. Their cultural identity is rooted in the past, their vision turns toward the future.

The social and cultural contradictions and tensions of modern Iran were dramatically catapulted into international attention by the 1977-1979 revolution, which ousted the Pahlavi dynasty. The revolution drew on two legacies: the repeated attempts at a bourgeois revolution (1905, 1952), and the repeated use of religiously phrased protest. The factions joining in the revolution disagreed sharply over the ultimate goals and definitions deriving from the Islamic and secular legacies. It is particularly with the religious legacy that this book is concerned, and more generally with the transformation of the Islamically informed consciousness of the majority of Iranians.

The town of Qum is the focus of study because it is Iran's university town for religious leaders. Even if much of what is taught there is denigrated by some of the youth as scholasticism, it is nonetheless the central reference point for the elaboration of other interpretations of Islam held by the various segments of the population. Chapters 3 through 5 of this book have circulated since 1976 under the title "The Qum Report." They remain essentially as written at that time: a portrayal of pre-1978 Iranian Shi'ism under a monarchy that tried to repress it. Qum has a particular mystique. It is a repository of the Shi'ite tradition, a center of conservatism rejected by many Iranians and lauded by others; and it served as a focus of opposition to the shah on moral grounds. The atmosphere of Qum in 1975 was one of siege and courageous hostility to a state perceived to be the stronger, but morally corrupt, opponent. The ambience was picturesquely and symbolically marked in the garb of past centuries still worn by the religious leaders: the turban, beard, *qaba* and *'aba* (under- and over-cloaks), and open-heeled slippers. Under Reza Shah Pahlavi (1925-1941) this traditional dress was forbidden to all except the clergy, in part a concession and in part a marking for slow destruction of what Reza Shah found backward and repugnant. The research on which The Qum Report is based was conducted in Iran during 1975 as part of the Islam and Social Change Project of the University of Chicago, under the direction of Professors Leonard Binder and Fazlur Rahman. Funding was provided by a Ford Foundation grant. Professor Shahrough Akhavi, a research partner in Iran, is preparing a complementary volume.

In 1977 chapters 1 and 2 were added and the title was changed to "Persian Paideia" to focus attention not only on the traditional education system of the madrasa (Islamic seminary or college), which is rooted in a common tradition with our own Western traditions, but also on Shi'ism as a moral tradition, as a nationalist tradition, and as a pedagogy of the oppressed. Its powerful psychological ambivalences—the dialectic between reliance on both reason and faith, between adoration and hatred of the West, between assertion of dignity and fear of inferiority—is not unlike the similar economic, psychological, and cultural dominations analyzed by Frantz Fanon, Abdullah Laroui, O. Mannoni, and Albert Memmi. That paideia is a Greek rather than a Persian word was appropriate to the long-standing debate between Iran and the West, honored in the madrasa curriculum through the continued study of the peripatetic philosophers and the response found to them in the Persian mystical philosophies of illuminationism (*ishraqi*). (The title was as well a tribute and an aspiration to emulate in a small way Werner Jaeger's magisterial *Paideia: The Ideals of Greek Culture.*)

In February 1979 chapter 6 was added to sketch the Shi'ite symbolic structure of the revolution. Fuller studies of the revolution will be needed in the future to sift out the many enigmas and premature interpretations behind what has been watched on television by a fascinated world. One thing is reasonably certain: Iran will continue to be a model, in the 1980s as it has been in the 1970s, for thinking about the developing world. In the 1970s the country was a major test case for modernization theory. It was the case where the constraint of capital theoretically was removed and which therefore was thought to have the best chance of relatively rapid transformation from a third-world country into the modern industrial first world. Many reasons will be adduced for the failure of this model in Iran. Among them are what I have playfully called the "oriental despotism paradox": the contradiction between using top-down "directed social change" to speed development and protect against reaction, and the local level initiative and commitment on which self-sustained growth eventually depends. The paradox is trying to suppress and stimulate local initiative at the same time. Oil revenues essentially made the government independent of any need to be directly responsive to its citizenry. In the 1980s Iran will continue to be a major test case of conditions of rapid social change and demographic explosion (half the population is under seventeen), where people feel themselves oppressed by an alien culture or world economy and use their traditional religious and cultural heritage as a vehicle of moral protest. What is at issue is the construction or reconstruction of a meaningful world in which people do not feel devalued by an alien culture, but can feel a sense of continuity with their own past and feel proud of their identity.

My interest in going to Qum grew out of an earlier research project in the town of Yazd during 1969-1971, a crucible of four major religious traditions of Iran: Zoroastrianism, Judaism, Bahaism, and Islam. In describing those four groups of people and their traditions, I wanted further to pursue Iranian Shi'ism to one of its pedagogical centers—as I had pursued Zoroastrianism to Bombay, Surat and Nausari in India—

not only because Islam was a multilayered and complex tradition, which could reward a lifetime's study, but primarily because Shi'ism was a powerful social force passively mobilized against the shah and critical to any understanding of the future social dynamics of Iran at the local level. The empirical field report, "Zoroastrian Iran between Myth and Praxis" (Fischer 1973), dealt with all four groups; the title was intended to underscore the construction of Iranian identity from its roots in a pre-Islamic Zoroastrian empire to its aspirations for the future. Religion, I had been trained to believe, provided a reservoir of symbolic terms people could use to create a meaningful world. Despite the powerful currents and antagonisms, Yazd and Iran in 1970 were symbolically stagnant: it was a world of myth not action. *Praxis,* Aristotle's term popularized by Marx, was an action which changed its agent, as opposed to *poesis* (of which *mythos* was one form), a fabrication which leaves agent and object separate. In 1970 Iran was poised for praxis. To be sure there was social change, and the shah attempted to elevate the Zoroastrian heritage into a nationalist symbolism, but the Islamic clergy (*ulama*) effectively blocked it from becoming a mobilizing vehicle: it was merely myth. In 1977-1979 an Islamic praxis began; wherever it leads it will probably leave Iranian Muslims and Shi'ism, as well as Iran, changed. The new constitution calls for territorial integrity, Islamic brotherhood of all men, political and economic unification of all Muslims, and establishment of Ja'fari or Twelver Shi'ite Islam—as well as other goals of social justice and internal organization: enough contradictions to generate lively debate for some time to come.

Many people have helped in the preparation of this study and in formulating my thinking. Special thanks are owed to my research assistant, Mehdi Abedi, a member of the young revolutionary generation, who in the final three months of the field work guided me expertly through the thickets of Shi'ism and the social networks of the ulama. He is responsible for much of my enthusiastic appreciation for Islam, an appreciation he had encouraged five years earlier during the previous field work in Yazd. Needless to say, although he served as a crucial soundingboard and helped mold my perceptions, he cannot be held responsible for my mistakes and misapprehensions. All of the Persian and Arabic texts and writings referred to have been translated with his help (and commentary).

Appreciation is owed to various helpful people in the Iranian Ministry of Science and Higher Education, in the several city and provincial agencies in Qum, and in the Office of Religious Endowments in Tehran and Qum, especially the staff in Qum who helped me circumvent the red-tape obstructions of their superiors.

Above all, this research could never have been pursued without the aid of the establishments of the three maraji'-i taqlid in Qum: Ayatullah Sayyid Mohammad-Kazem Shariatmadari, Ayatullah Sayyid Shahabuddin Marashi-Najafi, and Ayatullah Sayyid Mohammad-Reza Golpayegani. I am particularly indebted for the kind personal help I received from the first two and from Ayatullah Naser Makarem, Sayyid Hadi Khosrowshahi, Shaykh Mortaza Haeri-Yazdi, and Sayyid Shamin us-Sibtain Rizvi.

For help on various parts of the manuscript, I am grateful to Shahrough Akhavi, Said Arjomand, Mangol Bayat-Philip, Anne Betteridge, Leonard Binder, Michele de Angelis, Dale Eickelman, Shmuel Eisenstadt, Byron and Mary Jo Good, William Graham, Nikki Keddie, Muhsin Mahdi, Margaret Mills, Jacques Waardenburg, Nur Yalman, and Marvin Zonis. My understanding of events described in chapter 6 and the epilogue gained much from numerous discussions with Ervand Abrahamian. To anthropologists and linguists, especially to Mary Catherine Bateson and William Beeman, my apologies for not sticking fast to a transcription of Persian as it is spoken. Because the subject matter has direct linkages to Arabic, the language of the Qur'an and of religious scholarship, it was decided to use a transliteration. Contemporary names have been left as Persians normally transliterate rather than according to the scholarly system — Taleghani rather than Taleqani — with some exceptions for consistency: thus Khomeyni because shaykh rather than shaikh is used. For help with the transliteration I am indebted beyond adequate words to Wheeler Thackston, Jr. Full diacriticals, for reasons beyond our control, are preserved only in the glossary. Nonspecialists should be forewarned that some of the diacriticals are crucial: rawda is pronounced rawza.

Elaine Akhavi, in her passionate and intensely vital way, desperately wanted to share with Iranian Muslims the similar struggles which many East European Jews underwent in the last two generations. I hope this book, which she was not able to live to see, contributes to the dialogue she envisioned and conveys the sense of experiential reality she sought to capture in her art. I treasure her enthusiasm for chapter 3 of this book and her comment: "Don't let them make you change a word."

Finally and most importantly, two models and mentors have inspired and sustained me intellectually as well as emotionally for many years. In a number of ways, what follows about logic and validation, about history and social differentiation, and about liberalism and religious meaning grows out of a deep and continuing dialogue with a geographer and historian, and with a mathematician and geodesist: my parents, Eric and Irene Fischer.

Cambridge, Massachusetts   M.M.J.F.
Muharram 1400/1979

Contents

Illustrations

Figures

Tables

Chronology of Significant Dynasties

	Muslim Dates (A.H.)	Christian Dates (A.D.)
Pre-Islamic		
Achaemenians (Cyrus to Alexander)		558 B.C.-331 B.C.
Sassanians (Ardashir to Yazdigird III)		224-651
Early Islamic		
Rashidun (first four Sunni caliphs)	11-40	632-661
Umayyads	41-132	661-750
Abbasids	132-656	750-1258
Twelve Imams (Shi'ite)	11-260	632-872
Buyids (Shi'ite)	320-447	932-1055
Seljuks and Il-Khanids (Sunni)	429-754	1037-1353
Iran since establishment of Shi'ism as the state religion		
Safavids	907-1135	1501-1722
Afshars and Zands	1148-1210	1736-1795
Qajars	1200-1342	1785-1925
Pahlavis	1342-1399	1925-1979
Reza Shah (1925-1941)		
Mohammad Reza Shah (1941-1979)		

Calendars

Anno Hejirae or *Qamari* ("lunar"): the Islamic calendar, dated from the morning after the withdrawal (*hijra*) of the Prophet Muhammad from Mecca to Medina on July 14, A.D. 622. The year 1975 was A.H. 1395 or 1395 Q. The months are Muharram, Safar, Rabi' ol-avval, Rabi' os-sani, Jomadi ol-avval, Jomadi os-sani, Rajab, Sha'ban, Ramadan, Shavval, Zol-qa'da, Zol-hejja.

Shamsi ("solar"): the Iranian civil calendar, derived from the pre-Islamic Zoroastrian calendar, beginning each year on March 21. The year 1975 was 1353-54 Sh. The months are Farvardin, Ordebehesht, Khordad, Tir, Mordad, Sharivar, Mehr, Aban, Azar, Dey, Bahman, Esfand.

The New or Atabegi Courtyard, built in 1883, of the Shrine of Fatima, Hadrat-i Ma'suma, sister of the eighth Imam. Nobles and ministers of the Qajar dynasty are buried along the sides. Entry to the shrine is through the mirrored portal and under the gold dome. The present dome was constructed under the Safavids and gilded by the Qajars. Four Safavid shahs are buried in a mosque behind the main shrine, as are three leaders of the Qum center of learning. Behind that mosque is the new A'zam or Borujerdi Mosque, a major teaching space for the highest level of study, the *dars-i kharij*. Two Qajar shahs are buried to the right of the shrine in the Old Courtyard, behind which are two more courtyards, turned by the Safavids into the Madrasas Dar al-Shifa and Faydiyya, centers of political activity in 1963, 1975, and 1977-1979. See diagram, page 110.

1

Culture, History, and Politics

> Do not step on a Persian carpet
> or a mulla for it increases its
> value.
> —Persian proverb

*A*N ANTHROPOLOGIST is as much a character in the arena of research as the people from whom he tries to learn. Recognizing this fact is important to readers of an anthropological analysis because of its bearing on the objectivity, validity, and comprehensiveness of the description from which the analysis proceeds. More important, any interchange between anthropologist and respondent—the questions posed, the answers supplied—constitutes a micro-model of how culture is constructed. Compare, for instance, an encounter I had with a teacher in a madrasa in Isfahan in 1975 with one between a Christian and a Muslim in the eighth century as reconstructed by H. A. Wolfson.

I sat down in Madrasa Jada Buzurg. A couple of mullas immediately came to ask who I was and to sit and debate. Aqa Hajj Mohammad Beheshti then came and took over, aided by a younger man, Mulla Abdullah Said Sharifi. A crowd gathered. They kept pressing me on the absurdity of the Trinity: three is one and one is three. While pointing out that I did not believe in the Trinity I tried to suggest, first, that religious language is symbolic, that is, it has multiple meanings, and requires exegesis—to which they agreed; second, that man's limited mind cannot describe God—to which they agreed; and, third, that the Trinity is a formula for God's mystery—which they rejected. They insisted that any division into two already implies division into three, five, nine, seventeen, and so on: two fingers are divided by a space and thus are three things, three things are made distinct by two more divisions (and so are five), five by four (making nine), nine by eight (seventeen). In other words, anything but the unity of God implies polytheism, Hinduism, idolatry. I could not resist asking jocularly what was wrong with polytheism—all aspects of the world are divine. More seriously,

1

however, I countered by refusing to allow implication of the sort they were using, maintaining that the Trinity is simply a formula for God's mystery, and scored my only minor triumph by interrupting Aqa Beheshti at one point to say, "Look, it is you who keep insisting on the phrase 'God is three'; I say he is one!" Everyone laughed. Afterwards we three debaters shared a watermelon and agreed to meet under more quiet circumstances — there were well over fifty students crowded around — to discuss more fully.

Obviously, the argument could not proceed in any but a trivial way until I learned more of the tradition of argumentation invoked against me. Upon my return from Iran, I discovered that Wolfson (1976: 129-131) provides a clue that, had I been able to employ it at the time, might have shifted the debate to a deeper plane than that of monotheism and polytheism or the absurdity in ordinary common sense of "three is one." The clue is this: argumentation about the Trinity derives from the Greek neoplatonic triads of being (*esse*), living (*vita*), and reason (*logos, intelligentia*). This Greek tradition conditioned the controversy in Islam, Christianity, and Judaism over the attributes of God. In tracing the development of the controversy, Wolfson sketches a "typical debate between a Christian and a Muslim," drawing on the *Disputatio Christiani et Saraceni* of John of Damascus (d. ca. 754):

> The Christian presumably begins by explaining that . . . in the Trinitarian formula . . . by Father is meant what is generally referred to by both Christians and Muslims as God, and by Son and Holy Spirit are meant the properties life and knowledge or life and power or knowledge and power. Turning then to the Muslim, the Christian asks him if he has any objection to the Christian application of these properties to God. Immediately, the Muslim answers that he has no objection, adding that the Koran explicitly describes God as "the living" (*al-hayy*), as "the knowing" (*al-'alim*), and as "the powerful" (*al-qadir*) (Sura 2:256, Sura 2:30, Sura 30:53).

The Christian then establishes that these hypostases are distinct from the essence of God but inseparable from it. The Muslim finds nothing in the Qur'an to contradict this. The Christian then wishes to call anything that is "eternal" God, and prove these three Gods are but one God. The Muslim cites the Qur'an (Sura 5:77) against this: "They surely are infidels who say, God is the third of three, for there is no God but one God."

Wolfson's sketch is but a variation of my encounter.[1] Would that I had been able to sketch out for Aqa Beheshti the history of the debates over the attributes of God and perhaps even included the Nestorian reworking of the Trinity, which is more in accordance with Muslim formulations!

For the present purpose, however, my anecdote not only shifts the burden of ignorance onto me but raises the question of how we use assumptions and metacommunications (commentaries about the form or level of messages). From a contemporary Western point of view, Aqa Beheshti is the quaintly ignorant one. Language philosophy or the use of metalinguistic analysis ("The Trinity is but a formula for the mystery of God") to establish a common ground for the comparison of different belief systems has not yet been learned in the madrasas of Iran. To us, the mullas appear at times backward and literalist: they have not yet learned of Ludwig Wittgenstein or J. L. Austin, of Wilhelm Dilthey or Alfred Schutz. At other times they are as sophisticated as we, in, for instance, finding multiple levels of meaning in poetic metaphors and in analyzing the rhetoric of Islamic discourse. The problems arise at the boundaries of belief systems or in the comparison of belief systems. To them, it is we who are ignorant: secularists who do not understand what was distinctive and essential to Christian doctrine.

Another element in the encounter is the political need to convince the other. The mullas feel themselves engaged in a life-and-death defense of the coherence, rationality, and integrity of a culture under seige. For us, the use of metalinguistic analysis is a sine qua non for genuine cross-cultural communication and thus for global modernization; otherwise we are each locked into the limited cultural frames of our accidental and different backgrounds. The tragedy of the mullas is that they would be able to defend their heritage much more effectively if they could make use of the tools of linguistic analysis.

The mullas, of course, are simply wrong when they argue that there is a simple, unambiguous "essence" to Christian doctrine. Western journalists have shown themselves to be similarly wrong and ignorant in their coverage of the 1977-1979 Iranian revolution when they expected the slogan "Islamic republic" to refer to an unambiguous catalogue of doctrines and rules for behavior. Doctrines, interpretations, even general perspectives or world views, are defined in terms of contrasts to alternatives held by political competitors; thus they always have a historical context. This does not mean there is not also an internal logical structure to beliefs and ideologies. Both the internal logic and the external defining contrastive features go into the construction of a distinctive culture or cultural form.

We need to examine, at least briefly, these three basic terms of analysis: culture, history, and politics.

Culture, Common Sense, and Symbolic Structures

"Culture" is the term American anthropologists have long used to label their distinctive object of study. What culture is, how it is constructed, and how one can capture it for study and analysis are major problems that have undergone refinement over the past century. The effort has been to combine what the nineteenth-century Germans called the "human sciences" (*Geisteswissenschaften*), a historical-linguistic approach, with the criteria of objectivity and validation appropriate to science. In the European tradition this goal is usually referred to as the objectivity of socially constituted intersubjective worlds, or simply inter-subjectivity, in which even knowledge of oneself is achieved through publicly accessible semantic categories.[2] In other words, an individual's subjective experiences are in large part, if not entirely, formulated by his social participation, by his use of language, and by his use of cultural symbols. Insofar as communications between individuals are understood or have agreed-on meanings, those communications are public and objective and available (at least theoretically) for analysis. Viewing culture as relatively crystallized communication patterns with longer duration than messages repeated only a few times makes the notion of culture highly dynamic. Individuals have different positions in society, different perceptions, interests, and roles. Out of the negotiations and conflicts among them emerges a plural social universe in which many opposed outlooks may coexist and compete.

Two of the most interesting portions of culture are symbolic structures and common sense. Symbols (as the term is used here) contrast with signs and metaphors: a sign is a relation between a word or other signal and one reference or meaning; a metaphor establishes a relation between two meanings; a symbol usually has more than two references.[3] One of the important objectives in dealing with symbolic structures (sets of inter-related symbols) is to control the complex resonances that a particular symbol, action, or statement has for the actor or speaker.

Shi'ism, the established form of Islam in Iran, and its several forms of expression, such as preachments, passion plays, and the curricula and debates of the madrasa, can be viewed as cultural forms composed of symbolic structures. Within this perspective Islam is not a set of doctrines that can be simply catalogued. It is a "language," used in different ways by different actors in order to persuade their fellows, to manipulate situations, and to achieve mastery, control, or political position. There are in Iran at least four main styles of using Shi'ism: the popular religion of the villages and bazaars; the scholarly religion of the madrasas or colleges where the religious leaders are trained; the mystical counterculture of Sufism; and the privatized, ethical religion of the upper classes. One might add as a fifth style, the combination of the second and fourth, which Dr. Ali Shariati's followers have argued is the ideology of the 1977-1979 revolution.

More subtle than symbolic structures but just as important is common sense, often thought of as the underlying assumptions of everyday life. The rhetoricians of classical times defined common sense as the right way of talking about things: one feels satisfaction, competence, and aesthetic closure from saying things right. But that satisfaction is bought at the price of constraint on individual creativity: the individual may make some statements or assertions, or propose some ideas, that the culture or community finds ill-formed, repugnant, ugly, or untrue; and the individual either yields or is perceived as deviant. What is puzzling and what presents a challenge to anthropological explanation is why constraints are placed where they are. Why do the Aqa Beheshtis of the world accept certain kinds of argument and not others?

Perhaps the most interesting example of the shifting of the boundaries of common sense in Iran is to be found in the speeches and writings of Dr. Ali Shariati, the hero of Iran's youth in the 1970s and one of the patron saints, as it were, of the 1977-1979 revolution. Shariati attempted to bridge the gap between traditional Shi'ism and contemporary sociology. In the 1970s, when he was still alive and reformulating his positions, he found that he had to constantly shift his formulations toward conformity with those of the traditional clergy. After his death, and during the revolution, his teachings were appropriated by the more progressive wing of the religious movement, although a close reading of his texts with reference to the practical political questions of the day reveals that they were quite conservative. Indeed the the striking contrast between Shariati and culturally analogous figures in the 1930s and 1940s who also wished to purify Shi'ism and make it consonant with modern life raises the question of why such a figure had to be less secular in the 1970s than a generation earlier. (The answer has less to do with religious revivalism and more to do with the suppression of open political discourse by the Pahlavi regime, which forced politics into a religious idiom.)

The reorganization of culture, it should be clear, is an elusive quarry to try to pin down for study. Several accounts of religion and political conflict in Iran have been written, including an earlier effort of my own.[4] To say that most of them fail to convey accurately the nuances of religious sensibility and its transformation would be imprecise and ungrateful, for without those efforts this one would have been much more difficult. The problem has been partly theoretical—failure to use a sufficiently rich concept of culture—and partly a matter of method, that is, of presenting description in such a way as to allow the reader to see the sources of validation of generalizations. Modern historians and Orientalists studying Iran tend to spend as much time in the country as do anthropologists; yet there is often a curious difference in flavor in the writings of those whose myopia is focused on the written word, on piecing together documentary fragments of a past reality, and those whose myopia is focused on oral expression, on the nuances of reference, social allusion, and style, which make up the rich web of lived-in experience.

A minor example may illustrate. In recent years it has become popular for Orientalists and historians to claim that according to Shi'ite doctrine all temporal states are illegitimate.[5] This (false) claim they then use to ex-

plain why the religious leaders have a proud record of public opposition
to state tyranny, including the participation of many (but significantly
not all) in the Constitutional Revolution (1905-1911). The legitimacy of
any given ruler has always been the subject of political discussion by
Shi'ite religious leaders. All agree that were an Imam manifest in the
world,[6] he would be the only legitimate ruler. According to traditional
Shi'ite interpretation (modified, as we shall see, by the reinterpretation of
the followers of Shariati), the last Imam went into occultation in the
ninth century (he is not dead, merely not manifest in the world); hence,
Muslims are faced with the obligation to live as best they can by the
Qur'an and its principles of doing good and avoiding evil.[7] Any state that
attempts to govern according to Islam is therefore accorded a degree of
legitimacy. The religious leaders claim a right, based simply on study and
knowledge of Islamic law, to advise and guide. When a ruler goes wrong,
it is the responsibility of any knowledgeable Muslim to say so. What
Shi'ites reject is the legitimacy of the caliphate[8] or of blanket divine-right
claims of the sort that the Safavid and Qajar kings asserted with their
title "God's Shadow on Earth."[9] In other words, kings should not be
followed blindly, but that does not necessarily mean that whatever kings
or other temporal governments do is illegitimate and wrong.

According to the followers of Shariati, an Imam is a charismatic figure
who arises out of the people and expresses the general will. For Shariati
himself this is only a translation of the traditional theological term, Imam, into the Weberian sociological category, charismatic leader. For the
revolutionaries of 1977-1979, however, a problematic logic allows them
to apply the title Imam to Ayatullah Ruhullah Musavi Khomeyni, the
symbolic leader of the revolution and the charismatic leader who expresses the popular will. How far infallible knowledge, an attribute of
the theological Imam, is to be accorded Khomeyni remains to be resolved. Khomeyni himself, while never denying the title Imam, has his
official portraits carefully captioned "Nayib al-Imam" (Aide to the Imam). Moreover, Imam in Arabic usage among Shi'ites in Iraq and
Lebanon—but not in pre-revolutionary Persian usage—is a proper title
for leaders of a religious community as an extension of the term of
reference for a prayer leader (imam).

There are two reasons, one political and one cultural, for objecting to
the Orientalists' facile generalization that Shi'ism doctrinally denies
legitimacy to all temporal governments. Politically, the objection is important because though the religious leaders (the ulama) would like to
appropriate a monopoly on learning and moral guidance, doctrinally
they cannot do so, except in the trivial sense that anyone who studies
Islamic law is a religious leader ('*alim*). This means that a king or other
government can wage a moral battle against the ulama on the grounds
that the ulama have perverted Islam—for example, by misappropriating

religious endowment funds, by blind traditionalism, and by self-interested political activities (charges used by both the Pahlavi regime and by Shariati followers against the majority of the ulama) — while the government has been attempting to implement such Islamic values as equality, social justice, and economic opportunity. When used by the Pahlavi kings the argument was not persuasive, but under other circumstances it could be.

Culturally, the objection to the Orientalist generalization is important insofar as historians often selectively pick out rhetorical items in religious preachments to support their claims about the illegitimacy of any temporal government. Accounts such as that by A. K. S. Lambton (1964: 120-121) of Ayatullah Khomeyni's opposition in 1963 to the shah's White Revolution stress Khomeyni's use of words like *zulm* (hurt, oppression, injustice) and *'adalat* (justice) and his comparison of the shah to Yazid (according to Shi'ites, the archtyrant and transgressor against Islam). Lambton seems to suggest that *zulm* is such a loaded term that Khomeyni would use it only to indicate that quite suddenly "injustice had passed all reasonable bounds," and that Khomeyni's comparison of the shah to Yazid was so provocative that "the government had no choice but action." Although not in itself incorrect, Lambton's presentation is overstated. What is missing is the specific flavors that such terms and comparisons hold for believers. I will develop the notion of a Karbala paradigm (Yazid was the villain at the Battle of Karbala) in order to explore these flavors and how certain terms come to be emotionally charged.

Zulm, for instance, is not just contemporary tyranny. It gains its rhetorical power in circumstances like those of 1963 because it expresses an existential, almost cosmic, situation which at certain times sheds its vague general truth value and becomes an exact description of contemporary events. In Shi'ite rhetoric, Muslims have since the time of the Battle of Karbala been subjects of oppression and injustice. (Unless otherwise indicated, "Muslim" always means a Twelver or Ja'fari Shi'ite, a spiritual descendant of those who opposed Yazid, one who continues to uphold the ideals of the first and third Imams, 'Ali and Husayn.) 'Adalat, the term for justice, also has several meanings depending on context; when used as a criterion of being a king or other office holder (including being a religious leader), it means in part the equipoise of Greek philosophy to which Lambton refers (1962, 1964): that is, finding compromises between conflicting interests, balancing just causes, coordinating the various impetuses to good ends. But 'adalat has a narrower theological formulaic definition: never having committed any major sin (such as adultery) and trying to avoid the minor sins (such as shaving or dressing like a non-Muslim). In other words, behind these more or less critical terms lies a structure of thought full of traditional formulas, standardized metaphors, allusions, and implications, which are taught in the madrasas and are familiar to Shi'ite believers but so far have not been tapped for English readers.

My aspiration is to tease out this structure of thought. This aspiration is more than a wish for ever more rich detail, or "thick description."[10] To understand a cultural form requires an appreciation of its internal symbolic structure, its historical boundaries, its sociological boundaries, and its lines of cleavage or change. The Shi'ism of the Qum madrasas is a medieval religious structure, a symbolic structure, quite similar to medieval Catholicism and the Judaism of not so long ago. To say that some kind of epistemological revolution separates this medieval world view and the modern perspective is nothing new. But to have it be more than self-congratulation, to specify what is meant, what is systematically different, one needs first of all to describe the medieval perspective and its sources of validity, some of which are intellectual and some institutional. One needs to describe rhetorical frames of meaning, such as the Karbala paradigm, how they are elaborated, and how the elaborations become either beautiful arabesques of mental agility or sterile scholastic exercises. Their validity is demonstrated insofar as members of the community will correct those who try to change the formulation or interpretation. Such frames of meaning exert a certain intellectual force in a community, even over those who are critical but must communicate with others; as long as they are central to discourse, they constitute part of everyday common sense. There are always critical minds, dissidents, unbelievers, people with different backgrounds; these people are held in check by social constraints until they become sufficiently numerous or powerful to break away from, or to erode, the previous common sense. Schools like the madrasas are more than places where people learn the frames of meaning in their fullest and most coherent form: the schools are themselves political arenas in which success is demonstrated by ability to use the frames.

In sum, the current anthropological notion of culture involves sensitive elicitation of native conceptualizations; attention to language as a medium of social activity; analysis of action as skilled performances which are episodic, are interpreted retrospectively, have results that are not always intended, and are embedded in sociocultural structures over which the individual has little control. Culture is dynamic, with symbolic structures that grow and decay through repetition and the addition of meanings to symbols, or through the reduction of polysemic symbols into mere signs. This dynamism requires sociological and historical context for comprehension.

History, Politics, and the Sociology of Iranian Islam

The transforming of Shi'ite sensibilities is an emotionally charged battle. It is perhaps no more tense than the similar struggles, which the Germans called the *Kulturkampf*, in the West during the eighteenth and nineteenth centuries, but those battles are by and large behind us.[11] The political struggle over religion in Iran has at least two dimensions: a class dimension and a related but separate dimension of state control.

Under Mohammed Reza Pahlavi (1941-1978) the state—a neo-patrimonial form of monarchy relying heavily on built-in rivalries, overlapping responsibilities in the bureaucracy, and secret police terror to concentrate power at the top[12]—attempted to control or neutralize religion, while the religious leaders struggled to preserve a narrowing sphere of autonomy. The struggle between the state and the religious authorities becomes highly subtle and interesting as soon as one realizes that the relative success of the state in suppressing overt political opposition and critical discussion made religion the primary idiom of political protest.

Religious opposition to the aggressively modernizing state was not simple fanatic adherence to outworn ideologies of a bygone era, as the shah would have liked one to believe. Much was valid in the religious opposition. The tragedy was that it was difficult to separate valid criticism of oppressive state interference from reflexive traditionalism. The effect of suppressing political discourse was that arguments became diffuse and fuzzy. Generalized alienation against the state was heightened by the religious discourse, without much creative thinking about social change. To be clear and fair, the point is not that there was no creative thinking about social affairs—given the repression, a surprising number of courageous and stubborn innovative thinkers persisted in being vocal in public. Rather, as the Iranian educated classes argued, there could have been much more creative thought, it could have been more incisive and constructive, and it could have had a broader social base had the state been less repressive.

A case in point is that of higher education in Iran.[13] Refusal to allow the teaching of social science as a relevant set of policy sciences, or to allow university people in general to debate the course of social development, meant a highly disaffected student body and intelligensia. The state, however, needed people trained in policy making. The solution was to train much of its technocratic elite abroad.

The Shi'ism of political protest within this patrimonial state was not an undifferentiated form. Different social classes constructed different ideologies from a common religious grounding. Three broad ideological orientations will be considered: those of the secularized educated middle and upper classes, the traditionally educated religious students, and the popular folk. For an understanding of the common religious grounding, the learning of the religious students is pivotal. The religious center of Qum has itself been an arena of combat between the religious leaders and the state with its middle-class allies.

There were few heroes in this combat as it existed in 1975. The middle classes (professionals, bureaucrats, technocrats), particularly in Qum, were bitter opponents of the religious leaders, viewing them as ignorant and reactionary, manipulative misleaders of the masses. On the other hand, there was sympathy for the religious leaders as representatives of the personal heritage of members of the middle classes, many of whose grandfathers had been religious leaders. But for the modern middle classes, heritage is something to build upon and to grow from, not something to be reproduced. In the battle with the religious leaders, the middle classes were the implementers of state policy. Yet the state was trying to hold back the forces leading to a more popular distribution of power and decision making, keeping the pressures for socioeconomic change under its own aegis; in this endeavor the middle classes were potential opponents and unwilling accomplices, co-opted by the necessities of earning a living.

The religious leaders, though courageously speaking out against the repression in this sort of state (and to that extent uneasy allies of the middle classes), seemed to be able to draw only on romantic visions of the past and to have little creative sociological imagination. This is not to say that Shi'ite Islam as they preached it did not contain a valid ethical perspective, but general ethics are no substitute for social understanding. Nor is it to say that Shi'ite leaders were not socially innovative in practical ways where they were allowed to be so, especially in establishing channels of welfare and medical aid. The criticism of the religious leaders is directed to their preachments and to conceptual formulations in their teaching.

The situation is complicated in a further way, one that needs more exploration than it has been possible to present here: the interaction between the religious institution and the life cycle experiences of young people reveals an emotionally powerful dialectic between conformity to tradition and self-reliant free thought. The followers of the religious leaders—whether madrasa students or merely devout Muslims—frequently undergo a life cycle development from narrow fundamentalist belief as highly articulate and argumentative youths (argumentation is encouraged by the system) to a gradual liberalization of belief and understanding as adults. Many do not develop this more liberal outlook, however; they constitute a constant conservative drag on religious leaders, who might be more liberal if they did not fear losing their constituency. The madrasas have the potential for focusing the energies needed to break this circular effect; but in the pre-1978 situation the madrasas were forced to remain largely (though with important exceptions) stagnant, both for internal reasons and because of external pressures by the state.

The historical nature of the symbolic structure I call the Karbala paradigm has been highlighted by the 1977-1979 revolution. One begins to see that its coherence depended in part, for one set of meanings, upon certain political and cultural contingencies. When these changed, a new coherence and set of symbolic structures were needed. The Karbala paradigm had been honed over the years into a device for heightening political consciousness of the moral failings of the government. With the revolution, certain interpretations, such as the reformulation of the term *Imam*, suddenly took on a meaningfulness not previously possible, and the Karbala paradigm as a whole became politically less relevant than other parts of the cultural symbolism of Shi'ism and Islam. The events related in chapter 6 follow easily from the climate of Qum in 1975, as described in chapters 3 through 5. Future chapters in the religious and political history of Iran may well look quite different.

Cultural structures such as the Karbala paradigm, however, have multiple uses. The *rawda*—the form of preaching which draws on the Karbala paradigm and is used on occasions of death memorials, religious commemorations, and communal gatherings—may continue to play an important role in the emotional life of many Iranians, serving, for instance, to model and channel expressions of grief or to instill an attitude of quiet determination and humility in the face of life's tribulations. Cultural structures, because they are multifaceted, are both relatively changeable over time and extraordinarily tenacious. This is not a paradox, merely a challenge for controlled analysis.

2

Rise and Decline of the Madrasa

Call thou to the way of the Lord with wisdom
[*hikmat*, "philosophy"], and admonition [*maw'iza*,
"preaching"], and dispute with them [*jadilhum*,
"reasoned debate"] in the better way.

—Qur'an 16:126

*T*HE MADRASA SCHOOLS are a form of education well known
to Western tradition, for they are essentially the same as the Jewish yeshiva and the Catholic medieval studium. The dynamics of
the growth of all three examples of what I call "the scriptural school" are
the same and are perhaps most clearly illustrated by the development of
the yeshiva. All three had lost their creative vitality by the thirteenth or
fourteenth century. In Christian Europe the Protestant Reformation, the
requirements of the Prussian bureaucracy, and the industrial revolution
combined to produce the modern university, which grew out of the
universities of Halle and Berlin, not directly from the old medieval
centers of Paris, Oxford, or Bologna. The Jewish yeshiva carried on
through the nineteenth century in Eastern Europe and still exists in a
parochial form, though essentially encapsulated, isolated, and pushed
aside from the mainstream of intellectual life. The same thing is happening to the Islamic madrasa today.

The madrasa is a symbolic structure as well as an educational forum.
In order to understand the stability over time of the educational and symbolic content of the madrasa, one needs to understand how Shi'ism is
construed by its believers, especially how they think it differs from Sunni
Islam.

Shi'ite Islam

Three sets of information are basic to an understanding of Shi'ism: (1)
information about the founding legend or history, which I will call the
Karbala paradigm, and which others such as R. Strothman (1953) have
not inappropriately called by the name of the Christian parallel, the Passion; (2) information about the establishment of Shi'ism as the state

12

religion by the Safavid dynasty in 1501, an establishment that continues to the present and has always involved a struggle between religious partisans of the state and religious opponents of the state; and (3) information about the formation and defense of the legal, theological, and mythological canon.

The Karbala paradigm is the story of Husayn, the third part of the origin legend of Muhammad, 'Ali, and Husayn. It is the part that is the most emotionally intense and concentrated, and is the reference point for almost all popular preaching. It is, however, only intelligible as the climax to the story of 'Ali. Its focus is the emotionally potent theme of corrupt and oppressive tyranny repeatedly overcoming (in this world) the steadfast dedication to pure truth; hence its ever-present, latent, political potential to frame or clothe contemporary discontents. The complete origin legend, which might be called the paradigm of the family of the Prophet, focuses rather upon model behavior. Muslims should model themselves on the behavior of Muhammad, 'Ali, Fatima, Husayn, and Zaynab (the Prophet, his cousin and son-in-law, his daughter, his grandson, and his granddaughter).

THE KARBALA PARADIGM AND THE FAMILY OF THE PROPHET

According to the Shi'ite account,[1] when the Prophet Muhammad died, leadership of the community was to pass to his cousin and son-in-law 'Ali. Muhammad had raised 'Ali as a child, adopting him even before his marriage to his first wife, Khadija. 'Ali was one of those to whom the Prophet dictated his revelations (the Qur'an); he was a constant aide and a champion warrior in Muhammad's cause. When Muhammad withdrew from Mecca under the cover of night, forewarned of an assassination plot, 'Ali remained behind as a decoy in Muhammad's bed.

Among the many indications put forward by Shi'ites to demonstrate that the prescribed and proper succession was to go to 'Ali are the following six, preserved in the form of hadith (traditions).[2] First, when the Prophet called upon his kin to accept Islam and promised that the first to do so would become his successor, all hesitated except 'Ali, who was then declared Muhammad's successor and vice-regent. Second, Muhammad reaffirmed the succession after 'Ali led an exhausting but victorious battle against the Jews of Khaybar and the Bani Ghatafan in A.H. 7, seven years after the *hijra*, Muhammad's flight from Mecca (in A.D. 622). Third, the famous hadith of the mantle relates that 'Ali, who had been left in charge of Medina while the Muslim forces invaded Tabuk (A.H. 9), complained to Muhammad of a whispering campaign against the Muslims in Medina. Muhammad thereupon took his family (his son-in-law, 'Ali, his daughter, Fatima, and their sons, Hasan and Husayn) under his cloak and received the revelation of Sura 33:33, "People of the House, God only desires to put away from you abomination and to cleanse you." This verse relates to the doctrine that the family of the Prophet ("the five pure souls" under the mantle and later the Imams, descendants of 'Ali and Fatima) are immaculate and sinless (*ma'sum*). At the same time the Prophet again affirmed that 'Ali was to him as Aaron to Moses and would be his successor. Fourth, during the effort to convert the Christians of Najran (A.H. 9), 'Ali was reaffirmed as the successor upon the revelation of Sura 3:53.[3] Fifth, upon Muhammad's return from his final pilgrimage to Mecca, he stopped at a watering place called Ghadir Khumm to declare that he was leaving for the guidance of the community the Holy Book and his family, raising 'Ali's hand at that point. He invested 'Ali with the title Amir-ul-Mu'minin (commander of the faithful) and had the assembly swear allegiance to 'Ali. Sixth, and finally, there is the hadith of the pen and ink: upon his deathbed Muhammad tried to reaffirm in writing the succession but was foiled by 'Umar, who claimed that Muhammad was delirious.

Muhammad died in A.H. 11. 'Ali was with him at his last breath and was designated by the Prophet to wash the body, Muhammad having cursed anyone else who should look on the nakedness of the corpse. The burial was done in the house of 'A'isha, Muhammad's youngest wife. While 'Ali and the true Muslims ('Abbas, Zubayr, Salman, Abu Dharr, Miqdad, and 'Ammar) were engaged in mourning Muhammad and giving him a proper burial, Abu Bakr and 'Umar hurriedly held an election for the leadership. Abu Bakr, with 'Umar's support, emerged as the choice. He was a father-in-law of the Prophet (the father of 'A'isha), and as the senior male close to the Prophet he was a natural choice in a traditional clan-oriented leadership election. 'Ali's response was characteristic: he refused to yield his claim and withdrew from active politics so as not to split the community, but he gave freely of his advice when asked. He spent his time teaching quietly and compiling an authoritative edition of the Qur'an.

For 'Umar, 'Ali's behavior was unsatisfactory: he came to 'Ali's house to demand a public swearing of allegiance. In his rough approach, he opened the door violently, pushing it into Fatima's side and breaking her ribs. Fatima, who was pregnant, subsequently was delivered of a stillborn son (Muhsin). Although 'Ali was willing to swear allegiance in the interest of community solidarity, Fatima adamantly opposed all breaks with her father's injunctions: 'Ali was the rightful caliph. Nor would she remain silent: she delivered a public sermon on the wrong judgment Abu Bakr made in not allowing her to inherit the gardens at Fadak. He had judged that they were not the private property of her father but had been held by him in trust for the community.

In Shi'ite rhetoric, *Fadak* has come to mean the rightful domain of the family of the Prophet; that is, Abu Bakr decided by his acceptance of the caliphate to deny the validity of the Prophet's message, and his judgment about Fadak serves Shi'ites as a symbolic statement of this denial. Abu Bakr is not generally regarded by Shi'ites as an evil man; rather, in their view he shows by his faulty decisions that he was unsuited for the leadership role. He cut off a thief's left hand instead of the prescribed right hand; he had a man burned to death inappropriately; he could not remember what share of inheritance a grandmother receives; he excused one man for the same crime for which another was executed.

Abu Bakr died after two years. 'Umar succeeded him. Again in the Shi'ite view 'Umar's faulty decisions showed how unsuited he was for the leadership. He stoned a pregnant woman and a crazy woman (these categories of people are not to be so punished). He outlawed things that are permitted in the Qur'an: temporary marriage and pilgrimage to Mecca out of season. Shi'ites say he had libraries in Egypt and Iran destroyed, on the grounds that if their contents disagreed with the Qur'an they were inimical to the community and if they agreed with the Qur'an they were superfluous. In a gesture of distributing wealth, he had valuable Persian carpets cut up into valueless little pieces that could be passed out. He distributed funds from the community chest inequitably, leading to incipient class conflicts. Before he died, he nominated six men to choose the next caliph, hardly a democratic procedure, as Shi'ites sarcastically comment.

There were two leading candidates in this election: 'Ali and 'Uthman. Both were asked whether they would abide by the Qur'an, the rulings of the Prophet, and the rulings of the two previous caliphs. 'Ali replied that he would, of course, abide by the first two, but only those rulings of the latter that accorded with the Qur'an and the rulings of the Prophet. 'Uthman replied that he would abide by all four, so he was appointed. Under 'Uthman, evidences of bad government, which had begun to show under 'Umar, grew worse. There was conflict in Kufa and Basra, the two great Arab garrisons of Iraq: conflict between the ruling clans from Mecca and Medina, on the one hand, and newer converts, on the other; and conflict between Arab Muslims and non-Arab Muslims. 'Uthman was eventually assassinated by soldiers who had come to him to seek justice: although 'Uthman had promised them redress, they discovered that secretly he had ordered their death.

'Ali was finally elected the fourth caliph and began to put the house of Islam in order. But so many conflicts had been created that he had to spend most of his brief rule fighting, especially against the governor of Syria, Mu'awiya, a brother-in-law of the Prophet. Mu'awiya and 'A'isha (the widow of the Prophet, who bore grudges against 'Ali)[4] demanded that the death of 'Uthman be avenged. 'Ali, who had been elected with the support of the assassins and their defenders, was placed in a difficult position. The assassins argued that 'Uthman had not ruled according to Islam and so had been legitimately killed, for which there must be no revenge. 'A'isha's troops were defeated by 'Ali's forces at the Battle of the Camel, but at the Battle of Siffin, Mu'awiya's forces put Qur'ans on their lances, bringing the battle with 'Ali to a stalemate and forcing arbitration. 'Ali's representative was outwitted, and Mu'awiya was declared caliph, something 'Ali did not concede. A group of erstwhile supporters of 'Ali (the Kharijites) were so incensed that 'Ali had even agreed to the arbitration procedure that they determined to kill 'Ali, Mu'awiya, and Mu'awiya's lieutenant 'Amr ibn al-'As, all on the same day, so that one could begin anew and live according to the Qur'an. 'Ali was assassinated on the nineteenth of Ramadan A.H. 40 while praying in the mosque of Kufa. Mu'awiya and 'Amr ibn al-'As, however, escaped death.

The details of 'Ali's martyrdom — his foreknowledge that he was to be slain, his generosity toward his assassin, Ibn Muljam, during the three days it took him to die — plus his courage in battle, knowledge of Islamic law, humility as an office holder, and wisdom as a judge (in contrast to the three previous caliphs) are celebrated today by the Shi'ite community, especially during the month of Ramadan. For instance, a contrast is elaborated between the deaths of 'Umar and of 'Ali. 'Umar, when struck by his assassin (Firuz, the Persian), cried, "Grab that Magian who has killed me!" 'Ali, when struck by his assassin, cried, "O God, most fortunate am I!" The contrast is between one who saw death as the end and one who saw it as the beginning of a return to God. This contrast and their respective stories serve as much-discussed parables of truth versus justice and generosity versus revenge.

First the death of 'Umar: Firuz was a Persian artisan, a slave of an Arab who unfairly confiscated all of Firuz's outside earnings. Firuz appealed to the caliph 'Umar, introducing himself as a maker of many things. 'Umar asked what Firuz could make for him, and Firuz replied, "A mill turned by the wind." Seeing that 'Umar would give him no relief, Firuz made a two-bladed dagger with the handle in the middle and with this he killed 'Umar. He then ran out of the mill where the act had been committed. 'Ali happened to be sitting outside; as Firuz ran past, he rose and changed his seat. When pursuers came to 'Ali, they asked if he had seen Firuz. 'Ali replied, "As long as I have been sitting on this spot, I have not seen him." Having provided a temporary alibi for Firuz, 'Ali then advised Firuz to return to Iran and quickly take a wife. With a special prayer 'Ali transported Firuz to Kashan, normally a journey of several months. There he was welcomed and married. When his pursuers arrived in Kashan several months later inquiring about a certain Firuz recently come from Iraq, they were told that there was such a man but he had come several months ago and had married then, so he could not be the one they sought. Firuz's windmill, then, was the wind-borne news caused by his double-bladed slaying of 'Umar, which spread from the eastern to the western ends of the world.

The moral theme is that whatever is done for the good of society is of a higher value than absolute truth spoken regardless of consequences, often expressed in the words of Sa'di: *durugh-i maslahat-amiz beh az rasti-i fitna-angiz* ("a well-intentioned and calming lie is better than a truth that brings calamity"). Humane pragmatism rather than an impersonal rationalized system of rights and wrongs is what is valued.

The story of 'Ali's death is rich with detail and associations: On the thirteenth of Ramadan, 'Ali told Husayn that he would soon die and would not be able to participate in the hajj that year. When he told the Muslims that Ibn Muljam would kill him, they asked permission to kill Ibn Muljam first, but 'Ali refused, saying that revenge before the event was not proper. (According to the version in Rumi's *Masnavi*, Ibn Muljam himself asked to be killed and 'Ali responded that such a preventive killing would not be in defense of Islam but merely a personal defensiveness: see note 5 for the same argument in a different part of the story.)

The night before his assassination, 'Ali went on the roof to sing *munajat* (literally "whisperings," a form of elegaic prayer). He sang to the stars and moon that they should intensify their light because he himself was leaving the world. When he warned his family that he would be killed on the morrow, his daughter pleaded that he not leave the house but he replied that one cannot stop death. Even an animal attempted to block his path as he left the house for the mosque. Then his sash got caught in the door and his robe fell open. All to no avail. As he retied the sash, he remarked to himself, " 'Ali you must be dressed and ready when you are called." When he came to the mosque, he found Ibn Muljam sleeping on his stomach. 'Ali roused him and told him, "Sleep on your back like the Prophet, or on your right side like the Imams, or on your left side like the governors, but not on your stomach, for that is the sleep of the devils. Now arise and desist from what you intend: if I wished, I could tell what you have hidden [a sword under the clothing]."

They both stood for prayer. At the second *sijda* (prostration) Ibn Muljam struck 'Ali in exactly the same place as the sword of 'Amr ibn Abu Da'ud had once struck 'Ali.[5] 'Ali fell forward into the *mihrab* (the niche in a mosque wall which orients one toward Mecca). He took some dirt from the floor of the niche to put on his wound. The angel Gabriel filled the air with the cry that 'Ali was slain and the *muezzins* (those who call the faithful to prayer) took up the cry from the rooftops.

Ibn Muljam fled through the alleys. A man, awakened by the tumult, went into the streets; seeing a man with his cloak over his head running, he challenged him. The man replied he was in a hurry. Again he challenged the man, this time with the words "Have you not heard that 'Ali is slain?" The man replied that he had more important things to do. To this the man jestingly suggested, "Then it must be you who are the murderer." Ibn Muljam admitted it and at that moment a gust of wind raised his cloak to reveal the bloody dagger. They wrestled and Ibn Muljam was brought to the mosque. There 'Ali asked Ibn Muljam if he had been such a bad Imam; and Ibn Muljam, embarrassed, exclaimed that God had created him for hell; could anyone change his fate so that he should go to heaven? 'Ali ordered him detained but comforted him that if he, 'Ali, survived, Ibn Muljam would be set free. Each time 'Ali's sons brought him food or drink, 'Ali insisted that Ibn Muljam be served first. When it became clear that he would die, 'Ali remarked that it was a shame that for the sake of Islam Ibn Muljam would have to be killed; otherwise he would like to release him. As he died, 'Ali ordered that Ibn Muljam be executed with one blow only, for he had struck only one blow, and that Ibn Muljam's family not be molested.

Aside from the rhetorical form of tragedy in which the moral themes of generosity, fairness, and appropriate punishment are embedded, two ritual features intensify and support the rhetoric. First, 'Ali was stabbed at the second prostration of the stylized namaz prayer. One meaning given to the prostrations is that the first refers to "from dust we are created"; the worshiper then sits back, resting upon his haunches, which represents life; the second prostration refers to "and to dust we return"; the concluding rising to one's feet represents the final judgment. Thus 'Ali's putting of dirt on his wound reinforces the second prostration. Second, the details of the story were collected from several popular preachments (*rawda*) given during the month of Ramadan, between the nineteenth when 'Ali received his fatal wound and the twenty-first when he died. After the words " 'Ali took the dirt of the mihrab to put on his wound," the preacher next recites the verse from the Qur'an about man's being from dust. In one of the preachments the story is ended, "Husayn cried, and Hasan cried, and Zaynab cried; but 'Ali told Zaynab not to cry, to save her tears for Karbala." The story then turns to the mourning by Zaynab for the martyrs at Karbala.

Shi'ites draw many other contrasts between 'Umar and 'Ali, ranging from simple knowledge of the law, to ability to search out the truth in judicial cases, to proper government administration. Rather than depending on government by force, of which Shi'ites accuse 'Umar, 'Ali wrote to his governors not to extract taxes until they were sure the productive capacity of the land could sustain a given amount of taxation, and he appointed governors, such as Salman Farsi in Khuzistan, who refused to inhabit costly palaces but humbly placed themselves among the common people. Salman Farsi is said to have rented half a shoemaker's shop as his gubernatorial office. 'Ali himself is said to have worn poor clothing, eaten poor barley bread, and ridden on a donkey, that there be no Muslim envious of him. 'Ali's martyrdom was tragic above all because since then there has been no truly just government. Nevertheless, 'Ali's martyrdom was not the key martyrdom of Shi'ism.

After 'Ali's death, Mu'awiya became the uncontested caliph (A.H. 40-60). 'Ali's elder son, Hasan, was too weak to make an effective bid for the political leadership of the community. He therefore came to an understanding with Mu'awiya and was sent off with a handsome pension to live in Medina: when Mu'awiya died, the caliphate was to revert to the family of the Prophet. The understanding was not honored. First, Mu'awiya had Hasan poisoned; second, he made his own son Yazid his successor even while he was still alive. Husayn, the second son of 'Ali, refused to swear allegiance to Yazid. Mu'awiya was shrewd enough to ignore this, but after his death Yazid was determined to force the issue.

It is alleged by the Shi'ites that Yazid sent assassins to mingle with the pilgrims at the hajj. At the same time, Husayn received messages from Kufa in southern Iraq to come and lead a revolt against the tyranny of Yazid. To avoid bloodshed during the hajj, Husayn cut short his pilgrimage. Foreseeing his martyrdom, he released his followers from any obligation to follow him. With his family and seventy-two men — thirty-two horsemen and forty on foot — he made his way toward Kufa. Meanwhile, in good Oriental despot fashion, Yazid was able to coopt the Kufan leadership and the Kufans abandoned Husayn. As Husayn approached Kufa on the first of Muharram A.H. 61, he was intercepted by forces loyal to Yazid under the command of Hurr, and forced to camp on the desert of Karbala. Negotiations to secure Husayn's submission to Yazid failed. Husayn's forces were even denied access to water (the Euphrates was nearby).[6] On the tenth of Muharram, a bloody battle was joined in which all but two of the males in Husayn's party were slain, Husayn's body was desecrated, and the women were taken prisoner. The details of this battle at Karbala form the key imagery of the Passion of the Shi'ites. "Much more than the blood of 'Ali who was murdered by a single Kharidji it was the blood of Husayn who perished under the swords of the government troops that was the seed of the Shi'a church" (Strothman 1953: 534).

Husayn's martyrdom occurred at noon on Friday the tenth of Muharram. The details heighten the significance of Yazid's tyranny and desecration of the sacred and proper order of life and Islam. Not only had Yazid usurped the caliphate and not only was he using that office tyrannically, but he had attempted to desecrate the hajj, he had desecrated the time of communal prayer (Friday noon), and he had destroyed one by one the elements of civilized life: water, an elementary human need that by the desert code of honor is never refused to thirsty individuals, was denied not only to warrior opponents but to women and children; three sons of Husayn were slain: the infant 'Ali Asghar, the five-year-old child Ja'far, and the twenty-five-year-old youth, 'Ali Akbar. Destruction of family, community, government, and humanity are all themes of the Karbala story, retold and relived today in every religious gathering and reaching dramatic and emotional crescendo during the month of Muharram when the events of A.H. 61 are re-enacted, day by day.

Only two males survived the slaughter: the ill twenty-two-year-old fourth Imam and his four-year-old son (the fifth Imam). It was a woman, Zaynab, the sister of the third Imam, who kept the Shi'ite cause alive until the fourth Imam was sufficiently well to give a famous sermon that shamed the audience, a sermon that is repeated today in the Muharram mourning ceremonies. The body of Husayn was trampled in the mud and his head was taken to Damascus, where the caliph Yazid is said to have beaten it with a stick in a vain attempt to keep it from reciting the Qur'an.

Among the more heartrending stories are those of the marriage on the battlefield of Qasim, the son of the second Imam, to a daughter of the third Imam, and his immediate shedding of his earthly body; the attempt by 'Abbas, half-brother of Husayn, to fetch water, his success in filling a waterskin and refusal to drink himself until the women and children had water, and the loss of the waterskin, his arms, and his life to the slashes of bullying Syrian soldiers; and, above all, the crying of Husayn's three-year-old daughter, who demanded to know what she had done that her father had gone away and would not come to her and, upon being shown her father's head, became quiet, fell asleep, and died.

After Husayn there were nine more Imams. The last, a young boy, is said to have gone into occultation when his father died in A.H. 260. Withdrawn from the world, he does not provide daily social leadership, although occasionally he manifests himself to individual people. He is the Imam al-Zaman (the present Imam, the Imam of all time) and the messiah, or Mahdi, who will usher in the final battles leading to the day of judgment. One prays for his return. Aside from the twelfth Imam, the sixth Imam, Ja'far al-Sadiq, is probably the most important; he is the source of many hadith and was the teacher of learned men in both exoteric and esoteric knowledge. Of the twelve Imams only one is buried in Iran: the eighth, Imam 'Ali al-Rida (Imam Reza), is buried in Mashhad; his shrine is the greatest in Iran. His sister Fatima is buried in Qum, and this is Iran's second shrine. Otherwise these last nine Imams, intriguing as they may be for the historical development of Shi'ism (see Hodgson 1955), are of relatively less importance for the Karbala paradigm. Within that paradigm they are the carriers of the spirit and knowledge of Husayn; they are the true guides for men. Since 260/872, when the twelfth Imam went into occultation, or rather since the brief subsequent period during which he gave instructions through four special representatives (the period called the lesser occultation), proper knowledge has been the possession of those who study, the ulama.

PARADIGM, PASSION, AND DRAMA

There are two reasons for preferring the term "paradigm" to "passion." First, it focuses attention upon the story as a rhetorical device rather than on either the (albeit important) emotional component or the theological motifs common to Islam and Christianity (such as epiphany and parousia). The story can be elaborated or abbreviated. It provides models for living and a mnemonic for thinking about how to live: there is a set of parables and moral lessons all connected with or part of the story of Karbala which are themselves not obviously contradictory and to which almost all of life's problems can be referred. The story can take on dramatic form: during the first ten days of Muharram, shabih or ta'ziya plays are performed re-creating the events of the Battle of Karbala and other events, such as the Joseph story, which are related to Karbala: Jacob is told by the angel Gabriel that his suffering is nothing compared with the sufferings the family of 'Ali and Husayn will endure; those who lose their lives at Karbala compare themselves to Joseph, leaving their bloodied cloaks "of many colors" (bodies) behind while they go on to a world of plenty. (See Appendix.) During these ten days there are processions with floats representing the events of Karbala, interspersed with double columns of black-shirted young men chanting and rhythmically flagellating themselves with two-pound chains or beating their chests with both open palms and occasionally slashing their foreheads with knives (this last was banned by the Pahlavi government). The flagellants represent the Kufans repenting their abandonment of Husayn and, more generally, all Muslims who bear responsibility for not helping the Imam institute the true, just Islamic society. Muharram, and especially 'Ashura (the tenth of Muharram, when Husayn was slain), is the emotional high point of the ritual year. But throughout the year religious preachments (rawdas) have a stylized form that frames the subject of the preachment in references to Karbala. (Muharram and the rawdas will be described in chapter 5.)

The second reason for preferring the word "paradigm" is that it provides a way of clearly demarcating Shi'ite understanding from Sunni understanding of Islam and Islamic history. To Sunnis, Abu Bakr, 'Umar, and Mu'awiya were good caliphs, men without whom the survival of Islam would have been in question. For Shi'ites they are three of the key men who perverted Islam so that from then till the present, Islam has been unable to fulfill its promise as a just social system. For Shi'ites, 'Uthman and Mu'awiya also attempted to pervert the Qur'an and hadith, 'Uthman refused to accept 'Ali's authoritative Qur'an, and Mu'awiya instituted a Ministry of Hadith Fabrication. The esoteric or rather private passing of knowledge through the Imams circumvented these Sunni attempts. The exoteric Qur'an, standardized by 'Uthman, is not challenged (see Pooya 1971), but the meaning of the verses is. The sifting of correct from false hadith is a major task of the ulama.

But let us now hear the tale of the first four caliphs as it is usually told by Western historians, drawing upon Sunni rather than Shi'ite perspectives.[7]

Muhammad had created a system of alliances among Bedouin tribes that controlled the trade between the three great agriculture-based empires: Byzantium, the Sassanian empire, and Abyssinia. Each of these three empires had Arab clients and mercenaries. Muhammad's attempt to reform the Meccan ritual cult according to the call he believed himself to have received produced a dynamic of expansion. Mecca was an important trade crossroads and its cult was a ritual technique of allying not only its local clans, but expanding the alliance to include outside tribes. This cult seems to have been losing ground to the Christianity and Judaism of the three empires. Muhammad's call was to institute a comparable confessional faith that would help preserve the independence of the Arabian trade area rather than subordinate it to ideological systems whose centers were in these other empires. The resistance he encountered in Mecca eventually led to his famous withdrawal to Medina, the *hijra*. Although Medina was originally a Jewish Arab oasis, various pagan tribes had settled there, and no unified cult had been worked out to prevent the town from being plagued by feuds. Muhammad brought a solution to this local problem. The Meccans who came with Muhammad (the *Muhajirun*, "emigrants") were paired as guests with the new Muslim converts of Medina (the *Ansar*, "helpers"); but for material support the Muhajirun were sent out to raid caravans and later to take tribute from oases. Tribes that converted became part of a new alliance system, gradually replacing the old Meccan system (Mecca itself was taken in 9/630); tribes that resisted had heavy tribute exacted. When Muhammad died, this delicate polity of alliance and protection began to fall apart and tribute from various tribes stopped.

'Umar was the architect of reconsolidating and expanding the polity. He nominated Abu Bakr, a gentle and well-meaning soul even in Shi'ite accounts, as caliph, both because he was the senior kinsman and because he was one against whom few could object while the wars of the Ridda (bringing back the apostates) were conducted. Abu Bakr died after two years, having appointed 'Umar his successor. 'Umar took the title Amir-al-Mu'minin (commander of the faithful). Under him expansion proceeded quickly: the Fertile Crescent, Egypt, and much of Iran were conquered. Byzantium had ceased supporting the frontier Arabs in Syria, and the Syrians fairly readily joined with the Muslim advance: Arab mercenaries in the Byzantine army defected; Syrian Jews had been persecuted by the Christian Empire and Syrian Christians had been persecuted for their refusal to accept the leadership of the Greek church. So the conquest of Syria was fairly easy. Iraq proved also to be easy for similar reasons. The Sassanians had dismantled their Arab vassal frontier state of Lakhmid, and the huge, centrally run irrigation agriculture of the Mesopotamian plain had fallen into disarray owing to the civil wars following their latest defeat by Rome and a shift in the course of the Euphrates. The local population had little direct stake in the system; they were mainly Christians, Jews, and Manichaeans, and suffered disabilities under the Sassanian Zoroastrian hierarchy. The upper classes also had no direct stake in the local economy, being based rather on the Iranian plateau. The soldiers were largely Arab.

'Umar established a state based on the separation of the Arab military garrisons from the conquered populations. His governor in Syria, Mu'awiya, commanded from Damascus, but elsewhere garrison towns were established: Kufa near Ctesiphon, Basra on the Gulf, Fustat at the head of the Nile delta. A register of Muslims was established so that from the booty of war and revenue from lands conquered, these garrisons could be paid. In time this system would cause problems: with fewer conquests, less booty came in; there were complaints about social distinctions, reflected in the amounts to which one was entitled through the register, based on when groups had become Muslims. The Muhajirun and Ansar still formed a ruling aristocracy; below them were the other Arab Muslims; much more disadvantaged were the growing numbers of non-Arab Muslims. Under 'Uthman, all these problems and competing interests began to come to the fore. 'Uthman's solution to the problem of control was to rely increasingly on his own clansmen, the Umayyads. This raised further complaints of nepotism. There was pressure to be allowed to buy land or control its revenue directly rather than through the register and pressure to be allowed to compete in mercantile enterprises with the local merchants. In an attempt to enforce at least symbolic unity, 'Uthman imposed a standardized Qur'an. This too led to resentment, especially among the Qur'an reciters who had their own variants. 'Ali apparently became a center of opposition to several of these policies. 'Uthman, as already related, was assassinated in 36/656 by mutineers from Egypt, who proclaimed 'Ali caliph.

'Ali's caliphate might possibly be seen as an attempt to stabilize the state by using the religious position of Imam to strengthen the secular position of Amir-al-Mu'minin (Shaban 1970). It did not work: stronger measures were required. The Prophet's widow, 'A'isha, and Mu'awiya, still governor of Syria, demanded revenge for 'Uthman's death; through the arbitration following the Battle of Siffin and the assassination of 'Ali by the Khariji Ibn Muljam, Mu'awiya prevailed. He was a brother-in-law of the Prophet, but his state was based less on kinship or religious loyalties than on Syrian-based power. The Syrians appear to have been relatively satisfied with his government, and Muslims elsewhere seem to have recognized that disunity could threaten their precarious position as overlords. The real center of power, however, was not in Syria: most of the army and most of the revenues were in Iraq. Eventually, with the Abbasid Revolution, the political center of power would shift there, to the new capital of Baghdad.

Mu'awiya had his son Yazid appointed his successor in his lifetime, for bringing in anyone else, with other family ties, might have upset the delicate balance of political forces established in Syria. The Hejaz refused to recognize Yazid, and Kufa in southern Iraq invited Husayn to lead a revolt there, a revolt that failed before it started, ending in Husayn's death at Karbala. A revolt in the Hejaz under 'Abdullah ibn al-Zubayr had been almost crushed, when Yazid died. For a time Ibn al-Zubayr was the most widely recognized caliph, even by a major part of Syria. But eventually Marwan (who had been 'Uthman's chief adviser and was a cousin of Mu'awiya) established supremacy. Marwan, and his son Abd al-Malik, the latter with the help of a strong governor in Iraq, Hajjaj, who was not afraid to use terror, firmly established a hereditary dynasty (the Umayyads), which lasted almost a hundred years.

What is at issue in Sunni and Shi'ite accounts is not history per se but the abstractions from history and the different valuations. Sunnis focus attention on the life of Muhammad; Shi'ites, though they too cite Muhammad's life, are much more concerned with the lives of 'Ali and Husayn. For Sunnis there is a hadith that Abu Bakr, not 'Ali, was the first man (after Khadija, Muhammad's first wife) to accept the Prophet's call to Islam; 'Umar was a great statesman; election was the proper procedure for succession; Hasan died of consumption not poison; Muhammad (at least according to popular Egyptian tradition) died of natural causes not by poison, as Shi'ites maintain;[8] the tenth of Muharram is merely a day of voluntary fasting, which has to do with Muhammad's career and nothing to do with Husayn; and so on.

The difference in ritual calendars perhaps shows the contrast most clearly. Take, for instance, the month of Ramadan, the month of fasting. Muhammad first instituted a fast on the tenth of Muharram, adapting the Jewish Day of Atonement (*asire* or tenth of Tishre); when his relations with the Jews became strained, he made that fast a voluntary one and instituted a month of fasting in Ramadan, but still with many features reminiscent of the Jewish practices.

For Sunnis, Ramadan is a month primarily concerned with the career of Muhammad and the day he selected to commemorate the revelation of the Qur'an (the revelation occurred over a long period), which he compared to the bringing down from Sinai by Moses of the second set of tablets. (The tenth of Tishre is the day God forgave the Hebrews for the golden calf; the second tablets then follow on the sixth of Sivan.) According to al-Biruni,[9] the sixth of Ramadan is the birthday of Husayn, the Prophet's grandson; the tenth is the death day of Khadija, the Prophet's first wife; the seventeenth is the Battle of Badr (Muhammad's first important military victory); the nineteenth is Muhammad's occupation of Mecca; the twenty-first is the death day of both 'Ali and Imam al-Rida (the eighth Shi'ite Imam); the twenty-second is the birthday of 'Ali; and the twenty-seventh is the day of revelation.

According to Shi'ites in Iran today, however, Ramadan is a month primarily concerned with the martyrdom of 'Ali: he was struck by Ibn Muljam on the nineteenth, he died on the twenty-first, and Ibn Muljam was executed on the twenty-seventh (a day celebrated with a kind of trick-or-treat procedure called *dust ya 'Ali dust*).[10] The happy occasions are removed to other months: 'Ali's birthday to the thirteenth of Rajab and Husayn's birthday to the third of Sha'ban. The other important death day, that of Imam al-Rida, is also removed, to the twenty-seventh of Safar. The night of revelation is important, but it is by design unknown whether it is on the nineteenth, twenty-first, twenty-third, or twenty-seventh. It is said that prayers on that night are worth a thousand prayers on any other night; therefore, to encourage people to pray on all nights, the date remains unknown. The dates of the Battle of Badr and the occupation of Mecca are acknowledged but not ritually marked.

The recognition of such systematic differences between Sunni and Shi'ite versions of history is but the essential first step to a recognition that Shi'ism today is not so much the expression of partisan struggle on behalf of a political faction (as it perhaps was in Umayyad and Abbasid times). It is rather a drama of faith (*iman*). (That this is a problem for those concerned with fostering pan-Islamic unity is something to which we shall return.) Believers are witnesses (*shuhada*) through their acts of worship (*'ibadat*) to the metaphysical reality which is hidden (*gha'ib*). This is the meaning of the Karbala paradigm. Note the play with the words. *Shuhada* means both martyrs and witnesses. Husayn, knowing he would die, went to Karbala to witness for the truth, knowing that his death would make him a martyr, an enduring, immortal witness, whose example would be a guide for others. *Gha'ib* refers to a series of inner truths: a God who is not visible, a twelfth Imam who is in occultation, a personal inner faith, and the special light that created Muhammad, 'Ali, Fatima, Hasan, and Husayn. *'Ibadat* is the formal acts of worship such as prayer, fasting, and pilgrimage; further, it is the ten items of *foru' id-din* or religious duties: the five daily formal prayers (*namaz, salat*), the fast in Ramadan, the one-fifth tax (*khums*), alms (*zakat*), the hajj, the defense of the faith (*jihad*), the urging of people to do good (*amr bi-maʻruf*), the dissuading from evil (*nahy az munkar*), the defense of those who support the message of God and the Imams (*tawalla*), and the avoidance or fighting of those who are the enemies of God and the Imams (*tabarra*);[11] further yet, worship is everything a Muslim does. For *iman* is not just faith or conviction, it is also professing with the tongue and acting according to the principles of Islam.

There is a hermetic, recursive quality to the Karbala paradigm. It can be expanded or elaborated. Thus there is a cosmological part to it associated with the so-called *nur* (light) doctrine.[12] In the beginning Muhammad, Adam, and all the prophets (of whom there are 124,000) and Imams were created from a ray of divine light. These divine sparks were breathed into human form at appropriate points in the unfolding of history, often making for a miraculous birth. Thus, Fatima, the wife of ʻAli, went bathing one day and when she emerged from the water she was pregnant with Husayn. That pregnancy lasted only six months. In the sixth month her womb glowed with incandescent light; just before the birth the angels Azrael, Michael, and Gabriel came to her; at the birth Muhammad took the child from the midwife and placed his tongue in the child's mouth, whereupon Husayn began to suck.

This nur doctrine provides a way of connecting all the prophets. They have come to different peoples with essentially the same message, and at times God gives them foreknowledge of their successors, especially of the tragedy of Karbala. Al-Burqani[13] gives the following account of Adam:

> When the Prophet Adam, may peace be with him, descended upon the earth, he was looking for Eve around the world until he traversed to the Desert of Karbala. When he entered the Desert, waves of sorrow and sadness approached him. When he reached the death place of the Martyr Imam Husayn, may peace be with him, his foot caught a rock and blood started to flow from it. Then he raised his head to Heaven and said: "O Creator, I travelled in all the lands and I experienced no sadness and misery which has come to me here. Have I done any sin that you are punishing me for it?" Then God replied, "O Adam you have done no sin, but a son of yours shall die here from injustice and oppression. I wanted your blood to flow on this land the way his blood shall flow here." Adam asked, "O Creator, is Husayn a Prophet?" God answered, "[Husayn] is not a Prophet, but he is the son of my Prophet Muhammad." Adam asked, "Who is his murderer?" God replied, "His murderer is Yazid whom the people of Heaven and Earth curse." Then Adam asked Gabriel, may peace be with him, "What should I do?" Gabriel said, "Curse Yazid." The Prophet Adam cursed the Damned One [Yazid] four times.

Similar revelations of Husayn's martyrdom were made to Noah, Abraham, Ishmael, Moses, Solomon, Jesus, Muhammad, and ʻAli. Some of these have been elaborated into passion plays for Muharram. The analogy between Joseph and the martyrs at Karbala has already been mentioned. Similarly the sacrifice of Ishmael[14] has become a standard lesser analogy for the martyrdom of Husayn.

The doctrine of the immaculate sinlessness and perfect knowledge of the family of the Prophet (Fatima, 'Ali, and the Imams) dovetails nicely with the nur doctrine. In Qur'anic terms it is grounded in Sura 33:33, the verse of purification revealed under the mantle of Muhammad, whence the family has gained the title "the five pure souls."

There are, then, three parts to the notion of paradigm: (a) a story expandable to be all-inclusive of history, cosmology, and life's problems; (b) a background contrast against which the story is given heightened perceptual value: in this case, primarily Sunni conceptions, but other religions at times serve the same function; and (c) ritual or physical drama to embody the story and maintain high levels of emotional investment: the rituals of daily worship (prayer, purity rules, dietary rules); pilgrimage to the tombs of 'Ali in Najaf, Husayn in Karbala, the other Imams, and the hajj; preachments (*rawda*), mourning processions (*ta'ziya*), and passion plays of Muharram (*shabih*).

THE ESTABLISHMENT OF SHI'ISM AS A STATE RELIGION

After the defeat of Husayn there were a number of revolts in southern Iraq and Iran under Shi'ite banners using one or another descendant of the Prophet or of his family as a figurehead Imam. An early attempt in Kufa to avenge Husayn's death under the banner of his half-brother Ibn al-Hanafiyya was directed primarily against Ibn al-Zubayr. Somewhat later a descendant of 'Ali's father raised an even more important revolt, also based initially in Kufa but forced to retreat to Iran. The most important took hold first in Khurasan, and moving across Iran overthrew the Umayyads and established the Abbasid dynasty in A.D. 750.

From a Shi'ite point of view, as soon as the Abbasids established themselves, they sold out the ideals of Shi'ism, for they did not establish the rule of the Imam; so Shi'ite revolts and underground resistance continued. But the Abbasid Revolution was an early major use of the Karbala paradigm as an ideological tool of mobilization; with black flags, prophecies, legends, and slogans. The revolt was in the name of *al-rida min al Muhammad* (a member of the house of the Prophet acceptable to all), and the leader took the name Abu Muslim 'Abd al-Rahman ("Father of a Muslim, he who worships the Compassionate"). The famous, probably apocryphal, story about the first Abbasid caliph, al-Saffah, has a Shi'ite elaboration: after slaughtering every member of the Umayyad family he could find, he pretended to relent and invited those who remained to a banquet of forgiveness. When they were seated, attendants killed them; carpets were spread over them and the banquet continued. The Shi'ite elaboration is that al-Saffah was incited to this bloody act by listening to the poet Sudayf read *mathiya*(s) (dirges of more than a hundred couplets) about Karbala (Javaher-Kalam 1335a/1956:20).

The period of the later Umayyads and the Abbasids was when Shi'ism began to crystallize into a definable set of sectarian groupings. The sixth Imam, Ja'far al-Sadiq (d. 148/765) — a contemporary of the founders of the Sunni legal schools, Abu Hanifa (d. 150/767) and Malik (d. 179/795) — was the most widely recognized leader among all Shi'ite groups (the succession after him being disputed, most importantly by the Ismailis) and the source of many authoritative traditions. In the third/ninth century Zaydi principalities were established in northern Iran (Daylam around present-day Qazvin, and Tabaristan in the Caspian area). These were succeeded by Twelver Shi'ite principalities. Most important, the Shi'ite Buyids ruled most of the Fertile Crescent and much of Iran for over a century (320-447/932-1055) just before the Seljuq invasions. Under them the four major collections of Shi'ite hadith were codified (a full generation after the Sunni collections):

al-Kafi fi 'Ilm ad-Din (A compendium of the science of religion) by Kulayni (d. 328/939);

Man la Yahduruhu'l-Faqih (Everyman's lawyer) by Ibn Babuya (d. 381/991);

Tahdhib al-Ahkam (Corrections of judgments) by Shaykh al-Tusi (d. 457/1067);

Istibsar (Examinations of differences in traditions) by Shaykh al-Tusi.

Mu'izz al-Dawla, the Buyid king who captured Baghdad, instituted the first public ceremony on record commemorating Husayn's death, in 352/936; observance of the ceremony continued until the Seljuq rule of Tughril, over a century later.[15] For a very brief period during the reign of the Il Khanid Uljaitu Khudabanda (703-716/1304-1317) also the state religion was Shi'ite.

These various Shi'ite struggles are primarily of interest here to make one point: before A.D. 1501 the religious situation in Iran was one of multiple Islamic groups, Shi'ites dominant here and there (including Qum), the four Sunni schools dominant in most places, with cities factionalized between these several groups and loyalties shifting from time to time.[16] It is a fascinating period in its own right, but in 1501 the situation was dramatically changed and simplified. Shah Isma'il Safavi, upon seizing power, proclaimed Shi'ism to be the state religion.

The Safavids originally had been a Sunni mystical sect but gradually during the fifteenth century had assimilated a messianic version of Shi'ism. The leaders of the sect began to claim not only descent from the seventh Imam but to be the current link in the chain of divine inspiration passed from God through the Prophet to 'Ali and the Imams. Shah Isma'il and his successor, Shah Tahmasp, even had themselves treated as deities. With the establishment of the Safavid state and the need to expand their popular base these extremist enthusiasms subsided into a more orthodox form of Shi'ism. At most a Safavid ruler claimed to be the vicar of the twelfth Imam and to reign as "God's Shadow on Earth." Their form of Shi'ism was gradually transformed from a messianic ideology, capable of motivating a fervent fighting force that could seize power, into a political tool to counter the Sunni Ottoman empire to the west and to unify their own state internally. Shah Isma'il is said to have known relatively little about the orthodox tradition he was raising to dominance and to have had difficulty in finding books on the subject. The *Qawa'id al-Islam* by Ibn al-Mutahhar al-Hilli (648-726/1250-1325) is said to be the only book he could find, and for this he had to send to Anatolia.

Shi'ite ulama were invited from what is today Lebanon and southern Iraq. Theological colleges were endowed for them, and some were given posts within the state organization. The highest of these posts was the ministerial post of Sadr, in charge of the propagation of Shi'ism, the administration of religious endowments, some supervision of judges (though the state stressed customary, or *'urf*, law over religious, or *shar'* law and judges in general were under the supervision of the Divanbegi), the appointment of *shayks-al-Islam* in the major towns, and the appointment of heads of the sayyids (or naqibs).

In all this enthusiasm for Shi'ism there was considerable persecution of Sunnis, Sufis, and non-Muslims. As the influx of ulama continued, a critical mass or class of religious men was formed apart from the state. Only toward the end of the Safavid period was an officer appointed to head them, the *mulla-bashi*.

It is often claimed that under the Safavids, Shi'ism was altered to be more nationalist and less universalist. The anti-Ottoman posture, at least, encouraged an upsurge in denigrations of the first three caliphs. Said Arjomand (1976: 83, 92) points also to the interest shown by the Mulla-bashi Muhammad-Baqir Majlisi (d. 1700)—the greatest, if also one of the more intolerant, of the Safavid mujtahids—in details of eschatology, such as proving that there will be physical resurrection at the end of time, rather than in such concerns as the nature of God's attributes, reason, and faith, which were usual among earlier mujtahids. That is, he argues, there was a kind of theological involution toward fundamentalism. Majlisi also elaborated concerns with shrine pilgrimages rather than the hajj. Arjomand gives the following page counts as a rough measure: the four great hadith compendia spend the following ratios of pages on hajj and ziyarat (pilgrimages elsewhere than to Mecca): 197:42, 149:39, 198:0, and 493:118, but in Majlisi's encyclopedic *Bihar al-Anwar* (Oceans of Light) the ratio is just the reverse: 387:1055. Arjomand argues that this change also indicates a shift from universalism: the psychological effect of the hajj is to stress the worldwide

Islamic community and the unity of God, whereas local shrine worship, even of the Imams, stresses individual concerns for intercessors with God. In any case, the revival of intolerant orthodoxy under Majlisi had the ultimate result of contributing to the downfall of the Safavids: by interfering in Sunni Afghan affairs, the destructive Afghan invasions were provoked.

With the fall of the Safavids in 1722, many ulama emigrated to the shrine towns of southern Iraq.[17] They also became predominantly literalist, emphasizing transmission of knowledge (*naql*) rather than use of interpretive reason (*'aql*). The Akhbaris, as the holders of this orientation to knowledge were called, were dominant until Aqa Muhammad-Baqir Bihbahani (1705-1803) reenergized the more aggressive *Usuli* position. His students became the great religious leaders of the Qajar period. The Qajar monarchs, especially Fath-'Ali Shah (1797-1834) curried the favor of the ulama, which together with their newfound assertiveness gained them a position of popular power. Isfahan was still the main center of the ulama in Iran, as it had been under the Safavids. The most powerful of the Isfahan ulama was S. Muhammad-Baqir Shafti, who settled there in 1801 and remained until his death in 1842. An index of his assertive use of his mujtahid status is that he condemned to death between eighty and a hundred offenders of religious law. He was also perhaps one of the richest ulama in history: endowed by a khan of his natal village near Rasht, he owned four hundred caravanserais and over two thousand shops in Isfahan, plus many villages near Isfahan, Burujerd, Yazd, and Shiraz (Algar 1969: 60). He was strong enough to support the ultimately unsuccessful claims of Husayn-'Ali Mirza Farman-farma to be king against Muhammad-Shah; until his death he opposed the Sufi-leaning Muhammad-Shah and used bands of *luti*s (toughs) to create disturbances.

The ulama in the Qajar period steadily moved toward an oppositional role. Under Fath-'Ali Shah they were favored and there was a kind of alliance with the monarchy. Under Muhammad-Shah both the king and his vizier, Haji Mirza Aqasi, leaned toward Sufism, and whatever alliance had been forged was loosened. Nasir al-Din Shah (1848-1896) was religious but in a popular style that did not appeal to the ulama. More important, his ministers began Western-inspired reforms and the state became heavily indebted to the British and Russians. The ulama opposed this subordination to foreign unbelievers. The most dramatic and impressive of their protests was the successful boycott of tobacco in 1891-1892, which forced the cancelation of a tobacco monopoly concession to an English firm. The Tobacco Protest in a sense marks the beginning of the agitation for a constitution.[18] The constitutional revolution was sustained by an alliance of intellectuals, merchants, and ulama, though there was considerable division among the ulama both about whether to support the constitutionalists against the king and about the ultimate goals of a constitutional revolution. The constitution itself is a monument to the accommodations made in an alliance of groups with opposed goals. The constitution specifies that five mujtahids should pass on the legitimacy of all bills proposed to parliament on the grounds of their acceptability by religious law; that the king and ministers and judges must be Ja'fari or Twelver Shi'ites; and that education and freedom of the press should be so limited that nothing repugnant to Shi'ism would be allowed. Yet as Abdul-Hadi Ha'iri points out (1973: 437), although ostensibly the constitution is a document of compromise in which the liberals yield to the religious forces, clauses on the judiciary are formulated ambiguously so as to set the stage for the undermining of religious power by allowing appeal against ecclesiastical courts.

Under the Pahlavis (1925-1979) there was at first an outright attack on the powers of the ulama in jurisprudence, education, and supervision of public decorum. Secularization later became less strident, but the constitution was largely window dressing (not only for religious affairs), and the state attempted to enforce a separation between religion and state. This was a constant source of outrage to the ulama and their followers.

In sum, perhaps the most important observation about the notion of religious establishment in Iran is that despite its legal status by Safavid decree and in 1906 by a written constitution, the pressures and sanctions to behave in proper Shi'ite fashion come less from the state than from public opinion. Public opinion in Iran — not uniformly, but nonetheless in widespread fashion — shows deep respect for the ulama and the madrasa, despite much public and private cynicism and joking about the corruption, outmodedness, ignorance, and charlatanry of many of the ulama. Again, therefore, the common sense needs to be explored.

FORMATION AND DEFENSE OF THE CANON

Codification of the several elements of Shi'ism began long before the Safavids. The Qur'an was given its definitive form in the caliphate of 'Uthman (A.D. 644-656). The hadith were collected during the seventh through ninth centuries (the first three centuries of the Muslim era), were codified for Shi'ites in the ninth century, and are still undergoing critical classification. The popular, dramatic forms of mourning Husayn were introduced in the tenth century, though *marthiyas* (mourning dirges) and similar poetry may well be older. The passion plays, however, seem to have taken form only in the seventeenth century under the Safavids, and became important in the eighteenth and nineteenth centuries under the Qajars, especially under Nasir al-Din Shah, who built a royal stage for their production in Tehran. A glance at the traditional madrasa course of study, outlined in the appendix, will show that most of the texts of jurisprudence used today have been composed over the past four centuries—since the Safavids—but they depend directly upon older texts.

Defense of the faith takes place on three levels or in three spheres: the popular, the political, and the scholarly. These three levels are clearly separable only analytically. The most scholarly of the ulama claim to oppose the passion plays and the flagellation. Yet their prime means of communication to their lay following is through the preaching of their students, if not themselves; these preachments depend in part on learning citations and proper argumentation and in part on stirring the emotional chords of the Karbala paradigm.

Shi'ism is defended in the streets, from the pulpits, and in books; but the center of the defense in a very real sense is in the madrasa. The populace at large knows the Karbala paradigm, many of the hadith, and some of the legal and theological argumentation. Its knowledge is continually renewed by popular preachers and sometimes by study circles (*hayat-e madhhabi*) in which the Qur'an and religious poetry may be read and discussed. The preachers and scholars of the traditions, however, are educated in the madrasas.

The Scriptural School Form

The history of the madrasa system is most interesting when seen in comparative perspective and in the context of three issues of general significance: epistemology, pedagogy, and politics. By *epistemology*, here, is meant the degree of openness or closedness encouraged by a particular style of thought. It is a common opinion of both outsiders and Islamic modernists that the madrasa inculcates a mentality that for the modern world is overly closed.[19] One need only recall the twelfth-century intellectual vitality of Islam to recognize that this is not a static feature of the madrasa or of Islam but a historically contingent state of decay. The question of the relative openness of a style of thought shades into issues of dogma, fundamentalism, formulation of common sense, and social control of belief and expression. Shi'ism since the sixteenth century has elaborated a symbolic world ever more focused upon the events in the lives of the first and third Imams. This cultural involution is a process of intellectual closing rather than opening. In 1962 a group of Shi'ite leaders—including future leaders of the 1978-79 revolution, such as Engineer Mehdi Bazargan and S. Mahmud Taleghani—began to discuss the urgent need to revitalize the clergy, to throw off the stagnation and scholasticism of the past, to create a modern interpretation of Islam not only compatible with but relevant to a fully modern technological society. What is important at the moment is to formulate the concerns of these modernists more generally, as concerns about the form of pedagogy—what I will call the scriptural school—and the kind of understanding it produces.

Jacques Derrida (1967) has made the radical suggestion that the very nature of a scriptural tradition and of writing as the major medium of culture has a determining effect on the way people think and specifically leads to monotheistic theologies. In a much weaker form, the Derrida thesis is widely accepted: that there are radical differences between mythopoetic-oral cultures, literate cultures, and the emerging electronic, nonlinear, postliterate civilization.[20] Within Iran, these three modes of formulating and inculcating cultural perspectives may be represented by the priestly tradition of Zoroastrianism,[21] the scholarly tradition of the Islamic madrasa, and the new secular mass education.[22] The madrasa is but one example of the scholarly tradition and the scriptural school. Two comparable examples are the Jewish yeshiva and the medieval Catholic studium. (The Buddhist sanga colleges and the Chinese mandarin system provide interesting variants but will not be considered here.)[23]

Let us first deal briefly with the contrasts and then turn to the similarities in order to gain an understanding of the scriptural school form. The contrast with priestly training is fairly sharp. Descriptions of priestly training usually mention mnemonics, inspiration, rote learning, hereditary recruitment, and lack of importance attached to whether or not the priest understands or is a scholar. By contrast, in the madrasa type of education, though ritual accuracy and rote learning may be important, understanding and scholarship are never incidental; they are the most valued goals to be attained. There is a practical reason for this importance. The madrasa or yeshiva is not merely a place of preparation for a ritual leader. It is also a kind of legislature and judiciary. To varying extents, depending upon the nature of the state within which the scriptural school is set, the opinions of the scholars have the force of legal and judicial decisions. In the case of the Jewish yeshiva, from the destruction of political autonomy to the establishment of the modern state of Israel, this has only occasionally posed a political problem.[24] For Islam the political problem has been endemic because there have been two sources of authority, located in the madrasa and in the royal court.

The contrast on the other side with mass education is also fairly clear. Mass education is concerned with training a labor force, with institutionalizing scientific innovation, with mobility, and with citizenship training. Education has become separated from the other functions of the madrasa or yeshiva. In the madrasa or yeshiva, though there is active concern with society and citizenship, with justice and welfare, the focus of concern is the relation between the individual and God or the social collectivity and God, not the labor force and scientific truth per se. The proper training of the labor force and the fullest understanding of nature at best are demonstrations of the harmony between man and God.

If one looks at the evolution of the scriptural school, one finds that the three examples are similar in the way their textual canons were compiled; in their pedagogical styles of disputation; in their scholarly apparatus of

Table 2.1 Chronology of education until the twelfth century

DATE	IRAN	ISLAMIC	JUDAIC	GREECE	EUROPE
	Zoroaster Cyrus				
500 B.C.			586: First Temple destroyed		
400 B.C.			516: Second Temple built, mass meetings, synagogue readings, Knesset Gedolah		Roman laws of the Twelve Tablets
300 B.C.			Bet ha-Midrash (Soferim) Zugot	390: Isocrates 387: Plato's Academy 335: Aristotle	
200 B.C.	Centers of learning: Susa, Antioch in Mesene, Seleucia on Tigris		165: Maccabees		
100 B.C.					
0			75: Secondary schools 64: Elementary schools 70: Second Temple destroyed	End Peripatetics	
100			*tannaim*		
200				138: Chairs of rhetoric established by the state	

Year	Persia	Islamic world	Jewish	Byzantine / Greek	Western / Christian
300	Jundishapur (Shapur 241-271)				
400	439: Byzantium closes school of Edessa and it moves to Persia		220: Mishna complete *amoraim*		Monastic schools Episcopal schools: Lérins, Marmoutier
500	532: 7 Neo-Platonists come to Iran for one year		Closing of the Gemara	Neo-Platonists 529: Justinian code 580: Slavonic invasion	Presbyterial schools
600					
700					
800					Charlemagne's schools Alfred's educational reform
900		Ma'mun's Bayt al-Hikma Legal schools of Abu Hanifa, Malik, Shafi'i, Ibn Hanbal; Ja'far al-Sadiq al-Azhar			
1000		Dar al-Hikma, Dar al-'Ilm (Egypt) 1066: Nizamiyya	Rashi (1030-1103)		
1100					Secular schools: Laon, Chartres, Paris Universities: *studia generale*
1200		1258: Mongols sack Baghdad			

logic, hermeneutical rules, and appeals to authority; and in the substance of their theological and legal argumentation. This similarity is hardly surprising, since Judaism, Christianity, and Islam developed in constant historical dialogue. With regard, for instance, to their common theological problems, I would draw attention to Wolfson's selection (1976) of six central theological issues — attributes of God, the nature of the scriptures, creation, atomism, causality, and predestination — and his brilliant demonstration of how the three traditions played chess with the possible solutions so that no one would be caught taking the same position as an opponent yet so that each one could defend his choice. Each tradition also built upon itself, usually encompassing, but occasionally excluding, what had gone before. It is fascinating that not only were solutions in one period reversed in the next but that similar battles should be fought repeatedly, especially over how literally to interpret the scriptures and what kinds of critical controls to place on freedom of interpretation: the repeated battles in Christianity over the literalness of transubstantiation (the body versus the spirit of the Word), in Islam over methods of interpreting the Qur'an, and in Judaism over *peshat* (simple explanation, sticking to the original intent of the scripture) versus *midrash* (allegorical, mystical explanation).

The form of pedagogy and the scholarly apparatus in the three traditions are similar in evolution; they converge, and they have been in dialogue with one another. Each tradition needed first to establish a textual canon and then to develop methods for deriving laws from the canon, methods for dealing with inconsistencies in the texts and among commentaries on the texts, pedagogies for introducing elementary students to ritual duties and ideological justifications, other pedagogies for initiating advanced students into both the canon and the legal techniques, rules for disputation that could serve either to stimulate exploration of a subject or to set boundaries on what was permissible to query, and degrees for competence.

Finally, if one looks at the transition from the scriptural school to the modern university, one finds in all three traditions more discontinuity than continuity. The case is clearest for Christianity, since it was in Christian Europe that the transition first occurred and both Jewish and Islamic scholarship have had to adapt to that precursor. The argument is that the modern university is not a direct outgrowth of the medieval universities of Paris, Bologna, or Oxford, but rather of Halle (founded in 1694) and Berlin (founded in 1810). What is unique about Europe is the complex historical fact that there the threshold of the industrial revolution was first crossed. The modern university system is associated with that transition in the basis of civilization and in the nature of social-class organization. It was not so much the original industrial revolution (c. 1770-1840) of textiles, heavy machinery, and iron goods (in which Britain was the leader) but rather the second or scientific industrial revolution (1870-1890) of chemicals, explosives, electrical engineering, and steel, which was sustained by and required a new mode of education. In this new education Germany was the leader. Fearing itself lagging behind Britain, Germany made a commitment early in the nineteenth century to a state educational system. As the second industrial revolution developed, Germany had the technical personnel to sustain its expansion. It took France two defeats by Prussia, in 1866 and 1870, and England until the 1902 Education Act to make similar commitments. Indeed, it is striking how many scholars of the early twentieth-century universities in England, France, and the United States received at least some of their training in Germany.

Iran today is undergoing a similar transition to mass education and industrial civilization. A few statistics may serve to establish the structural difference between Iran today and Germany in 1885 and thus help throw light on one source of the extraordinary tension in contemporary Iran. In 1885 Germany had 47 million people; today Iran has 36 million. Yet the number of students in the upper levels of the mass education system in Iran is several times what Germany had; Germany's system was much more exclusive or elitist as one proceeded into the higher grades.

	Germany, 1885[25]	Iran, 1965	Iran, 1974-75[26]
Primary	7,500,000	2,181,600	
Secondary	238,000	493,700	
Gymnasium	128,000		
Other	100,000		
Higher education	31,400	28,900	135,300 in Iran
University	27,000		+ 30,000 in
Technical			U.S. and G.B.
institutes	2,500		(others in
Other			India,
institutes	1,900		Germany)

The economic expansion of Germany in that era was extraordinary. It is unlikely that Iran's expansion today is qualitatively similar, and a problem is that the system rapidly produced a swollen bureaucracy rather than a highly productive labor force.

Our interest here is not the manpower problem itself—the lack of vocational and management training, and so on, for which there is a specialized literature available[26]—but rather the fact that the madrasa system does not link into this modern educational vortex of energy and attention. Not only are the madrasa students excluded, they are viewed by the newly professional elite as an embarrassment that should be helped to wither away as quickly as possible. In terms of numbers (a total of about 11,000 students) the madrasa students have already become an encapsulated and bypassed minority, a fact that adds to their existential anxieties.

The power and influence of the madrasa today, then, does not depend either on size or on any institutional centrality in Iranian society. No longer does the madrasa supply the teachers, notaries, judges, lawyers, scientists, or physicians of society; all these professionals are recruited now from the universities, domestic and foreign. The influence of the madrasa depends upon Shi'ite Islam's still being part of the common sense of everyday life and hence it is politically potent.

THE ISLAMIC MADRASA

The conventional date for the beginning of the madrasa system is A.D. 1066, the date when the Seljuq vizier, Nizam al-Mulk, opened the Nizamiyya College in Baghdad. This was the first of a series of *nizamiyya*s across the Seljuq empire, publicly endowed with stipends for students and salaries for teachers. The purpose was to strengthen Sunni Islam. Important figures such as al-Ghazali (1058-1111) taught at these nizamiyyas; al-Ghazali taught for four years at the one in Baghdad and then for a short time at the one in Nishapur; Sa'di (1194-1291), the great Persian poet of Shiraz, studied under a fellowship at the Nizamiyya College at Baghdad.

What is important about the nizamiyya system is that it is a "nation-wide" public system of education. There had been madrasas before this. Al-Azhar in Cairo had been founded in 970 by the Fatimids to institutionalize their version of Shi'ism. Mehdi Nakosteen (1964: 43-44) gives a list of fifty-nine denominational madrasas in Eastern Islam (Iran and Iraq today) between 1050 and 1250. (They are listed in table 2.2) But these were individual and local efforts. The nizamiyas were a kind of culmination of the first five centuries of Islamic education. That is, they mark the end of a period of creativity and are a first early attempt to introduce a widespread system and reduce diversity of opinion. They mark a kind of division in the history of Muslim education.

The earliest period of Islam was a period of collecting and translating manuscripts. There is a now-discredited legend that the first years involved destruction of ancient centers of learning. The caliph 'Umar is alleged to have replied to his commanders in Egypt ('Amr ibn al-'As) and Persia (Ibn Waqqas) that if the information in the books in the libraries were in agreement with the Qur'an, the books were superfluous, and if

Table 2.2 Denominational colleges in eastern Islam, A.D. 1050-1250[a]

SECT AND LOCATION	NUMBER	SECT AND LOCATION	NUMBER
Shi'ite		Sunni: Hanafi	
Kashan	4	Baghdad	3
Qum	8	Isfahan	1
Rey	7	Sunni: (school unspecified)	
Saveh	2	Baghdad	1
Varamin	2	Gorgan	1
Sunni: Shafi		Hamadan	1
Baghdad	2	Isfahan	1
Balkh	1	Kashan	1
Basra	1	Kirmanshah	3
Herat	1	Merv	1
Isfahan	1	Nishapur	5
Mosul	1	Rey	1
Nishapur	1	Shah Jahan	2
		Yazd	5

[a]Adapted from Nakosteen (1964).

the books disagreed with the Qur'an, they were not worth preserving; in either case the books should be destroyed. The manuscripts of the libraries of Alexandria are said to have provided fuel for the city's baths for six months. But the Persian center of Jundishapur survived until the tenth century, and much of its activity had shifted closer to the Islamic centers of Baghdad and Samara by the end of the ninth century. At least by the time of the later Umayyads the collecting of ancient manuscripts had begun; it grew into an important full-scale activity under the Abbasid caliphs al-Mansur, Harun al-Rashid, and al-Ma'mun. Translation and library centers such as the Bayt al-Hikma founded in Baghdad by the Caliph al-Ma'mun in 213/833 provided also the grounding for creative extensions of knowledge in the sciences, mathematics, medicine, and history. Many of the translators were non-Muslims: Jews, Mazdians (Zoroastrians), Nestorians, and new converts from these older religions to Islam.

The period between the victory of Islam and the establishment of the nizamiyyas, thus, is one of reconstruction and creativity generated by attempts to solve puzzles thrown up through the activity of translation and collation of ancient manuscripts. As Franz Rosenthal (1947) puts it, a creative tension arose from the conjunction of several sources of intellectual interest: a dialectic between acceptance of Greek authority and a critical attitude, stimulated above all by attempts to harmonize Plato and Aristotle while recognizing that there were fundamental differences between the two; the feelings of the superiority of Persian civilization (the so-called *shu'ubiyya* movement); and the feeling, interlinked with submission to Islam, of an Arab supremacy based on the revelation of the Qur'an as the true source of all knowledge. The tenth century (fourth century A.H.) saw a movement to stress the oneness of intellect, based on a hadith that the Prophet had said, "If Aristotle had lived to know my message, he would have adopted my religion." This sort of resolution and harmonizing grew eventually into the noncritical, all-encompassing, mystical strains of Islam, known loosely as Sufism.

What is important about this early creative period is that, aside from the caliph-supported centers of translation, education and intellectual activity centered on individuals and depended upon possessing particular manuscripts. Places of education attracted students or declined in popularity as particular scholars were present, moved, or died. Such fluctuation is to some extent true of all educational systems, but it is crucial in systems that do not have institutionalized schools that continue irrespective of the comings and goings of particular individuals. Perhaps less obvious to the contemporary mind is the dependence on manuscripts in an age before the printing press. Rosenthal (1947) cites al-Biruni's forty-year search before he found a copy of Mani's *Safar al-asrar* (Secret journey), Ibn Rushd's desire to consult certain Mu'tazilite works but inability to find copies of them, and the Christian scholar Hunayn's unsuccessful search for a Galen manuscript. Hence the emphasis among students on taking careful notes on their professors' lectures,[27] the repetition of older sources in new works, the tremendous loss occasioned by the destruction of a scholar's personal library, and the peripatetic lives of scholars traveling great distances in search of knowledge, that is, of manuscripts.[28] The following description of an Italian Renaissance university applies equally well to Muslim colleges even today in Iran and would have been absolutely true a century ago before the printing press was introduced in Iran in the late nineteenth century:

> [The students] had no notes, grammars, lexicons, or dictionaries of antiquities and mythology to help them. It was therefore necessary for the lecturer to dictate quotations, to repeat parallel passages at full length, to explain geographical and historical allusions, to analyze the structure of sentences in detail, to provide copious illustrations of grammatical usage, to trace the stages by which a word acquired its meaning in a special context, to command a full vocabulary of synonyms, to give rules for orthography and to have the whole Pantheon at his fingers' ends. In addition to this, he was expected to comment upon the meaning of his author, to interpret his philosophy, to point out the beauties of his style, to introduce appropriate moral disquisition on his doctrine, to sketch his biography, and to give some account of his relation to the history of his country and to his predecessors in the field of letters . . . Scores of students, old and young, with nothing but pen and paper on the desks before them, sat pa-

tiently recording what the lecturer said. At the end of his discourses on the *Georgics* or the *Verrines*, each of them carried away a compendious volume, containing a transcript of the author's text, together with a miscellaneous mass of notes, critical, explanatory, ethical, aesthetical, historical, and biographical. In other words, a book had been dictated, and as many scores of copies as there were attentive pupils had been made. The language used was Latin. No dialect of Italian could have been intelligible to the students of different nationalities who crowded the lecture-rooms. The elementary education in grammar requisite for following a professorial course of lectures had been previously provided by the teachers of the Latin schools which depended for maintenance partly on the State and partly on private enterprise. (John Symonds, cited by Laurie 1903: 35)

For a description of the Iranian madrasa, merely substitute "Arabic" for "Latin."

The process of reconstruction of ancient knowledge and its creative extension is conventionally said to have peaked by the end of the eleventh century. Thereafter scholarship became repetitive compilations of encyclopedias rather than innovative. Religious orthodoxies set in and reduced the intellectual freedom of expression. In the sixteenth century, with the establishment of the Safavid and Ottoman religious ideologies, political conditions also reduced tolerance for diversity of opinion. Internationally, after the eleventh century the Arabic translations began to be retranslated into Latin and generated a creative impulse for the development of the Renaissance and modern European universities. The torch of creative scholarship was passed from the Muslim world to Europe.

Madrasas continued to be built by the rulers. Most of the old madrasas of Qum were initially constructed and endowed by the sixteenth-century Safavids. At the same time the religious leaders attempted successfully to separate the actual administration of the madrasas from state interference. Here the development in Iran differs radically from that in the Ottoman empire, where the madrasas were integrated into the bureaucratic structure. But in both cases the result was a kind of religious involution: an intellectual stagnation and an elaboration of the kind of religious learning consisting of commentaries on hadith and the Qur'an and commentaries upon commentaries, usually in the form of notes upon one's teacher's lectures, which in turn were his notes upon his teacher's.

Although the madrasa system that developed in Iran was not a state system on the nizamiyya or Ottoman models, yet it was statewide and international. There was a standard curriculum. There was teacher certification: ijazas or letters of permission were given by recognized scholars to certify that one was qualified to teach specified items. Students started their ABCs in the local maktab (elementary school), often run by women. Boys might proceed from the maktab to provincial towns for the lower levels of education. Then they went to the larger cities for the upper levels, ultimately trying to go where the most reknowned scholars lectured. The madrasas and students were supported by religious "tithes" (the sahm-i Imam, or "share of the Imam," that is, half the one-fifth khums tax), by private endowments, and by endowments from high officials, including the king. At times the royal court attempted to supervise these endowments through a Ministry of Endowments, but the sahm-i Imam and voluntary contributions have provided a major source of independence for the religious institution, although paradoxically also a source of anti-innovative conservatism.

The Jewish Yeshiva

Three points of comparison between the yeshiva and the madrasa are worth considering: the social role of the scriptural school, that is, the legislative and judicial role, and how this role varied; the pedagogical system, that is, the sequencing of study, the rules of method, and the degrees obtained; and the evolution of the form of schooling, both its rise and its decline. It is not surprising that early Muslim scholars should have adopted Judaic techniques of legal and theological argumentation (and that both should have been influenced by the Greco-Roman world): the scholarly tradition of Islam arose in Mesopotamia shortly after (in part concurrently with) the talmudic and rabbinic tradition. (In the medieval period the debt would be repaid, with Jewish scholarship borrowing from Islamic.) Indeed according to Marshall Hodgson (1974: I, 310), "A significant part of the population that accepted Islam in its formative centuries was composed of Jews, whose narrative traditions, called *Isra'iliyyat* (Israelitics), dominated the popular legendry of early Islam." The same should hold for scholarship.

Similarly, at the modern end of the scriptural school's development, the yeshiva was confronted with the Enlightenment and the modern university before the madrasa was. In both cases a process of isolation and parochializing ensued, with the brightest and most socially mobile students leaving for the modern educational system. But even long before this, both systems had been relegated to primarily religious studies and so had stagnated. Shlomo Dov Goitein (1971) points out that even religious leaders in Jewish medieval Cairo tended to come from scientific, and especially medical, training. (Maimonides was the example par excellence.) Despite the claims of the madrasa and yeshiva to be based on creative disputation, it is practical affairs that ensure creativity. Both the yeshiva and madrasa, through the late medieval and early modern periods, served as guarantors of a certain amount of literacy, the yeshiva much more successfully than the madrasa, for a reason that I think has to do with the nature of the synagogue liturgy.[29]

The history of the yeshiva begins with the destruction of the Temple, or with the destruction of the priestly tradition of Judaism.[30] This was a long process extending from 586 B.C.E.[31] (the destruction of the first Temple by Nebuchadnezzar) to 70 C.E. (the destruction of the second Temple by Titus). Just as the completion of the madrasa system is conventionally said to have been instituted in 1066, so the yeshiva is conventionally said to have begun in 70 C.E. with what was known as "the vineyard" at Yabneh, established by Johanan ben Zakkai. In both cases the conventional date is the culmination of an important preparatory transition.

After the Persians conquered Babylonia, Cyrus the Great allowed Nehemiah and Ezra to return to Jerusalem to rebuild the (second) Temple (completed in 516 B.C.E.). An academy (*bet ha-midrash*) was built near the Temple. Although the majority of the population which had been removed by Nebuchadnezzar to Iraq remained there, and although there seem to have been academies in Iraq, this bet ha-midrash quickly became the premier academy, drawing students from everywhere. There were apparently several early academies in Palestine as well, but these merged into the one at the Temple, with two heads (the *zugot*, or "pair"): the *nasi* (president) and the *ab bet din* (head of the court).[32] From this academy were recruited the seventy members of the great assembly (Hebrew *knesset ha-godol*, Greek *sanhedrin*), headed by the high priest, and the members of the several lesser courts of twenty-three members.[33] At the same time as this academy began to take shape, Ezra organized mass meetings at which the scripture was read and instituted readings in synagogues four times a week (Monday and Thursday mornings and twice on Saturday); a quorum of ten was required, and the readings were done in both Hebrew and the vernacular Aramaic, which had been adopted in Babylonia.

This was the period of the canonization of the Bible, the creation of the synagogue liturgy, and the evolution of methods of deriving the law from biblical texts (*midrash halakhah*, the parallel to the later Islamic discipline of usul or methods of deriving the fiqh or law from Qur'anic verses). The nature of the community was quite different in this "second commonwealth" from that under the first Temple; no longer were there prophets, the tribal divisions no longer had meaning, the Temple contained no Ark of the Covenant, and rather than a king and nobles, a council of sages headed by a high priest led the community. The community paid tribute to the Persians, then the Greeks, the Ptolomies of Egypt, and the Seleucids of Syria. In 165 B.C.E. the Maccabbee revolt established the independence of the state of Judea with the high priest as king. This theocratic rule lasted until 37 B.C.E., although the kingdom lost its independence to Rome in 63 B.C.E.

Toward the end of this period, around 75 B.C.E., Simeon ben Shetah, nasi of the sanhedrin and brother of the queen, Salomeh, instituted secondary schools to prepare students for the academy. This reform seems to have been connected with the dispute between the Pharisees (*Perushim*, "separatists"), the traditionalist faction led by Simeon, and the Sadducees (*Zedokim*), who rejected the Oral Law, invoking the slogan to return to the Torah alone and thereby attempting to restrict the sphere of religious law so that there might be greater freedom to emulate Greek civilization.[34] The educational reform, systematizing preparation in the school rather than in the home, instituted to protect the faith, had the effect of producing so many students that the great academy split into two: the famous academies of Shammai and of Hillel, the first two *tannaim* ("repeaters" or transmitters of what they had learned, parallel to the later Islamic "transmitter," or ravi).[35] These two leaders and schools figure continually in the Talmud as the sources of opposed opinions on any given subject.

Indeed, one of the first subjects of dispute for an account of the development of education is their opposed positions on who is to be educated. The Talmudic tract *Aboth* begins: The men of the great assembly "said three things: Be deliberate in judgment, raise up many disciples, and make a fence around the Law" (*Aboth* 1:1). But later there is a comment upon "raise up many disciples": "For the school of Shammai says: One ought to teach only him who is talented and meek and of distinguished ancestry and rich. But the school of Hillel says: One ought to teach every man, for there were many in Israel who had been sinners and were drawn to the study of Torah, and from them descended righteous (*saddiqim*), pious (*hasidim*), and worthy folk" (*Aboth* 1:3).

The school of Hillel eventually won out. The school of Shammai continued the old practice of charging student fees. Hillel opposed fees: teaching and learning are religiously meritorious and ought not to be subject to fees; a scholar should not support himself by teaching if he can otherwise earn a living.[36] This shift toward open education for all quickly went to its logical conclusion. No longer was there a primacy accorded to those of priestly, noble, or wealthy ancestry. Indeed the leaders of the sanhedrin after Simeon ben Shetah were two men of proselyte origin (Shemaya and Avtalyon).

Nearly a hundred years later a system of elementary schools was introduced by Joshua ben Gamala (64 C.E.). Those parents who refused to send their children were disparagingly called *'amm ha-arez* (peasants, hicks).

In 70, Jerusalem was taken by the Romans, and the story goes that during the siege Johanan ben Zakkai, a student of Hillel, had himself smuggled in a coffin through the lines to the Roman camp. From Vespasian he obtained the pledge that he could establish a school in Yabneh, for Jews were to be excluded from Jerusalem. This yeshiva exercised the functions of the sanhedrin: setting the ritual calendar, being the supreme court, collecting financial support. After the death of Johanan, yeshivas were established in several places so that if one were closed by the Romans, others could continue. As the yeshivas had different teachers with slightly different styles and interpretations, students would move from school to school.

There were no fees, but Johanan tried to establish admission procedures. However, student pressure was so great that these were abolished. The custom of standing to listen to the lecture (out of respect for the word of God) was also abolished and semicircular benches were introduced.[37] In the front were three rows of twenty-three seats assigned to the advanced students, called shield bearers, men who could defend their opinions (similar to Muslim mujtaheds). Behind them came less advanced students, and in the back the rest of the students, with first-year students and common people seated on the ground. This semicircular pattern resembled a grape vine, and the "vineyard" metaphor was employed; it reproduced as well the arrangement of the sanhedrin, where priests and Levites had been seated in the front rows. Support for the yeshivas were obtained by sending messengers to various communities to take up collections, replacing in part the annual obligations of Temple sacrifice dues. There was an ordination (*smicha*) leading to the title *rabbi* ("master") already introduced under Hillel and Shammai, as well as certifications of expertise (*reshut*), which did not carry the title rabbi (parallel to the later Muslim mujtahid and ijaza).[38]

Thus the institution that had emerged by 70 C.E. was, first of all, a three-tiered system of public education, graded and with certifications of several sorts (reshut, smicha), and open to all. Second, its masters (rabbis), both in councils (sanhedrin, yeshiva, *havurot ha-sedeq*)[39] and in courts (*bet din*)[40] were the legislative and judicial authority for the community. To be sure, the rabbis did not exercise political authority. In Palestine, political authority was placed by outside powers upon the nasi or patriarch, and in Babylonia upon the exilarch (*rosh galuta*); later the title in Cairo became *nagid ra'is al-yahud* (leader of the Jews).[41] And so, despite the claim of religious law to be all-encompassing ("not only a religion but a way of life"), a de facto distinction arose between religious and secular law, exactly as would be the case in both Islam and Catholicism.

The education itself consisted of a tripartite curriculum. The elementary level (*miqra*) began, after mastering the alphabet, with the Pentateuch, the Prophets, and the Hagiographa, all of which were extant before the second commonwealth began (c. 500 B.C.E.).[42] The child or older beginner memorized and translated or paraphrased into the vernacular (Aramaic or, in Alexandria, Greek). An interesting practice, established at least by the time of Rabbi Akiba (40-130 C.E.), was that one begins the Torah not with Genesis but with Leviticus, that is, not with the legends of creation but with the rules of sacrifice and purity. Various reasons have been given, the most probable being that the Pharisees wished to emphasize the separation of Jews, in opposition to the assimilation into Hellenic culture being promoted by the patricians and many of the Sadducees. In any case the practice continued into modern times in the yeshivas of Eastern Europe.[43] The Talmudic reason given for the practice is that "children are pure, sacrifices are pure, let the pure (children) study the pure (sacrifices)." In the nineteenth-century elementary schools (*heder*) of Eastern Europe, the Pentateuch was still the basis of the learning, together now with the commentaries of Rashi (1030-1105); the Prophets and Hagiographa were usually left for the student to learn by himself.

The most immediate purpose of this elementary education is not literacy per se, but to prepare a boy[44] to take part in the synagogue (as the *scholae cantora* of Europe were to train priests to sing the Offices, and the Muslim maktab to give a child the minimal knowledge of the Qur'an). Goitein (1971) suggests that the heavy stress on memorization derived from a period in which there was a need to preserve not only an exact reading but also the proper cantilation; hence the Talmudic line "The world exists solely through the breath of the school children." (Compare the Muslim apologia that the authenticity of the Qur'an is guaranteed by the oral memorization of numerous early Muslims.) By the eleventh and twelfth centuries, however, Goitein points out, the ambiguity of the Hebrew alphabet (an ambiguity from which Arabic also suffered) had been resolved by notations for pronunciation and cantilation. (Arabic also evolved notation for vocalization, and the Qur'an too gained cantilation notes.) Further, by this time the Targum (Greek translation) had become not a translation aid to understanding the Hebrew but yet another obscure text to be memorized. Reading was learned but not writing: writing was only an aid to learning, and those who did not continue their studies often could not read or write the cursive script. The reward for studying well was to be allowed to ascend the platform in the center of the synagogue (*bimeh, anbol, minbar*)[45] and read a portion of the week's section of the Torah.

The intermediate level of education revolved around the Mishnah (from *shanah*, "to repeat") or Oral Law. In the early days (until 200 c.e.) this followed the order of the Pentateuch. Thus, Nathan Drazin (1940: 85-90) gives the following example: when one came to the verse "The seventh day is a Sabbath unto the Lord thy God, in it thou shalt not do any manner of work" (Exod. 20: 10), the teacher would recite:

> The main classes of work are forty save one: sowing, plowing, reaping . . . how much must a man build to become culpable? He is culpable who builds [on the Sabbath] aught soever, or who at all hews stone, or wields a hammer, or chisels, or bores a hole. This is the general rule: if man performs

work on the Sabbath and his work is enduring, he is culpable . . . he is culpable who writes two letters (of the alphabet), whether with his right hand or his left, whether the same or different letters, whether in different inks or in any language.

Note the use of numbers as mnemonics (thirty-nine classes of work). In 200 C.E. the Mishnah was reorganized by Rabbi Judah ha-Nasi Rabban into six orders, each divided into tractates, totaling sixty-one. This then became the standard text. The text, however, is but a summary of the teachings of the tannaim (from Shammai and Hillel to the Rabbis Akiba and Rabban), an aid to oral teachings. And so the tannaim (repeaters) were followed by the *amoraim*, or "interpreters" (c. 200-500), who made additional compilations of traditions and explanations; with chains of transmission going back to Moses (parallel with the *isnad* of the Muslim *hadith*), and developed critical methods for evaluating and applying the Oral Law. This then is the period of the development of the *gemara* or the two talmuds, the Babylonian and the Palestinian. They contain sermons by the sages, records of debates, and explanations. After the completion of the two talmuds, the amoraim were succeeded by *gaonim*, scholars who replied to questions about the law. In the eleventh century in France, Rashi produced a definitive recension with commentaries of the Babylonian Talmud, which is accepted to the present. Further commentaries were produced in the twelfth and thirteenth centuries (the *Tosafot*) and then not again until the sixteenth century in Poland.

The Talmud was the subject of study for the highest level of education: the yeshiva. The distinction between the intermediate studies and the advanced studies was not so much the subject as the detail and subtlety of exposition. Even each letter of the text might be examined.[46] Various critical rules were established: Hillel had listed seven hermeneutical rules, Rabbi Ishmael (a contemporary of Akiba) established thirteen rules for interpreting legal decisions (halakhah) and thirty-two rules for interpreting legendary material (haggadah) rules such as *gezerah sharah* (deriving the meaning of a word in an unclear passage from its meaning in a clear passage), and *kal va homer* (deducing from a minor to a major case, or from a concrete case to a general law). In the nineteenth-century yeshivas of Eastern Europe there were two school terms (April-July, October-June) during which there would be a daily assembly with the president in the chair and the students standing around him.[47] The president or head of the yeshiva (*rosh yeshiva*) would give a lecture, followed by an argumentation called *hilluk* or *pilpul* in which the contradictions in the Talmud and commentaries would be pointed out, solutions proposed, these solutions shown to be contradictory, and further solutions proposed, until the subject matter was fully explored (compare the *bahth* of the Muslim madrasa). Toward the middle of the term there would be less pilpul and more attention to textual materials, and toward the end of the term the students would be allowed to try their hand at pilpul (Gamoran 1925). The varieties of interpretation are endless, though a traditional mnemonic classifies them into four levels: PaRDeS ("orchard"), an acronym of the first letters of *peshat, remez, derush,* and *sod,* referring to "the plain, the typological, the homiletical, and the symbolic method of interpretation" (Avi-Yonah 1968).

The yeshivas of the early gaonim period were three major academies, one in Palestine and two in Iraq (Sura and Nehardea). In Iraq the scholars were dispersed among the various Jewish communities of Mesopotamia and Iran, but they would gather twice a year for study and making decisions. The *gaon* or head of the yeshiva would announce which sections of the Talmud would be discussed at the following semiannual meeting so scholars could study ahead. The gaon's exposition would be carried to the large audience by interpreters who would also relay questions. At the spring assembly questions would be discussed that had been sent from various parts of the world (students and inquiries came to Iraq from as far afield as Italy and France). The Palestinian yeshiva had no such semiannual convocations, but the scattered members would meet to discuss communal and religious issues on pilgrimages to Jerusalem, particularly at the Feast of Tabernacle (Sukkoth). In 1071, when the Seljuks conquered Jerusalem, the Palestinian yeshiva moved to Tyre, then to Damascus, and finally to Cairo (1127), where it lasted as a continuous institution until it was replaced by a school formed around Maimonides in the late twelfth century. A Jewish convert to Islam, Ya 'qub ibn Killis, became vizier to the Fatimid caliph in the 970s and presided over the beginnings of al-Azhar. The Fatimids also provided financial support to the yeshivas for a brief period.[48]

In the tenth to thirteenth centuries, heads of the local congregations in the Mediterranean were nominated by the congregations and appointed by the heads of these three yeshivas. In Cairo some congregations followed the Palestinian yeshiva, others followed the Babylonian yeshivas. Although there was competition for membership, the public chest, courts, and endowments were jointly administered. When the Palestinian yeshiva moved to Cairo, it remained composed of seventy members, but an unlimited number of scholars were associated. Only a person occupying a seat in the rows was allowed to participate in the disputations; each row had a head (*rosh ha-seder*) who in turn might be the head of the lesser academies or *midrashim* (compare Islamic madrasa). These lesser colleges sprang up all over the Mediterranean, and as the schools in Baghdad began to decay in the tenth century, those in Tunisia (Qayrawan) and elsewhere began to grow. The Iraqi yeshiva was finally reduced to relative insignificance at the time of the Mongol invasions.

Regional differences in competence arose, depending upon political conditions. Europeans had less legal autonomy and so became better

Talmudic scholars but poor judges.[49] The concentration on Talmud in Europe led to a neglect of precision in knowledge of the Bible and its pronunciation, skills that were maintained in Egypt and especially in Yemen. For Europeans the Talmud was more practical than the Bible: it had more about prayers, family law, and commerce. In Cairo, on the other hand, Jews were more integrated into national life, and their religious concerns focused on problems of adjudicating legal cases and on theological issues.[50] In the tenth and eleventh centuries the gaonim (heads of the yeshivas) began to write monographs on aspects of the law, using Arabic or Islamic terms (compare the Muslim *taqrirat*); and the responsa or answers to questions of the gaonim began to be collected as the basis for local rulings (compare the *risala-i tawdih al-masa'il* of Muslim mujtahids).

To recapitulate, Rabbi Jehuda ben Tema said that at five years of age one should begin the Torah, at ten the Mishna, and at fifteen the Gemara.[51] A thirteenth-century description is more detailed (Gamoran 1925: 9):

At age 5:	First month — alphabet
	Second month — vowels
	Third month — syllables
	Leviticus and the weekly Torah portion
7:	The Targum
8-9:	Prophets and Hagiographa
10:	Mishna and Torah
13:	Youngster can be taken to the house of the devoted to study
16:	Duty of separation for study in the yeshiva for seven years: two years each for Mo'ed, Nashim, Nezikim, Kodashim

The focus of study is always the Torah and Talmud, but other things might be added. Goitein remarks that the eleventh-century *kuttab* taught little writing or arithmetic, but Hay Gaon (d. 1038) allowed both arithmetic and Arabic calligraphy. The Talmud speaks of the experiments of Rabbi Simon b. Halafta who examined ants to verify a biblical assertion that the ant has no chief, overseer, or ruler, and the disciples of Rabbi Ishmail who dissected the cadaver of an executed prostitute to discover the number of bones, 250, in a woman's body (Drazin 1940). A twelfth-century Spanish curriculum claims to include the Bible, Hebrew poetry, the Talmud, the relations of philosophy and revelation, the logic of Aristotle, Euclid, arithmetic, the mathematics of Nicomachus, Theodosius, Menelaus, Archimedes, optics, astronomy, music, medicine, natural science, and metaphysics (Gamoran 1925: 10). More seriously, Goitein points out the importance of physicians both as community leaders and as religious scholars, of which Maimonides is the outstanding case; of the ten named Egyptian nagids between 1050 and 1400 all were physicians. Even sticking narrowly to Talmud and Torah, the method of study stressed the multifaceted nature of truth, pragmatism, and reducing social dissension. Pilpul or dialectics may eventually be self-defeating, but it is not simply dogmatics.

THE CHRISTIAN STUDIUM

Like the yeshiva and madrasa, Christian education in western Europe began with scriptural schools.[52] In the Byzantine East, classical schools continued and Christians attended them—albeit with much unease, for the method of teaching was inextricably bound to the pagan content. In learning to read, one went from syllables to the names of gods and then to the various poetical forms, the content of which was not only pagan figures but the values of a pagan age. Tertullian went so far as to forbid Christians to be teachers in such schools; and when the Emperor Julian banned Christians from teaching what they did not believe, the two Apollinari (father and son) tried to write new texts using the classical literary forms but with Judaeo-Christian contents: the Pentateuch in the style of Homer and the historical texts of the Old Testament as drama, for example. These and the attempts of Origen to establish Christian schools with both catechism and theological exegesis were short-lived reactions. Christians took part in the classical education. Parallel Christian schools were eventually established in monasteries and by the patriarch, their curricula including theology, rhetoric, grammar, philosophy, and mathematics. In 1453, with the conquest of Constantinople by the Turks, this tradition of Christian education was broken and priests resorted to local scriptural schools, as had the early Christians of Western Europe.

In Western Europe, where classical education collapsed along with the Roman political authority, schools were set up in monasteries to teach monks to read the scripture (*lectio divina*) and in cathedrals to train priests. Encouragement of these schools, established first in the fourth and fifth centuries, was later given by Charlemagne and Alfred (ninth century),[53] and until the thirteenth century the Church more or less had a monopoly on learning. The process of building a textual corpus for education was not very different from that of the yeshiva and madrasa. The first need beyond the catechism, plainsong, psalms, Canonical Hours, and the Bible itself, was to make available at least extracts from writings of the early Church fathers. This was the task of Alcuin at the court of Charlemagne. Inconsistencies in the texts led to commentaries, to distinctions between the letter and the spirit of a text, and to systematizations. The development of the Gloss, or standard commentary on the text (*sacrina pagina*), was similar to that for the Mishna and Talmud; indeed when textual criticism became important in glossing, Jewish rabbis were freely consulted, both for the Hebrew and for historical context, in order to clarify the meaning. This consultation, in fact, apparently reintroduced to Jews a number of forgotten Hebraic traditions preserved in the patristic writings (Hailperin 1963: 6).

The standard commentary, *Glossa Ordinaria*, was begun by Anselm. The next generation then glossed the Gloss. Physically the texts, like those of the Talmud and Islamic commentaries, became crowded with marginal notes, which in turn became authoritative. *Quaestiones* on theological matters began to be separated out with their answers as separate texts. Of these Abelard's *Sic et Non* set the style: a compilation of 158 questions, each followed by a series of quotations from the Church fathers giving conflicting views and arguments, with no solution attempted. Peter Lombard, a student of Abelard, used the same form in his *Sentences*, which began as questions raised during his glossing of Anselm (the *Magna Glosatum*), but he indicated the accepted solutions. The *Sentences* became the universal textbook of theology. In law, a similar style of codification occurred. Irnerius (c. 1113) compiled a digest of *responsa* of the classical jurists, and thereby made civil law a full-time course of study, separate from the liberal arts. Slightly later (1142-1151) the monk Gratian compiled the *Decretum* or *Concordantia Discordantium Canonum* in the manner inaugurated by Abelard's *Sic et Non* and doing for canon law what Peter Lombard's *Sentences* was to do for theology. That is, on every disputed question in ecclesiastical law, he listed all the authorities on either side and indicated those doctrines that are to be preferred for their superior authority, more recent date, or reasonableness. Not only did this help differentiate canon law from civil law as a separate course of study, but Pope Gregory IX used this model to publish five books of his own and his predecessors' *Decretals*, which he then sent to the universities of Paris and Bologna to be taught, thereby to create an international legal training such as had been provided by Roman law for the old empire. Even medicine (particularly at Paris) relied on this scholastic style of presenting opinions.

Systematization in this scholastic mode, using syllogistic reasoning to support the accepted opinions on disputed issues, is conventionally said to have culminated, at least in theology, with St. Thomas Aquinas (d. 1274). The thirteenth century began to see the recovery of many new Aristotelian and other classical texts, through the efforts of translation from Arabic, especially at Toledo under Archbishop Raymond. One way of characterizing the turning point of the thirteenth century is given by Richard McKeon (1975: 185):

> If you wanted to know what the culture of the twelfth century was, you could list, let's say, three thousand quotations that every intellectual would know. And you would have a method by which to deal with these quota-

tions because each of the collections of canon law and the *Sic et Non* gives the method. If you have a pair of statements which seems to be contradictory on the same question, you consider who said it, to whom, under what circumstances, and for what purpose . . . So the culture of the twelfth century is easier to describe than the culture of any other period that I know because you can tabulate it. By the thirteenth century, this is totally changed. It is changed because three thousand quotations are no longer enough. The new translations bring in new data . . . there is a multiplicity of methods.

With this explosion in materials to be worked with, the cathedral schools had begun to evolve into universities. The *scholasticus*, or canon in charge of training priests, had become a chancellor of a university with three senior faculties—in theology, law, and medicine—and one preparatory faculty—in arts. The university[54] became, by charter of the Pope, a place that offered a *studium generale* (open to all, foreigners and native, laymen and clerics) and gave degrees *jus ubique docendi* (the right to teach in the same faculty at any university). At the beginning of the thirteenth century there were three main *studia*: Paris for theology and arts, Bologna for law, and Salerno for medicine. By 1650 there were thirteen to seventeen universities in France (depending on how you draw its boundaries). The first Papal bull of *jus ubique docendi* was issued in 1233 to raise Toulouse to equality with Paris and Bologna. Other new universities obtained similar bulls, and in 1292 they were formally given to the old universities of Paris and Bologna. (Oxford and Padua did not receive bulls, but were declared *studia generalia* "by custom"; Paris, however, refused to recognize Oxford degrees without further examinations, whereupon Oxford repaid the compliment in kind.)

To take Paris as the example of this evolution,[55] the university grew out of the cathedral school of Notre Dame. The Lateran Council of 1179 had decreed that each cathedral school endow a master to teach gratis, that no fee should be exacted for a license to teach, and that the license should not be refused any qualified applicant. A scholasticus-chancellor supervised the licensing to teach. From about 1170 there was a guild of masters who asserted the right to strike and in 1200 received a charter of privileges from Philip Augustus, including the right to protection from the provost of Paris (against the chancellor, if need be); and in 1209 Pope Innocent III allowed the guild to appoint a representative in Rome to represent them in disputes with the chancellor. Involved in these constitutional developments were major disputes between the chancellor, the masters, and the city. In the 1250s further disputes developed, this time over the role of Dominican and Franciscan monks in the university, since they operated their own houses of teaching and demanded licenses to teach without being subject to the guild rules. One of the results of this conflict was the founding of residential colleges for secular theologians, such as that of Robert Sorbonne, chaplain to Louis IX, as rivals to the religious houses. The conflict over privileges and jurisdiction eventually led to the destruction of the university as an international institution: under Louis XI, in the latter part of the fifteenth century, the rector (the title that replaced scholasticus) had to swear loyalty to the crown, and foreign students were expelled. Gradually the quality of education declined and the universities were overshadowed by Protestant and Jesuit educational ventures.

It is interesting to look at the life of students in these universities and discover the centrality of disputation (like the bahth of the madrasa and the pilpul of the yeshiva). At the beginning there was little regulation of the sequence of studies and students wandered from school to school. Abelard (1079-1142) was one of the masters who drew students to Paris in its early days, though he too wandered from place to place and was twice ousted from his chair at Notre Dame.[56]

John of Salisbury studied in France from 1139-1149: first, logic in Paris for two years; then the quadrivium[57] in Chartres for three years; and then theology again in Paris. He has left a description of the grammatical lectures of William of Conches at Chartres:

> After questions on parsing, scansion, construction and the grammatical figures or 'oratorical tropes' illustrated in the passage read, the Lecturer noticed the varieties of phraseology occurring therein, and pointed out the different ways in which this or that may be expressed — in short subjected the whole diction of the author to an elaborate and exhaustive analysis . . .
> He then proceeded to comment on or explain the subject matter, enlarging upon any incidental allusions to physical science or any ethical questions touched on by the author. The next morning the pupils were required, under the severest penalties, to repeat what they had been taught on the preceding day; and there was daily practice in Latin prose and verse composition in imitation of specified Classical models. (Rashdall 1895: I, 65)

In the next century, things became more regularized. A boy aged fourteen or so would come to the university. There he would begin Latin grammar; or, if he already had some training in the liberal arts (which were more widely taught in the provinces than the higher subjects), he would go to the arts classes, where he would sit on the floor around the lecturer's desk (benches were introduced in the mid-fifteenth century). To get the bachelor's degree he had to "respond" in December (have a disputation with a master in grammar or logic); next he had to be examined by a board of examiners; and finally in Lent he had to face a "determination" (a disputation in which he defended a thesis against an opponent) to which many came, since the candidate provided drinks and a feast. The bachelor then became an assistant teacher, going to classes but also taking part in disputations and giving some lectures. At age twenty he could apply for a master's degree. This involved an examination, a disputation, a second examination, an inaugural lecture, and a feast. He then had duties of public disputations for forty days and lecturing for two years (though by the mid-fourteenth century this requirement was dropped). A master's degree in theology could be taken at age twenty-five after six years' study (four on the Bible and two on the *Sentences*). A doctorate of theology could be obtained at age thirty-five. Inception, the admission to being a master, was marked by giving an inaugural lecture seated in a magisterial cathedra and being invested with the insignia of an open book, a ring, and a cap (*biretta*).

Peter the Chanter (c. 1170) has left a famous description of scholastic learning which could just as well be a description of what goes on in the madrasas of Qum:

> The practice of Bible study consists in three things: reading (*lectione*), disputation, preaching . . . Reading is, as it were, the foundation and basement for what follows, for through it the rest is achieved. Disputation is the wall in this building of study, for nothing is fully understood or faithfully preached if it is not first chewed by the tooth of disputation. Preaching which is supported by the former, is the roof, sheltering the faithful from the heat and wind of temptation. We should preach after, not before, the reading of Holy Scripture and the investigation of doubtful matters by disputation. (Smalley 1964: 208)

Lectures (the reading and glossing of a text), repetitions (special discussions of particular questions, often led by *bachelarii* not yet qualified to lecture on the scripture itself), and disputations (a thesis is maintained against all comers) were separate teaching devices. Students took notes on their teachers' lectures, and these became the basis of their own lectures. Interpretive senses were often distinguished into four, as by St. John Cassian in his classic example of the meanings of Jerusalem: "Jerusalem, according to *history*, is a city of the Jews, according to *allegory* it is the Church of Christ; according to *anagoge* it is the heavenly city of God which is the mother of us all (Gal. iv. 26); according to *tropology* it is the soul of man, 'which under this name the Lord often threatens or praises' " (Smalley 1964: 28). Or into three senses, as by Peter Lombard: "This historical sense is easier, the moral sweeter, the mystical sharper; the historical is for beginners, the moral for the advanced, the mystical for the perfect" (Smalley 1964: 245).

Tables of meanings of words with texts illustrating the several senses (*distinctio*), parables (*exempla*), glosses, and concordances, all aided in exposition and teaching. As in Judaism or Islam, there was always danger that during the process of "grinding the corn of scripture into the bread of tropology" or moralization, one would be accused of doing violence to the meaning of the text; vice versa, too literal an interpretation of the text or acceptance of too many of what Jews identified as literal meanings led to accusations of Judaicizing and perverting the message of the Lord.

Decline of the Scriptural School Form

A variety of factors contributed to the decline of the scholastic universities: continuing discovery of more and more classical texts, the rise of national vernacular literatures, the nationalization of the universities away from an international system nominally coordinated by the Pope, the rigidifying of scholastic methods, and the Protestant Reformation. Histories of Western education and culture tend to stress the first and fourth of these factors, but the rise of the Protestant minister is perhaps equally important, both in indicating social changes in the basis of public sensibilities and in changing the style of education.

Preaching is an activity for which madrasa and yeshiva students are trained, as were the medieval friars. In medieval Europe there were collections of parables, sermon manuals, and canons issued by bishops that priests must preach the ten commandments, the creed, the Lord's Prayer, the seven sacraments, the seven virtues, and the seven deadly sins. An outline from the popular fourteenth-century *Fasciculus morum* is given by Wenzel (1976: 38):

Theme	"You should follow in His footsteps" (I Peter 2:21)
Simile from everyday life	Masons, carpenters and writers all need a model. If you want to go to heaven, you also need a model: the life of Christ.
Restate theme	Hence after the blessed words of Peter: You should follow Christ, who like a good leader went before us on a three-fold path:
Divide theme in three	Humility and obedience Poverty and patience Purity and continence
Restate theme with a quotation from the Bible	"Let my Lord pass before His servant, and I will softly follow in His footsteps"

(Compare this with the Shi'ite *rawda*, or preachment, described in chapter 5.)

Various devices were used to enliven these sermons: anagrams from key words, verbally painted pictures of abstract ideas, and versified "preachers tags" for both wit and rhetorical persuasion. To illustrate that pride can be overcome by thinking about death, the Latin word for death (*mors*) is used to talk about four words, each beginning with a letter of *mors*, indicating things associated with death: *mirum speculum* (mirror), *orologium* (clock), *raptor* (thief), (s)*citator* (summoner). Or an abstract concept is allegorized by describing a person with a series of attributes related to the concept. Finally, versified tags not only could sum up a point but could add the flavor of a divine voice or a wail of a damned soul: "Whoso will not when he may, He shall not when he would; Alas, alas, that I was born, Both life and soul I am forlorn." By 1500, comments Wenzel (pp. 49-50), denouncing the vices (and commending the virtues), "with its innumerable proof texts and illustrative stories, had been heard so many times that it would no longer stir an audience to contrition, but lull them into a peaceful doze."[58]

The Protestant minister reacted against the routinization of the Church message, the overritualization of the liturgy, and the corruption of the Church itself. Instead he emphasized a message of personal conversion, simplicity of expression, and active dedication to spiritual goals in one's social life. The typical career of an English Protestant minister still began at the universities of Oxford and Cambridge, but financial support for his lectures increasingly came from local communities and the rising bourgeois merchants. Several strands of thought reinforced each other: the anti-Catholic and the humanist. As early as 1524, Martin Luther sent a letter to German municipalities asking them to provide their own schools and not depend on the Church. Vitorina da Feltre (1378-1446), the Brethren of the Common Life in the Netherlands, and Erasmus (1467-1536), though critical of the Church, were not hostile to it; yet their emphasis on the classics sowed the seeds of non-Church-related schools. Indeed at one point, dismayed at how efforts to secularize ecclesiastical property resulted in closing many grammar schools, Erasmus complained that where Lutheranism flourished, learning decayed. But the Protestants—Melanchthon (1497-1560), Trotzendorf (1490-1556), Sturm (1507-1589)—slowly began to found their own schools and universities. As a counter, the Society of Jesus was founded in 1534 and set up one of the most disciplined and effective systems of education, refurbishing the old scholasticism and also concentrating on the classics. Latin ceased to be the language of learning, and royal academies in France and the Ritterakademien in Germany began to attract more scholars than the old universities.

Of the various efforts at creating a new educational system, that of Germany was the most dramatic and was to provide a model for reformers in France and England and the United States.

In 1694 the University of Halle was founded to train "servants of the state," breaking with scholastic tradition by teaching in German and by the direct concern with staffing the state. "Servants of the state" was a category outside the traditional estate system and included doctors, lawyers, and syndics; even Fredrick the Great called himself a servant of the state. In the eighteenth century the Prussian state gave royal grants to set up schools (1736) and decreed compulsory school attendance (1763). Civil service exams were introduced in 1794. Universities similar to that at Halle were founded at Frankfurt (1731), Gottingen (1734), and Jena (1790). The attempt by the state to establish full control over education was resisted in the name of academic freedom, so in the early nineteenth century a Ministry of Culture was established to supervise relations with the educational institutions. The *Abitur*, or secondary-school leaving examination, was standardized and made a prerequisite for entry to the university (1812). About the same time the University of Berlin was established, with Johann Fichte as the first rector (1810). It became the model for the modern university. The Abitur was the school leaving examination for the Gymnasium, a secondary school that taught the full complement of Latin and Greek. The Realschulen, or secondary schools that focused on math, natural science, German, and foreign languages, channeled students to positions in commerce and industry rather than to the university. Knowledge of the classics now became a badge of social class, of belonging to the academic elite. The system was modified during the nineteenth century, but it was sharply tracked: in 1885, there were 7.5 million primary school students, yet less than 333,000 students went on to secondary school and of these only about half to the Gymnasium; only 27,000 were enrolled in the university, plus 4,500 more in other institutes of higher learning.

In England, state concern with education began a century later than in Germany: in 1832 small annual grants were first established for school buildings; later a Committee of Council on Education was set up, grammar schools were organized, and a pupil-teacher system was introduced. But not until 1902 was a fully integrated state educational system attempted. Meanwhile public schools were established with special ties to particular professions: Wellington was a training ground for the army, Marlborough for the Church, and Haileybury for the East India Company. The public schools rapidly became the way of absorbing the rising middle class into the elite. As in Germany, the classics were emphasized and used in the open civil service examinations introduced in 1870 for the highest category of administrative class. The public schools stressed gentlemanly manners, and there was an increasing emphasis on custom, tradition, and etiquette. The operation of the system is shown by a few statistics. Of 69 cabinet ministers between 1885 and 1905, 46 were from the public schools; in 1928, public schools had educated 152 of 225 senior administrative class officials, 33 of 45 senior Indian civil servants, 30 of

47 dominion governors, and 52 of 56 bishops. As long as Oxford and Cambridge continued to stress the classics, so did the public schools. In 1905 Eton had 32 masters of classics, 14 of math, 9 of modern languages, 4 in science, 1 in history, and 1 in drawing. In 1936 classics dons still were half the faculty. In 1932-1936 27 percent of foreign service recruits were Etonians. Although chemistry was taught at Cambridge and Oxford and natural science programs were established in the 1850s, the first impetus for scientific training at the university level came from the new civic universities supported by private merchant and citizen collections (Manchester, Liverpool, Nottingham, Sheffield, Leeds, and Birmingham). Even so, commercial firms often imported scientists and engineers from Germany.

In sum, the eighteenth and nineteenth centuries saw a reorganization in education. It involved, first, what the Germans call a *Kulturkampf*, the struggle to free education from the church. Second, it involved the gearing of education to the expanding bureaucratic and scientific needs. And third, both of the former implied a change from scholasticism to a humanism based on the classics and then to a scientific episteme. Whereas the state was substituted for the church as the organizing agency of education, the rising merchant and urban classes played an important role in supporting the Protestant reformation, especially in England, and then the demand for scientific training.

The fight to wrest education from church control, the demand for professional education, and state-supported education have all come to Iran too. By the turn of the twentieth century there had already been a series of new educational initiatives. In 1811 the first student was sent abroad for study by the government, though by 1851 only twenty-nine students had so been sent. In 1851 the Dar-ul-Fanun was established to train government officials: it was free, was meant for elite sons aged fourteen to sixteen, and included a curriculum of foreign languages, natural science, math, history, geography, engineering, medicine, pharmacy, geology, and military sciences. Several more schools were opened: a school of languages (1873), military colleges in Isfahan and Tehran (1883, 1886), a school of agriculture (1900), and a school of political science within the Ministry of Foreign Affairs (1901). In 1918 some five hundred Iranians were studying in Europe, and in 1930-31 this figure had risen to fifteen hundred. Meanwhile a series of lower level modern schools had been established by Zoroastrian (1850s), Christian (1880s) and Jewish (1920s) philanthropic agencies. Local Muslim leaders also established new schools, starting with those of Rushdiyya (see chapter 4). In 1935 the University of Teheran, incorporating some of the earlier professional schools, opened. It was followed in 1949 by the Universities of Tabriz, Isfahan, Mashhad, and Shiraz; and then by Ahwaz in 1955, Jundishapur in 1956, National University in 1960, and Aryamehr Technical University in 1966.

By 1979 twelve more universities had opened or were under construction. There are also a large number of nonuniversity institutes of higher education, so that in 1975 only 45 percent of students in higher education were enrolled in the universities.

The lower levels of education have also seen a series of dramatic developments. Since the 1920s both public and private education has been expanding systematically. In 1963 as part of the White Revolution, high school graduates were drafted into the army to form a literacy corps and were sent out to staff village schools. By 1966 the school attendance of urban seven- to fourteen-year-olds was estimated at 75.8 percent. The rapid development of the mass education system quickly led to structural problems in relation to the labor market. In 1966 high school graduates had a higher rate of unemployment than did the illiterate. There has been increasing pressure in number of high school students seeking places in the universities: 45,000 for 17,000 available places in 1968, 300,000 for 30,000 places in 1976 (Eicher et al. 1976). University graduates expect and often find employment only in some state bureaucratic agency. The education system is failing to adequately supply the productive part of the economy, where industry and business suffer a lack of middle level management and technical personnel. This is directly reflected in poor quality control of products such as textiles, so that despite large-scale production, export capacity is inhibited. In 1965, the primary and secondary school system was overhauled in an attempt to track students toward the needs of the economy. And in 1974 all education was declared free if students promised to serve the state two years for each year of free education from the upper grades of high school on. This was an attempt to stem the brain drain of the educated to more rewarding or better-paid jobs abroad.

The various problems and dynamics of the mass education system vis-a-vis a changing social structure are interesting in their own right and deserve separate treatment elsewhere. For instance, although elite students have many advantages — from better initial training to being able to pull strings and to having powerful aid in finding initial jobs — university recruitment is to some extent meritocratic.[59] An analysis of the medical students at the University of Teheran showed that in 1976 only 31 percent of their parents had incomes of over Rls. 240,000 per year ($3,600), only 20 percent of their fathers had at least a B.S. degree, 20 percent had a high school education, and 10 percent were illiterate (Ziai et al. 1976).

What is of primary interest is to recognize that the madrasa students have become a small isolated minority, many of whom are trying to get a secular education also so that they will have more job options. Although in 1976 some 300,000 people competed in the entrance exams for 30,000 university places, there were only some 11,000 students at all levels in the madrasas. The power and influence of the madrasa lies elsewhere than in numbers or institutional centrality. It lies in a symbolic centrality. It is the repository of a tradition out of which the various religious ideologies of the several Iranian social classes are constructed.

3

Madrasa: Style and Substance

We have a hadith: The people are dead except the ulama.
The ulama are dead except those who practice their
knowledge. All those who practice their knowledge are dead
except the pious ones, and they are in great danger.

— Agha Najafi-Quchani

*T*HE PEDAGOGICAL IDEAL of the madrasa is posed by its members as a criticism of the secular education system, which is spreading at the expense of the madrasa system. The madrasas have been deteriorating in quality and scope of curriculum despite efforts to stop the deterioration and to accommodate to modern demands. But as long as the state and the religious establishment each considered the other a threat to its own legitimacy, no serious thought could be given to an independent quality development of the madrasa ideal.

The Madrasa as a Free University

The picture that members of the madrasa system draw of the secular schools stresses their coercive and antilearning nature in contrast to greater freedom and more learning for learning's sake in the madrasas. In the state institutions students are forced to take classes they do not like. They are pressured to study for grades and for diplomas rather than for knowledge. Both teachers and students anxiously await release by the bell at the end of the class period. Students and teachers often do not respect each other. Teachers pontificate; students are captive audiences rather than partners in learning.

The pedagogical ideal of the madrasa is just the reverse. There are no grades, so students study only for learning's sake. Students who do not study are not flunked out, but neither are they elevated by bribery or favoritism. For each there is a place according to his capacity and inclination: a village preacher (*akhund*) need not be a legal expert (*mujtahid*). Students study with teachers of their own choice. There is thus never a disciplinary problem or a problem of lack of respect for teachers. Indeed the bond of respect and devotion of students for their teachers is

Ayatullah Sayyid Mohammad Kazem Shariatmadari (in the black turban that indicates sayyid status) in a characteristic daily activity: receiving visitors, inquiries, requests for advice and guidance.

proverbial in almost the sense of the Indian term *guru*. Teachers do not pontificate; rather, all teaching is on a dialectic principle of argument and counterargument in which students are encouraged to participate insofar as they have the preparation to do so.

That is the ideal, and to a greater or lesser extent it is also what in fact exists. Teachers, of course, have their different styles, some of which encourage more and some less interruption. For example, to turn to the madrasas in Qum, Ayatullah S. Mohammad Kazem Shariatmadari tends not to interrupt the flow of his discourse; he hears interjected questions from the audience but responds to them in his own time. Ayatullah S. Mohammad Reza Golpayegani, on the other hand, stops and listens to each question and answers it as it comes up. Style of give and take also depends upon the level of the class, there being more freedom and reason for questioning and debate at the most advanced levels. When, after a break of several years, Naser Makarem reopened his classes in *'aqa'id va-madhahib* (doctrines and religions), he found himself forced to rule many questions out of order and to demand that only people with a certain level of training come to class; otherwise the debate could never get off the ground.

Two styles of pedagogical discourse can be briefly illustrated. First, an example from the most advanced level of teaching, the so-called *dars-i kharij* ("external studies" or studies beyond the strict sequence of textbooks). In Qum this occurs in the great mosque built by Ayatullah S. Hoseyn Borujerdi adjacent to the Shrine of Fatima, Hadrat-i Ma'suma (sister of the eighth Imam). Several parts of the mosque are simultaneously used by different classes, each teacher seated upon his minbar (a set of stairs that serves as lecturn, or podium) and the students seated on carpets around him. The three important dars-i kharij (given by Shariatmadari, Golpayegani, and Marashi) are scheduled so that one can attend them all. The students range from youths approaching their twenties to whitebeards in their eighties. The serious students take notes; others may occupy their hands with worry beads, or may even doze.

Ayatullah Shariatmadari is discussing the status of intention (*niyyat*) in the formal namaz prayer, enjoined on each Muslim to be performed five times a day. There are prescriptions for ablutions preceding the prayer, the number of prostrations to be performed at different prayer times, the direction of prayer, and the words to be used. The issue is whether one can do a ritual perfunctorily, or how much conscious intent there must be at each step of the ritual. We shall follow the discussion as it progressed over a few days, merely to get the flavor of the debate. We begin with some fine points of scholastic casuistry, involving first the two meanings of the word *'ibadat* (worship).[1] Namaz, of course, is the most strict meaning of the word; but it also means simply worship of God, which need not be confined to a ritual form. When worship does not take a ritual form, then obviously intention is all important. But when one follows all the prescriptions of a ritual form, does a lapse in consciousness of the purpose invalidate the worship, forcing one to begin anew? And from what point does intent become important?

The question (posed by Shariatmadari): Does wudu' (the ablution beginning the namaz) require deliberate intention (*niyyat*) or no? There is no riwayat (tradition) specifically on intention; rather, over time the consensus (*ijma*) of the religious authorities came to regard intention as mandatory (*wajib*). Does this then mean that, strictly speaking, intention is not really necessary?

A strategy: Now if we can show that the ablution is technically part of 'ibadat (worship), then ipso facto intention is shown to be mandatory, because for 'ibadat to be valid, there must be intention.

One answer (Shariatmadari continues): We have a riwayat that says that worship is composed one third of ablution (*wudu'*), one third of recitation (*rak'at*), and one third of prostration (*sujud*). Namaz begins with wudu'.

Query from the audience: Maybe wudu' should be considered as something done before namaz?

Answer: There is no word "before" in the riwayat: when you do the namaz, you begin with wudu'. It is part of the preliminaries of namaz together with knowing the right time to do it, knowing the direction of the *qibla* (orientation to the Ka'ba in Mecca), wearing of clean clothes, not wearing clothes made of skins of animals one is forbidden to eat or clothes belonging to someone else, and not praying in spots where the owner has not given permission.

Shariatmadari then throws in a pragmatic caveat:

But all of this is not fiqh (law) but kalam (theological casuistry) and is of use only to those who are waswas (overly fastidious ritualistic people). Waswas is the thinking of the devil. In the Qur'an it says that God wants heaven for us, not difficulties.

The castigation of waswas ("doubt," extreme concern with ritual precision) is an interesting concern of teachers about their half-educated students, and the lore on the subject is considerable. There is a story about the nineteenth-century marja'-i taqlid (supreme authority on the law) Shaykh Mortaza Ansari that one day when he went to the baths, he saw a student at the pool making the same sound over and over. He inquired what the youth was doing. The youth replied that he wanted to say the niyyat (intention) for a ghusl (full ritual ablution). Shaykh Mortaza asked who his teacher was. The youth replied that Shaykh Mortaza Ansari had taught him about the necessity of proper niyyat, that he continually fell into doubt as to whether or not he had the proper intention, and that as long as one doubted one could not proceed to the ablution proper. Shaykh Mortaza replied curtly: I do not hold niyyat to be mandatory (*wajib*); get on with it, get it done.

In Yazd, the folk story is told of the student who had *sawda* (the Yazdi term for waswas). His fellow students decided to cure him. They took a dog, sprayed it with water, and then let it loose in the student's room. Now, dogs are ritually polluting and water conducts pollution. The dog shook itself, thereby making everything from books to carpet najis (ritually unclean), at least to one fanatically concerned with ritual cleanliness. The poor student had only one recourse: he shut his eyes and said, "May God will, it was only a goat (*insha' allah buz bud*)." (Goats are not polluting, and *insha' allah buz bud* is the saying for occasions when someone does not want to face reality.)[2]

The disease of waswas is common. Even the late marja'-i taqlid Ayatullah S. Hoseyn Borujerdi (d. 1960) is said to have fallen under its influence as a student.[3] The reaction of pragmatic Muslims is encoded in a story of 'Ali, the first Imam, that when he went to urinate, he would always sprinkle a little extra water on his garments so that in the event a little urine splashed on them, he could say it was the water and there would be no major commotion over a minor ritual matter. (Urine, like dogs, is one of the ten or twelve items of pollution.)

Shariatmadari's discussion of niyyat and what sort of intention makes worship valid or invalid continues:

There are three reasons why people might pray: (a) for fear of hell, (b), for hope of heaven, (c) for love of God. Sayyid Ibn Ta'us issued a fatwa (opinion) that the first two reasons invalidate prayer and only the third makes prayer valid. But the fatwa is wrong for four reasons: (1) There are very few people who could live up to the fatwa, that is, pray only for love of God all the time, maybe 'Ali could, maybe Sayyid Ibn Ta'us. But such a ruling would make most people's prayers batil (invalid). (2) The Qur'an talks of heaven and hell as reward and punishment. (3) the Prophet Muhammad said of himself, "I am the bringer of good and of frightening news." (4) There are hadith going against the fatwa of Ibn Ta'us. On the other hand, it is clear that praying for the love of God is more valuable than praying out of fear of hell or hope of heaven. 'Ali said that slaves worship out of fear; shopkeepers worship out of hope: I will worship you, and you will give me beautiful female houris in heaven; but worship for love of God is the real thing, worship of God.

Student objection: When Husayn and Hasan were taken ill as children, their parents, Fatima and 'Ali, vowed to fast for three days if the boys became well. After the three days of fasting, each time they wanted to break fast and prepared food, some poor person would come to the door and they would give away their food. The verse of the Qur'an revealed after this was, "These people asked no reward for their good deeds."

Answer: But what precedes and follows this aya (verse of the Qur'an)? Fear of God.

Another day, Ayatullah Shariatmadari, in order to make the issues even sharper, introduced niyyat in the case of *'ibadat isti'ari* (the namaz prayers said on behalf of someone else, such as the prayers said on behalf of a recently deceased person to make up prayers he might have missed during his life, prayers for which the reciter earns a fee). The issue became so heated that the students constantly interrupted and the debate did not move very far forward. Some supported Sayyid Ibn Ta'us, others argued that 'ibadat (worship) has intrinsic value. But Shariatmadari would not allow them to ignore the problem of self-interested prayer:

> Do you mean that namaz for a wish is batil (invalid)? What about when the Qur'an says, "For wish, fear of hell?" Do you override the Qur'an?

We need not follow the debate further. The elements of the style of debate are evident. The subjects of debate in such classes have become a standard sequence: purity rules (*taharat*), prayer (*salat*), fasting (*sawm*), pilgrimage (*hajj*), and manumission from slavery (*'itq*), although the last is usually omitted. There are no set texts. One is assumed to have mastered all the basic works of law (*fiqh*) and principles of legal deduction (*usul*, or how one derives the rules of fiqh from the Qur'an and hadith). One calls upon these standard sources as well as all other sources one can command: the opinions of various scholars, the etymology of technical terms, the context of Qur'anic and hadith injunctions, the validity of the sources, and one's own ingenuity. The drama can be heightened when two mujtahids play off one another, as happened in the 1920s in Qum when Ayatullah Shaykh Abdol-Karim Haeri-Yazdi and his assistant, Ayatullah S. Mohammad-Taghi Khonsari, would cite arguments against each other (Razi 1332/1953: II, 57).

A second style of discourse can be illustrated from the *dars-i 'aqa'id va-madhahib* (course in doctrines and religions) of Naser Makarem. This course is an elective. It is not based directly on the standard series of books that every student must master but on a freer sort of debate. *'Aqa'-id*, or kalam (theological casuistry), is a sort of free reasoning — what sort will be indicated later. This particular course is designed for middle level students, those who have at least begun reading the *Kifayah* of S. Mulla Mohammad-Kazem Akhond-e Khorasani and the *Makasib* of Shaykh Mortaza Ansari. Just as for the dars-i kharij, students sit around the minbar. Nearly eleven hundred students signed up for the course in both 1974-75 and 1975-76; attendance at the weekly sessions runs on the order of seven hundred. A mimeographed outline of the evening's subject is handed out at the door. It is usually divided into four parts: statement of the problematic concept; description and research (dictionary meanings, usages in other religions, historical context, Islamic usage); sanad or proofs (citations from Qur'an, hadith, other Muslim writings); and results, the clarified philosophy of the concept.

One of the first subjects Makarem took up in 1975 was the troublesome issue of predestination, fate, free will, and causality. Predestination and lack of free will do not exist in Islam. This was clarified by using determinists, Zoroastrians, materialists, and Communists as contrastive straw men. Makarem's argument, in brief, was as follows:[4]

> If all is simply determined by the will of God, what is the point in Islam of stressing taklif (duty), the virtues of striving, heaven and hell, jihad (defense of the faith), making promises, questioning and judging? Fate is *qada-wa-qadar*. The terms *qada* (ordering) and *qadar* (measure) are technical terms in the philosophy of creation (*takwini*) and the philosophy of duty (*tashri'i*). In the former, cause and effect are part of qada: a window is broken by a stone; the size and force of the stone are its measure (*qadar*), the breaking of the window by a stone is the law of nature, causality, creation (*qada*). There is no opiate to free will here but rather a stimulus to learn how the world works, so as to be an effective agent within it. Six aya (verses) in the Qur'an are cited as proof of this usage of the terms.[5] The usage with regard to duties is parallel: the command to pray is the qada, to do seventeen *rak'at* (units of namaz prayer) is the qadar. One 'aya and three hadith testify to this usage.
>
> 'Ali is supposed to have credited idolators with originating the notion of determinism (*jabr*) and Satan with being the leader of determinists, for it is said in the Qur'an that Satan complained to God, "You caused me to lose my way." Zoroastrians, Makarem adds, are also determinists, for all good is caused by Yazdan and all evil by Ahriman. Clearly, neither is man fully free nor fully determined (*hadith* of Imam Ja'far al-Sadiq), and materialists go to absurd lengths when they attempt to account for drinking a glass of water through changes in body chemistry producing thirst (an example attributed to Dr. Arani, former leader of the Iranian Tudeh party).
>
> To try to account for all of history for economic reasons is equally absurd. If a man observes the Ramadan fast in summer, may he not refrain from drinking Dr. Arani's glass of water? Communists deal adequately with causality but not with individual responsibility; the individual is submerged in the social. In Islam everything turns on individual efforts (five aya confirm this).[6] Lazy people who excuse themselves for defeat by citing fate are counted as bad in the hadith literature. There is a hadith that 'Ali rose from sitting by a crooked wall and sat under a straighter one. He was asked if he was trying to run from God's qada, for surely God could make the straight wall fall as easily as the crooked. 'Ali replied, "We run from the divine order to the divine order, for God gave us reason to use."

Other subjects discussed in Makarem's course also display this pragmatic ethic:

Zuhd (asceticism) does not mean a turning away from the world, but that one not be captured by materialist interests, money, or ceremony. Without zuhd, political leaders and judges cannot be trusted but will be corrupt and oppressive.

Ruhbaniyat and *dunya-tarik* (monasticism and world rejection) are evil because they are a separation from society and lead the individual to mental illness. It is a negative reaction to defeat; the positive reaction would be to analyze the causes of failure and correct them. Separation from the world in the name of piety also opens society to domination by colonialists. Sufism is thus bad.

Sabr (patience) does not mean resignation but persistence in the face of odds.

Taqiya (dissimulation) is acceptable under three conditions: (a) You should not throw yourself to martyrdom by your own hand when among hostile people; rather save yourself to fight another day. (b) You should not waste your breath with those who are intellectually incapable or whose minds are closed. (c) In the interest of common goals, you should forget differences with other branches of Islam, though you may argue the differences in a friendly way.

The argument is always couched in the framework of sanad (citing of Qur'anic, hadith, and later authorities) and tafsir (alternative exegeses). After the discussion on monasticism, I approached Makarem privately with three queries:

1. Given the importance of Sufi orders in Islamic political history, I was surprised that he castigated them as world rejectors.
2. Was the comparison with Christian monks, which he had drawn as the case type of monasticism, really apt to his purpose? It is true that monks are supposed to be celibate, but otherwise many orders are meant to serve in the world not leave it. They have set up hospitals, schools, and so on.
3. If one wished to speak of world rejection, should one not rather refer to Hinduism or Buddhism? But even in Hinduism one is supposed first to become a householder and raise a family.

His response was to devalue my historicism and to insist on the meaning for Islam. In early Christianity, he said, monasticism meant being a hermit off by oneself; the Dominicans and Jesuits are relatively recent. Yes, *tariqats* (Sufi orders) have been important in Islamic history as a kind of political party, but that does not make them correct. Sufism is an accretion from Hinduism and has nothing to do with real Islam.

I tried a second tack: Leaving history aside, there is a philosophical issue having to do with differences in interpretation as one becomes more knowledgeable and having to do with the esoteric/exoteric (*batini/zahiri*) distinction. Yes, he acknowledged, the great mystical poet Rumi spoke of the seed and the skin, (*maghz va-pust*), the skin for the animals, the seed or brain for us; but that is nonsense. There is no *batini/zahiri*, no esoteric/exoteric, distinction in Islam.

I persisted: In the West there is much interest in the analysis of symbolic language; religion is symbolic and always requires exegesis whether the core text be the Bible or the Qur'an. He replied: Of course, but there is a danger in treating things as symbolic. That is precisely what the Sufis do. Do you mean that every man can build meanings for himself? he asked. We have a hadith that begins, "You should eat red meat and [golden-] red wheat, for they are healthy." Sufis interpret the two red things as the two lips, and so interpret the hadith as an injunction that you should observe silence. My last thrust before changing the subject was the comment that tasawwuf (Sufi doctrine, mysticism) is taught in the al-Azhar curriculum in Cairo. He replied: In classes on beliefs and doctrines we have a section on tasawwuf as we do on Christianity, on Bahaism, and so on. We debate tasawwuf; it is in the curriculum; but that does not mean we accept it.

The issue of the limits of acceptable freedom in interpretation is an extremely important one. The degree of limitation is perhaps nowhere clearer than in a new genre of book issued now by any major mujtahid who lays some claim to being a marja'-i taqlid. Called *Risalat tawdih al-masa'il* (Explanatory text on problems [of Religion]), the books are supposed to be compendiums of legal opinions on problems of ritual and religious duty. The first such book was issued by Ayatullah Borujerdi; it was compiled by Ali-Asghar Kalbazchi (now a high-school principal in Tehran) as a kind of abstraction from and commentary on S. Kazem Yazdi's *'Urwat al-wuthqa*. What is new about this genre is that the books itemize rules and opinions succinctly, with no justifying arguments; each is a short guide on how to act as a Muslim. What is striking and revealing is that there is very little variation between the *Risala* of different mujtahids, for the opinions are not the free opinions of different men: they are the disciplined elucidation of the intent of the Qur'an. That is the meaning of ijtihad (exercise of interpretive reason), of being a mujtahid. One almost feels that a mujtahid could hold two opinions, one his own and one the result of his technical skill in a disciplined form of deduction. Of course, for any believing Muslim the latter must take precedence; it would be the difference between whim and reason. There is, however, also another rationale: for new opinions with political impact, like the outlawing of tobacco in 1891 or the making of Pepsi Cola religiously undesirable (*makruh*) in the 1950s,[7] mujtahids attempt as far as possible to maintain a united front so as not to dissipate religious authority.

To any Westerner conversant with post-Hegelian theology, the most striking thing about Shi'ite theological debate surely must be the refusal to deal with theological discourse as itself a social and linguistic phenomenon in a wider sense than the rhetoric and hermeneutics internal to Islamic belief. So many things that are still dealt with in the Muslim world as questions of truth (and therefore also questions of heresy: believer versus unbeliever or at best misguided believer) could be handled as modes of expression, as symbolic idioms. One does not abolish truth by adding a new consciousness with a metalanguage tool; on the contrary. Perhaps to admit this, however, would diminish what is left of political authority in making things forbidden (*haram*) or undesirable (*makruh*). Part of the problem is the distinction between the initiated (the *khass*) and the uninitiated (the *'amm*), and between believer and nonbeliever (dealt with under the rubric of *taqiya* or dissimulation). The issue can be illustrated through a remarkable series of questions elicited by Naser Makarem from his students in doctrines and religions in the fall of 1975.

The questions fall into several groups. There are simple points of information:

1. What *madhhab* (religious school) is *Majus* (usually Zoroastrian)?
2. When was Wahhabism founded?

There are questions asked by future preachers wanting to know what to answer to popular questions:

3. Why was the Prophet illiterate?
4. Why did the Imams practice taqiya (dissimulation)?
5. If generosity is makruh for women, why was Fatima al-Zahra so generous?

The answers to these questions have implications for dogma. That the Prophet was illiterate is part of the proof that the Qur'an is divine, for Mohammad could not have written it. The question about dissimulation becomes more involved, for the immediate answer is that in times of real Shi'ite weakness it was important to the very survival of the doctrine that people not reveal themselves and not be martyred. Dissimulation is permissible under a limited set of circumstances; it is not permissible if the religion is thereby endangered, however — if, for instance, there is danger that the youth will not be taught properly. In the last two decades Ayatullah Ruhollah Musavi Khomeyni has insisted that Islam is precisely in this danger and that therefore Shi'ites must not dissimulate. During the time of several of the later Imams the reverse was the case: by keeping publicly quiet and conformist, the doctrine could be passed on secretly. The problem is, as some of Makarem's students asked, why God did not give the Imams more power so that they could institute a just society on earth; that, of course, involves all the problems of individual responsibility past and present. The generosity-of-women question has to do not only with female codes of behavior — that they should not make themselves conspicuous — but perhaps more with the notion that a woman should not be too free with her husband's wealth; Fatima never overstepped such bounds. Generosity per se is never bad.

Some of the questions give a glimpse into adolescent concern with working out what truth is, a concern intermingled with enjoyment of scholastic games. All these questions are found in the hadith, many come from Greek sources:

6. Can God create something like himself?
7. Can God create a stone so heavy he cannot lift it?
8. Can God miniaturize the world?
9. If creation is material and God is immaterial, how could He create a material world?
10. We must know God with our reason; our reason is limited; God is unlimited; how can we know God?
11. How does one reconcile the Qur'anic verse saying that whoever is more pious is more loved by God with the verse saying that an educated man (*'alim*) is worth more than seven thousand worshippers?
12. Since most people go to hell and only a few to heaven would it not have been better if God had not created us at all?
13. If Muslims go to hell, what is the difference from being a *kafir* (unbeliever)?
14. Why were not all men created equal?

Many of the questions have to do specifically with the articulation of symbolic domains: that is, with social boundaries, the application of theological formulas, and the juxtaposition of different modes of categorical thought. Simplest are the questions about social boundaries:

15. Who are the Shaykhis and what are the reasons for opposing them?
16. If piety (*taqwa*) exists among Jews and Christians, why are they unclean (*najis*)?

More interesting are the questions having to do with teleological boundaries:

17. Why does not Mohammad's being the last prophet mean that men do not need prophets any more?
18. How do we know the Qur'an has not been changed?

Islam is a teleological structure of the form: if everyone acted according to the divine and immutable rules dispensed through Muhammad, society would be just and equitable. Insofar as one accepts Islam, Muhammad's prophethood is ever-continuing. To say that men do not need a prophet any more is to say that Islam belonged to a historical stage of the past. Question 18 has the form of a factual question, but its answer has to do with the defense of the revealed word (see Pooya 1971).

Connected with these fundamental questions are those that touch on the development of the teleological scheme:

19. The Qur'an says prophets committed sins; why do we protest so much that they never sinned?
20. Why did Husayn go to Karbala when he knew he would be killed?
21. Are heaven and hell currently in existence?
22. Is it mandatory (*wajib*) to believe everything about resurrection?

Question 19 in part has to do with the proof that the Old and New Testaments have been tampered with: how could they be the original divine books when they say that the prophets were such sinful people? The allegations of drunkenness and incest of Lot, adultery by David, idolatry of Aaron and Solomon, and so on, are counted here as evidence that the Jews, in particular, tampered with the divine book. Question 20 is the key question around which popular Shi'ism is built. People were abandoning the true religion; Husayn had to witness for Islam and thereby shock people back to the true path, to serve as an example throughout the ages that sometimes death can create a lasting testament that people will remember. Question 21 provides an opening for existentialist interpretations of the variety favored by Bishop Ian Ramsey (1969): Hell as a place of physical torture after death is morally repulsive, cosmologically implausible, and theologically contradictory with the Christian doctrine of God's mercy; but hell as the separation between self and other which occurs when one does wrong makes eminent sense. Fundamentalists of course will play the question another way, drawing on the rich physical imagery of the Sirat Bridge leading to the other world.[8]

Many of the questions reflect category confusions:

23. If ghusl (ritual ablution) has to do with microbes (or cleanliness, a justification added by popular apologists), what does niyyat (intention) have to do with it?
24. Why is human excrement najis (unclean) when the food eaten is clean?
25. The Imam al-Zaman (messiah), can he fight atomic weapons? (When he returns he is supposed to wage war against the unjust and then establish a period of peace and justice on earth.)
26. How can we believe in metaphysical things we cannot see?

Lewis Carroll's Red Queen, of course, went even one step further in answering question 26: every morning before breakfast she practiced believing in three impossible things.

Still other questions have to do with social issues and general intellectual issues of the day:

27. Given that Islamic law is not practiced in the world, isn't communist law the next best choice?
28. Why do we say Islam fits all societies, but no country has Islamic law?

29. Why is the character or morality of Muslims no better than that of non-Muslims?
30. Why should women get only half an inheritance share, and why should women not participate fully in society?
31. If Darwin is incorrect, with what do we replace his theory?
32. What has religion done for us? The advanced societies are without religion.

The final category of questions has to do with their own educational system and profession:

33. Why do not ruhani (religious leaders) work? Why do those who do not work eat the sahm-i Imam (a portion of the religious tax)?
34. Why does the *hawza* (religious college system) not give diplomas?
35. Why do the ruhani not make use of television, radio, and cinema?
36. Why are those who have studied Arabic for sixty years unable to speak it?
37. Why do the ruhani disagree? What is the road to unity among the ruhani? Why do the maraji'-i taqlid (leaders of the community) not issue *fatwa shaura* (joint opinions)?
38. Why are the ruhani and the people at odds?
39. Why is the prohibition against riba (usury) and maybe against interest of all kinds discussed so little?
40. Does not the law of khums (the portion of the religious taxes that should support poor descendants of the Prophet) promote a kind of aristocracy?

Many of the questions 33–40 will be dealt with in the following pages. These forty questions are only a sample of more than three hundred collected by Makarem, but I think they provide an insight into the nature of the thought of the students, as adolescents and young adults and as questioning young professional religious leaders.

Another insight, perhaps focusing a little more on one of the sources of student dissatisfaction, came from a discussion I had after the first session of Makarem's course I attended. Seven students invited me to their rooms. They wanted to make sure I was introduced to the proper Islam and did not mistakenly assume that the dry Islam taught in the madrasas and by Makarem was all there was. "Dry" (khuskh) is a frequent word of disdain: dry preachers (akhund-i khushk), dry religion (din-i khushk). They gave me a list of names of important members of the religious counterculture: Dr. Ali Shariati, Shaykh Mohammad-Taghi Falsafi, Professor Mortaza Motahhari, S. Mahmud Taleghani, Gholam-Reza Saidi, Engineer Mehdi Bazargan, Jalaloddin Farsi, S. Abdol Karim Hashemi-Nezhad. They were pleased that I was already familiar with these names and offered to supply me, one by one, with the books of these authors (those of Shariati, Taleghani, Bazargan, and Hashemi-Nezhad being banned by the government).[9] They then engaged me in a discussion that though inconclusive and unstructured was friendly and enjoyable on all sides.

We began with *tawhid* (unity). Tawhid does not mean merely that God is one; to say only that is to play with a word, a kind of word worship, and thereby to be *kafir* (an unbeliever). Tawhid involves the unity of self-society-nature, thus the living of a just existence. Land, for instance, does not belong to individuals or countries per se but should be for the use of society, and individuals should be free to develop their abilities. I suggested that this was not far from socialism, the only difference being that they insisted on referring to God whereas socialists couldn't care less. They became rather animated at this: socialism was essentially good, but there was a significant difference. We never really resolved what that difference was, because we got hung up along the way on the existence of the soul (*ruh*).

The example was given of two individuals, one alive, one recently deceased: what is the difference between the two? Their answer was the absence of ruh. I took the position that there is no distinction between body and spirit, that the dead individual is merely a machine that has stopped working: that the cells are natural, and they decay and contribute to further life. (The students recognized the word "entropy"; we had a bit of trouble with "cell," but I think we agreed; RNA and DNA were beyond us: I was trying to include the attempts to synthesize the latter.) We got to the point where I had a young sayyid, who had emerged as their debate captain, agreeing that *ruh* was merely a word for something metaphysical. Where did the ruh go at death? He did not know. So, then, I asked what was really different between his saying that there is a ruh and we do not know what happens to it and my saying that whether there is or is not a ruh is unknowable. OK, he said, forget the word *ruh*, that is a matter perhaps of philosophy. Merely of language, I countered. OK, conceded he, of language; well, forget the word *ruh*. What is the referent of "I"? Is it my head? my finger? What is the *insaniyyat* (being, personality, character) of an *insan* (person)? In reply, I began to speak of socially molded and learned perceptions, behavior, and so on. The conversation shifted to the difference between man and animal. First, however, another student wanted to pursue the question of the ruh and the electricity analogy, but the sayyid immediately saw the fallacy: the source of electricity is in the generator and is not a parallel to the cessation of a sentient being.

The students insisted on a sharp man/animal distinction: animals cannot talk, think; this was to be an argument for something special about ruh. I countered with the chimpanzee Sarah who can communicate with men and possibly do some very simple grammatical thinking. But they said it took four thousand years to do that. So I said, if man's thinking capacity was so great, why couldn't he design a just society? To this the response of course was that the design exists in the Qur'an; what proper Muslims do not have is power: if I grab a piece of candy from you, it does not mean you would not know what to do with it if you had the power to keep it. There are people who know how to live and operate a just society. So I asked whether such a society has ever existed, trying to suggest that man-made societies were imperfect not only because of man's inability to think them through but because social forces have their own imperatives. Yes, they replied: at the time of the Prophet. (They took the position that before the Prophet the Arabs were savages and that the Prophet and Qur'an transformed them overnight into a just society.) For but a few years, I retorted. No, no, they said, down to the present day, wherever people understand the Qur'an.

Just one example, I said: The Qur'an says riba (usury) is haram (forbidden); now what about interest in the bank? They brought up a distinction between riba and *i'tibarat* (credit), denied that this was a distinction in amount (a just versus an unjust return on money), and cited the notion of an Islamic bank (which gives no interest and charges none on loans). But they rapidly capitulated, pleading ignorance of economics, when I pointed out that the Islamic banks were funded as a kind of charity by capitalists and that under current conditions to return the same face value of money to the lender (which was what they meant by *i'tibarat*) would cause the lender to go broke, given that an egg that cost 2 rials two years ago costs 5 rials today.

A standard conscious contradiction contributing to a feeling of alienation among religious students can be seen in this exchange. On the one hand there is a faith in Islam as a guide for a just society: people have been unfairly dispossessed and thus there is no just society; Muslims have not been allowed the power to mold society; if they were, they would create a just society. Statements are frequently made that had the 1963-1971 land reform not occurred (that is, had private property not been unjustly confiscated), Iran would have no need to import food today. On the other hand, as the capitulation on the issue of bank interest shows, the students realize they are not getting the technical education that could allow them to defend their faith in pragmatic terms. The problem of agriculture in Iran is serious; even government experts and foreign advisers debate whether it could not have been handled in a better way. For instance, had the same scale of monetary credit, protection, and technical aid been given agriculture as has been given to industry, perhaps a whole series of less drastic and more immediately productive options could have been utilized. Not all landlords were bad, and many still retain an important and appreciated role as buffers between villagers and the bureaucracy; the religious students' protest underlines this. It is self-deception, however, to think that the agricultural sector did not need upgrading and transformation.

We shall return to student alienation. The point here is that there are limits to debate. One limit is a conscious limit of knowledge and a forced reliance on authority figures who presumably know more. In the realm of social issues this limitation has become an open source of student dissatisfaction. A second limit is again a conscious one, the marking of certain things as questionable and other things as explicable only through traditional procedures. A middle level student put it this way: "Among *ahkam* (actions one is enjoined to do) there are things that should be done and not questioned (*ta'abbudi*); that is, they may have ultimate reasons, but if one begins to question them without the proper learning, it will be counterproductive. These are such things as the unity of God, prayer, fasting. But there are also *tawassuli* or things that should be explored and understood. There is a riwayat (tradition) that all learning should begin and end with an appreciation of God: *awwal al-'ilm ma'rifat al-jabr wa-akhir al-'ilm ta'wid al-amr li'llah*." A third limit is less conscious, the force of the dramatic aesthetic. Shi'ite idiom is elaborated around the events of the lives of the first and third Imams in particular; anything that reduces the dramatic impact of these stories is strongly resisted.

The Institution: Students, Innovations, Problems

Ali is a high school dropout from Mashhad. His parents forced him to take up religious studies, but he learned to like it and after three years he decided to move to Qum to get the best possible training. He seems like a very sharp student and evidently is doing well. His roommate, Mahmud, also a high school dropout, worked for his father for a few years until a mulla discovered him, praised him as *zerang* (clever), and encouraged him to become an akhund (a cleric). Hasan is the son of a weaver. He chose to become an akhund and would now be at the level of dars-i kharij, if he had not preferred to do research on his own. He is associated with Dar-i Rah-i Haqq, a missionary institute that sends out a kind of correspondence course to Muslims in Iran and publishes various tracts, including a series on Christianity (in Persian) which it vaguely hopes will somehow convert someone. Hasan is not of the missionary sort and feels a sense of anomie. He is marking time because the army refuses either to issue him exemption or to draft him; he refuses to pay the requisite bribe to get the exemption, partly because he does not have the money but partly because as a man of religion he cannot countenance it. He was almost engaged once, but the marriage negotiations fell apart.

Mohammad is a middle level student, the son of an akhund, who came to Qum because it is the best place to be trained. He would like eventually to be trained to go abroad to do missionary work, ideally in Europe or America. He studies religious subjects during the day and at night attends secular high school to complete his diploma. Abbas is a village boy; five lads from his village, with their parents' encouragement, came to Qum. Abbas has been continuing his secular education at night and will get his diploma this year. Although in mu'min (believer) style he keeps a stubby beard, he does not wear religious garb. He plans to go to university next year, or perhaps the year after, since anti-government demonstrations caused him to miss a set of examinations. He is leaving the religious life.

Ahmad completed his religious studies in Qum and teaches various subjects tutorial style, including several European languages. He attends philosophy classes at the University of Tehran's Faculty of Literature, testing the secular waters, as it were. Reza is from a family of weavers. After six years of education he too became a weaver; then at age seventeen he began religious studies in a provincial town. He has a job as a clerk in that town and slowly over fifteen years has reached Ahhund-i Khurasani's text in *usul-i fiqh*, the *Kifaya* (see the traditional course of study outlined in the appendix). During the troubles over Ayatullah Khomeyni in 1963, although technically exempted, Reza was seized on the streets and pressed into the army.

Mohammad-Reza is a high school dropout from Tehran. He styles himself a "missionary to the youth" and is active in several religious circles in Tehran. He studies in Qum. He does not wear religious garb, so as not to put off the modern youth. Volatile and enthusiastic, he would make an ideal undercover agent provocateur for the secret police.

Then there are the foreigners: the son of a missionary in east Africa; the Tanzanian who will return home to teach Islam during the hour for religion in high school; the serious Afghan who regards with disdain popular Iranian Shi'ism — particularly its rawdas and dastas (preaching and flagellation) — but views Qum as a mecca of learning; the Pakistani who has been kicked out of Najaf and regards Qum as second best; and the Pakistani who has selected an Iranian Ayatullah as his personal "His Holiness" and light of inspiration. Then there are the occasional Europeans: the anthropologist who is to be treated as a dangerous germ; the ex-hippie who has kicked a drug habit, found religion, and now wants to find out what it is he has found; and the wandering scholar without degrees who has been converted to Sufism and wants to learn Arabic and Persian but can get into no formal university program.

In 1975 there were over 6,500 students in Qum, approximately 1,800 in Mashhad, 1,000 in Isfahan, 500 in Tabriz, 250 in Shiraz, and 300 in Yazd.[10] In Yazd it is estimated that 80 percent of the students come from rural backgrounds; Shiraz also receives a large percentage from rural and small-town areas toward the Gulf.

For Qum the figures can be broken down somewhat further (see table 3.1). Of the 6,414 students listed in the registers in the fall of 1975, a quarter (1,574) were sayyids (descendants of the Prophet); more surprisingly, apparently only a quarter were unmarried. If one includes a liberal area northwest of an arc from Kirmanshah to Qazvin, Turkish-speakers accounted for nearly a third of the students. Refugees from Iraq (since 1970 the Iraqis have been expelling foreign religious students and teachers) were the second largest group after Azerbaijanis. Foreign students constituted only a small percentage of the student body but were significant connections to other parts of the Shi'ite world. In rough order of number of students, they were Pakistan, Afghanistan, India, Lebanon, Tanzania, Turkey, Nigeria, Kashmir, and Indonesia.

The father's occupation, unfortunately, could be obtained only from smaller and possibly biased samples. The largest was a sample of 236 students at the Madrasa Golpayegani (table 3.2). This sample was geographically somewhat skewed in favor of students from the central plateau. Well over half were of rural background (125 farmers, 2 poultry farmers, 1 shepherd); not quite a quarter (56) were of ruhani (clergy) background; nearly as many were from the bazaar: 24 shopkeepers, 18 craftsmen, 2 barbers, and a merchant. The Golpayegani school was an innovative one designed to prepare younger students for entry to the higher levels of the madrasa system. It had a preparatory two-year program (210 students in 1975) and then a five-year program (312 students). The director had a degree from the Faculty of Theology of the University of Tehran and served as an Arabic teacher in the secular high school system as well.

A second new innovative madrasa, Haqqani, yielded an even smaller sample of 30. The skewing in this case resulted from a rather careful admission procedure, which selects for well-educated, intelligent students. Consequently, father's occupation ran strongly in an urban direction with craftsmen and white-collar workers leading (7 each), ruhani (6), shopkeepers (5), and only 5 rural. The students were older than the Golpayegani students, ranging in age from fifteen to thirty-one, half being between seventeen and nineteen years old. Of the sample of 30, one had a B.A. degree, 12 had completed high school, and 19 had had at least half of the secular high school course (first cycle).

Finally in a nonscientific random sample of 35 students in the more traditional sections of the madrasa system (ages ranging from sixteen to twenty-five, except for one thirty-two-year-old), father's occupation split evenly between ruhani (14) and farmers (13), with craftsmen (2), shopkeepers (1), manual laborers (3), and clerks (1) trailing.

One may conclude from these figures and from impressions of people in the madrasa system that the two major sources of students are sons of farmers and sons of ruhani. To what extent the religious elite is drawn

Table 3.1 Qum talaba (1975), by place of origin, sayyid status, and marital status

PLACE OF ORIGIN	TOTAL NUMBER	SAYYIDS	UNMARRIED[a]
Azerbaijan[b]	1,118	223	222
Iraq[c]	780	206	155
Khorasan[d]	564	153	199
Isfahan	479	121	135
Mazandaran	469	119	112
Qum	392	181	44
Zanjan	322	79	34
Arak	301	72	45
Rasht	286	50	64
Tehran	245	63	44
Hamadan	243	39	28
Qazvin	146	49	19
Yazd	125	41	22
Kerman	116	10	12
Shiraz	107	41	15
Kashan	95	20	26
Khoramabad	62	11	8
Ahwaz	51	29	7
Saveh	51	9	2
Kermanshah	47	8	9
Bandar Abbas	32	1	7
Unknown:[e]			
at Madrasa Kirmani	8	11	—
at Madrasa Haqqani	123	27	—
at Madrasa Mahdiyya	52	11	48
at Madrasa Mu'miniyya	200	—	—
(no stipend; bread only)	—	—	400
Total[f]	6,414	1,574	1,657

[a.] That these students were unmarried is inferred from the fact that they received 5 *man* of bread each month from Ayatullah Mar'ashi-Najafi; married students received 10 *man* (1 *man* = 3 kilo).

[b.] Includes 6 Turks.

[c.] Includes 32 Afghans, 34 Pakistanis, 13 Indians, 18 Lebanese, 2 Kashmiris, and 4 Africans.

[d.] Includes 28 Pakistanis, 18 Afghans, 13 Indians.

[e.] Out of a total of 122 at Madrasa Kirmani, all but 8 are distributed by place of origin; the 11 sayyids are a total for the 122 students. No geographical distributions available for Madrasas Haqqani, Mahdiyya, and Mu'miniyya.

[f.] In this population there were 57 deaths and 21 changes in marital status over a 17-month period.

Table 3.2 Madrasa Golpayegani students (1975): social background, education, origin (N = 282)

Father's occupation		Town of origin (In order of places sending 5 or more students)	
Rural: farmer	125	Qum	38
poultry farmer, shepherd	3	Isfahan	28
Clergy (ruhani)	56	Yazd	24
Urban: merchant, broker, clerk	7	Golpayegan	17
shopkeeper	24	Hamadan	16
craftsman	18	Amol	10
laborer	20	Arak	9
other	3	Damghan, Malayer, Tabriz	7 ea.
No information	26	Kirman, Qazvin,	
		Shahreza, Tehran	6 ea.
		Mahallat, Shiraz, Shahrud	5 ea.
		Other	80
Religious education prior to Qum		**Secular education**	
5 years (or more)	1	High school diploma	2
1 to 4 years	105	Primary school (6 years)	197
Less than 1 year	16	5 years	36
None	129	1 to 4 years	10
No information	31	None	11
		No information	26

from the latter group will be explored in the next section; although many observers think that the proportion of ruhani is declining and that of the rural folk is increasing, the data are insufficient to draw any conclusions.

The schools are attempting to innovate to meet not only the needs of a possibly changing student body composition, but also of a changing society. The traditional course of study is detailed in the appendix. It is organized into three levels corresponding to three levels of student stipend. To pass to a higher level of financial support, a student must pass a written and an oral examination. Stipend levels in 1975 were around 150 tomans (10 rials = 1 toman), 260 tomans, and 470 tomans monthly, plus an allotment of bread. These were cumulative sums from all sources: in Qum seven leaders distributed stipends and each student could take from each leader (see table 3.3). In 1975, the largest amounts were given by representatives of Ayatullahs Khoi and Khomeyni (who themselves resided in Najaf), followed by Shariatmadari, Golpayegani, and Khonsari (the last residing in Tehran), and trailed by Amoli; Ayatullah Marashi-Najafi followed the old tradition of giving bread coupons instead of cash: 5 *man* (15 kilos) for unmarried students, 10 *man* for married students.

Table 3.3 Stipend levels of unmarried students, in tomans (1975)

SOURCE	LEVEL		
	1st	2nd	3rd
Khoi	40	60	100
Khomeyni	40	60	100
Golpayegani	20	40	80
Khonsari	20	40	80
Shariatmadari	20	40	80
Amoli	10	20	30
Total	150 (= $22)	260 (= $38)	470 (= $69)

The madrasas of Qum are listed in tables 3.4 and 3.5. The less traditional schools — Golpayegani, Dar-al-Tabligh, Haqqani, Amir al-Mu'minin, and even Razaviyya — are set up to serve needs not supplied by the traditional system. The goals of the Golpayegani school have already been indicated: to train younger and religiously unprepared students for entry into the Qum system, which considers itself to be essentially a university, a place of higher learning. With the improvement of transportation, more lower level students have been coming directly to the great centers of learning (Qum, Mashhad, Isfahan) rather than first studying as far as they could in the smaller provincial centers. Schools like the Golpayegani school and now the Razaviyya school are intended to deal with this population. In order to be accepted in the Golpayegani school, a boy must be introduced by someone of known character, who is held responsible should the boy misbehave or not attend classes. The course of study is a slightly simplified version of the traditional course of study (see appendix). Theoretically the program can prepare a student up to the third level (*dars-i kharij*), although the middle level training may be somewhat less thorough than one would get in the traditional madrasa classes.

The Madrasa Haqqani was founded with a slightly different conception. It is aimed toward research students and thus is a kind of alternate and modernized hawza-i 'ilmi (center of religious learning) in itself. When fully complete it will provide a sixteen-year course, the first ten of which are formal classes, the rest guided research and reading. Again the lower level classes are modeled on the traditional course of studies, but simplified with new books: for instance, *Sarf-i Sada* (Etymology Made Easy) and *Nahw-i Sada* (Syntax Made Easy) were produced for use here, and Allama Tabatabai wrote *Bidayat al-Hikma* (Beginnings of Philosophy) and *Nihayat al-Hikma* (Results of Philosophy) to be used as the philosophy texts here. Modern languages — English and spoken

Table 3.4 Madrasas in Qum: Traditional

MADRASA	FOUNDED	REBUILT	ADMINISTRATOR	T	R[a]
Faydiyya[b]	Safavid (934/1527): Shah Tahmasp I	Qajar (1213/1798): Fath 'Ali Shah Pahlavi: Yazdi, Sadr, Borujerdi	Golpayegani (and others)	x	x
Dar al-Shifa	Safavid (1055/1645): Shah Abbas II	Qajar: Fath 'Ali Shah Pahlavi: Yazdi, Sadr, Borujerdi	—	x	
Mehdi Qoli Khan	Safavid (1123/1711)	Pahlavi (1378/1958): Borujerdi	Borujerdi's son	x	
Hojjatiyya[c]	Pahlavi (1366/1946)	Qajar: Nasir al-Din Shah Pahlavi (1376/1956): Borujerdi	Hojjat's son	x	
Razaviyya[d]	—	—	—		x
Mu'miniyya	Safavid (1113/1701): Sultan Husayn	Pahlavi (1284/1964): Mar'ashi	Mar'ashi-Najafi	x	
Mar'ashi	Pahlavi: Mar'ashi	—	Mar'ashi-Najafi	x	
Mahdiyya	Pahlavi	—	Mar'ashi-Najafi	x	
Jani Khan	Safavid	Qajar: Nasir al-Din Shah Pahlavi (1373/1953): Borujerdi	—	x	
Fatima	Pahlavi: Shariatmadari	—	Shariatmadari	x	
Vahidi	Pahlavi (1392/1972): Vahidi	—	Vahidi	x	
Amoli	Pahlavi: Amoli	—	Amoli	x	
S. Sadeq	Pahlavi	—	S. Sadeq's son	x	
Kirmani	—	—	—	x	

a. T = teaching; R = residence.
b. Until June 1975 riot, the center of the hawza-i 'ilmi; after Khomeyni's return in 1979 his center of operations.
c. After June 1975, center for dispersing student stipends; residents largely Azerbaijani.
d. Being transformed into a modern madrasa.

Table 3.5 Madrasas in Qum: Modern

MODERN TEACHING SCHOOLS	FOUNDED	STUDENTS (APPROX.)		ADMINISTRATOR
		MALE	FEMALE	
Dar al-Tabligh	1965	400	150	Shariatmadari
Golpayegani	–	500	–	Golpayegani
Haqqani (Muntaziriyya)	1964	186	30	Qoddusi
Imam Amir al-Mu'minin	1975	1096	–	Makarem

Arabic — are stressed. Great emphasis is placed on recruiting well-trained students: at first most students were of rural background; by 1975 the figures were reversed and the principal (Mr. Qoddusi) was proud that he had attracted not only a large number of students holding high school diplomas but some with university degrees. In 1974 there were 340 applicants of whom 30 were admitted. Thirty is the target size of each class, though in the past for lack of space not every year had a class; in 1975 there were 186 students. When the school's program is complete, it is hoped there will be twelve major subjects (see appendix), including the moral sciences, to be composed of morals, psychology, sociology, and Islamic economics. The last three did not yet exist in 1975: not enough material existed to construct a program. Dr. Ali Shariati (d. 1977), the French-trained idol of the religious youth, who attempted to formulate the beginnings of an Islamic sociology, was, in the opinion of the teachers in Qum, not Islamically well informed, and one would not want to begin a program using his flawed texts. Presumably the course texts will have to be developed out of the higher level studies in the madrasa itself (years eleven and on). Associated with the Madrasa Haqqani there is even a new school for girls: in 1975 it had 30 students and 5 female teachers.

The Madrasa Haqqani is thus almost a complete cell set apart from the rest of the hawza structure. Its students do not participate in the general stipend system but get their stipends directly from the school, and those stipends largely come from the Mashhad establishment of the late Ayatullah Milani. The philosopher Allama Tabatabai is the father-in-law of the school's director and intellectually has had an impact upon the formulation of the school's identity through the texts he has written for the school. This school is one of an interesting set of four in the Milani establishment. Milani's largest school in Mashhad, physically razed in 1975 by the government to make way for a green belt around Mashhad's shrine, was similar in conception to the Golpayegani school in Qum; it had an eleven-year program and trained many of the Mashhadis who have subsequently come to Qum for higher level studies. Milani set up two other kinds of madrasa in Mashhad. In 1971 the Madrasa 'Ali-Husayni was opened as a specialized institute of higher learning to train *mubaligh* (missionaries, preachers); there were plans to send students to Africa and Pakistan for training in English and then to use them abroad. In 1974, the Madrasa Imam Sadiq was opened as a second and parallel specialized institute to train mujtahids.

In Qum, the Dar-al-Tabligh, set up in the mid-sixties by Ayatullah Shariatmadari, was a cross between the modern lower level schools and the Madrasa 'Ali-Husayni. It had a five-year program (see appendix), organized on a credit system with course exams. There was also a four-year preparatory program for those unable to pass the entrance exams. In 1973 a parallel school for girls was set up, and two years later there were 150 students; male teachers spoke from behind a curtain, using a seating chart to aid them in directing questions. Foreign students were a source of pride to the Dar-al-Tabligh, and through a semiformal arrangement with the passport office the Dar-al-Tabligh acted *in loco parentis* for all lower level foreign students.

The Dar-al-Tabligh was, in fact, the center of an interlocking series of propaganda activities. It itself trains preachers. Together with Dar Rah-i Haqq, it produces a correspondence course on Islam: short lessons are sent out in the mail with questions to be filled out and returned for correction. Four journals are produced in association with it, three in Persian—*Maktab-i Islam* (School of Islam) for adults, circulation 60,000; *Payam-i Shadi* (Glad Tidings) for children; *Nasl-i Naw* (New Generation) for adolescents—and one in Arabic, *al-Hadi*. A circulation of 60,000 for *Maktab-i Islam* may seem modest for an Iranian population of 34 million, but it has excellent distribution and arguments in the bazaars invariably will lead someone to pull out a copy to use as an authority. *Nasl-i Naw* often translates items from foreign journals like *Readers Digest*. *Al-Hadi* not only finds its way to the Gulf and Iraq, but serves as a link to Muslim institutions as far afield and as otherwise unconnected as the new Jam'iyya Nizamiyya college in Ceylon. Books are also published by the Dar-al-Tabligh, usually in runs of 50,000 copies. Finally, Dar-al-Tabligh provides a letter answering service on queries about religion and morality, in Persian, Arabic, Urdu, and English. Perhaps the major frustration of the activities centered on the Dar-al-Tabligh is an inability to develop—outside the two Pakistani staff members—sufficient expertise in English to really engage in discussion with Western audiences.

The last and newest of the madrasas in Qum is the Madrasa Imam Amir al-Mu'minin opened in 1974-75 by Naser Makarem. Its major activity is the large course in *'aqa'id va madhahib* (doctrines and religions). It also teaches English and Qur'an reading, has a letter-answering service and a publishing section, and supports a group of aides to help Makarem with a tafsir commentary on the Qur'an.

The picture thus was one of a functioning traditional madrasa system with a series of complementary newer institutions being built around it.

How well the enterprise as a whole functioned was a matter of opinion. No one appeared to think that things did not need improvement; the major difference of opinion was whether the major obstacles lay within the madrasa system or in the government hostility to any religious revival.

Those who stressed the internal problems included Mortaza Motahhari (1341/1962), a graduate of Qum who taught in the Faculty of Theology at the University of Tehran and was assassinated on May Day 1979 in Tehran when he was a leading member of the Revolutionary Council. They pointed to lack of matriculation examinations, inadequate guidance counseling, bad language teaching methods, failure to update the teaching of fiqh, contraction of the curriculum (the almost complete lack of mathematics, medicine, and science; the decline in teaching of philosophy and morals), and lack of a proper financial base. By lack of a proper financial base, Motahhari meant in part the loss of madrasa endowments (either from their having been converted, over time, to private holdings or, more recently, by their falling under government control); primarily, however, he referred to the paradoxical fact that though the funds came largely from tithes (the sahm-i Imam, which is half of the khums) and were independent of the government, such funding had conservative and anti-innovative force. For instance, he cited the frustrated desire of Shaykh Abdul Karim Haeri-Yazdi in the 1920s to send some young ruhani to Europe to learn the foreign languages and introduce Islam abroad; Tehran bazaaris threatened to cut off their payment of the sahm-i Imam if he went forward with this plan to send youths to learn kafir (unbeliever) ways. Subsequently the marja'-i taqlid, Ayatullah Abdol-Hasan Esfahani, refused to allow pedagogical innovations in Najaf, citing what had happened to Haeri-Yazdi. Motahhari cited al-Azhar in Egypt as the opposite side of the paradox: because the rector is state appointed, he can lead rather than follow public opinion, but he has no independence from state policy. Thus we had—though Motahhari did not say this—the sad spectacle during the Nasser period of al-Azhar convocations and publications producing crude propaganda, which made a mockery of Islamic scholarship. Indeed it is a supreme article of pride among Shi'ite ulama that they are the only body of ulama in the world who have not been reduced to state functionaries. The cost, as Motahhari pointed out, is a problem of a different kind.

Those who stressed the constraints of government hostility and government designs to control the ulama and the madrasas pointed to the repeated exile from Qum of teaching personnel for either actual or alleged political stands; to the attempts by the government to divert religious endowments from the madrasa system; to attempts to introduce government examinations and control over curriculum; to threats of drafting students into the army, of imprisoning them for any political activity, or simply intimidating them; to the closure of religious innovative institutions such as the Husayniya-Irshad in Tehran; to the efforts to establish government religious leaders through bribery, the Sipah-i Din (religious corps) and the Murawwij-i Madhhabi (religious aides); and to efforts in general to isolate religious personnel. These government activities will be discussed in greater detail in chapters 4 and 5. They provide a clear context, however, for the alienation of students who feel they have been led into an educational cul-de-sac: lack of technical training, lack of diplomas recognized by society at large, and thus lack of access to jobs and means of self-improvement outside the religious institution.

The hawza leadership in 1975 — Qoddusi, Shariatmadari, Golpayegani, Makarem, and (before his death) Milani — were moving cautiously to respond in positive directions, despite the polarized climate between an anxious and alienated student body deeply suspicious of government goals, and a government which perceived repeated evidence that the madrasa population was refusing to be anything but a recalcitrant opponent of its modernization goals.

The Ruling Elite and the Role of the Marja'-i Taqlid

Picture the marja'-i taqlid (leading mujtahid) as a grandfatherly man with a white beard and twinkling eyes seated on a mat in a small room amid piles of books, or seated upon a wooden platform in a courtyard amid pomegranate trees, or seated against a wall of a simple carpeted room amid attendants and visitors also arranged along the walls. Glasses of tea are served to visitors before they approach.

A group of akhunds (clerics) enter, one of whom is an Arab sayyid who has been in East Africa. Greetings are conducted with the intimate joking of long familiarity. The sayyid moves closer to the marja', claiming to be hard of hearing. The marja' retorts that obviously he hears what he wants and not other things. The sayyid claims not to hear. They all laugh. The marja' asks him if he is going to preach (it is Ramadan). The answer is affirmative. Has he been getting a good response? Affirmative. Does he talk for a full hour? No, not so long. Does he read a rawda for the people (a tear-jerking account of the martyrdom of Imam Husayn)? No, says the sayyid, his heart is not strong and he himself gets worked up by rawdas.

An old man comes in with a 400-toman sahm-i Imam (portion of the khums religious tax). He is a caretaker of a mosque: he says he has given some of the khums to poor sayyids in the neighborhood but is bringing the rest here. The marja', seeing the man is not well off, takes the money and says, "I accept this as a sayyid and return it to you." Several young students come with similar offerings from villages in which they have been preaching and are similarly treated.

A woman enters and is politely ignored until she arranges her pieces of paper and her veil. She lists all her possessions and income and asks that her khums be calculated and the receipts of previous payments be subtracted. The marja' does this quickly, giving a bank account number to which she may deposit further payments. The woman asks what kind of monthly payments should be made and is told that she should see how her situation is; the work of God does not proceed on monthly payments; whenever she has it she should contribute. The woman then gives him an apple to say a prayer over for her heart condition. This he does and returns the apple.

An old shaykh from a village of Isfahan comes to say that the village prayer leader has died; having studied in Qum, he (the shaykh) wishes to get written permission from the main ayatullahs (the *aqayan*) to take the post; the mosque should not remain empty (an indirect plea for money accompanies the phraseology). The marja‘ puts him off, saying he will look into the shaykh's education and for the time being only affix his seal. He adds, bringing grins to the onlookers, that if not enough people were coming to the mosque a good imam could milk the jinn.

A young Arab comes to ask for help in claiming his father's house. The marja‘ says he does not know his way around such administrative problems. An akhund volunteers that you advertise in the newspaper that so-and-so has died, and unless other heirs come forward with claims — The Arab interrupts protesting that he does not know Persian. The akhund replies, "For that there are lawyers."

A seventy-year-old Shirazi, a man of the old school of rural gentry perhaps, enters in a shabby suit, the zipper on his pants broken, a knit cap on his head, and an old-fashioned collarless white shirt, with a wad of money pinned in a pocket inside the shirt. He has brought 6,000 tomans to help support the students. He lists also the other contributions he has made to the Bayt al-Mal (community chest), contributions for preaching, and so on. He asks if he has given enough or if he may give more, say for passion plays on Ashura. The marja‘ says he should give more, especially in these days when the *fa"aliyyat-i Wahhabi* is so widespread (those who scorn popular styles of devotion: preaching, passion plays, shrines). The two are good friends. The marja‘ asks after the family and is told that the children are not behaving properly, especially the educated one. The wife is to blame. For twenty years they have been having daily fights. The family is becoming so irreligious that in his own house he cannot even say *shukrullah* (thank God). The Shirazi breaks into a sob: even his own trust in God has become little. He says his prayers and means it when he says, "O God, only your help do I need." But it is all a lie; he knows he needs the help of others too. He had gone to Aqa Mahallati (the leader of the Shiraz community) and the latter tried reading some hadith to him but it did not help. Finally, to comfort him, the marja‘ says he (the Shirazi) has now given money to support 7,000 students, which with their dependents is some 20,000 people. In praise of being allowed such a good work, the old man does a prostration (*sijda*) toward the qibla (the Ka‘ba in Mecca). He asks for a memento and is given an agate ring.

There is a theory prevalent among Shi'ites that at any given time there should be only one marja'-i taqlid (leading mujtahid). This theory appears to be neither very old[11] nor firmly grounded, since it is a duty of every man to follow his own reason as far as he is competent and to seek expert advice where he is not. Although it is admitted that, beyond the certification of mujtahid status, the question of who is the most learned of all is merely a matter of opinion, the theory holds that a consensus slowly emerges. Shi'ites today do attempt to trace a line of maraji'-i taqlid back to the time of the twelfth Imam (see appendix). That is, they claim that before the twelfth Imam went into occultation he first selected four special assistants (*nayibha-yi khass* or *nuwwab-i arba'a*); after them, leadership passed to those most learned in the law or nonspecified assistants (*nayib-i 'amm*).

In 1975 there were six first-rank maraji'-i taqlid: Khoi and Khomeyni in Najaf; Golpayegani, Shariatmadari, and Marashi-Najafi in Qum; Khonsari in Tehran; (Milani, the seventh, in Mashhad, died in August 1975). The term, however, is also used more loosely to refer to people who administer the several hawza-i 'ilmi (learning centers), who give out student stipends, and who thereby are really patrons. Though there were many more maraji' in this sense, these six remained the most important, having the most funds to distribute. Funds are a way the Muslim public votes for maraji'-i taqlid, so the roles of intellectual leadership and administration are not distinct. Some intellectual leaders do no administration, the philosopher Allama S. Mohammad-Hoseyn Tabatabai being the most prominent; there is, however, no marja' who does none. This is as it should be: the greater part of the funds given the maraji' are counted as fulfilling the religious tithes, which should be given to the most religiously qualified person available.

Among maraji' there is at least tacit administrative cooperation: each student on stipend receives funds from them all. Intermarriage and tactical cooperation on selected issues also bind the leadership together. But for the time being it stops short of issuing joint opinions, as has been urged by a number of writers (see, for instance, the essays of Motahhari, Taleghani, and Jazayeri in Tabatabai 1341/1962) but opposed by others on grounds of reducing the flexibility of the law and internal checks on questionable interpretations (Ziai n.d.).

A second popular theory, stemming from people's cynicism about the corrupting influence of position and power, is that sons of the major religious leaders (*aqazada*) almost invariably are intellectually lazy and morally corrupt. They are at best functionaries in their fathers' establishments and rarely become leaders in their own right. This is used at times to argue that the recruitment to the religious elite is democratic, achievement-based; not a case of a closed nepotistic caste. The democratic theory is partially confirmed by the few first-rank leaders who rose from village boys, the most prominent recent example being the founder of the present hawza-i 'ilmi in Qum, Shaykh Abdol-Karim Yazdi-Haeri. Naser Makarem is a case of someone making it to near the top from a non-ruhani background. Both Shariatmadari and Golpayegani came from modest, if religiously educated, backgrounds. It is furthermore true that although all the first-rank maraji' today are sayyids, it is not true of the historical list of sixty-odd maraji' through history.

On the other hand, the elite do tend to intermarry and to recruit new talent to their marriage alliances as well as to their work. Shaykh Abdol-Karim Yazdi-Haeri is a particularly clear example (see figure 3.3). If one looks at the historical list of maraji' (see appendix), one sees many sets of relatives. For example, at least five maraji'-i taqlid appear in the ancestry of the late marja'-i taqlid Ayatullah Hoseyn Borujerdi (figure 3.1). Again, the Shirazis not only count four maraji' within two generations, plus the current marja' of Kuwait, but are intermarried with the Mahallati-Shirazis (the leaders of the Shiraz community) and with a cadet line of Marashis (figure 3.2).[12]

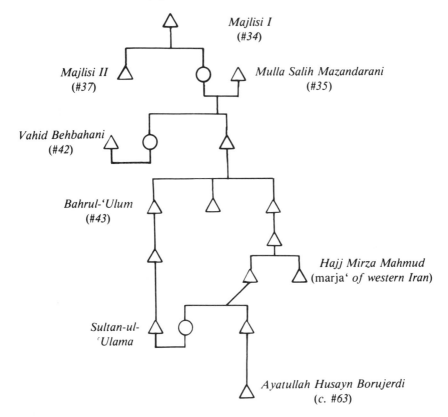

Figure 3.1 *Maraji' in Borujerdi's ancestry (numbers in parentheses refer to the list of maraji' taqlid given in Appendix 2).*

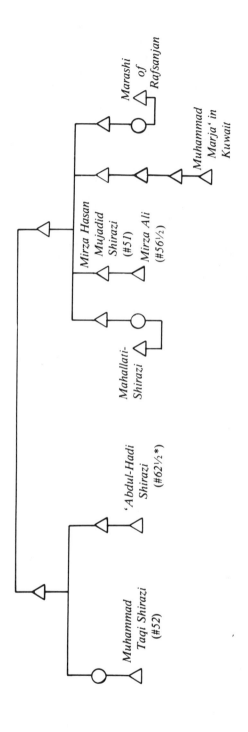

Figure 3.2 *Shirazi maraji' (numbers in parentheses refer to list of maraji' taqlid given in Appendix 2; a person identified with a ½ number was not accepted by the compiler of the list as a marja'-i taqlid and so is not included; if he were, his name would fall in the numerical position indicated).*

Far more impressive is the interrelation of contemporary maraji'. Although the links between Ayatullahs Hojjat, Marashi, and Milani are relatively distant, all seven first-rank maraji' of 1975 can be put on one genealogy, as in figure 3.3. On this simple diagram (essentially two generations) there are twelve first-rank maraji', four second-rank maraji', six other leading teachers, and two professors. Extensions could easily be made: the late marja'-i' taqlid Khonsari (a cousin to the current Khonsari), the marja' of Rey (a son of Milani), and four important teachers of the Mashhad hawza (two sons and a grandson of Milani; a brother of Shariatmadari).

It may be objected that close kinship is only prima facie evidence of any meaningful cooperation. Similarly that Golpayegani, Shariatmadari, and Khomeyni were classmates in Qum is only circumstantial evidence. But it is an observable fact that second-rank aides and friends freely circulate in the establishments of the maraji', so that there is constant communication. During the 1963 opposition to the enfranchisement of women, the maraji' and leading mujtahids met together and sent joint protest telegrams (see Davani 1341/1963 for an incident-by-incident description).

Mild competition, of course, also occurs. A minor case, but one that went on for several years, occurred after the death of Ayatullah Hojjat over which of his two sons should receive the right (and the 10 percent administrative fee that goes with the right) to administer the Madrasa Hojjatiyya. One son was supported by Shariatmadari and Zanjani, the other by the two great leaders in Iraq at the time, Abol-Hasan Esfahani and Zia'oddin Eraghi. The issue was claim by primogeniture versus claim by intellectual superiority. The Endowments Office, backed up (but never used) by the open and secret police, appointed the latter candidate.[13]

More important is the friendly rivalry in setting up new schools, hospitals, missionary activities, and so on. Indeed it was almost as if Qum were divided into three territorial sections with the Azerbaijanis and Shariatmadari to the southwest (upriver: the Sahami Hospital, the Dar-al-Tabligh and its library, Dar Rah-i Haqq, Maktab-i Islam, Madrasa Hojjatiyya), Marashi in the center (his library, tekke, and madrasa, with further to the southeast another madrasa and married student housing), and Golpayegani to the northeast (downriver: his hospital and two schools). (See figure 4.1). The territorial division was more apparent than real: the main Golpayegani school was upriver, a Shariatmadari dormitory was downriver. The apparent competition also arises in activities abroad. Shariatmadari through the Dar-al-Tabligh and the journal *Al-Hadi* was perhaps the best known to non-Persians; visitors came from Lucknow and Karachi in the east, and from Cairo and Fez in the west. In Lucknow at the several Shia colleges, however, except for

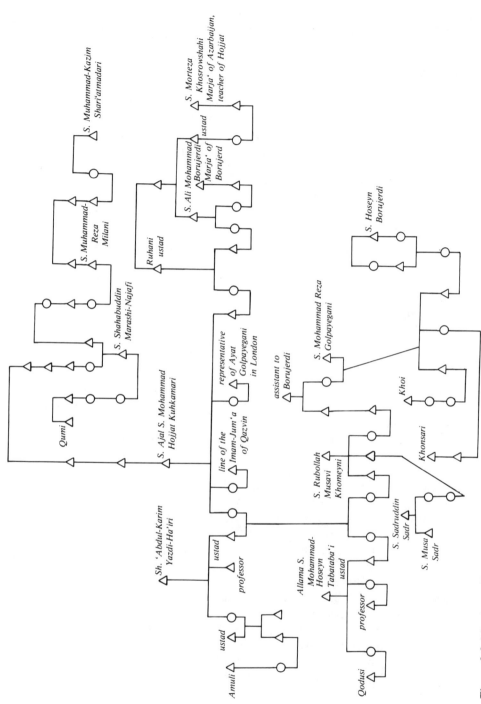

Figure 3.3 *Marriage alliances among the ulama elite*

the top leadership, people in 1975 were very vague about a marja'-i ta-qlid: pressed to haul a name out of their memory, several came up with Hakim, then dead nearly five years; a few said Shariatmadari, and a few said Khomeyni "because originally he is from Kashmir and so is an Indian" and because a few Indian students in Najaf had written that he was the best. Golpayegani in the 1970s began more active efforts abroad: he built a mosque in London, began giving *shahriyya* (monthly stipends) to students in India, bought land for a madrasa in Kashmir, and claimed in 1975 to be negotiating for a similar madrasa in Tibet. Marashi was primarily known abroad through his scholarship in *rijal* (biographies) and exchange of *ijazat* (certifications) with numerous religious leaders, Sunni, Shia, Zaydi, and Ismaili alike. He has a small institute, Lajna-i Ihqaq al-Haqq, which collects and publishes Sunni hadith and writings favorable to Shi'ism.

Perhaps more important than either the internal cohesion of the elite or its friendly competition is the degree to which it is interrelated with the political and economic elites, for here it clearly emerges how closely tied to a passing order the elite is (see table 3.6). Links to the bazaar—especially to the wholesale merchant class—are most clearly evident in the Shariatmadari genealogy, but they also exist in the Marashi, Milani, and to a lesser extent Golpayegani genealogies. Golpayegani instead comes from a family of small landowners and ruhani (as did Borujerdi) and married into a family of shopkeepers and ruhani.

There is a tendency for the new category of professionals to grow, a tendency illustrated schematically by the fortunes of the former royal family, the Safavids. Originally, the leadership of a militant Sufi sect, they became Shi'ite (or explicitly Shi'ite), seized power, made alliances with various religious and government elites (including the Marashi family), then lost the throne, becoming themselves religious leaders, and finally in the last two generations, through a brief one-generation flirtation with military careers, became professionals.

Of all the families, the Mar'ashi record is the most fully preserved, thanks to the labors of Ayatullah Shahaboddin Mar'ashi. It illustrates, moreover, changes in the organization of society at large. The ancestors of the Mar'ashi, descendants of the third Imam, first lived or ruled in northern Iraq, then moved to Rey and Mazandaran where they served as naqibs (chiefs of the "guild" of sayyids as it were). Later, through warfare, religious propaganda, and marriage alliances with local notables, they became kings of Tabaristan. Qavamuddin "Mir Buzurg," the first of fifteen Mar'ashi kings of Tabaristan (A.D. 760 to c. 1007), began as a *darvish*, heir to an important popular following which was feared by the local king. When attempts to humiliate Qavamuddin and defeat his followers failed, he seized the throne; marriage alliances with the Kia Jalalian, Kar Kia, Yazvaran, and Kayomars families helped stabilize the

Table 3.6 Males in genealogies of religious elite, by generation and occupation

Occupation	Shariatmadari			Marashi			Milani			Golpayegani			Total
	E[a]	O	Y	E	O	Y	E	O	Y	E	O	Y	
Ruhani	3	6	1	12	5	5	13	4	12	2	19	23	105
Merchant (*tajir*)	7	7	0	6	11	5	1	11	3	2	1	4	58
Industrialist	0	0	0	0	1	0	0	0	0	0	0	0	1
Shopkeeper	2	5	0	0	4	0	0	2	2	0	3	0	18
Landowner	0	0	0	2	2	2	0	0	0	0	6	0	12
High government	0	0	0	3	2	0	0	0	0	0	0	0	5
Professional	0	0	1	3	2	8	0	1	7	0	1	8	31
Clerk	0	0	1	0	0	0	0	0	0	0	0	3	4
Military	0	0	0	0	3	0	0	0	0	0	0	0	3
Other or unknown (but not ruhani)	3	2	0	9	8	2	2	7	1	0	2	2	38
Subtotal	15	20	3	35	38	22	16	25	25	4	32	40	
Total		38			95			66			76		275

[a] E = elder, ascending generations; O = own generation; Y = younger, descending generations.

political balance. War, defeats, and accommodations with Timur followed. Mar'ashis became mutawalli (administrators) of the Shrine of Imam Reza in Mashhad.

Meanwhile a Mar'ashi, Mir Najmuddin, married the daughter of the naqib of Shushtar, succeeding to the post and to some lands. The fifth Mar'ashi in this post, Mir Nurullah (d. 925/1519) began to convert the people to Shi'ism. When Shah Isma'il, founder of the new Safavid dynasty (see chronology facing page 1), arrived in Shushtar, he confirmed Mir Nurullah's position and gave him more lands. Mir Nurullah's grandson, Qadi Nurullah, after being educated in Mashhad, went to India and served as minister and military judge in Akbar Shah's court. (Exposed as a Shi'ite, he was later killed by Jahangir Shah.)

In Iran under the Safavids, Mar'ashis served as viziers to the kings and intermarried with them: daughters of Shah 'Abbas II, Shah Tahmasp II, Shah Sulayman, and Shah Sultan-Husayn. They continued to serve as mutawalli of the Imam Reza Shrine, and one (Mirza Sayyid Muhammad, "Shah Sulayman II") even seized the throne in Mashhad for forty days from Shahrukh, whom he blinded in the process—for which deed Mirza Muhammad's tongue was removed. Mar'ashis served as naqibs in Rey and Tabaristan, and as *sadr* or mutawalli of all religious endowments in

Iran. Under the Qajars one married a daughter of Fath-'Ali Shah, several became court doctors, one was an ambassador to Istanbul, and a number were ayatullahs.

These various exalted positions illustrate, first, something of the quasi-hereditary nature of posts like naqib and mutawalli and, second, possibly something about the changing interrelation of the religious and political elites. It is possible to argue, as Ayatullah Mar'ashi himself on occasion will, that his line of the family is the religious line and has little to do with politics.[14] He himself certainly tried to steer clear of overt politics, although he refused, for instance, to give youths positive permission to study social science at university because it seemed clear that such professionally trained people would be corrupted and used by the immoral Pahlavi government system. Yet his grandfather and uncles were court doctors and a great grandfather was an ambassador. These men clearly were of the Qajar nobility if not professional politicians. Again the argument is that though kin linkages are only prima facie evidence, certain of these linkages are observable in action. The political linkages probably ceased under the Pahlavis: that was one of the changes in society at large, namely, that top bureaucrats were recruited from the university rather than from the madrasa. In 1975, a Mar'ashi happened to head the government's Endowments Office in Tabriz, but he was of the new secular bureaucratic class. The linkage between the new professional class and the religious leaders is one of replacement or new occupation not one of support, as was the linkage with the old political elite and is still today with the bazaar merchants. These latter links with the bazaar are quite observable: Tabriz merchants who come to pay their respects (and monetary contributions) to Shariatmadari; merchants who serve as intermediary links between the general public and the maraji' (if you need to get past Ayatullah Khonsari's attendants, say Hajji Hoseyn sent you). Nor is the linkage one of uncritical support. A merchant, asked whether he gave khums to the *aqayan* (religious leaders) or dispersed it himself, put it this way: "I do not give money, but rather I say may I donate a new door to such and such a mosque to replace the one that is broken, or may I donate a piece of equipment to your hospital."

The role of marja'-i taqlid is thus both an active dual leadership — intellectual and administrative — and socially limited by its supporters, the students and the financial backers. A Tabriz mujtahid of the same generation as Shariatmadari noted that the limitation has become stronger recently for another reason: in the past many of the religious elite were landowners and could thus be gentlemen scholars. After land reform, not only was it less possible to be a gentleman scholar, but that route of recruitment to the religious elite was closed.

The Pahlavi government also limited the role of marja'-i taqlid and lesser provincial ayatullahs. The role of marja'-i taqlid is ideally suited to setting up social services, but social services became an area of competition with the state. When a major flood destroyed many homes in 1933, Shaykh Abdol-Karim Yazdi obtained from the Endowments Office a ninety-nine-year lease on Mobarakabad, a suburban village of Qum, and organized the rehousing of the victims. He was also instrumental in starting the Sahami and Fatimi hospitals. Both he and Ayatullah Borujerdi agitated until finally the government built flood walls along the river. Ayatullah Golpayegani later executed Yazdi's plan to build a hospital for Mobarakabad by getting a forty-nine-year lease from the Endowments Office and facilitating its building. Similarly when the Sahami Hospital began to fail, it was taken over by Shariatmadari and was rebuilt.

Libraries are another facility that the religious leaders have provided for community use, not only in Qum. Rationalized welfare programs are another area of activity. Perhaps the most impressive program was the one organized by the Mahallati establishment in Shiraz: based on pledge cards (with some 2,000 contributors in 1975) and giving regular aid in rent supplements and medical needs, some 300 families were being helped month by month. Welfare applicants were first thoroughly checked out, and there was a staff of nine to collect pledges. This *Daftar-i Khayrat-i Islam* (Office of Islamic Charity), nine years old in 1975, had by then built twenty-five houses for needy families and was building a further five; other families were helped to buy houses. A clinic was connected to the Daftar and there were plans for a hospital, but the family planning section of the clinic had been closed at government request in an effort to systematize and not duplicate. A similar but less formal welfare program was operated in Qum by Shaykh Mortaza Haeri-Yazdi (the son of Shaykh Abdol-Karim Haeri-Yazdi). Another area of endeavor was to encourage Islamic banks (which neither charge nor give interest and are primarily used for small loans to set up shops, pay for weddings, and the like).

Both the welfare and Islamic bank endeavors in part were attempts to aid the truly needy and those who can be helped, separating them from those merely looking for a handout, and thus avoiding confrontations that reflect ill on all, scenes like the following, which I witnessed in 1975.

The mosque in the Tehran bazaar was not very full for evening prayers. A sayyid walked in and did a couple of prostrations. The young man sitting next to me went up to him and obviously asked for money. He was refused and returned to his place next to me cursing the sayyid aloud: "He says he has not brought any money. These bastards collect the money from the people and then eat it. We have nothing and they drive to the mosque in a [Mercedes] Benz. In the days of 'Ali this would not have happened, he who ate poor barley bread." He explained that he was unemployed because there was something wrong with his foot; he had been to the hospital but the foot was not better. Not only had the sayyid not given him any money; he had told him to go to work. Several others also tried to get money and were turned away. An aide then announced that those who had come for money should return on Saturday; today there was none. The ayatullah then came in and took his place in the front row. Some money was handed out to a few people who came up and apparently were known. Prayers began immediately.

Of course, rationalization involves its own problems of bureaucratic and status procedures trampling on the dignity of charity recipients. The traditional dignified style of giving charity is to slip some money to the recipient as unobtrusively as possible. That is hard to accomplish with a bureaucracy, as the following scene in Shiraz demonstrates.

Donors and one better-dressed recipient were offered tea immediately upon their arrival; the regular recipients did not get any. The clerk was brusk and firm with the obviously poor. One old couple was given money for his eyeglasses but not for medicine. Another old woman was given something for an eye doctor and apparently was expected to contribute some money herself (the bill would run 300 to 400 tomans); this she said she did not have. She was sent away after some moral admonitions to see what she could do and return to let the office know what had happened. An amputee was turned away: his case had not been researched. He refused to leave and just sat. Five tomans were offered; he refused them. The five tomans were put into his hand; he sat some more and then got up on his crutches and walked across the room to return the money. He left the office, but sat on the steps outside to await the ayatullah. He had at least been given tea and the explanation that his case had not been researched; he replied that he had applied some time ago and had been back several times, yet nothing had happened. After he left, the clerk explained that there were two kinds of people: those who were really needy, often not even pressing their legitimate claims, were good people; and then there were those, like this man, who ran their troubles as a kind of business and even would use children as a way to extract money. Thus the need to check out each case.

Although these endeavors are praiseworthy from a humanitarian point of view, the Pahlavi government apparently found their too open success a threat; it placed various limitations on the kinds of medical facilities it would license and in general attempted to provide all major services through its own bureaucracy. The situation in 1975 was ill-disguised competition on both sides. Government medics scoffed at the quality of service the religious hospitals could offer. The ulama spoke of the hospitals "we built" without acknowledging the help of others, including the lands acquired at no cost from the government Endowments Office.

The Vocal Elite and the Role of Wa'iz

In 1935 Reza Shah was mounting a campaign to persuade people to dress like Europeans. Since 1928 men had been ordered to wear the Pahlavi cap and Western trousers; now the Pahlavi cap was to be replaced by the fedora hat and women were to unveil. In Fars, the religious leaders Ja'far Mahallati and Sayyid Nuroddin protested and were punished by having their waqf (endowment) pensions taken away. At first there was newspaper propaganda and lectures, and only schoolgirls were unveiled. But toward the end of 1935 the police began to order veiled women off the streets and out of public places such as cafes, cinemas, and hospitals. On 8 January 1936, Reza Shah, accompanied by his unveiled wife and daughter, made a speech on the emancipation of women. Social events were organized, which government officials (and increasingly others) were required to attend with their unveiled wives. Even members of the ulama received such invitations and a British diplomat, Urquart, described their dilemma: "There is much talk of how the various mullahs wept over this rape of Islamic tradition, and people are enjoying with a morbid horror and indignation definitely cautious, the prospect of some of the religious leaders dying of grief and strain, or else committing suicide . . . it is rumoured that a sayyid, prominent at Khoi, in resisting the order to unveil was arrested, shaved and sent home wearing a European hat, and that he was found dead in bed on the following morning."[15]

Pressures came to one climax in 1935 on the twentieth anniversary of the Russian bombing of the Imam Reza Shrine in Mashhad. A little mulla, sent by Hajj Mirza Hoseyn Qummi to talk against the unveiling of women, climbed onto the minbar in the Gawhar-Shad mosque of the shrine. To gain attention, he pulled off his turban and squatted over it. The place quieted and he began to speak, demanding repeal of the orders about male headgear and female emancipation, demanding that taxes be lowered, and abusing the shah and local officials. A few people shouted slogans to help emphasize his points. Navvab Ehtesham and other shrine officials snatched off and ripped up their official headgear. The police arrived and were greeted with insults and missiles. Infantry (200 strong) and 50 cavalrymen blocked off the shrine. As the British consul, Day, reported it: "A fracas occurred during which the general officer commanding was pushed into a water channel. He appears to have lost control of himself and ordered machine gun fire to be opened."[15] The official death count was 32. Appalled at what he had just done inside the sacred precincts, Sartip Iraj Khan pulled his troops back and notified Tehran. The shah ordered the shrine cleared by persuasion, failing which by sticks and rifle butts, and only failing that by bayonet. Crowds gathered during the three days it took to consult Tehran, beating their breasts to the chant "Husayn protect us from this shah." Villagers began to come into town armed with sticks, sickles, shovels, and daggers. The bazaar closed. The garrison, largely in sympathy with the populace, was disarmed and confined to barracks, with the exception of one detachment. That detachment was given a feast and then, at 2:00 A.M. on the fourth night, it forced the door of the shrine, opened fire with machine guns, and cleared the shrine. Officially 28 were killed. Unofficial sources claimed 128 were buried in trenches prepared before the event. Some 800 were arrested and flogged. Blame for the event was pinned on Asadi, the caretaker of the shrine, who, after torture, confessed and was executed.

Amid the chaos of the first day, the little mulla, Bahlul (Shaykh Mohammad-Taghi Sabzevari), slipped away and fled across the Afghan border, beginning a forty-year exile from Iran. He had, however, become a folk hero. "Bahlul" is an affectionate nickname. The original Bahlul pretended to be crazy when the sixth Imam (Ja'far al-Sadiq) was imprisoned, as a way of spreading the Imam's message. When people thought about what he said, they realized that he was not crazy. For instance, one day Abu Hanifa was preaching about the problem that if God is not visible how can one know something is there to be worshiped? In the course of his argument he elaborated on the notion that like objects cannot irritate one another. Bahlul threw a clod of dirt at him and hit him on the forehead. Abu Hanifa took Bahlul to court, complaining that his head hurt. Bahlul responded: if there is a problem about worshiping God because we cannot see him, show me your pain. Furthermore, you say like cannot irritate like; you are from dirt, as was the clod, so your pain cannot come from it. There are many such Bahlul stories and the contemporary Bahlul, "crazy" for having sat on his turban, revels in the comparison. He is known as not particularly learned but with an excellent memory for all the stories and rhetorical devices that amuse audiences. Indeed he himself says he had gone to Najaf to become a mujtahid under Hajj Mirza Hoseyn Qummi, but the latter seeing that he would never become a good mujtahid sent him to preach instead. Nor is he known for his elegance of speech; on the contrary his folksy Khurasan accent and style endear him to his audiences.

He is a folk hero not only for his style but for his courage in defense of Islam against the state. He had been sent by Qummi to make his way from town to town to preach against unveiling but to leave if trouble threatened. Response among the populace had to do not only with veiling and headgear, but also with economic conditions: regressive taxes squeezing the lower classes, state foreign trade monopolies squeezing the merchants, printing of money increasing the cost of living, unfavorable state-monopoly wheat prices to the farmer and forced closing of bakeries, making bread prices rise 20 percent. And, with the growing police state: the army of informers, the crackdown on the free market (smuggling). After Bahlul fled Iran, his image was bolstered with stories of how he settled in Afghanistan as a farmer and raised a number of orphans to become doctors and teachers, and how earlier when he had gone to study with Qummi he had carried his aged mother on his back from Mashad to Najaf that she might make that pilgrimage. Nor was his image damaged by briefly broadcasting for Nasser from Cairo against the shah. In 1975, he had made his peace with the shah and was again in Iran and allowed to preach, as long as he stayed away from political topics.

There are two main terms for the preaching role. *Wa'iz* is the more respectable and means really a lecturer. Professors who are well-known lecturers on the religious circuit—like Javad Managhebi—are *wa 'izin*. The other term *rawda-khwan* or *akhund*, refers literally to the reading of the dirges about the tragedy of Karbala. *Akhund* has come also to be the common term for a cleric; it is not particularly respectful, but it serves as the colloquial term rather than, say, *mulla*. *Ruhani* is the respectful term for those who wear religious garb. Terms for what is delivered follow a parallel semantic structure: a wa'iz delivers a speech (*sukhanrani*), a rawda-khwan "reads a rawda," an akhund may do either. A khutba (sermon) is not a didactic event in Iran; khutbas are given by the *imam-jum'a* after Friday noon prayer, but they are not important events. (This would change after Ramadan 1979).

The didactic event in Shi'ite Iran is the rawda. This begins with an aya (verse) of the Qur'an; at each mention of the Prophet's name, and at other signals, blessings (*salawat*) are chanted by the audience; a speech or sermon forms the body of the performance; and the closing is always a turning (*guriz*) to the events of Karbala (the rawda proper), during which the audience engages in the pietistic exercise of weeping. One wishes to weep for the martyr of Karbala so that on Judgment Day he will intercede and one's sins will be weighed more lightly and with compassion. The capacity to weep with true repentance, humility, and regard for Husayn is called *hal-i khosh* (the good state). One who makes a pilgrimage to an important shrine but is unable to weep in this fashion will sadly comment, "I stayed ten days, but I could not find the good state (*hich hal-i khosh payda nakardam*)."

Of interest is the fact that with a few exceptions—Khomeyni in particular—the maraji-i taqlid do not go onto the minbar to preach, though they support preaching to commemorate the death of, say, Ayatullah Borujerdi or during the months of Ramadan and Muharram. Instead, there is a whole other set of prominent names associated with this activity: Bahlul, Shaykh Mohammad-Taghi Falsafi, Dr. Javad Managhebi, Rashed, Sayyid Abdol-Karim Hasheminezhad, Dr. Ali Shariati, Engineer Mehdi Bazargan, Shaykh Ahmad Kafi, Abdol-Reza Hejazi, Fakhroddin Hejazi, Mohammad Khasali, and so on. The youth know these names and their stylistic idiosyncrasies the same way they know movie actors. It is in this role that the passion of Shi'ism is most clearly focused. Consequently, the Pahlavi government took great care to monitor such speeches. An occupational hazard of being a minbari was the possibility of being silenced or jailed from time to time. In early 1975 Falsafi was not being allowed to speak, S. Abdul Reza Hejazi was in prison, Khasali was banished to Baluchistan, Shariati was in prison, Bazargan and Hasheminezhad were not being allowed to speak. But Bahlul, after his forty-year exile, was back and speaking. Shariati was released from jail later that year, so seriously ill that he died within two years. Another akhund — Ghaffari — allegedly died in jail under gruesome conditions.

Despite this occupational hazard — though if one remained totally bland, talking only of general ethics as Rashed did, there was no hazard — the role had its elements of glamour for the madrasa students. This for most was to be a major element in their professional lives. Even as students, they supplement their incomes in an important way during Ramadan and Muharram by accepting speaking engagements. Villages often solicited rawda-khwans through the maraji'-i taqlid or provincial ayatullahs. Ayatullah Milani initiated a regular service to take students on circuit around the villages of Mashhad on Thursdays and Fridays to lead prayers and deliver rawdas (though for this program the students were not allowed to accept fees).

The dean of the wa'izin was perhaps Shaykh Mohammad-Taqi Falsafi. Regarded as a careful researcher of sources, his collected lectures served as a basic reference on issues of psychology and personal development from childhood to adulthood. Students also respected him for having been in the center of social issues of his day. During the disturbances over Bahaism in the mid-1950s, Falsafi was one of Ayatullah Borujerdi's main spokesmen in Tehran. The religious establishment at that point in Mohammad Reza Shah's reign was strong enough to intimidate the government, not only to allow Falsafi to regularly broadcast against Bahais on radio but to get the leading members of the government to publicly support the hysteria against the Bahai threat to Islam.[16] Falsafi happened also to be on the minbar at the death memorial for Ayatullah Fayd (the rebuilder of the Qum hawza) in 1951 when shots rang out and General Razmara, the prime minister, who only the day before had threatened the nationalists in the parliament if they did not support his compromises with the British over Persian oil, was assassinated by a member of the fanatic Fida'iyan-i Islam. Falsafi's freedom to speak on the minbar was finally taken away after a speech in Tehran, at a gathering in 1970 convened by Ayatullah Khonsari to protest the expulsion from Iraq of Persian nationals and to protest the attack on Najaf, which those expulsions represent. The speech, to which ambassadors of the various Muslim countries were invited, was taped for radio broadcast but was edited in several places before it went on the air. One of the deleted sections is alleged to have contained the taunt that when Muslims throw

stones at Satan in the ritual of the hajj, they only think they are stoning
Satan, but when Iranian students threw rotten eggs and tomatoes at the
shah in Germany they were really stoning Satan. The government is said
to have responded by circulating a doctored photograph of Falsafi in bed
with a naked woman; to which Falsafi allegedly retorted:

> Kun-i' dawlat para kardam;
> Hala mikhwahand vaselin bimaland.
>
> I buggered the government;
> Now they want to soothe it with Vaseline.

1975 was but prologue to 1977-1979. The madrasa and its alumni were
but microcosm to the society at large. Just as the members of the
madrasa defended their institution as a free university in contrast to the
regimented state schools, so they also saw freedom, flexibility, and
ultimate moral modernity as riding with the custodians of the Iranian
Islamic heritage, not with the state. Just as the madrasa was perceived as
having been hampered and constricted in its development, so too the
promise of a just Islamic society. To reap the fruits of the promise would
require hard work and learning from the modern world. Thus the revolution of 1977-1979 would use the network of preachers and the administrative structure already in place, but it would not hesitate to utilize
an alliance with people outside the ulama hierarchy.

Khomeyni would be the leader, the only marja' who consistently, from
1963 on, did go on the minbar and preach, sending tapes of his sermons
and speeches to Iran, criticizing the shah. But Khomeyni would be
openly or tacitly aided by a variety of other maraj'i-i taqlid, ayatullahs,
and figures of lesser rank. Shariatmadari would be vocal, as would the
two Mahallatis (father and son) in Shiraz, and Ayatullah Shirazi in
Mashhad. The modernist wa'izin—Ayatullah Sayyid Mahmud
Taleghani, Engineer Mehdi Bazargan, and the numerous followers of
Dr. Ali Shariati—would play a crucial role. Indeed, one of these
followers, Dr. Ebrahim Yazdi—who as a young man had been groomed
by Bazargan, had spent years in the United States as a medical researcher
and as a devoted preacher to the Islamic students there, and would
become first deputy prime minister for revolutionary affairs and then
foreign minister in 1979—rescued Khomeyni when he was deported from
Iraq in 1978 and refused entry to Kuwait. Yazdi convinced Khomeyni
that in Paris he could become a focal point for a modern media revolution: not only could tapes and written statements be easily mass
reproduced, but easy access could be had to the international news
media, above all the BBC. For weeks during the revolution, in Shiraz and
other towns of Iran, preachers would end in time for people to go home

and catch the BBC Persian broadcasts. It all would have happened without the BBC, television coverage, tapes, and telephones: these were just modern, speedier accessories of an old system, symbolically focused in the person of Khomeyni and in the town of Qum.

4

Qum: Arena of Conflict

> There are a number of things which kings should learn. One
> is digging with a shovel and earning his bread, so that he
> will not lightly take the bread from the hands of others;
> another is for him to suffer the pains of torture so that he
> will not without good reason order anybody tortured;
> another is that he should experience hunger so that he will
> give to the hungry; and another is that he should know the
> toil of traveling on foot so that he will no longer make peo-
> ple go on foot to where he goes.
>
> — *Darabnameh*

QUM IS THE RELIGIOUS HEART of Shi'ite Iran; what happens in Qum has national importance. Insofar as Iran has a fairly centralized political structure, the social pressures operating in Qum are not very different from those operating elsewhere. In these two senses Qum's unique characteristics provide both a kind of local color to patterns observable elsewhere in Iran and a special access to the religious aspects of those patterns.

The task now is to place Qum and the religious personnel of the madrasa system in the context of a modernizing, nondemocratic state: to show how the provincial town of Qum as a unit of the state has been transformed; to show where and how in that transformation the freedom of maneuver (power, leadership, control) of the religious personnel has been circumscribed, and to indicate how in the transformation classes differentiate themselves in religious idiom.

Qum has a peculiar set of reputations in Iran. Foreigners and even many Westernized Iranians avoid it as a hotbed of fanaticism. The hagiographies of the town portray it from its earliest Islamic days as a Shi'ite refuge and stubborn stronghold. For shrine goers, only Mecca, the 'atabat (the shrine towns of southern Iraq), and Mashhad surpass Qum as a site of experiential intensity. In the popular folklore of character types Qummis are *bad gens* (bad types, clever, scheming, two-faced).

Despite the census claims that Qum has a population of over 200,000 people, it is a small town with practically no industry. It is still a very traditional town based on farming, weaving, some herding, some carpentry, brick making, selling to pilgrims (garrish pottery, prayer beads, souvenirs), and services to the sizable madrasa and shrine population.

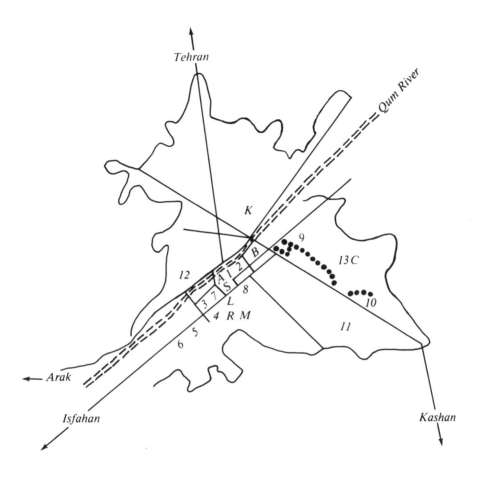

Figure 4.1 *Qum location map*

Key: Major mosques
 A A'zam (Borujerdi)
 B Imam
 C Jum'a
Madrasas
 1 Faydiyya
 2 Dar al-Shifa
 3 Hujjatiyya
 4 Dar al-Tabligh
Other major institutions
 S Shrine (Hadrat-i Ma'suma)
 R Dar Rah-i Haqq
 L Mar'ashi Library

M Maktab-i Islam
K Mobarakabad
●●●● *Bazaar*

5 Imam Amir al-Mu'minin
6 Golpayegani
7 Mar'ashi
8 Khan
9 Kirmani
10 Razaviyya
11 Mu'minin
12 Haqqani
13 Jani Khan

Opium and prostitutes (primarily the former) are still the major forms of male entertainment, rather than alcohol and cinemas.

Although Qum has a long madrasa tradition — traced back to the third century A.H. — the current set of madrasas are only some fifty years old. Their growth and social power has had a decided effect in making the town more puritan, more conservative, less amenable to change than it would otherwise be; the effect is by no means appreciated by all Qummis and was perhaps intensified unintentionally by the Pahlavi government's anticlericalism. During the sixties and seventies, government efforts to introduce changes in social welfare (education, health care), physical planning (parks, modern buildings, roads, diversified economic opportunities), and civic administration (price control and political party maneuvers) gathered momentum, making the madrasa system increasingly a backwater.

Evolution of the Shrine Town: Shi'ite and Royal

Qum's historians revel in its reputation as an obstreperous Shi'ite center, tracing this posture back to the early Shi'ite resistance to the Umayyads. Abu Musa Ash'ari, the ineffective and somewhat stupid representative of 'Ali,[1] visited Qum in A.H. 23, but Qum remained Zoroastrian and paid *jizya* (the tax on protected minorities). Indeed the great Sassanian ritual fire in the nearby village of Mazdijan was extinguished only in A.H. 288 by Bayram Turk, the governor of Qum. Nonetheless, Qum and Kashan became refuges for opponents of the Umayyads. After Mutraf ibn Mughira's revolt against the governor of Iraq, Hajjaj ibn Yusuf Thaqafi, failed (66-67/685-687), a group of his followers, the Bani Asad, came to settle in a village outside Qum, called Jam Karan (now an important secondary shrine of the area). A decade later refugees from the unsuccessful jihad (holy war) of 'Abd al-Rahman ibn Muhammad ibn Ash'ath (governor of Seistan) against Hajjaj also came to Qum (c. 78/697). 'Abd al-Rahman's army had included seventeen *tabi'in*[2] (disciples of the Prophet's companions), and among the refugees who came to Qum were the sons of Sa'ib who had fought with Mukhtar in the unsuccessful attempt to revenge Husayn in Kufa under the banner of his brother, Muhammad ibn al-Hanafiyya. The first of 'Abd al-Rahman's followers to arrive in Qum were the brothers 'Abdullah and Ahwas Ash'ari. They were welcomed by the Zoroastrian, Yazdan Fezar of Abrastigan Qum, and were given a village, Muhammadan, apparently in recognition of aid the Ash'aris had previously given Qum in efforts to stay independent of the Daylamis. The alliance was short-lived, however: a quarrel broke out, the Ash'aris were asked to leave; instead they slaughtered the leading Zoroastrians. The other Zoroastrians began to leave or converted to Islam. Among the Ash'ari sons were twelve rawi (transmitters of riwayat or hadith) of Imam Ja'far al-Sadiq, the sixth Imam.

From these beginnings Qum next developed a reputation for resisting Sunni governors and their tax demands. S. Hoseyn Modarresi-Tabatabai (1350/1975) lists five occasions in the third century A.H. alone when the town had to be militarily reduced before taxes could be collected. In contrast, a Shi'ite governor was given so much cooperation that he was removed by the caliph lest he claim independence. During the third century there were 266 Shi'ite ulama and 14 Sunni ulama in the town; among the former were the Babawayh family and their most renowned son, the marja'-i taqlid (number 2 in Appendix 2). Shaykh al-Saduq ibn Babawayh. On these grounds, Qum lays claim to being an older hawza-i ilmi (center of religious learning) than Najaf, although the scholarly tradition had periods of virtual disappearance.

It was to this Shi'ite town that Fatima, the sister of the eighth Imam, 'Ali al-Rida, came when she fell ill in Saveh (a Sunni town) en route to visit her brother in Mashhad. She died in Qum, and over the years her grave has come to be the second most important shrine of Iran: the Shrine of Hadrat-i Ma'suma, Fatima. The first mutawalli (administrator) of the shrine appears to have been a representative of the eleventh Imam; he was of the Ash'ari family.[3] The first dome was constructed over the grave in the sixth century, and the shrine apparently served as a pilgrimage site for Sunnis as well as Shi'ites. The dome was redone in the Safavid period and gilded in the Qajar period. Fatima's sister has a smaller shrine in the uplands village of Kohak, a place that at times competed with Qum for predominance.

By the ninth century A.H. Qum's identity had begun to crystallize: it became, in addition to a Shi'ite center and a shrine, a place of royal interest. Jahan Shah, Uzun Hasan, Sultan Ya'qub, Alvand Sultan, and Sultan Murad all used Qum as a winter hunting capital (Uzun Hasan was visited here by envoys from Venice), Sultan Muhammad Bahadur briefly established a semi-independent state centered on Qum. Jahan Shah Qaraquyunlu issued the earliest extant *farman* (royal order), dated 867/1462, naming S. Ahmad Nizamuddin as mutawalli of the shrine and naqib (local head) of the sayyids. He also sponsored *majlis wa'iz* (preachments) in Qum. From later farmans it becomes clear that the two jobs of naqib and mutawalli always went together and were assumed to be hereditary in the Razavi sayyid family of Musa Mobaqa, which had come to Qum in the third/ninth century. (This family has a large set of mausoleums on the edge of town.)

The Safavid shahs Isma'il and Tahmasp continued the tradition of using Qum as a winter capital. But the Safavids built Qum into something much grander than it had ever been. The tombs of Shah 'Abbas II, Shah Safi, Shah Sulayman, and Shah Sultan-Husayn were placed here, near the Shrine of Fatima, Hadrat-i Ma'suma. The shrine was refurbished, and two of its four courtyards were turned into the Madrasa Faydiyya with a small hospital behind for pilgrims, the Dar-al-Shafa.

Important teachers were brought: Mulla Muhsin Fayd, Mulla 'Abd al-Razzaq Lahiji, Mulla Sadra Shirazi, Mulla Tahir Qummi, and Qadi Sa'id. Several administrative arrangements were tried: for a while the governor was the mutawalli; for a while there were three mutawallis, one each for the tombs of Fatima, Shah 'Abbas II, and Shah Safi. But the main mutawalli was Mirza S. Habibullah ibn Mir S. Husayn Khatim al-Mujtahidin and later his descendants; he had been brought from Lebanon by Shah Tahmasp with his father and two brothers. The two brothers were made mutawalli of the Shah 'Abd al-'Azim Shrine in Rey and the Shah Safi Shrine in Ardebil. These jobs remained hereditary until 1965 when shah Mohammad Reza Pahlavi ousted them.[4] Whether the custom is older is unclear, but under the Safavids the shrine became a place of sanctuary (*bast-nishin*), where one could take refuge from the law until a judgment thought to be unfair could be sorted out. At times this legal recourse tended to degenerate into a device used mainly by debtors.

The Qajars continued the tradition of placing royal and noble mausoleums at the shrine of Fatima, with the tombs of Fath-'Ali Shah, Muhammad Shah, and the many Qajar ministers: Qa'immaqam and Mirza 'Ali-Asghar Khan, among others (see figure 4.2). They rebuilt sections of the shrine, the grand Sahn-i Jadid (new courtyard) being built by Amin al-Sultan in 1883. The bast (sanctuary) tradition continued despite efforts by the prime minister, Mirza 'Ali-Asghar Khan, to abolish it. The madrasas, however, lost their vitality after the death of the scholar Mirza Qummi in 1231/1804, although several of them were rebuilt under Fath-'Ali Shah (1797-1834), and the Jani Khan Madrasa was rebuilt under Nasiruddin Shah (1848-1896) (see table 3.4).

The Religious Establishment and the Expanding Bureaucratic State

In the twentieth century two social vectors became increasingly important: First, the hawza-i 'ilmi (center of religious learning) was reestablished in Qum, but this time not through royal or aristocratic patronage. Second, the state began to eliminate or reduce, one by one, the spheres of influence claimed by the religious leaders: law, education, endowments, registry of contracts, and, through control of television and radio, even the dissemination of religious propaganda.

On the national level education began to be removed from ulama control at the turn of the century: secular schools were established beginning in 1897; laws were passed in 1907 and 1911 making all schools, including religious ones, subject to the Ministry of Education (Akhavi 1980). From 1926 on, the jurisdiction of religious courts was more and more limited until nothing was left. In 1932 the lucrative notary republic and registry functions were made secular (although under state supervision ruhani were still usually the ones who registered marriages). From 1934 on, state supervision of religious endowments became increasingly stringent. Regarding the dissemination of religious propaganda, the state claimed the right to regulate the curriculum of religious schools, but the regulation remained ineffective. The state monitored rawdas, still a key medium of religion, but the intimidation value of the monitoring varied. Television and radio, however, are new media; under Mohammad Reza Shah they purveyed a nonpolitical programming on religion congenial to a modernizing state: the leading wa'iz on the radio, Rashed, confined himself to general ethical pronouncements; television coverage of ritual events and studio programming, much of which were very good, were both handled artistically and presented as "our cultural heritage."

In brief, the recent history of the ulama can be summarized as follows. Under Reza Shah (1924-1941) the ulama were openly under attack and on the defensive. In the following period (1941-1963) under Mohammad Reza Shah they were freer and able to take some open stands, issuing fatwas (opinions) in favor of nationalizing oil (in the 1952 period), against the emancipation of women (in the 1962 period), and so on, although in 1949 a large meeting had been convened by Ayatullah Borujerdi to urge the ulama to eschew political activism (Akhavi 1980). From 1963 until 1978 they again came under pressure, perhaps with less openly avowed hostility than in the 1930s, but perhaps with more covert police measures.

We turn to Qum. The date 1920 is the one usually given for the modern founding of the Hawza-i 'Ilmi of Qum. That is the date of the arrival of Shaykh Abdol-Karim Haeri-Yazdi from Arak (Soltanabad) and before that from Iraq. It was part of the exodus back to Iran by Shi'ite leaders who were concerned that the uncertain transition between Ottoman and British rule in Iraq might jeopardize their position in the 'atabat (shrine towns of Iraq). Shaykh Mortaza Ansari earlier had sent Mir Mohammad-Ali Shushtari-Jazayeri to reconnoiter Qum and Mashhad. Then in 1916 Ayatullah Fayd Qummi, joined later by others, returned to Qum to reclaim the old madrasas to their original purpose. Shops and storage areas had to be converted back to student rooms in the Madrasa Faydiyya. Even wheat bakeries had to be set up. Over the course of a full century—since the death in 1815 of Mirza Qummi, author of the *Qawanin* (Laws)—Qum's madrasas had fallen into disuse and ruin and the town had suffered what a leading editor and pedagogue calls "an intellectual famine" (Rahimi 1339/1961). After establishing a minimal basis for a hawza, Ayatullah Mirza Mahmud Ruhani and Shaykh Hoseyn Qummi were dispatched to Arak to invite and persuade Shaykh Abdol-Karim Haeri-Yazdi to come. He did so, bringing with him a large following, including those who were to succeed after his death (in 1935): Ayatullahs Shaykh Mohammad-Ali Haeri-Qummi (d. 1939), and S.

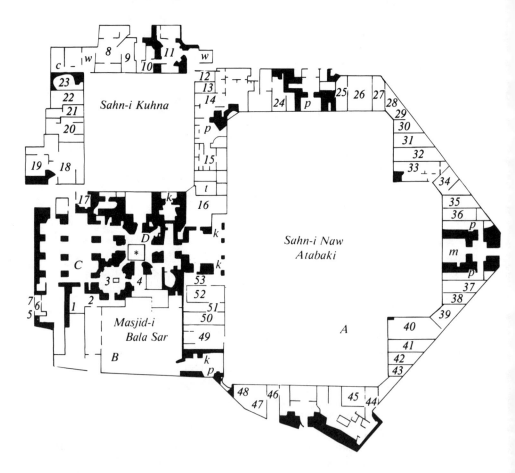

to Madrasas
Faydiyya &
Dar-al-Shifa

Adapted from: Astana-i Muqaddas-i Qum 1354/1975

Figure 4.2 *Shrine of Fatima, Hadrat-i Ma'suma, Qum*

* Holy Shrine	c candles
A Where Mar'ashi-Najafi leads festival prayers (namaz-i 'id)	w water
	p passage
B Where Shariatmadari leads daily prayers (formerly the Museum courtyard; now the Museum Mosque)	k left shoes
C Where Mar'ashi-Najafi leads daily prayers	m mosque
D Old Treasury	t teahouse

Masjid Bala Sar
1 Shah Sulayman
2 Shah Sultan-Husayn
3 Shah 'Abbas
4 Shah Safi
5 Shaykh 'Abd al-Karim Ha'iri-Yazdi
6 Sayyid Sadruddin Sadr
7 Sayyid Muhammad-Taqi Khwansari

Sahn-i Kuhna (Old Courtyard)
8 Fath-'Ali Shah
9 Qahraman Mirza
10 Sadr al-'Ulama
11 Mustawfi al-Mamalik
12 Mudabbir al-Dawla
13 Salar Muharram-i Tabrizi
14 Vuthuq al-Dawla
15 A'lam al-Saltana
16 Mirza 'Ali-Asghar Khan Atabak
17 Fuladvand
18 Muhammad-Shah
19 Mahd-i 'Ulya
20 A'in al-Mulk
21 Amir Afkham
22 Amin al-Dawla
23 Manuchihr Khan

Sahn-i Naw Atabaki (Atabegi New Courtyard)
24 Hajji Sarkeshik

25 Mu'avin al-Sultan
26 Sa'd al-Saltana
27 Hajj Shaykh Fadlullah Nuri
28 Shaykh al-Mulk
29 Isfahaniyyan
30 Diya' al-Mulk Tafrushi
31 Hajj Amin al-Darb
32 Mawlavi Nahavandi
33 Thiqat al-Islam Borujirdi
34 Mirza Muhammad-Husayn Sakana
35 Sayyid Mahmud Kashi
36 Baha' al-Mulk
37 'Abd al-Rahim Nahavandi
38 Zafar al-Sultan
39 Sarhang Murtada-Quli Khan
40 Khazin al-Khalvat Hajji Rabi' Agha Fariburz
41 Beglarbegi
42 Hajj Sayyid Radi Rashti
43 Nusratullah Khan Bakhtyari
44 A'zam al-Saltana
45 Mushir al-Saltana
46 Mu'in al-Dawla
47 Hajj Mirza 'Ali Sarraf
48 Shukuh-Nizam
49 Hajj Mu'in Bushihri
50 Hajj Aqa Nuruddin
51 Varatha-i Asghar Khan
52 Hajib al-Dawla
53 Qayimmaqam

Mohammad Hojjat Kuhkamari came immediately as did the then young
S. Ruhollah Musavi Khomeyni and S. Mohammad Reza Golpayegani; S.
Ahmad Khonsari came in 1923, S. Shahaboddin Marashi and S.
Mohammad-Kazem Shariatmadari in 1924, and Ayatullah S. Sadroddin
Sadr in 1930. Almost immediately upon the reestablishment of the Qum
hawza, it was able to play host to refugees from Iraq: Shi'ite resistance to
the British caused for short periods both the voluntary and nonvoluntary
exile of students and teachers.

How much of a change the growth of the madrasas made to life in
Qum can only be estimated from a series of incidents: the campaign of
Ayatullah Bafqi to keep men from cutting their beards, the staging by
Nurollah Esfahani in Qum of calls for the ousting of the dictator Reza
Shah (1925), the clash between Bafqi and Reza Shah over the veiling of
the royal women in the shrine, the burning of wine shops, the opposition
to modern schools, opposition to the enfranchisement of women, the
student harangues against the Tudeh party, and the opposition to the introduction of the cinema and television.[5] Not all the acts of the religious
leaders, however, were conservative in this sense: their leadership in
building hospitals, welfare systems, libraries, and flood walls have
already been mentioned. Indeed some of the conservatism was reaction
to Pahlavi government-led anticlericalism. As one official in the
Religious Endowments Office put it, "They [the ulama] fall behind on
their own, and we help kick them back whenever we can."

The burning of the wine shops is perhaps a good example of the
dynamics of one kind of conservative pressure. (For similar cases of
displacement along "religious" lines, see Fischer 1973: appendix 1.) Just
after Reza Shah abdicated in 1941, an Armenian from Qazvin had the
temerity to open a liquor store near the shrine. Ayatullah Bafqi, freshly
released from exile in Rey, led a campaign to buy him out and close the
shop, or simply destroy the shop. Meanwhile, a chronic civic disturbance
erupted over the division of the river water between Qum and Mahallat.
Being further downstream, Qum began to get less water, so the farmers
marched on the congregational prayers of the ulama, stopped the prayers
by seizing the *muhr*,[6] and demanded that something be done. An akhund
managed to seize leadership and shouted that this was no way for
Muslims to behave: the farmers should pray themselves, should not attack the ulama, but should attack the real enemies, the liquor stores.
Some youths got some gasoline and the crowd set the Armenian store on
fire; then they crossed the river to the new town and gutted the remaining
liquor stores and whorehouses there. Ever since, liquor has been
available only through private houses: the police will not license a liquor
store. The government quelled the disturbance with firearms—a few
were wounded, some perhaps killed, and others were arrested. After this

release of frustration, Ayatullah Fayd brought together the various parties to the water dispute and worked out a solution.

A different sort of case, but also illustrating this religious "overdrive," seems to be the expulsion from Qum in 1975 of a woman school principal at the wish of one of the maraji-'i taqlid.[7] It began with the principal's support for her mother's brother's son (her cousin, with whom she had been raised) in his plea for a divorce on the grounds of his wife's infidelity. The judge, a friend of one of the wife's alleged lovers, kept continuing the case, until the principal used her middle-class credentials to insist on action. The wife then accused the principal of wanting the man herself, a cultural, if not a psychological impossibility since *hamshir* (those suckled at the same breast) may not marry and sexual relations between them constitute incest. In any case, the wife complained to the marja' who in turn complained to the Office of Education that the principal — who incidentally had tutored the marja''s own daughters — was of loose morals and should be dismissed. The Office of Education, to minimize possible conflict with the religious establishment, transferred her to Tehran.

Schools — and more recently the visual mass media — have long been an arena of ambivalent hostile acceptance by the religious population, for slightly different reasons of conservative dynamics than those described for the wine riot. The alleged contradiction in the behavior of the marja' in the story of the school principal — summary condemnation without investigation of a teacher formerly trusted with the education of his daughters — perhaps fits the patterns of ambivalence.

Before the first government school opened in Qum in 1919, seven private modern schools had been started, the first in 1898 by Mirza Hasan Roshtiyya, an ex-cleric, the third in 1906 by S. Mohammad Bagher Mesbah-Towliyat, the head of the shrine and later a friend of Shaykh Abdol-Karim Haeri-Yazdi. Despite the involvement of some ulama and their friends in these efforts, people who grew up in Qum tell stories of having to dodge heckling talaba (religious students) on their way to school, especially, of course, the girls. The ambivalence may have something to do with the growth of the government regulatory function in education and in the administration of endowments. From their early days the Offices of Education and Endowments contributed funds to private as well as government schools; indeed all schools had to be licensed by the Office of Education; it officially opened an office in Qum in 1915, and in 1925 the Office of Endowments was joined to it. Secular education beyond elementary school did not exist until 1935, and the big push for schools came in the next two years: a coeducational school opened in 1935; that same year Reza Shah ordered adult education to be offered and fifteen schools were opened in 1935-36; by 1937 there were three high schools.

These were, however, also the years of great pressure against the religious establishment. The great struggle over dressing like Europeans and unveiling women came in 1935-36. Attempts were made to license those who had a right to wear religious garb, and the number of religious students in Qum began to decline, reaching a low of 500 or less at the end of Reza Shah's reign in 1941 (Razi 1332 Sh./1954: II, 119). When Haeri-Yazdi died in 1935, not only were laws in effect against rawda-khwani preachments, but a formal death memorial for him was disallowed (though the inpouring of people to Qum to chant in the streets could not be prevented). In 1938 the government tried to introduce examinations for the religious students in order to regulate their progress and to formalize procedures for exemption from the army. The examinations were evaded by a plea from the *hawda* leadership that the date set for them had fallen upon the anniversary of the death of Shaykh Mohammad-Ali Qummi and the students had to convene a memorial service. The government acquiesced and did not try to reinstitute the examinations. In 1975 those who were at least middle level students and had six years of secular education could ask a committee of hawda teachers to certify to the Office of Education that they were students in good standing. The Education Office forwarded this document, with the student's letter requesting deferment from the army, to the gendarmerie draft board. Direct control over religious students thus was abandoned in favor of informal surveillance. Resistance to open procedures had led to expansion of covert procedures.

In the area of endowments, feelings of being encroached upon, being made redundant, and having traditional moral leadership challenged are similar to those in education and even more central. An endowment (*vaqf*, pl. *awqaf*, or *mawqufa*) is a donation of property for specific purposes; its administrator (*mutawalli, tawliyat*) has, by Muslim law, rights to 10 percent of the annual income.[8] General supervision of awqaf has always been a duty of the state, but since in the past the ulama have provided state councillors, have often served as mutawalli, and have been legal and notary specialists, there is a lingering feeling of proprietorship over endowments for religious purposes. Degree of centralization of control, corruption, misuse of funds or misregistry so that awqaf were turned back into private holdings have varied. In a famous exchange, Nadir Shah (1736-1747) asked the 'alim who served as the last Safavid minister of endowments (*sadr-i sudur*) what he did with the funds; the reply was: disperse them to the ulama that they may pray for the king. Nadir Shah noted that it had not done the Safavid kings much good against the Afghan invasion (1722) and dismissed the man.

Under the Pahlavis, state administration of awqaf operated under sets of regulations issued in 1934, 1942, 1945, and 1968. The Office of Endowments was separated from the Ministry of Education in 1964 and was overseen by an eleven-member council under the prime minister. The council included the head of the Endowments Office, representatives of the Ministries of Interior and Education and the Office of Land Registry, two law professors, and four notables or mujtahids. It intervened whenever there was no mutawalli, when it was unclear who the mutawalli was, when the Endowments Office had been named as mutawalli, or during interim periods between the death of one mutawalli and the appointment of a new one. It also could suspend a mutawalli for not adhering to the terms of a deed of endowment. In 1966 a form of administration by council for some awqaf was approved. These *hay'at-i umana* (councils of honest men) consist of three to twelve persons acceptable to the local mayor and, if an ancient monument is involved, to the Archeological Service. The Shah Cheragh Shrine in Shiraz, for instance, was administered under such an agreement (A. Betteridge-Sadeghi, personal communication), as is the Jam Karan Shrine outside Qum.

From 1965 to 1979, the Shrine of Fatima in Qum was under a mutawalli appointed by the shah, but the Endowments Office retained budgetary review powers, providing an interesting example of overlapping responsibilities: the mutawalli had two masters. For instance, in 1974 the local Endowments Office in Qum refused to approve the budget of the shrine on the grounds that it included a series of items that had no justification in the deeds of endowment or in precedent. Specifically, objections were raised to the large figures for medicine, miscellaneous, a jeep, flood victims in Bangladesh, and a salary rise of 20 percent over the previous year. Eqbal, the mutawalli, replied, not to the head of the office in Qum, but to the latter's boss in Tehran, that the jeep had been approved by the Tehran Endowments Office, the salary rise was a general government policy, and he had a direct order from the shah to use the money for flood victims and medicine. The complications became more involved between the 1974 and 1975 budgets: at the shah's order, land in Qum was sold and the proceeds invested in the Cement Company of Fars and Khuzistan. This transaction is registered in the 1974 budget; income from the investment is given as "unknown." In the 1975 budget, however, these shares (worth Rls 12 million or $176,470) do not appear at all.

Holdings under the shrine and directly under the Endowments Office were handled with a view toward productive growth: for instance, in Tehran a ruined little mosque with no income was turned into a large office building; in Qum the little shops along the shrine square (Maydan-i Astana) were being replaced in 1975 by modern hotels and shopping arcades. More funds thus became available for all sorts of needs, ranging from the traditional upkeep of the shrines and increased support for hospitals and schools to humanitarian gestures like food and medicine for flood victims in Bangladesh and famine victims in the Sahelian region of Africa.

The old, pre-1965, administration of the shrine was accused by the post-1965 administrators of being corrupt and inefficient. Mohammad Mehran's indictment of the old order after he came to reorganize things in "the dawn of 3 Esfand 1344" (1965) is a marvel of technocratic horror (Astana Muqaddas Qum 1346/1967: 4-7):

Rls 4 million outstanding in back salaries, with some employees unpaid for 19 months

Rls 390 total assets

Money taken in for shoes, candles, and the right of burial merely eaten by the caretakers (except the 10 percent paid to and collected by the mutawalli)

No personnel files of any kind

No systematic documents files

No budget

Lapse of the ceremonial khutba (an invocation including a blessing of the shah, sung at changes of the watch)

Loss of an illegal sale of valuables belonging to the shrine

Within two years Mehran claimed to have righted all this: he set up personnel files, paid off all debts, introduced double-entry bookkeeping, raised salaries, reinstituted celebrations of national and religious occasions, reinstituted the twice-daily khutba with its praise and prayer for the shah, issued two sets of clothing per year to the caretakers, opened adult education classes for illiterate caretakers, opened dining facilities for the caretakers, and registered all the graves (p. 17). He also began to rationalize the personnel; over the next few years a number of caretakers were eased into retirement. In 1968 when Abdul Wahab Eqbal took over, a new darih (latticework guard around the tomb) was unveiled by the queen and a new "dusting off" (*ghubar-rubi*) ceremony was initiated of inviting officials to the annual opening of the darih and counting of the contributions left by pilgrims. The shrine was thus rejuvenated ceremonially as a state-linked religious center, as well as being reorganized administratively.

There is no doubt that the pre-1965 mutawalli was something of a rogue. Silk brocade (*termeh* from Yazd) covers on the graves and fine carpets in Shah Abbas's tomb were sold off. He misrepresented letters from Ayatullah Borujerdi as support for his election to parliament (where he represented Qum for fourteen years). He seized land outside of Qum and preserved his ownership of it, despite the post-1963 land reform laws, by declaring it "mechanized agriculture." (Later he sold much of it but became a partner in a development corporation for the land.) On the other hand, the traditional administration of the shrine was an organic part of Qum society, relying on informal procedures not so different in kind from the Eqbal-shah relationship. Whole families of caretakers had hereditary positions in the shrine dating back at least to Safavid times. And presumably the mutawalli acted as a patron to all. Local opinion, at least, was divided: there was indignation over the issues raised by Mehran in the new middle class; there was also amused, nostalgic tolerance by some of the older shrine employees.

The rejuvenation of the shrine as a state-linked religious center and the expansion of control by the Endowments Office were viewed by the religious establishment as parts of one process directed against its claims to leadership in all religious and moral matters. The Endowments Office litigated all possible loopholes in endowment deeds to establish itself as administrator or at least supervisor. Religious leaders claimed that for this reason people stopped making endowments and preferred to give funds directly to the maraji'-i taqlid. Funds thus flowed more informally and less publicly, adding to the ambience of underground resistance to the state. It remained unclear, however—though it was often alleged as a major reason for rerouting of funds—that government control in itself led to a serious decline in income to madrasas from endowment sources. The agricultural land and the nominal shop rents, which make up the bulk of the endowments, did not in Qum add up to very much wealth (as opposed to Mashhad's very rich endowments). It is likely that to some extent the government allocated discretionary endowment funds differently from the way religious leaders would have done. But surely a major reason for decline in funds available during the 1960s and 1970s if there was a decline, was that (unlike under the Safavids and Qajars) high officials of the state were no longer making significant endowments for religious purposes or putting under religious administration such endowments as existed.[9] The endowments of the royal Pahlavi Foundation were divided into five categories of which "religion" was one, but though no information is available on how this money was spent, clearly it was not spent by religious leaders; the other four categories were health, culture, the poor, and social problems (Mostafavi-Rejali 1351/1973: 159). In other words, there was no major inflow of new endowments to offset the decay of older endowments through abandonment, loss, or transformation into private holdings.

The question perhaps is really less one of simple diversion of funds by the government than whether, under less constrained conditions, the religious establishment could have organized the property productively in a capitalist sense as the Endowments Office was attempting to do; for example, would it have insisted that agricultural land remain agricultural and not be upgraded (on the reasoning that what was donated was agricultural land in perpetuity and not something else). Part of the answer would depend on the position taken on interest: can money earn interest; is that a violation of the Qur'anic prohibition against usury? Opinion is divided, but at least one mujtahid argued there was no real theoretical obstacle to investment, and another provincial ayatullah had set up his "Islamic Bank" as an account within the Bank Saderat, a private commercial bank. Furthermore, while the terms of a deed of endowment are supposed to be inviolate, there is a principle of *tabdil* (substituting something better). So the real complaint was not loss of funds per se but loss of control of opportunity.

The government response was that proper mutawalli are free to administer their endowments, subject to the terms of the deed, without interference. Furthermore, those endowments made specifically for the support of students under Endowments Office control were used as specified. It was not the fault of the Endowments Office if these endowments were small. For instance, in Mashhad, twelve of the twenty-six madrasa were administered by the Endowments Office; of these twelve, only four had sufficient income to give out some monthly stipends to students. To qualify, the students must have passed the *muqaddamat* examinations (preliminaries). Thus in 1975, 80 of the 180 residents in Madrasa Navvab got 80 tomans per month; in Madrasa Baqirayya all 38 residents got 100 tomans; in 'Id al-Khan 48 of 78 residents got 50 tomans; and in Sulayman Khan 55 residents got 200 tomans per month. A similar situation existed in Shiraz. In Qum the situation was slightly less clear: all the madrasas were administered by the religious leaders, though the endowments were supervised by the Endowments Office. The shrine and the Endowments Office both claimed to make monthly payments to religious students (*talaba*). The 1974 shrine budget listed Rls 1,750,000 ($25,735) aid to pilgrims and talaba. The head of the Endowments Office, a source of wild misinformation, claimed to give monthly stipends to half of the 13,000 talaba in Qum in 1975. His clerks suggested instead that some 300 ruhani got 200-300 tomans per month, but directly from Tehran.

Government regulation of endowments was not simply autocratic but operated through a set of negotiable bureaucratic and litigation procedures,[10] as illustrated by two contrasting cases, one in which the government secured control and one in which it did not.

Since at least 1804 there had been a dispute over a small piece of land originally donated by Shah Sultan-Husayn (1694-1722) for the upkeep of a little shrine, Imamzada Khak-i Faraj. In 1804 Muhammad Khak-i Faraj, the descendant of the original mutawalli, complained to Fath-'Ali Shah that the mutawalli of the great shrine (Hadrat-i Ma'suma, Fatima) was trying to take over. Fath-'Ali Shah confirmed Muhammad Khak-i Faraj's right. Beginning in 1955 the Endowments Office decided to contest the claims of Muhammad Khak-i Faraj's descendants on the grounds that it was never specified in any of the documents that the position of mutawalli was a hereditary job. The court had repeatedly ruled in favor of the Endowments Office, but as late as 1975 the case was still being appealed.

Far more interesting and amusing is the case of what is now the new Madrasa Mu'miniyya, rebuilt during the 1960s by Ayatullah Marashi. Originally a madrasa built by Mahmud Gavanlu at the end of the Safavid period, it fell into disrepair and became known as Madrasa *Tawilkhana* (stables). In 1943 the place enters the records of the Endowments Office. The nominal mutawallis (the Azadegan brothers) complain that despite their objections one S. Hasan Maktabdar has taken over the madrasa using one of the rooms as a maktab (religious elementary school), that the Endowments Office has confirmed him as the *khidmat-guzar-i maktab* (one who is doing public service by running a school), and that he has been given as his *haq-i khidmat* (fee for the title) the fruit from the trees in the courtyard. They complain that S. Hasan is a bad character, the place is dirty and unfit for children, he is lazy and does not clear the snow from the roof, and he is using the bricks of the madrasa to build his own house.

The next year (1944-45) Mortaza Azadegan, a bookseller, is confirmed by the Endowments Office as the *sarparast* (overseer) of the madrasa. He suggests that he collect rent from S. Hasan and from a policeman who has moved in. He complains the madrasa has become a locus of gambling and prostitution (*qumar* and *'amal-i nashayista*); he names three gamblers, has the police arrest them, and then asks forgiveness for one of them. One of the reasons for the deterioration of the madrasa, he says, is that the neighbors' drainage gutters run off into it.

In 1945-46 a certain Hasan Bashiri rents three *hujra* (rooms) for a school. Two more policemen move in as squatters; they agree to a rental fee but refuse to pay. S. Hasan meanwhile has locked up his school and gone away. In 1947 there is newspaper propaganda to rebuild this eyesore as a public elementary school (*dabistan*). Hasan Bashiri complains the place is a den of iniquity and demands reimbursement for three thousand rials he has put into the building (he has never paid his rent). The following years see more complaints about the den of iniquity (*arajif* and *arazil*). In 1957 someone complains that Arbab Hasan is storing straw in a hujra. Ali Dastpak then rents the whole madrasa for nine years. People complain that he is using it for his sheep. Ali Dastpak in turn complains about the squatters who now include a woman and her daughters. Ali Dastpak's contract is canceled.

Finally in 1959 the Endowments Office begins thinking seriously about turning the place into a school. It asks Ayatullah Marashi's opinion. He says no: we need the space for housing for talaba; the building is sound and only needs some repair; you repair it and give it to us. Tehran decides that Marashi is right: it is a madrasa and cannot be turned into something else; but the Endowments Office has no money for repairs, so Marashi should do it. Two years later the Qum office is still trying out projects: maybe turning part of the madrasa into shops would get some income flowing. But again it is decided that this would be illegal unless

the property were producing no income at all, the ulama were un-
interested in it, and the buildings were irreparable. In 1965 Marashi finally begins rebuilding it; he gets the plot number from the Endowments
Office so he can reregister it as waqf under his administration; he rents it
for nine years and the Endowments Office tells him to apply the rent to
the utility bills.

In this case, however much the government would have liked, it was
unable to alter the use of the plot. Intermediate between these two cases
is that of the old Madrasa Ghiyathiyya, built in 938/1531 in the reign of
Shah Tahmasp by Ghiyathuddin Mansur and given into the trusteeship
of the Razavi Borgai sayyids as mutawallis. Completely ruined by floods
in 1044/1665 and 1313/1933, by 1975 it had been turned into a kind
of caravansery—a place for off-loading trucks and work areas for
carpenters. Again the government first attempted to build a school on
the site, but financing was not forthcoming and the plot was finally auc-
tioned off on a fifty-year lease. Over the course of time only four-sixths
(four *dang*) of the property has remained waqf; two-sixths is held
privately.

If government initiatives in education and endowments were felt to be
attacks on the prerogatives and leadership of the ulama, potentially even
more direct threats were in the plans of the Endowments Office in the
areas of the madrasa curriculum, the Religious Corps (*Sipah-i Din*) and
the Religious Aides (*Murawwij-i Dini*). State control over the madrasa
curriculum remained in the talking stage. Curriculum reform was attempted only at the Theological Faculties of the universities, which now
follow an essentially Western style reading list and have nothing to do
with the Endowments Office; and at the Madrasa Sipah Salar in Tehran,
which was a kind of royal court-sponsored madrasa. The Religious
Corps (Sipah-i Din), on the other hand, though instituted, was completely subverted from its purpose. Intended to train religious leaders
who would take to the villages a progressive religion in line with the state
modernization ideology, it became instead a make-work program for
university graduates in theology, political science and law, geography,
and sociology. Established in 1971 by a royal farman, by 1975 there had
been four classes, of 39, 49, 42, and 50 students. They served tours of
duty as clerks in the Endowments Office. The Murawwij-i Dini
(Religious Aides) consisted in 1975 of 460 ruhani who had agreed to
work for the Endowments Office, to go out to the villages and help coordinate the upkeep of mosques and shrines, and incidentally to support
government programs in birth control, sanitation, education, and so on.
Again the program was not pursued with any great vigor.

Despite the lack of vigor in these three programs, they contributed to
the perception of a noose being tightened around the independent ulama.
Was such a noose merely the unavoidable side effect of modernization,

of building a nation-state? The sometimes vague, sometimes oppressive sense of the noose was not confined to the ulama, and was one of the powerful emotional strings upon which they played for wider popular support. In education, not only were the madrasas under pressure, but the semireligious schools, such as the 170 Ta'limat-i Islam schools established by Shaykh Abbas Eslami over the previous several decades[11] and similar schools established by Hajj Abedzadeh in Mashhad, were being absorbed by the government, as in the 1970s were all private schools. The process was gradual: after the banning of foreign-run schools by Reza Shah during the thirties, private schools received state aid in teachers' salaries and personnel; by the late 1970s tuition was being made free for those students who signed promises to work for the government, and being raised for those who refused. In the marketplace, the political arena, and city planning, similar incentives and punishments were explored.

In the marketplace, the government struggled on several levels to provide rational planning. Periodically, however, it launched an anti-inflation campaign singling out "parasitic middlemen" as villains for such practices as overcharging or hoarding. Since the government itself could not supply the rotating credit functions of the middlemen, the campaigns tended to be unstable and punitive rather than constructive. The short-term logic of price control was based on the crisis management that worked relatively successfully, for instance, in England during World War II.[12]

After 1956, shopkeepers and craftsmen were gradually organized under government supervision into guilds. In 1974-75 an anti-inflation campaign was launched using the guilds as an enforcement mechanism. Price levels were lowered by fiat from Tehran, price lists being posted in shops and printed in newspapers. In Qum there were thirty organized guilds, the heads of which elected an executive council of seven; these seven elected a schoolteacher as their head. The executive council was to make policy recommendations and oversee a staff of ten people (mainly young schoolteachers) who daily checked the posting of prices and profit margins. In Tehran students and housewives were recruited to do the checking. Offenders were brought before a special court for fines or jail terms at 50 tomans per day until the fines were paid. The whole operation was overseen by a higher council composed of the head of the executive council, the governor, the chief of police, the head of SAVAK (the secret police), and the chief justice. This latter council issued exile orders against large and repeated offenders. For a short time the procedure worked, to some extent: at least the number of offenders brought into court dropped dramatically over a three-month period.

Qum is a small distributive bazaar (aside from carpentry and sweets, there is not much production or wholesale activity), so after a short time complaints were being filed not locally but against the suppliers in Tehran. By the end of the summer of 1975 the campaign began to falter. Quality goods were being hidden behind counters and sold only to known and safe customers. Many of the local guild councils were disbanded, including finally also the one in Qum, and the functions of policing the market were transferred to the mayoralty.

Part of this last shift was a tactic to disallow the crystallization of working relations between merchants and policing officials which might allow circumvention of the law. Keeping uncertainty about who was doing the policing, and how, was a way of extending the campaign. The same tactic was used in the political arena. Under the Rastakhiz party (established in 1975), nomination procedures initially were in the hands of local politicians; nominations then went to Tehran for approval. In 1975, twenty-eight people presented themselves as candidates for parliament from Qum. A commission was set up to pick three nominees on the criteria of who had a following and who owned property in the town. One of the twenty-eight filed a complaint that Bani-Fatima (head of the city council, head of Kamkar Hospital, and husband of the head of the local women's organization) was unduly exerting pressure on behalf of himself and a relative. The dispute went to Tehran where the committee for the Central Province, headed by Hushang Nahavandi (chancellor of the University of Tehran), crossed out all parties to the dispute and placed another name—the eventual winner—as one of the three nominees.

This action led a number of commentators to speculate that the party had been concerned to loosen the previous power structure in Qum to make Qum more directly responsive to Tehran policy initiatives. Not only was the city council leadership rebuffed, but the previous Qum representative in parliament (Dr. Shokrai, also director of health for Qum) was defeated by a proindustrialization candidate, the owner of the only textile mill then functioning in Qum. The facts that the as yet uncrystallized master plan for Qum called for industrialization and that some dozen factories were under construction only served to confirm the analysis.

At first sight city planning would appear to be the most innocuous of the arenas of expanding government control. The possibility of abuses under conditions of no planning seems self-evident. Benevolent coalitions could emerge, such as those that constructed the hospitals. The Fatima Hospital, for instance, was initiated by the son of Hajj Mirza S. Mohammad Fatima with money left by the father; Shaykh Abdol-Karim Haeri-Yazdi suggested it be used for a hospital. The government contributed a third of the cost. Haeri-Yazdi presided over the groundbreaking; the prime minister (Mahmud Jam) presided over the opening. Fatima made the lands of Masumabad *waqf* (endowment) to support the hospital.[13] Not-so-benevolent coalitions could also emerge such as the attempt by a mulla named S. Mehdi Rouhani to seize 32,457 square meters of land along the Tehran road. The land had been land of Arbab Jamshid (the famous Zoroastrian banker and money changer of the turn of the century). Arbab Jamshid gave the land to the government rather than pay taxes on it. In 1953 S. Mehdi Rouhani allegedly arranged with the head of the local office of the Finance Ministry and with General Zahedi for a poorly publicized auction of the land so that he could buy it cheaply. The plan was foiled by a newspaper, which publicized the proposed auction and even found another bidder. S. Mehdi moved to Paris where he claimed to be a representative of Ayatullah Borujerdi, a claim disavowed by Borujerdi to little effect (*Paykar-i Mardum*, 19 Esfand 1336 / 10 March 1958).

A candid city planner put the problem in 1975 thus:

> After land reform, agriculture declined because the new small holders did not have the money to keep up the water supplies. Therefore there was a great influx of people into town [see Qum statistical profile, in appendix, for population figures for the city and metropolitan areas between 1956 and 1966], and this together with the growth of industry led to a boom land situation. A number of big shots seized land and just began sellng it without concern for hospitals, parks, or other needs. A proper road system was not laid out, and so we have roads that just end, and all traffic is funneled through the center of town. A number of obvious things have to be done: complete the road pattern so there can be circulation; build a bus terminal on the Tehran road; create parking facilities for visitors to the shrine; map out a proper land-use zoning system.

Many of these projects were then under way. Qum was one of the last cities to get a master plan: sketched out only in the spring and summer of 1975 it was slowly making its way through the Tehran bureaucracy. By then some new parks, boulevards, public buildings, and a children's library had already been constructed. The religious establishment feared that other boulevards and parks would be driven through several of their important buildings; the bulldozing of madrasas in Mashhad to create a green belt around the shrine there was cited as a precedent and omen.

The past existence of chaos, corruption, and inefficiency—the problems the government claimed to be solving—was not disputed by the religious establishment. But that did little to lessen the sense of the closing noose of a growing bureaucratic state. In June 1975 the fears and frustrations erupted in a three-day demonstration.

The Demonstrations of 15 Khordad 1975

On the fifteenth of Khordad (June 5) in 1963, Ayatullah Khomeyni was arrested for leading opposition to the enfranchisement of women, the Local Council Election Bill of 1962, land reform, the six-point White

Revolution, and a major military loan from the United States including immunity from Iranian law for American servicemen. Three months earlier, demonstrations by the religious students had led to the occupation of the madrasas of Qum by security forces. Ayatullah Milani sent a widely publicized letter to Khomeyni remarking that the, "religious and national interests are threatened and violated by the corrupt Ruling Body . . . It would be strange for a Moslem to allow himself to remain silent under such circumstances and fail to defend Islam" (Zonis 1971: 45). On the fifteenth of Khordad, at the end of the emotional first ten days of Muharram that year, Khomeyni was arrested, and resistance among the religious students in the central Madrasa Faydiyya was quelled, a number of students losing their lives by being tossed by gendarmes from the roof of the madrasa down into the dry riverbed below. Within two hours of Khomeyni's arrest, crowds had also gathered in front of the Tehran bazaar; by 10:00 A.M. troops had fired upon them. For three days disturbances continued in Tehran, Qum, Mashhad, Isfahan, and Shiraz, and precautionary measures were taken elsewhere. Thousands died.

Twelve years later, the fifteenth of Khordad fell just after the new single-party state had been declared and during the registration for the first election under the new party. Khomeyni, exiled since 1964 (in Iraq since 1965), had smuggled into Iran pamphlets decrying the new party as nothing other than a tool for tightening the dictatorship. The secret police tried to keep systematic track of all akhunds who referred to the issue in their preaching. Rumors were spread of dire consequences if one did not join the party and register to vote, registration being used as a means of checking and renewing all adult identity cards. The threat was effective in corralling most people. At the same time the anti-inflation campaign was moving into high gear: names of violators, fines, and exiles were publicized; included among the violators were a sprinkling of prominent businessmen and industrialists. Publicity was also given to women's rights (an attack on the family in the conservative scheme of values).

The fifteenth of Khordad in 1975 was a Thursday. People began arriving for weekend visits to the shrine. In the evening religious students gathered for prayers in the Madrasa Faydiyya. After the prayers a number of the students began to recite 20,000 blessings (*salawat*) upon the defenders of Islam (Khomeyni) and *la'nat* (curses) upon the enemies of Islam (the shah), keeping count on their prayer beads. As word spread, the police moved quickly to disperse a crowd gathering outside and to arrest all students leaving the Faydiyya in case they intended to coordinate interior and exterior demonstrations. A water cannon was then brought up to the door to keep all the students inside, and the courtyards were filled with tear gas. When the tear gas came, students would scurry to their rooms "like mice for their holes," as one of them described it, only to reappear and continue the chant when the gas cleared. This went on until 7:00 A.M. the next morning. That day, after a few selected arrests, the police allowed free entry and exit.

Friday evening the demonstration renewed. From the roof of Madrasa Khan, across the square from the Faydiyya, students threw stones at the police, hitting one in the mouth. The police cleared the roof and stationed their own men upon it while the students fled into their rooms and doused the lights. A few windows were broken by overly enthusiastic police. This time the students in the Faydiyya were shut in by the water cannon for good, and the police called for military support.

On Saturday morning the police contented themselves with dispersing the crowds, arresting and beating with billy clubs and shields those religious students bold enough to appear on the streets in their distinctive garb. Around noon a dozen religious students, wrapped in headcloths against both the blazing sun and police identification, climbed onto the archway between the Faydiyya and Dar al-Shifa Madrasas and raised a flag. Subsequently red, white, and black banners were put on the walls with slogans: "Muslim brothers, stand up like men; it is three days since the Faydiyya was attacked"; "Death is better; war is our duty." Around 4:30 a green army helicopter reconnoitered the area; shortly thereafter gendarmes and a special commando unit attacked. The commandos are said to have marched around the roof of the Faydiyya five times shouting "Javid shah" (long live the king). They then descended to round up students, force them to say "Javid shah," and empty each room of people and books. Almost all windows and doors and, allegedly, a few lives failed to survive the commandos.

Rumors of deaths spread quickly: two students were said to have been thrown from the roof of the Madrasa to the riverbed below, others merely from the second story to the courtyard; eight were said to have been killed directly, five others to have been hospitalized in critical condition. Some three hundred students were arrested and sent to Tehran jails.

Their work finished, most of the eighty-five commandos were marched out of the area in columns, grinning and happy, their bus following behind. A small boy threw stones at them; one commando broke ranks to chase him good-naturedly. It was a beautiful, balmy spring riot day. The thirty-odd gendarmes were more discreetly removed in two trucks, leaving the police behind to guard the Faydiyya and disperse the crowd. Towards evening things again began to turn ugly, and there are stories of several severe beatings, one student expiring in a police car; but by midnight order was restored.

Not for another two days was any notice taken in the press. Then a front-page story, under headlines about masked red and black reactionaries, "Islamic Marxists," reported the finding of bombs and communist propaganda and made allegations that the students were responsible for the physical damage to the madrasas and that they were manipulated from abroad. The shah then referred to the disturbances in a nationally televised speech calling for an analysis of the problems in implementing the White Revolution (in 1975 called the Shah and People Revolution).

Within two weeks, at least half of the detained students were released. Exact counts of demonstrators killed and rumors of leaders being pushed out of an airplane over the desert began to fade into a general admission of lack of information as the intense emotions, paranoia, and antistate solidarity of the demonstration days faded. At a minimum, people now said students were identified by pictures taken during the demonstrations from the minarets of the shrine; those not sent to detention directly from the Faydiyya were picked up around the country. One destination was what was known as the Committee Prison in Tehran: two-man cells too small to stretch out to sleep in, wet and cold. Food and tea were given in single utensils to each pair; should your cell-mate be ill, you had to take your chances of contagion or forgo food. Mornings were grim and fearful, for interrogations were in the morning. Afternoons were more relaxed and gregarious. Lucky students were taken to the plush Evin Prison: large carpeted rooms for thirty or more, warm water, showers, cigarettes on request (but to be smoked and finished under guards' eyes), spoons without handles, cold foods ("cold" in the Galenic sense). Those released spoke gratefully of good treatment. Those uninvolved remained intimidated by the continuing occasional raids into the madrasas to take this or that person and by the examples of radically aged or changed ex-prisoners released in the past.

Three kinds of questions need to be asked: Why did the students demonstrate? Why was the response of the state so heavy-handed? And what was the meaning of the symbolic staging on both sides?

The why of the demonstration has already been indicated: worries about the direction of social change, feelings of a bureaucratic noose being tightened, and the deadendedness of religious education. There were many causes for worry about Iran's forced pace and mode of economic and physical change. Technocrats worried about bottlenecks—insufficient port capacity to handle the building material and equipment, insufficient truckers, doctors, managers, to keep things moving. Social critics worried about consequences of the state drive for modernity: galloping bureaucratization, not so creeping authoritarianism, proletarianization, destruction of the older amenities of family and neighborhood. More comprehensive analyses had to be phrased cautiously and indirectly inside Iran. Religious language was often used to express alienation if not any clear understanding. These ranged from S. Hossein Nasr, a university professor whose interest in Islam was internationally recognized but whose demands that society be restructured according to the Qur'an and not the Qur'an reinterpreted according to the needs of the day somehow never achieved more credibility than polite cocktail-party repartee. (He, of course, became a refugee to the United States from the 1979 Islamic revolution.) At the other extreme were the bewildered religious students who insisted that if only the government were placed under the supervision of the representatives of the divine Imam (already in 1975 many of Khomeyni's followers referred to him as "Imam" Khomeyni), sacrilege against private property (land reform) and family stability (equality of women) would cease, the income redistribution taxes of Islam would be instituted, and a just civilization would be achieved, one without exploitation, the taking of interest, or imperialism.

The vulnerability and confusion of these religious students was not merely unrealistic idealism: they were caught in a situation for which they did not bargain. The course of study in which they were apprenticed no longer had practical application, except as a solid grounding for preaching. It led to no degree recognized in the wider society which could serve, as does a high school diploma or a B.A., as a mark of aptitude for a variety of jobs or further study. The general society, furthermore, was coming to have increasingly little respect for their learning, appreciating only the entertainment value of their preaching; and the role of the average akhund was popularly dismissed as parasitic and often hypocritical. Many religious students were attempting to complete secular high school at night, but many also merely drifted.

The difference may be illustrated by two reactions to events of the fifteenth of Khordad. One student who had returned to Qum from Tehran on the third day reacted to the sentiment that it was lucky he had not been in his room in the Faydiyya by saying "*Badbakhtam!* (I am deprived, impoverished!) Would that I had been martyred with the others in the cause of Husayn; that is what Shi'ism is all about." The other reaction was of a younger student who told me that a mutual friend had been among those inside the Faydiyya; we commiserated for the friend, a villager who had just completed his high school degree at night; he was preparing for his college entrance examinations and planned to leave his religious studies behind. For him the missing of the examinations would mean at the very least the loss of a year. In the event, he was released after ten days.

The vulnerability of the students is clear, but what of the government? Why did it react with equal fear and paranoia? The problems of managing a volatile expanding economy and of using international expertise while still maintaining independence no doubt lent an aura of walking a tightrope. Equally to the point was the nature of the political system. Not a carefully centralized bureaucratic state with a dedicated party cadre like the communist model, Iran in 1975 was rather a menage of vaguely balanced and changing centers of power with overlapping responsibilities and multiple secret and open information gatherers. The attempt to control and run such a system from the top, even with a relatively efficient secret police and apparently loyal army, involved disarming potential loci of competitive power—in 1975, for instance, the demand that capitalists sell 49 percent of shares to workers and the public (including a state holding corporation on the public's behalf) and that merchants take only a government-fixed percentage over their purchase price of goods. Charges of dictatorship ran too close to home to be tolerated, especially if they came from several quarters at once.

On the fifteenth of Khordad 1975 university students in Tehran also staged a demonstration. Students there had vulnerabilities somewhat similar to those of religious students. There were not enough university places for all those holding high school degrees and wanting university places; those who did get in received for the most part education inferior to that of classmates who studied abroad—or at least the prestige of having studied abroad guaranteed a better job; the jobs available to degree holders were largely pencil-pushing rather than stimulating. University demonstrations had been going on all year. One complaint was about the government's forced reservation of seats in technical universities for army personnel, since the army was having difficulty competing with private industry in recruiting engineering graduates. Among the occasions for demonstration was the anniversary of the army's brutal invasion of the University of Tehran in 1963.

The government also had to contend with small groups of terrorists such as the eleven persons sentenced to death in January 1976 for the assassinations of three United States colonels, a Persian general, a Persian sergeant, and a Persian translator for the United States Embassy over the preceding two and a half years. And there were the adverse propaganda efforts of Persian students abroad.

The government thus attempted to portray the June affair as a conspiracy of communists infiltrating Qum and fomenting violent rebellion against the state. Proofs of communism were the red flag and red banner, and the various antistate tracts and pamphlets allegedly found in the students' rooms such as one named "The Necessity of Armed Struggle in Iran." Proofs of the violent intentions were the pamphlets, the bombs allegedly found, and the damage done to the madrasa buildings. One of the leaders named was an old man known for his opposition to the state because of the jailing of his son; he was a Qum character, hardly a guerrilla leader. The other names appear not to have had ready recognition value.

For the religious students, the events of 15 Khordad 1975 provided a validating drama of the Shi'ite persecution paradigm: idealism overrun, right determined by might, truth obscured in a maze of defensive maneuvers, sacrifice required for speaking out. The slogan "It is three days since the Faydiyya was attacked" referred both to the events twelve years earlier and the repeat of the three days of demonstration in 1975, focusing attention on the nature of the Iranian policy as a whole. The slogan "Death is better" is part of a well-known line from the story of Karbala: Husayn, the third Imam, says to those who warn he will be killed, "Death is better than life under oppressors." It is more likely that the red flag, identified by the press as marxist, was the red flag placed over the grave of an unavenged soldier killed in a holy war: ten of the eleven slain Imams of Shi'ism have green flags over their graves; one, Husayn, has a red flag.

Technocratic versus Religious Style

At issue was, in part, a conflict of styles. The growth of the bureaucratic state is not an indifferent social process: there was a component of hostility as well as a mutual patronizing "understanding." In the twenties and thirties Reza Shah had denigrated the ulama as skilled only in making people cry and had attempted to substitute public holidays of joy for the religious flagellation and mourning ceremonies. In 1936 the women of his family not only appeared in public unveiled but so entered the shrine in Qum. They were accosted by Ayatullah Bafqi who demanded, "If you are Muslim, why do you appear this way; if you are not Muslim, why have you come here?" Reza Shah went to the mosque — legend has it — with his minister Teirmurtash (in fact already dead by 1933). He entered the shrine without removing his boots, dragged Bafqi from the mimbar, and kicked him and hit him with his whip. The conflict of style, however, did not need to be this overtly hostile. Friendly repartee could also illustrate the difference in attitude.

The setting is a guild office during Ramadan 1975. No one is fasting; all are drinking tea on various excuses of illness. In the following dialogue Hajji is a small factory owner, G and H are school teachers, and MF is the anthropologist.

Hajji: Is alcohol *haram* or *halal* (forbidden or permitted) in Christianity?
MF: It is halal, but of course one should not drink too much.
Hajji: That is like makruh in Islam: eggs are makruh. You should not eat too many. But alcohol is haram because whatever is bad for the body is haram. (Takes out a cigarette.) Do you smoke?
MF: No thanks, I don't smoke. Why were cigarettes not made haram?
Hajji: They did not have cigarettes in those days.
H: Drinking a little as long as one does not bother anyone is halal.
Hajji: No it is not; it is haram.
H (to MF): He says that now because he used to drink, but he has become an old man and cannot drink any more, so he tells us not to.
G: You know the poem of Ibn Sina (Avicenna): . . . halal gashta ba fatwa-

yi 'aql bordan/ haram gashta ba dastur-i shar' bar ahmaq ("by the decree of reason wine is halal for intelligent people; by religious law it is
forbidden for the crazy or unthinking").

Hajji: 'Ali said that if a drop of wine falls into a well and a sheep drinks of
the water, I will not eat the meat of the sheep. Now who is higher, 'Ali
or Abu 'Ali (Avicenna; the name is a pun: Abu means "father of")?

Nonobservance of the fast among bureaucrats seemed more pronounced in Qum than in Yazd or Tehran. Perhaps this was an observer
effect, perhaps it expressed a need for stronger rebellion against the
psychological domination of religion in this shrine and madrasa town.
But the attitude to religion of deritualization and ethnicalization was
widespread. An engineer I invited to visit me in Qum observed he rarely
had reason to come to Qum. I suggested, "Come when you come on
pilgrimage (*ziyarat*)" — a picniclike recreation even for those who are not
ritually inclined. There was a pause, then a sharp reply: "I am not a
heathen, I do not worship graves."

This issue of so-called heathenism has been the subject of a running
battle for a long time. In the 1940s it was picked up by two well-known
writers, Ahmad Kasravi and Ayatullah Khomeyni. Kasravi, although he
tried to create a syncretistic religion himself, essentially stated the case
for a kind of puritan rationalism, appealing to middle-rank bureaucrats.
He accused Shi'ism (and each of the other religions in Iran) of irrational
superstition:

> Prayer, crying, vows, and so on, have no efficacy . . . People think God
> watches this country in particular and as soon as someone commits a sin,
> He sends a famine or flood or epidemic or a Ghengiz Khan. They think that
> God is emotional and that in response to a sheep sacrifice he will forgive.
> People learn all this from the preachers [*pishvayan*] . . . a mulla on the
> mimbar during Ramadan talking about famine . . . turned to the women
> and said: you go with bare legs without stockings and you go to the cinema;
> the famine is the result . . . I am surprised that no one stands up at least to
> protest that these are sins of women in Tehran and Tabriz: why should
> hunger strike the women of Bushire? . . . the beliefs in miracles . . . are
> blasphemies against God . . . If God does not answer prayers, what kind of
> God is He, they ask, and so are interested in fortune-telling and magic . . .
> *Du'a-nivis* (prayer writers), sayyids, and mullas who tell you to make vows
> in order to be cured do not know God. (Kasravi 1321 Sh./1943).

One of the faults of Kasravi and modern Shi'ite writers, almost
without exception, is that they misrepresent their opponents' position to
score cheap rhetorical points. Attacks on fortune-telling, magic, dealing
with the jinn, dealing with the occult, and so on, are supported by the
religious hierarchy too: such things are haram in Islam (Khomeyni
1363/1944). But to attack the various psychological supports of
religion — prayers for aid and cures, commemoration of significant past

and events and people, techniques to aid decision-making — is silly and counterproductive. There is refusal to agree on the grounds of argument.

Kasravi attacks the cognitive absurdity of customs like divination from the Qur'an, praying to the Prophet and the Imams for cures and wishes, and building shrines. Khomeyni defends the psychological uses of such practices and scores points against Kasravi's commonsense language with theological casuistry. Thus Khomeyni formulates the query of praying for cures and wishes to the Prophet and Imams as a query about *shirk*: is one making something other than God a partner with God, a heresy against the doctrine of *tawhid* (unity, monotheism). The answer, of course, is a linguistic sleight of hand and a shifting of the argument's grounding: if such prayer or request is worship ('*ibadat, parastidan*) of the invoked personages, then it is shirk; but if it is merely expressions of respect (*ihtiram, tawadu'*) and affirmations of solidarity with the Islamic path mapped out by these personages, then there is no problem.

The basic philosophy is, for Khomeyni as for Kasravi, that for whatever man can do himself he has no business asking divine aid. Khomeyni simply goes a step further to say that where man cannot help himself (as in the case of illness after all medical knowledge has been applied), or where there is no basis for deciding one way rather than another, prayers for cures and divinations from the Qur'an are psychological aids to avoid hopelessness and psychic paralysis. Furthermore, ritual props like shrines and the muhr (sacred soil from Karbala used in prayer) are visual aids to put one in a proper frame of mind and to recall to mind the martyrs of the past and the principles they died for. The charge that prayers of request are shirk because to request implies that God's mind may be changed is dismissed by Khomeyni as a childish question that can be answered only as one would answer a child: the changing states of the world are an unfolding of God's divine plans; what appears as a change to men (from deteriorating illness to health, say) is a continuous process from a universal point of view.

But Khomeyni undercuts his own arguments by his in-group rhetorical cuteness. Thus his attempt at redutio ad absurdum on the issue of the muhr: if one insists that use of a piece of dirt from Karbala or other sites in prayer is a kind of idolatrous shirk, then all namaz would be shirk and only those who do not pray would not be idolators (*mushrik*). But this is exactly the charge, and it is no argument to say that since everyone we call Muslim has adopted the custom of using the muhr, it is right, particularly since it is widely accepted that there are few proper Muslims in the world. The argument is rather that the muhr is an aid to mental recall and formation of religious intent, or more simply that because we do it, it is right, and it is legitimate because those who know the law do not find it wrong. Perhaps the clearest example of Khomeyni's directing attention in one direction while the argument really lies in another is his dismissal of citing hadith against the building of domes (*gunbad*) or shrines. There are hadith pro and con, but those against shrines use the word *sawiyyat* ("to level"), the opposite of "to mound up," and the context is the pre-Islamic practice of making a mound over a grave and putting an idol or statue on top; it is these domes as idol platforms and idols that are to be leveled. Muhammad, Abu Bakr, and 'Umar all built domes for their graves and the Imams never asked that these be leveled. But if one is willing to make the distinction between worship and respect, then the only rationale for allowing Islamic grave markers and destroying non-Islamic grave markers is that Muslims define non-Muslim practice as worship while they define their own practice as respect. If one is given the power to define boundaries of who is legitimate and who is not, then one can define them any way one wishes. (And indeed the Wahhabis of Saudi Arabia, like Kasravi, define Shi'ite shrines to be idolatrous worship.) The same process, but without any propositional argument at all, is clear in Khomeyni's demogogic rhetoric against the rationalist reformers:

> The intellectuals (*rawshan-fikran*) want progress (*pishraft*) and release from taqlid [in the pejorative sense, "blind imitation" of traditional models or of the mujtahids; in the positive sense, "following" the opinions of those who know]. But they are really followers of the camel-herding savages (*wahshi*) of Najd [the Wahhabis] . . . These arguments have been around since the beginning of Islam . . . They think that if we abandon religion, we will advance and catch up with Europe, but they do not realize what Europe has to offer is not civilization (*tamaddun*), but savagery (*tawahhush*). Nor do they realize that people in Europe are still religious, that the great men of Europe and America pray every morning . . . Nor do our writers realize how little progress there is in the deserts of Najd and the Hejaz: we should seek advice on development from them? (Khomeyni 1363/1944: 2-7).

The basic problem, of course, is an asymmetry in the right to interpret ideology, the insistence that Shi'ism is perfect, only flawed in practice, whereas all others (Wahhabis, the West) are fundamentally wrong. The style of debate thus relies heavily on sarcasm, arguments ad hominem, and other rhetorical devices, since direct confrontation (which would assume equality in the right to interpret) is ruled out:[14]

Kasravi (on the claims of the mujtahids to veto powers over laws passed by parliament and the differences of opinion among mujtahids): So, I am a mujtahid and I hereby give permission (*ijaza*) to parliament to do good things for the country.

Khomeyni: Great! Now all the problems have been solved. May he give similar permission to all governments that all the problems of the world be solved.

Kasravi: Whence comes the right of the mujtahids to judge the laws? For them to be legitimate in this function, parliament must pass a law to so acknowledge them.

Khomeyni: You have learned circular reasoning well. Who knows better, God or Millspaugh [American financial advisor to the Iranian government 1922 to 1927, and 1942]? Which do you say: Islam is not the law of God, or God does not know what is good or bad?

Kasravi: The rule that you can follow only the opinions of a living marja'-i taqlid means that when an old one dies, you have to read the book of the new one. What a waste of time.

Khomeyni: Big deal, maybe four maraji' die in a man's lifetime and the four books cost less than a novel or going to a film. Besides they are not new works but notes on previous works. We do not throw out the works of dead ulama; we perfect them.

Kasravi: Ruhani are parasites; they should work.

Khomeyni: If you want mujtahids, they must have time to study. Besides who is more of a parasite, lawyers or ruhani? Just look at their respective houses and life styles. Who is more patriotic? I know an 'alim who never used anything foreign. Lawyers use everything foreign including cloth for their children's clothing.

Kasravi: Why on the eleventh of Muharram should the radio still be filled with programs of mourning?

Khomeyni: May you go blind! You once were a rawda-khwan (preacher). Programming is so filthy, it hurts to have one program devoted to religion?

A relatively clear arena of stylistic differentiation among the traditional believers, the modernizers, and the state itself is mourning ceremonies. The differences are stylistic because the underlying philosophy and the justifying slogans of a Khomeyni or a Kasravi (and even of Reza Shah) are not so different: appeals to reason and acceptance that ceremony is useful in maintaining public health. Khomeyni specifically defends the psychological uses of ritual acts; Reza Shah tried to substitute happy national ceremony for religious mourning; Kasravi's followers used book burnings of "superstitious religious books" as a rite in his syncretistic religion *Pak-din*.

Three main kinds of mourning ceremonies (*'azadari*) have been differentially valued by the state, the modernizers, religious leaders, and the populace. The most dramatic are the passion plays (*shabih, ta'ziya*) in which the events of the Battle of Karbala and a few other associated events are re-enacted. Organized on the local level in villages and urban neighborhoods, these plays were also supported by the Qajar state; they were devalued by the Pahlavi state. They have always been looked at askance by the religious leaders. Shaykh Abdol-Karim Haeri-Yazdi explicitly disapproved of them. Under Mohammad Reza Shah passion plays were mildly discouraged until the late 1970s, when the court patronized them not as religion but as folklore.

On the other hand, Haeri-Yazdi and religious leaders in general supported rawdas, the style of preaching that is framed within the dramatic recitations about the Battle of Karbala. Among rawda-khwans (the preachers) a distinction is drawn. Some wail about the injustice of the world and the misfortunes that befell Husayn and Shi'ites and imply that Husayn will intercede on behalf of his partisans in the next world for sins they have committed in this world; these are the lower-class rawda-khwans, who sing in graveyards and do little preaching. More respectable and acceptable to religious leaders are rawda-khwans who stress Husayn as an example of bravery and courage in the fight for freedom rather than as a victim. The more middle-class oriented the preachers, the less of Karbala their talks contain, the less preaching, and the more lecturing. The Pahlavi state, of course, was suspicious of the political potential of both kinds of rawdas and attempted to monitor them, jailing or intimidating preachers who made political statements. To be so jailed became a badge of honor in the struggle against the state.

A third form of 'azadari is engaged in by dasta, the lines of breast-beating young men (during Muharram they also use chains to beat themselves on the back, and in the past used knives on their foreheads). This exercise, like the carrying of huge wooden structures representing Husayn's coffin (the naql) by several hundred men, was outlawed by Reza Shah in the 1930s. It remains a popular pietistic exercise as much as weeping during rawdas. Even religious leaders like Haeri-Yazdi in their youth took part, although in general it is rare for religious leaders to participate. Until 1955, Mohammad Reza Shah Pahlavi gave annual donations to dasta groups in Qum.

One might diagram the stylistic variation in terms of approval ($+$), disapproval ($-$), and ambivalence (0) thus:

	PASSION PLAYS	RAWDA	DASTA
Qajars	$+$	$+$	?
Reza Shah	$-$	$-$	$-$
Ulama	$-$	$+$	0
Populace	$+$	$+$	$+$
Mohammad Reza Shah	0	$-$	$-$

The role of the state in religious ceremonies should be given some attention: where there is loss of state support, ceremonies may atrophy or may even take on antistate characteristics (as the message of Husayn in the passion plays may or may not do); state support of religious activities on the other hand is a method of control. Pilgrimage is a case in point. There are two kinds of pilgrimage: the hajj to Mecca, which came to be completely state controlled; and *ziyarat*, or pilgrimages to shrines like those in Mashhad and Qum, which were only state coordinated on major occasions, in the sense that the police scheduled the different dasta groups entering the shrines. Group ziyarat provide an instructive contrast to the modern hajj, for they are organized through local religious meeting groups (*hay'at-i madhhabi*). These local groups are often run by bazaar merchants. During Ramadan they support public rawdas; during the year they may meet in members' houses with a cleric as leader to discuss the Qur'an. On the annual ten-day death memorial of the seventh Imam (the father of Hadrat-i Fatima who is buried in the Qum shrine) these groups in Qum go to Mashhad (as many as forty busloads). There is a Qum (upriver from the shrine). Similar activities go on in other cities. This bazaar-neighborhood organization provides the skeleton of much popular religion.

In the old days hajjis traveled with a guide (*hajj-avar, hamla-dar*). Being a good guide was good business; some even took people on credit or lent them funds on interest. By the mid-1970s all hajjis were flown by Iran Air to Saudi Arabia. Prospective hajjis had to register with the Endowments Office, pay their money into a bank, and get medical clearance from government doctors. Their numbers were regulated by Iranian and Saudi government quotas. The bureaucratic procedures allowed a fair amount of corruption (a recent national hajj leader was dismissed for embezzling five million tomans) and discrimination against lower classes: requiring repeated trips to town, with time deadlines that were often missed by villagers and shepherds, the sort of people who save all their lives to fulfill this religious obligation.[15] Nonetheless, gradually more preference was given to those who had not gone before and who were genuine hajjis. The number of hajjis rose steadily, from 12,000 in 1961 to more than 57,000 in 1972. Nearly a fifth of the peasants who wanted to go in 1972 (18,000 applied) were rejected by the doctors or at other steps in the procedure; nonetheless peasants still formed the largest group of hajjis (see table 4.1).

The contrast with the ziyarat is clear: the hajj has become a processing machine of vast bureaucratic dimensions, although hajjis are divided into small traveling units. The ziyarat organized by meeting groups (*hay'at-i madhhabi*) are totally local enterprises integrated as semi-permanent fixtures of community organization.

Table 4.1 Hajjis, by occupation (1972)

OCCUPATION	NUMBER	PERCENTAGE
Farmer	14,504	32.5
Shopkeeper	11,706	23.5
Worker	10,965	21.5
Retired	3,935	7.5
Clerk	2,734	6.0
Merchant	1,970	4.0
Ruhani	1,931	4.0
Army	405	1.0
Total	57,230	100.0

SOURCE: Sazman-i Awqaf 1353:140.

5

Discourse and Mimesis: Shi'ism in Everyday Life

Mulla shodan,	How easy to become a
che asan,	mulla [learned];
Adam shodan,	How hard to become
che moshkel.	Adam [a man].

— Persian proverb

*T*HE NOTION OF RELIGIOUS styles needs to be pursued in several directions: the degree to which there is class-linked patterning, the degree to which the discourses of the class-linkèd styles are hermetic and exclude one another, and the dilemma of individuals caught at points where two styles interact and contradict each other. A simplified three-class analysis should suffice at this stage: village and working-class communities; the traditionally educated, urban middle class — merchants, landowners, and the ulama; and the new middle and upper classes with modern secular education. I wish to stress the necessity of pursuing analyses of cultural styles. The three-class analysis here is emphatically simplified and is capable of refinement. It is only sufficient to demonstrate that there are different styles and that they are highly informative about social cleavages. Any analysis concerned with emerging class consciousness in Iran, or elsewhere in the Middle East, should take them into account. To rely instead on a tradition versus modernity dichotomy, as so many accounts of the Middle East do, relegating Islam to the former, is to ignore a wealth of socially critical information.

Religious settings in villages and old urban neighborhoods are many and cater to a variety of social needs: the mosque with its daily routine of prayer; the rawda with its homiletic entertainment; the *majlis madhhabi*, or weekly gatherings for religious discussion, recitation, or pietistic exercises; the annual passion plays, special pilgrimages,[1] celebrations on 'Umar's death, mournings on the death days of the various Imams and celebrations of their births; the zurkhana, or traditional gymnasium, used primarily by high school boys and craftsmen (but also others),

136

where the virtues of Islamic chivalry are acted out; the sufra (ritual feasts) attended primarily by women, for vows, cures, sociability, and homiletics; the tombs and stopping places of saints (*imamzada, qadamgah*), and the sacred trees and wells (where picnics may be brought) for vows and cures; the khaneqah or Sufi conventicles; the bazaar with its language of Islamic morality, its decaying Islamic commercial codes, and its fading taboos circumscribing non-Muslims; the Thursday afternoon ziyarat (visits, pilgrimages) to the graveyards to reaffirm ancestral ties and duties, including charity to the assembled beggars; and, of course, the gatherings for weddings and deaths.

Of these eleven settings, only four or five normally involve the ulama. Preachers (rawda-khwans, wa'izin) are involved in rawdas and, when they are invited to give rawdas there, in sufras, or ritual feasts. There are always low-level religious singers and rawda-khwans at graveyards. Ulama may be involved in majlis madhhabi if invited. They participate peripherally in weddings, to supervise the public contract, and centrally in the rawdas associated with funerals. The imam or prayer leader of the mosque is usually a member of the ulama by virtue of his dress and some formal madrasa training. The imam may even be an important community leader: the great ayatullahs all serve as imams.

On a slightly less elevated level an educated village imam can be an important community leader, as is a certain shaykh near Rezaiyeh in western Iran. The ideal place to meet this handsome shaykh, with a silvering black beard and flowing black on grey cloaks ('*aba* and *qaba*), is in his gardens amid the cucumbers. There he has a small shelter and a bench where he likes to sit and drink tea away from the flies of the village. The son of a line of ulama who originally came from Khonsar, he spent twelve years as a married student in Qum. He speaks elegant Persian and Arabic as well as the local Azeri Turkish. When the village water system broke down, he not only talked from the minbar about solutions but was deputed to talk to the relevant ministry. He is also a source of educated opinion on such subjects as sanitation and birth control. Regarding birth control, for instance, he has a pragmatic position: the government program to lower the birth rate is a misordering of priorities. There are enough resources to support new births if the resources are used sensibly. Islam teaches faith that God will provide for Muslims. Rather than an antibirth campaign, the government should do more to provide nursery care, schools, and social services. The government is shirking its responsibilities. He himself has many children, but finally his wife told him the factory was closing down. So now he practices birth control. This is an akhund who is not a social parasite: he works his own land, he contributes pragmatic leadership, he can lend his linguistic and educational skills to broker relations between the Turkish-speaking villagers and the Persian administration—and he can perform rawdas and lead prayers.

The position of *imam-jum'a*, or leader of Friday prayers, in big cities traditionally has been, and remained under the Pahlavis, a state appointment (although it may in fact also be quasi-hereditary); thus, unless the imam-jum'a was a person of unusual integrity and learning, he had little authority among the people. The last Pahlavi-appointed imam-jum'a of Tehran—Western educated, allegedly (at the beginning of his appointment) totally innocent of Arabic, allegedly addicted to sports cars, wine, and women in Switzerland—was a standing joke among religious folk.

The ulama under the Pahlavis were at the fulcrum of two social oppositions: First, they usually spoke for a conservative moral vision in opposition to the state's mode of modernization and to the notion that Islam and traditional religious forms are archaic. On the contrary, they would insist, Islam is perfect and has a design for the just society, which is in need of implementation not alteration. Second, they spoke for ideals that often transcend the possibilities of practical life. They were thus always vulnerable to the charges of hypocrisy and pretension. This vulnerability was recognized both by the many jokes about them and by the ulama themselves in their constant admonitions to the anthropologist not to judge Islam by their activity, for they were inadequate Muslims, not to do sociological investigations, but to study Islam itself.[2] There is a commonly used folk verse:

> Islam bi dhat-i khod nadarad 'aybi,
> Har 'ayb ke hast dar musalmani-i mast.

> There is no essential fault in Islam;
> Whatever fault exists is in us Muslims.

The vulnerability is evaluated in different ways, as shown by responses to a minor incident in Qum. Two young religious students approached two women in the square outside the shrine, mistaking them for prostitutes. The women screamed curses and injunctions of shame, and a crowd quickly gathered. The two students escaped in a taxi. Members of the crowd clucked at this display of vulgarity by persons wearing religious garb: "They should practice what they preach; so much for the defense of Islam these days." A young man replied that Islam was not tainted by the character of its preachers: "When you receive a letter, you do not inquire into the character of the postman before reading it." Another young man, sympathizing with the embarrassment of the two offenders, quietly confided to me that a major reason he had decided against a career in religious garb was precisely the elevated moral expectations imposed on a mulla and not on ordinary men. But the majority rejected these defenses, and people itemized the immoralities of the maraji-'i taqlid and especially of their sons and sons-in-law: one was photographed in adultery and was forced to appeal to the secret police for aid against repeated blackmail extortion; another had brought an actress-prostitute to Qum; another two were homosexuals; and the community's tithe money was being dissipated on fine cars, trips to Europe, and support of idle followers. A couplet from the poet Sa'di about a cuckolded stargazer, who knows what is going on light years away but not what is going on in his own house, was invoked to give authority and aesthetic punch to this line of reasoning. Indeed religious law (*fiqh*) supports this attitude by requiring justice ('*adalat*) as a criterion of a mujtahid, prayer leader, or other religious official. Lack of morality (*fisq*) is by definition a lack of faith.[3]

If the ulama only teach Islam and do not embody it, upper-class and Westernized Muslims have an even more tenuous relation to the traditional religious settings. Indeed their major contact often is only through forced attendance at life-cycle rituals, which may be quite artificial, though the following is extreme:[4]

> There is a tradition in my family to read a rawda on the twelfth day of the lunar month. While my great-aunt was alive, it was done in her home in Shiraz. When she died, one of my sisters picked it up. A guy comes, does a rawda, and collects twenty tomans. Happy-go-lucky mulla: turban, motorbike. I came back from Europe and went to my sister's. He is sitting in a room reciting; nobody is listening. So I said I would sit through one to show respect. It is supposed to be read to a group of people. This is ridiculous to have him sitting and doing it by himself. It is so commercial. There he was sitting doing his rawda, reading *Zan-i Ruz* (Today's Woman) magazine.

Religious feeling among many of these people remains quite strong, nonetheless, and often is expressed through the language of Sufism and Islamic modernism. What these upper-class and Westernized Muslims have to say about the beauty, value, and truth of Islam, however, is often angrily rejected by the more traditional classes, especially the madrasa students and religious high school and university students.

Sufism, Self-Development, and the Upper-Class Idiom

Sufism in several different forms remains important to the Persian consciousness: its poetry as constant epigrams to frame everyday life, its organized meetings as a kind of social club consciously apart from the religion of the ulama, its philosophy and cosmology as a contemplative frame for the intelligentsia, and its psychology as a moral referent in a corrupt world. In the past there were other forms: the pietistic and missionary Sufi orders, which threatened the legitimacy of local rulers and on occasion seized power (for instance, the Mar'ashis, the Safavids); the mendicants who wished to escape the duties of ordinary life; the lodges supported by the state as a mode of stable influence in the body politic. Organized orders today in Iran serve as weekly meeting places primarily for men in the wealthier, better-educated traditional occupations.[5] A few of the more exotic orders exist on the peripheries of the coun-try — especially in Kurdistan — but their influence is not on the same scale as in the Indian subcontinent or North Africa.

For upper-class and Westernized Persians the appeal of Sufism is rather in its links to metaphysics, psychology, and aesthetics. Two dif-ferent uses of Sufi idiom can be illustrated in the work of the Culture and Personality Circle and in the publications of S. Hossein Nasr. In-terestingly, although the latter is more religiously erudite, he is also more isolated from ordinary belief and practice.

The Culture and Personality Circle was a small group of Persian and American intellectuals in Tehran in the 1970s whose core members were two anthropologists (Mehdy Soraya, Mary Catherine Bateson), a psychoanalyst (Hasan Safavi), and a business school professor (Barkev Kassarjian). Various others, including myself, participated for shorter or longer periods. The purpose of the circle was to explore the socio-linguistic structuring of Persian behavior and attitudes. A file of taped discussions was collected and so far two short papers have been pro-duced; one is of relevance here because it, together with as yet unworked taped material, provides another kind of access than that provided by Nasr's books to upper-class Muslim usages of Sufism.

The paper, *Safa-yi Batin* (Inner Purity), in part is a corrective to descriptions of Persian social interaction as fraught with insecurity, fear of double dealing, and cynical expectations. *Safa-yi Batin* points out that these descriptions reveal only one pole of Persian conceptions of self-and-other. In a corrupt world, self-preservation forces one to play the game, to lie, to be dishonest, to take nothing at face value. But underneath this mandatory mask, the individual's self-respect depends on a view of himself as essentially pure, honest, and trustworthy. Fur-thermore there is a constant search to find others with whom one can be this true self. Such friendships are the strongest relationships there are; biddings will be done without question of motive.

Those rare individuals who can flout the normal protective devices of social interaction, who can always be open, trustworthy, hospit-able — these are the true Sufis or *darvish*. A darvish need not worry about proper clothes or rules of propriety; what is essential is his moral activity. *Safa-yi Batin* develops a series of character types who have more or less of these darvish qualities: *luti*, the neighborhood strongman who takes care of the weak and protects morality; *jahil*, the young street tough who gets into trouble but, as he grows older, may develop into a luti; *dash*, a lesser luti who has only strength and moral authority whereas a luti also has funds to distribute; and darvish, essentially powerless but simple and honest. A luti does not swear; his worst curse is *nakas naluti* ("you are a nobody, you are not luti"). If his desires overpower him (say he looks unchastely at a woman), he punishes himself (archetypically by chopping off a finger). He often speaks in the third person with the voice of community morality: "A man does not behave this way." A luti is supported by *nocheh*, men who are willing to sacrifice themselves (*fida*), to execute his orders, and to uphold community morality. A dash on the other hand does swear, and a jahil always flirts with trouble. If, then, the continuum between luti and jahil is one of morality, darvish belongs to the same pole as luti. But a darvish, unlike a luti, dash, or jahil, has no power. The character of being a darvish (*adam-i darvish*), as opposed to being a member of a Sufi order, has to do with humility. One may be rich and powerful, but if one ignores status distinctions, if one interacts with everyone as an equal, then one is a darvish. A darvish is the opposite of being *mutakabbir*, one who always invokes status distinctions, who refuses to talk to those below him.

The paper *Safa-yi Batin* and additional tapes make clear the use of these character types as mental frames in all spheres of life. Some examples: students consider me a luti professor; the general, despite his rank, behaved like a darvish; one who runs a firm has to be a bit of a luti; and so on.

These words, darvish and luti, are associated with an entire network not only of neighborhood strongmen and protectors but with the chivalry and physical prowess celebrated in the zurkhana (gymnasium) and the poetry and parables about its patron, 'Ali, as well as its heroes from the epic *Shahnameh (pahlavan*, for example, means both athlete and hero). Exercises in the zurkhana are done to the beat of a drum and chanting of the Shahnameh or other poetry. The exercises are prefaced and concluded with prayers and punctuated with salawat (praises to the family of Muhammad) and la'nat (curses upon the enemies of Islam). In the past ill people were brought to the zurkhana for particularly efficacious prayers and collections were taken up there for the unfortunate of the community. 'Ali, as early Islam's greatest fighter (his sword Dhu'l-fiqar was a wondrous double-bladed instrument), is the patron, but he is celebrated for his darvish and luti moral qualities as much as for his valor in battle: he ate poor barley instead of wheat bread, wore poor clothes, and rode a mule that others be not jealous. He treated all equally and always acted justly. Once having bested an opponent and being about to kill him, the latter spat in 'Ali's face; 'Ali released him and walked away, that he might kill him justly for God, not improperly out of personal anger. When his anger had cooled, 'Ali returned and killed the man. 'Ali rebuked the caliph 'Umar after a decision in favor of 'Ali and against a Jew, because 'Umar had not accorded equal respect to the

Jew during the proceedings. The notion of equality used to be architec-
turally enshrined in the zurkhana by the tiny entrance door through
which all had to stoop and squeeze, even the most powerful athlete.

Outward identification with the concept of darvish/luti is sometimes
marked by a large mustache, just as identification as a *mu'min* (believer)
is marked by a beard of at least three days' growth. The darvish and luti
images are powerful ones among all classes, and popular films make
much of them. Among the upper classes interviewed by the Culture and
Personality Circle, they provide psychologically positive self-images that
can be used with greater or lesser seriousness to establish masks for interaction with others; and they provide a positive moral image of Islam
(through 'Ali, Salman Farsi, Imam Ja'far al-Sadiq, and others) which
can be used as a framework to accept others in society. As a luti one is a
protector of social life: to what extent one prays oneself or goes to
rawdas or knows the minor trespasses of local ulama is not relevant; one
supports the women and believers for whom rawdas, sufras, funeral
meetings, and the distribution of charity are important. One of the infor-
mants illustrated with the story of a general who periodically let a poor
jinn-catcher rid the house of jinn in return for payment, although he did
not believe in jinn.

S. Hossein Nasr represents an entirely different usage of the Sufi
idiom, an intellectual elitism that manages somehow to be more discon-
tinuous with the lower religious classes than does the behavioral elitism
of would-be lutis. (For an elaboration of how protestation of simpleness,
directness, and so on, is used to disavow one's own superiority, see
Beeman 1976.) It is an intriguing discontinuity that operates on three
levels; least interesting and most obvious is the rejection by the religious
classes of someone who had become aligned with the Pahlavi political
establishment; more interesting is the constant definition and redefini-
tion of the differences between Sufism and Shi'ism, which in other situations may be allowed to blur; least explored is the hint by Nasr (1972:13)
that the Ni'matullahi order in the nineteenth and twentieth centuries experienced an important revival among the educated, a political current of
unclear significance. Understanding Sufism, says Nasr, is reserved for
the "intellectual elite (*khawass*) of the traditional classes" (p. 14), but its
message, if explained properly by someone as talented as Nasr, could
provide spiritual answers for modern men of both East and West.

The ad hominem objections to Nasr must be cleared away first so as to
allow the more interesting questions to emerge. The first objection is
political. Although Nasr briefly flirted with the group of reformers at the
Husayniyya Irshad around Dr. Ali Shariati, he was one of the first to
drop out when friction developed between the Pahlavi government and
this group. He was closely associated with the Pahlavi establishment, and
wrote such technically admissible (see below Khomeyni's 1943 opinion),
but politically unacceptable (to the vocal religious elements), statements

as: "As for political life, since Shi'ism in contrast to Sunnism does not accept the religious legitimacy of the institution of the caliphate and believes monarchy to be the best form of government in the absence of the Mahdi, the Persian monarchy possesses a positive religious aspect" (1975:112).

The second objection has to do with Nasr's self-association with a group of European (Swiss, French, Belgian) scholars of a mystical bent: Frithjob Schuon, Rene Guenon, Titus Burkhardt, Martin Lings, and—the only well-known academic—Henry Corbin. For the Westerner the objection is their partisanship in an ecumenical mysticism, albeit erudite, that obfuscates the historical and sociological dynamics of religion. For Persians the objection is that Nasr is associated with non-Persians, even a European Sufi circle deriving from a North African saint, who miss entirely what is a major element of Islam for ordinary believers: sociopolitical criticism of the state. Madrasa students in Qum have on occasion reacted quite heatedly to Nasr's name: "Nasr—you know why we do not like him, because he is trying to turn Islam into Sufism."

To this Nasr's response is that what is most valuable in Islam for the modern world is its esoteric psychology, philosophy, and eschatology. As to phrasing politics in Islamic terms, he says skeptically,

> Islam can only gain respect and even adherence among intelligent non-Muslims as well as young, Western-educated Muslims themselves by being expounded, not as another version of such Western ideologies as happen to be fashionable today, but as a clear-cut alternative to these ideologies . . .
> If Islam is presented, for example, as socialism or rationalism, then the thoughtful modern man who stands outside the world of faith will seek the purer form of socialism and rationalism in the Western philosophies and ideologies themselves, rather than in their Islamic imitation. (1968b: 60)

The rejection of Sufism by the Shi'ite hierarchy, Nasr argues (1972: 118), was a political phenomenon of the late Safavid period when the ulama reacted both to royal patronage of Sufis and to an increasing flood of charlatan mystics who claimed to be Sufis. The ulama then drew a sharp distinction between gnosticism or speculative mysticism (*'irfan*), which was acceptable, and Sufism (*tasawwuf*), which was not, a distinction that holds to the present. An excellent example of this now traditional boundary is given by the diatribe in a rawda of Javad Manaqebi, Professor at the University of Tehran and son-in-law of Allama Tabatabai:

> [Most Sufi chains of initiation go back to 'Ali, the first Imam.] Of 'Ali we know that he was born in the Ka'aba and that as a child he came to Muhammad before Muhammad had revealed the Qur'an and asked permission to read from it. [Poem of thanks to God composed by 'Ali's father is recited.] But do not think therefore that 'Ali is greater than the Prophet. The Prophet is the master, and 'Ali the student. However much we praise

'Ali, the Prophet is greater. It is too bad that there are a few who believe in 'Ali so much that they forget God and Muhammad. 'Ali says that we must pray, but they do not pray even two *rak'at*. 'Ali when he prayed sometimes fell to the ground like a stick of wood, so did he fear God. Some say that 'Ali is God and forget the Prophet and God.

In Mashhad I went to see a *murshid* (Sufi leader) in the Mahalla Gombad-e-Sabz. I began politely, greeting him in his own idiom, and I asked him how he had arrived at his station. He looked at me sideways as if I were a child. It took a great deal of effort, he said. For thirty years I did not go to the baths, not a drop of water fell on my body. And indeed he was right: his skin smelled like that of an animal. He was very dirty, his face was very dark, and his beard was all matted. But as for his stomach, he ate well enough: do not think that he had nothing to eat. I knew from the first that he would say some nonsense, but I wanted to engage him in argument. I asked him, "You never took wudu' (ritual ablutions) to recite namaz? You never experienced seminal emission?" He got angry and shouted, "You are a child, do not be rude, you have no cause to talk to a lover of God so. We have reached God. You are still on the way. We do not need wudu', ghusl, namaz." At this I too got angry and cried, "Fie upon you, you have grown up and need no prayer, but 'Ali whom you love prayed in the mihrab [and was martyred there]; so he did not reach God, but you have? [Shouting:] *la ilah 'llah . . . haqq hu haqq . . .* You have reached God but Musa the seventh Imam did not, he who imprisoned spent his days from morning till night praying and yet did not reach God!" At this point I saw his friends were coming to beat me and I left.[6]

If Sufism is intellectually the same field as gnosticism or speculative mysticism, Nasr can save it both on historical grounds and in terms of what is currently taught by the ulama. Important Sufis were members of the entourage of the Imams until the ninth Imam. Important theologians openly wrote of Sufism and gnosticism until, in an anti-Sufi campaign under the Safavids, Mulla Muhammad-Baqir Majlisi (number 37 on table in appendix) even denied the Sufism of his own father (number 35) (Nasr 1972: 103-114). Khomeyni was a professor of gnosticism in Qum, and Nasr likes to claim discipleship under Allama Tabatabai, the dean of the field in Qum, with whom he spent a number of sessions (1975b: 24). Not only can Nasr save Sufism, but by dismissing most of what is taught in the madrasas as transmitted (*naqli*) sciences, he can elevate it to central prominence as one of the intellectual (*'aqli*) sciences, and then say, "Most of the teaching of the Islamic intellectual sciences in Persia today is performed outside formal institutions and in private circles" (1975a: 109).

At its best, Nasr's exposition of Sufism as the intellectual core of Islam is an elegant antirationalist plea for a return to metaphysical play. He bemoans the impoverishment of man's mental universe by Western rationalism: "With the weakening of gnostic elements in Christianity, the rational faculty of Western man became gradually estranged from the twin sources of immutability, stability, and permanence: namely, revelation and intellectual intuition. The result was on the one hand the nominalist trend, which destroyed philosophical certainty, and on the other this reduction of man to the purely human, cut off from any transcendental elements, the man of Renaissance humanism" (1968a: 244).

There is even an occasional nod to those, like Mircea Eliade (1969), who in quite self-conscious terms state their goal as making the world pregnant with associations so that when the physicist steps out into the star-studded night, he can contemplate Greek, Chinese, or Hindu mythology and their aesthetic and moral realms as well as his ever more involved equations:

> [Traditional] cosmologies describe the whole Universe as an icon for contemplation; they are not childish attempts to find fantastic causes for natural occurrences (Nasr 1967a: 37).
>
> Razi, by rejecting prophecy and the process of *ta'wil* which depends upon it, also rejected the application of this method to the study of nature. In so doing he transformed the alchemy of Jabir to chemistry. That is not to say that he stopped using alchemical terminology or ideas, but in his perspective, there was no longer any balance to measure the tendency of the World Soul, nor any symbols to serve as a bridge between the phenomenal and noumenal worlds. The facts of nature were studied as before, but as facts, not symbols. (1967a: 93)

But for Nasr, "A symbol is not based on man-made conventions. It is an aspect of the ontological reality of things, and is as such independent of man's perception of it" (1968a: 247).

Nasr, to the charitable reader, avoids inconsistency in affirming the shari'at as divine revelation (1967a),[7] denying the value of ecumenicism (1970),[8] acknowledging that Islam is only one of the true religions (1972), asserting that symbols are ontologically given (1968a) and religion addresses that "which is immutable and permanent in man" (1972: 170) through the doctrine that there are many theophanies, infinite aspects of the one truth. In the same fashion he comments on the Shi'ite-Persian ethos and apparent conception of life as tragedy: "Few people are given as much to the enjoyment of life's pleasures and beauties as the Persians, but this attitude is always compensated for by the realization that a moment once gone never returns" (1975b: 106).

He cites the weeping while "chanting the Holy Qur'an" (he must mean rawdas or the incidental tear brought on by dilating on a fine sound) in beautiful surroundings, the sad quality of Persian music which is really nostalgia for the divine, and the repetition in poetry of the theme that theophanies never repeat: tragedy and sadness (*huzn*) alternate with but do not negate joy (*farah*) and "it is a tragedy based on the realization that the human condition contains an apparent contradiction. Man is in desperate need to realize the Divine and to become aware of his own spiritual nature. Yet this realization is made well nigh impossible by the distance that separates him from the Divine and by his need to await Divine assistance to accomplish this end" (1975b: 107). The divine assistance is by way of Sufi initiation, the esoteric instructions (*asrar*, "secrets") brought by Muhammad back from his ascent to heaven. These instructions take one's soul through the various stages and states of spiritual development.

The commonality between Nasr's use of Sufism and the moral-character use cited in the work of the Culture and Personality Circle lies in the concern with the self. It is quite irrelevant whether Nasr himself ever was initiated or knows any mystical secrets. It is a mind-expanding game of an intellectual, what the Germans called *Bildung*, with all the latter's connotations of developing virtue and learning high culture.

The contrast with the ulama, with the popular religion, and with popular Sufism becomes striking. In popular religion, the divine assistance is the intercession of the Imams, and Husayn in particular, on the Day of Judgment, plus the rules for social life given in the Qur'an. For Nasr it is ultimately ambiguous whether esoteric knowledge is passed down through a chain of adepts or whether it is learned from someone like Tabatabai, who claims only to be a philosopher, a scholar. But for popular Sufism, spiritual guides are of the essence, as the leader of the Qum Ni'matullahi group stated in a weekly meeting, but directed especially to me:

> Jews count no one as *ma'sum* (sinless, perfect) and so all their beliefs are batil (void) since anyone they follow might err. Christians count Jesus as ma'sum but they have no laws from him directly and count no one else as ma'sum, the result being the same as the Jews. Sunnis, our Muslim brothers, count the Prophet as ma'sum but no one else, so they are in the same boat as the Christians. Shi'a count the Prophet and the Imams to the twelfth Imam as ma'sum but no one after that, so they again are in the same boat. We believe that from Adam to Noah the rules were passed from hand to hand and thence to Abraham and on to the Imam al-Zaman, who went into occultation, and then on hand to hand to the present. ["Hand to hand" refers in part to the physical *bay'at* or oath of allegiance consisting of kissing a fist made of two right hands, a practice which went into abeyance among the Shi'a but was kept up by the Gonabad Ni'matullahi Sufis.]

For the ulama, gnosis is not a different realm of experience but only a deeper level of comprehension. For Khomeyni, *kashif-i asrar* ("revealing the secrets," which he titled his 1943 book) is merely the unfolding of explanations of the Qur'an's intent discovered over generations of scholars, esoteric only in the sense of expertise. Above all, ulama are less interested in the self than in society.

Social Utopia and the Religion of the Ulama

The religion of the ulama, beyond the rules of ritual, is essentially a moral and social ethic. Relative to Sufism it is concerned with the community rather than the individual, or with the moral person (*ensan*) — which by definition involves more than one — rather than the development of the individual soul (ruh). At points this becomes a difference of emphasis: both ulama and Sufis talk of perfection, unity with the divine, gnosis; but the interpretations are different. For the ulama the law (*shari'at*) is a sine qua non; for the darvish or Sufi the law is a mere foundation to be transcended. "Shari'at, tariqat, ma'rifat, haqiqat" (law, path, knowledge, truth) is their frequent counter to criticisms of failing to obey the letter of the law. The archetype opposition between the ulama and the darvish is the ulama attitude toward the *shath* (ecstatic statement) of Mansur Hallaj, who proclaimed "ana'l-haqq" (I have merged with, I am, the truth), for which blasphemy he was executed by the ulama. The higher ecstatic states of contemplation are, for them, loss of discipline, mere irrationality, and thus lapse into heresy. The concern of the ulama with justice and social morality, with rationality and community, is only natural given their training in the law and its principles, with, as Nasr complains, philosophy of the soul given secondary billing.

Their mode of communication is response to private queries, books, and, most important, preachments (rawda). One of their key didactic devices is the retelling of events in Islamic history and drawing of moral lessons, the reflection upon a utopia and consideration of how to make it practicable. To construct a just society, three major areas of concern are elaborated: politics, economics, and personal codes of conduct.

POLITICAL THEORY: 'ALI AND HUSAYN

There are two sides to Shi'ite political theory, appropriate to life with political power and life without political power. 'Ali's brief caliphate represented the former: procedures for reconstructing society along just lines are recorded in his letters to his governors and in the various traditions about him. For instance, he admonished his followers to first make the land productive and then worry about extracting taxes. In the case of lack of power, which is the rest of Shi'ite history, there are rules of accommodation without abandoning principle, represented by 'Ali under the first three caliphs, and rules of drawing the line where principle is endangered, represented by the martyrdoms of 'Ali and Husayn. 'Ali is the measure of governments, Husayn the model of perseverence in the face of injustice.

The style of popular discourse can be easily demonstrated. In Mashhad on Friday mornings, the courtyard of the Madrasa Milani near the shrine used to be covered with canvas roofing. Starting at about seven o'clock various men would go to the minbar and sing *munajat* (a genre of praise to God). Regular attenders and pilgrims attracted by the loudspeakers would gradually assemble, first sitting around the edges and then gradually filling in the central space in straight rows. All would stand in respect when Aqazada Mohammad-Ali Milani entered and proceeded to the minbar. A hefty man with a full black beard, he was the youngest son of Ayatullah Milani and ran the Milani establishment for the last few years of his father's life. On Friday morning he led the *du'a nudaba*, the prayer for the return of the twelfth Imam. Before leading the prayer, he would deliver a rawda.

One of the Fridays shortly before his father's death and shortly before the madrasa was razed by the Pahlavi government to make way for a green belt around the shrine (in 1975) he spoke of 'Ali, the paragon of religious knowledge and justice, using stories about him as illustrations.

> One day 'Ali sees a youth being led away and asks why. He is told that the caliph-'Umar ordered the boy to be bastinadoed because he had called a certain woman his mother. 'Ali finds it strange that this should be a cause for lashes and stays the punishment. He asks 'Umar to explain. 'Umar says the lad called the woman his mother, but she claimed to be a virgin. The lad had lied, and Islam provides a punishment of eighty lashes if a man in the bazaar or street should with maligning insinuation call a woman "Hey, mother of so-and-so, hey, daughter of so-and-so." One must take care of one's tongue. One's tongue must not rattle on with evil idleness (*zaban-i laghw nabashad*).
>
> [To stress the moral issue of male conduct, Milani here called for the audience to chant a salawat, a blessing upon the Prophet and his family: *allahumma salli 'ala Muhammad wa al-i Muhammad.*]
>
> The woman's brothers then testify to 'Ali that they had been so poor they had been unable to marry off their sister. 'Ali has a solution: he will marry the woman to the youth. He, 'Ali, will supply the dowry. The woman should go to the baths and prepare herself. At this point the woman speaks up. She fears the fires of hell and will tell the truth. She had married and become pregnant, but her husband died and her brothers refused to raise the child. They forced her to leave it in a pit. Secretly she watched over it and saw it rescued by some tribesmen. As it grew up, she kept watch from afar. Somehow the lad learned his origin, but she, fearing her brothers, did not acknowledge him. 'Umar at this point cried out, "Oh, how without 'Ali would 'Umar have caused justice to miscarry!" [Milani calls again for a salawat and follows it with the admonition: "May you and I until our last hour and dying day and until resurrection cry, Ya 'Ali!"]

Many such stories are told about 'Ali to demonstrate his ingenuity, knowledge, and fairness in contrast to characteristics of Abu Bakr, 'Umar, and 'Uthman,[9] and thereby establish the Shi'ite claims that the latter three were illegitimate caliphs. The stories also suggest indirect contrasts with contemporary society and indicate how justice should be administered. In another story, Salman Farsi, 'Ali's gubernatorial appointee, is contrasted with the rapacious governors appointed by other caliphs: Salman rented half a shoemaker's stall as his office. In another story it is related that 'Ali conducted business at night under a tree by candlelight; whenever some personal matter arose, he would extinguish the candle, for it belonged to the community. The stories of how 'Ali was cheated of his rightful succession to Muhammad are told with indignant resignation: it is the way of the world still that those who know are not asked, whereas the ignorant and unjust rule.

In theological terms this is the problem of the *uli'l-amr* (issuer of orders) and of the relation between imamat (guidance of the Imams) and the ulama. It became a major issue at the time of the 1905 Constitutional Revolution and continues unchanged in the minds of the ulama today.

According to Kasravi's account (1330 Sh./1946) during the struggles over the 1905 Constitution, the ulama took essentially three positions. Some—led by Mulla Mohammad-Kazem Khorasani, Hajj Shaykh Abdollah Mazandarani, and Hajj Mirza Hoseyn Tehrani—argued that since the Imam al-Zaman, the twelfth Imam, is not taking an active role in the world,[10] a constitutional government of the wise should replace the rule of the cruel. Others—led by S. Mohammad Tabatabai and S. Abdollah Behbahani—agreed with this ideal but argued that it could prove to be difficult to implement and that it was at least important to establish constitutional checks upon the arbitrary cruelty of the rulers, checks modeled on those adopted by the European democracies. Yet others—led by Shaykh Fazlollah Nuri—insisted on the establishment of a constitutional government, but constitutional in the literal sense of the word *mashruta* ("constitutional"), which comes from the Arabic root *shart* ("condition"): that is, conditioned by the Qur'an and sunna practices of the Prophet). Nuri's slogan was *inqilab-i mashrutiyyat-i mashruta*—a religious constitutional revolution.

Merely to follow the European model, he argued, was contradictory to Islam: a European taxation system was contradictory to the Islamic *zakat* and other taxes; European notions of equality before the law of all citizens was contradictory to Islamic insistence that Jews, Zoroastrians, Christians, and *kafirs* (unbelievers) not be equal to Muslims (enshrined in article 8 of the 1905 constitution); European notions of obligatory education to create an enlightened (indoctrinated) citizenry was opposed to the freedom of the individual and must in any case not prejudice Islamic teachings (article 19 of the constitution); European notions of freedom of the press would allow all sorts of scurrilous anti-Islamic, immoral, and antisocial ideas to be disseminated and therefore the press should be restricted to what is in Islam's interest (article 20 of the constitution). Finally it was Shaykh Fazlollah Nuri who proposed the amendment that no laws be passed by parliament until approved by a group of ulama as consonant with Islam; this became article 2 of the constitution.

There was of course a fourth group: the ulama in the pay of the shah, who were used to block moves to limit royal power. For instance, Mirza Abu'l-Qasim, the imam-jum'a of Tehran and son-in-law of the shah, Muzaffaruddin, was used as an agent provocateur in a meeting of bazaar merchants and ulama, called to discuss the government mismanagement of a price-control campaign.[11] The imam-jum'a urged Sayyid Jamaluddin Isfahani (father of the founder of modern Persian prose stories, Sayyid Mohammad-Ali Jamalzadeh) to go on the minbar. Although distrustful of the imam-jum'a, Behbahani said to trust in God and go ahead. Jamaluddin began by recounting the events that had closed the bazaar and said that if the shah were a Muslim he would join the protest, if − −. Here he was interrupted by the imam-jum'a: "O irreligious sayyid, what disrespect do you show the shah? O *kafir*, O Babi, why do you malign the shah?" Jamaluddin replied, "You do not even know what my next words will be." But the imam-jum'a cried, "Get him; kill him." Troops entered, there was bloodshed, the participants fled. The ulama led an exodus from Tehran to take asylum in the shrine of Shah 'Abd al-'Azim. The government reacted with two punitive measures: shops in the bazaar which refused to open would be broken open; the administration of the religious madrasas in Tehran were to be taken away from anti-shah and given to pro-shah people. The negotiations with the ulama and merchants who took asylum eventually led to the granting of the constitution, though in no direct or honest fashion.

The point is that though there were persons in religious garb like the imam-jum'a of Tehran (and the Mutawalli-bashi in Qum, if one stretches a point to include him in the religious personnel) who opposed the constitutional movement, the fluidity of politics made others adopt various stances; yet the Islamic position was clearly formulated and has been maintained to the present.

To deal first with political fluidity: Shaykh Fazlollah Nuri, a relative of the shah by marriage, did not join in the first exodus to the shrine of Shah 'Abd al-'Azim, although his son did. When the prime minister had the antiroyalist Muwaqqar al-Saltana imprisoned and forcibly divorced from the shah's daughter, who was then given in marriage to the imam jum'a, Nuri performed both the divorce and the marriage, the latter on the very day the administration of the madrasas Marviyya and Ibn Babawayh were taken away from their previous mutawallis and given to the imam jum'a. When the Russians wanted to build a bank in a graveyard and S. Mohammad Tabatabai refused permission for the sale, saying the land was waqf, Nuri agreed to the sale, saying it was waqf for the dead and produced no profit: another piece of land could be bought to replace it. The opposition ulama—seeing the bank as a colonialist foothold—marched on the bank and the Russians claimed damages from the shah. Nuri's reputation temporarily suffered. Yet Nuri, in the popular memory of religious people today, is remembered as the protector of the Islamic conception of state, selling out neither to a corrupt shah[12] nor to the Western imperialists. Again when the ulama debated whether or not to accept the proposed constitution, S. Kazem Yazdi sent a telegram from Najaf saying anything opposed to religion should be blocked; Akhund-e-Khorasani phrased the same sentiment in the opposite rhetoric: if a parliament is so formed as to help protect Islam, then it is a duty to support it (Kasravi 1330 Sh./1946:382). In popular memory, Khorasani is pro-constitution, Yazdi anti-constitution.

Nuri and Yazdi have become the heroes who foresaw that the constitution would be a meaningless trick allowing more, not less, European domination. Nuri's arguments have been repeated, down to the most recent Khomeyni work on the state, *Hukumat-i Islami* (1391/1971), and rawdas on *uli'l-amr* and *imamat* and *wilayat* (three differently derived theological terms for the leadership of the community). Essentially all three positions on the constitution can be seen as pragmatic versions of the Islamic position derived from the Qur'anic verse (Sura Nisa': 62): "O you who have faith, obey God, obey the Prophet of God, and obey the *uli'l-amr*" (literally, "issuer of orders"). Who is the *uli'l-amr*? The theory adopted by the Sunnis is that it is the sultan of the moment: that as long as a sultan rules according to Islamic law, Muslims should support him. This was also the theory adopted by the clerics aligned with the Pahlavi government (*akhund-i dawlati*) and by Nasr: that obedience to the shah was clearly indicated in the Qur'an. A few purists insist that *uli'l-amr* refers to the Qur'an; this would depoliticize the verse insofar as it would no longer point to any particular leader. Shi'ites, however, insist that *uli'l-amr* is clearly a term for the twelve Imams. Reason as well as the myriad references in the Qur'an and hadith to the role of the Imams and the necessity of following them indicate the necessity of a more secure successor to the Prophet than anyone as fallible as a king. Khomeyni (1363/1943: 132-153) gives a series of Qur'anic verses that, according to hadith recognized by Sunnis as well as Shi'ites, refer to the role of 'Ali and the Imams. The rhetoric used both by undistinguished rawda-khwans like S. Mahmud Khatami (rawda on the eve of Imam Husayn's birthday, 14 Ramadan / September 21, 1975) and by Khomeyni fails to do justice to the "sultan" interpretation of *uli'l-amr*, that support is demanded only so long as the sultan obeys Islam; they insist on talking about the absurdity of following kings who do evil (Khomeyni 1363/1943: 109-111; Khatami 1975). The stories of the mistakes in Islamic law made by the first three caliphs are cited in this context, and the evilness of Mu'awiya, Yazid, Mutawakkil 'Abbasi, and so on are referred to with curses. Man-made law must be imperfect, as is evident from its frequent changes (Khomeyni 1363/1943: 182). The Imams, by contrast, have perfect knowledge of the divine law, and in Khatami's account even miraculous powers:

> If he [an Imam] says to a wall or a tree, "Come here," it must obey. Imam Hasan raised the Ka'ba into the air. He struck the earth with his heel, and a lake opened up, complete with ships and fish — he gave some of the fish to friends and they could not consume all there were. For three days Imam Hasan went into the heavens and threw the stars about. On the minbar one day, Imam Hasan said that if he wanted, he could make Syria and Iraq change places, or make the heavens change places with the earth, or turn men into women. A man got up and said this was all nonsense. [Khatami tells of how Hasan turned the man into a woman, his wife into a man, and how their subsequent child was neither male nor female; the man repented.] The ninth Imam at age eight solved 30,000 difficult problems in one meeting. When 'Ali ibn-Ishaq came to ask some questions of the eleventh Imam, he was referred to that latter's two-and-a-half-year-old son (the twelfth Imam), who not only knew all the answers but the questions before they were asked . . . 'Ali destroyed the homosexual city of Lut by lifting it into the air and letting it drop and smash.

When the Imams are no longer active in the world, their role is taken over by the mujtahids or the *faqih 'adil* (just experts in the law).

At this point the logic of the dogma allows Khomeyni to formulate a theory of ethical opposition not far removed from opinions of those who would interpret the *uli'l-amr* as referring to the sultan or king: "Bad government is better than no government. We have never attacked the sultanate; if we criticized, it was a particular king and not kingship that we criticized. History shows that mujtahids have aided kings, even kings who did wrong: Nasir al-din Tusi, Muhaqqiq-i Thani, Shaykh Baha'i, Mir Damad, Majlisi" (Khomeyni 1363/1943: 187). And again (p. 189):

> Some say that government may remain in the hands of those who have it, but they should get approval (*ijaza*) from the legal experts (*faqih*). Yes, but a mujtahid can give such approval only under the condition that the law of the country is the law of God. Our country does not meet this condition since the government is neither constitutional nor the law of God. Yet bad government is better than no government, and mujtahids do not simply attack it, but if necessary help it as they did with semi-independent Iraq under the leadership of Mirza Mohammad-Taqhi Shirazi. The ulama always cooperate with the government if that is needed. The government made a great mistake in its hostility to the religious leaders and in trying to separate the youth from them. I cannot believe this came from the dry brain of Reza Khan, but he acts on the advice of others.

One is reminded of S. Mohammad Tabatabai's letter to Muzaffaruddin Shah saying, "We are often accused of being antigovernment; we are not. You are a good king, but you do not know what is going on"

(Kasravi 1330 Sh./1952: 86). One is reminded also of the meetings during the constitutional agitations convened by religious students to take up collections to liquidate the state's external debt (pp. 171-172).

There was a brief period in the early years of Reza Khan's rule (1924) when the ulama took an explicit position against republicanism and for constitutional monarchy, but this had to do with the strategic maneuvers in the 1920s for leverage in preventing secularization of the sort being provided by Kemal Ataturk in Turkey, and retaining some influence as a third force between Reza Khan and the British in Iraq (see Akhavi 1980). By 1971 Khomeyni's attitude had hardened and he called for non-cooperation with the then-current order and work toward creating a new order (Khomeyni 1391/1971: 205). The theory of Islamic government is nicely set out (pp. 52-53): it is neither authoritarian, allowing a ruler to play with people's money and punish and execute at will, nor is it constitutional in the modern sense, but conditioned (constitutional) by the Qur'an and sunnat. Since all Muslims wish to follow God's law, government does not depend on force but merely serves to map out programs. There are no castles or stipends for the royal family which eat up half the budget of the state. With all the oil, minerals, and other natural endowments, there should be no need for Iran to borrow from England and America. Justice should be swift and simple; cases should not drag on for a lifetime, providing only lawyers' fees and graft.

These ideas, which Khomeyni restated in 1971 in a series of lectures, published as *Islamic Government: Guidance by Religious Experts* (*wilayat-e faqih*), insist on the supremacy of the moral law. The theory of *wilayat-i faqih* proceeds from the debate over the *ulil amr*. Islam abolished absolute, hereditary monarchies: to recognize one man above all others is a form of idolatry (*shirk*, the sin against the doctrine of the unity of God). Rulers (*hakim-i shahr*)—monarchs or other leaders—must be subordinated to the moral law. We want to have a leader (hakim-i shahr) who would punish his sister for selling heroin (p. 179), a clear reference to Princess Ashraf, the shah's twin sister. Mujtahids or faqih know the moral law and can provide guidance. They do not seek power as an end; like the Imams, they should wait until opportunities arise which they can exploit to foster just government. Except for 'Ali, the Imams waited until the end of their lives for such opportunity. In 1979 Khomeyni found himself with such an opportunity. But how, he asks in 1971, does one begin to establish an Islamic government? With persuasion (*tabliqat*), by creating enough like-minded people to have the power to struggle and establish an Islamic government (p. 173). The role of the just and knowledgeable faqih is the same as that of the Imam or the prophet: to institute the divine law. It is the law which is supreme: no faqih can dismiss the opinions of other faqih, and so the guidance of the just government may be collegial.

Khomeyni's 1971 book was to become controversial in 1979 during the drafting of a new constitution. Just how much power should be given to the clergy? Should wilayat-i faqih be interpreted as a call for theocracy? Was there a distinction between general moral guidance and daily administration? Would the Islamic form of moral principles not be unacceptably restrictive of human rights, especially those of non-Muslims and secular Muslims? Would the particular living faqih of the moment meddle excessively in the affairs of government? Although Prime Minister Bazargan would feign surprise in October 1979 that Khomeyni was pushing for so many provisions for clerical supervision, and seemingly for so much personal control, in the new constitution, what was at issue was not the form of Khomeyni's arguments, which were the same as his 1971 arguments, and as those articulated by his predecessors in 1905. Rather, what was at issue was the interpretation and implementation. Ayatullah Shariatmadari and Ayatullah Nasser Makarem championed the interpretation that wilayat-e faqih could be accomplished very nicely under a fully democratic form of government, without multiplying boards of clerical overseers in all areas of government. A committee of five mujtahids, such as was provided for in the 1905 constitution, would be quite sufficient. This position of Ayatullah Shariatmadari in opposition to Khomeyni, plus his invocation of the right, as a faqih, to be consulted, caused a major crisis in the autumn of 1979.

Perhaps the most interesting parts of Khomeyni's 1971 lectures for non-Iranian readers who became aware of the book only in 1979 was the rhetorical vehemence against Jews, Zionists, and colonialists. But again it was fairly old standard rhetoric. The Jews from the beginning of Islam had been enemies. In recent times, even worse were the colonialists, for they divided the Muslims into competing nations, they introduced laws for organizing usury and fornication and endless legal processes, and they introduced an education which misrepresented Islam to Muslims as being incomplete and only concerned with rules of ritual purity, as not having the means for really organizing society. False religious leaders, who propagated these views and said that Islam should be separated from politics, were supported. Indeed the centers of religious education were now centers for the propagation of such false views, and there was a need to reform the clergy and retrain them.

The most interesting modern reformulation of the Shi'ite theory of state is that of Ali Shariati, a French-trained intellectual and Islamic reformer. He draws a distinction between the Western concept of politics and the Oriental notion of *siyasat*, which, originally, he claims, meant "taming a wild horse." Politics (from the Greek *polis*, "city"), he says, has a problematic of satisfying the citizens; it is essentially administrative, conservative, status-quo oriented, allocating the most happiness to the greatest number. In contrast, the problematic of siyasat is one of education, reform, bringing perfection into being. It involves leadership and force if necessary. The Islamic terms *ummat* (community) and *imamat* (leadership of the Imams) fall on the Oriental side of this distinction. They form a dynamic pair, derived, he claims, from *amm*, "decision to go." The emphasis on movement toward perfection (*takamul*), disciplining and teaching (*tarbiyat*), and an active society of believers (*ummat*) is radically different from the democracy of bourgeois capitalism. Backward people, like children, cannot be expected to be able to choose intelligently; they will always choose present pleasure over discipline for future improvement. Even in the West, vote buying and deception make a mockery of democratic ideals. Liberal democracy, not the government of kings and priests, bombarded Algeria and killed 45,000 people in Madagascar. Lenin said it took half a century to create a social revolution; the Chinese say it is an endless process; in the meantime one cannot depend on democracy.

At the end of the process of social development, Shariati concludes, one can have democracy and at the same time the Sunni and Shi'a theories will coincide, for then one can run society through democratic councils and the twelfth Imam will not have to be in occultation. In the meantime, one should beware of Western arguments to give up religious fanaticism (*ta'assub*, "tenacity of belief"): ta'assub is our integrity. The West wants us to accept a division between politics and religion; that is a way of making us impotent. The West wishes to make us assimilated men, who, Sartre has pointed out in the introduction to Frantz Fanon's *The Wretched of the Earth*, are emptied of their heritage and turned into mindless imitators. Such mindless imitators will desire to buy Western goods and thus will provide markets to keep Western capitalism going.

There are many problems with Shariati's formulations, but perhaps the most revealing is that despite his claim to being a revolutionary reformist voice in contrast to the backward-looking religious establishment, his message is essentially identical with that of, for instance, the supposedly nonpolitical scholar Allama Tabatabai (1341 Sh. b/1943):

Just as children, orphans and the insane need guardians, so society needs a supervisor. If there is only law and no head, society falls apart . . . The necessity of such a head is called *wilayat*, or in Persian *sarparasti*. (p. 74)
[Islam] is neither democratic nor communist. The lawmaker is God, and changes are not made by majority opinion . . . *haqq* (truth), not *khwastan-i mardum* (popular will). (p. 86)
What people want is the result of what they are taught. They can be taught to want what God wants. The abandonment of the sunnat was not a natural death (*murdan*) but murder (*kushtan*) by Arabs who substituted false for true sunnat. (p. 88)
For fifty years we've had democracy, but for all the glory it has given others it has brought us only grief. If one says we have democracy only in name,

we don't practise it, the same can be said of Islam. Is democracy perfection? Then why is it on the decline and being replaced by communism? (p. 89)

The ill done our part of the world by democracy is only a social form of what was done individually earlier by Alexander and Genghiz Khan . . . Now it is done more subtly by technology and psychology, so people do not even realize what is happening and are not aroused to revenge. (p. 91)

Again Shariati's notion of the active Islamic society and need for discipline and leadership is not very different from that expressed by the preacher Shaykh Mohammad Taqi Falsafi in a rawda on the expulsion of Iranians from Iraq (c. 1971): "Does man naturally turn towards justice? No. Man is first an animal and then a person . . . The verse I cited ['We send our Prophets with signs and miracles, a book and scales of justice'] is followed by 'and we created iron,' that is, the sword. Justice without the sword is impossible. Justice and freedom must be forced on people. Islam eased this by basing itself 90 percent on belief and 10 percent on force."

And in turn, how different is this from the position held by Mohammad Reza Shah that the Persian people were not ready for democracy; that they needed to be educated in civic behavior, that society needed to be transformed before democracy could be introduced, that democracy was not necessarily a good thing, that Persians wanted a strong father-figure; and that all of these attitudes are ingrained in Persian tradition and national character?

There is one crucial difference perhaps: the balance between force and legitimacy is reversed. The shah depended upon a good deal more force than the 10 percent Falsafi claimed for Islam. Theoretically this may be problematic: if Islam is divine and people do not wish to obey, may not force (*jihad*) be used to the utmost extent necessary? Doctrinally the answer is that all reasonable men will admit Islam's perfection and so force does not arise as an issue; historical examples to the contrary are really examples only of perversions of Islam. But even if one admits there was a convergence of political philosophy between shah, Shariati, and Falsafi, it should serve only to focus attention on strategies for development and on Islamic claims to having a more just way than either capitalism or communism.

ISLAMIC ECONOMICS

The protest from Nuri to Khomeyni and Shariati was not only generalized moralism: an Islamic economics goes along with the ideals of justice in political theory. For some reason, however — presumably owing to the lack of education in Western economic theory — discussion of Islamic economics seemed both less frequent and less sophisticated than in the more developed literature in Pakistan (see, for example, Qureshi

1946, Yusuf 1971, de Zayas 1960, Rahman 1964). Beyond the slogan that Islam was a third road between capitalism and communism, the faith that interest-free banks must be possible, and the unquantified assertion that Islamic taxes would be sufficient to run the state, debate seemed limited to the century-old *Makasib* (On Trade) (the manual of Shaykh Mortaza Ansari of rules for exchange in the bazaar). The only serious contemporary work on the subject was *Iqtisad-i Ma* (Our Economics, 1381/1961) by Mohammad-Bagher Sadr, which was translated into Persian from the Arabic; it seemed widely agreed in Qum that both the translation and the subject matter were incomprehensible. An incomplete version of S. Sadeq Shirazi's *'An al-Iqtisad al-Islami* was translated as *Rah-i be-suy-i Bank-i Islami* (Setting up Islamic banking, 1393/1973); the original was not allowed to be published in Iraq. Otherwise there are a series of popular books on the general philosophy of property and social commitment such as Taleghani's *Islam wa Malikiyyat* (Islam and Property, 1340/1942), S. Abdol-Karim Hasheminezhad's *Rah-i Sivvum Bayn-i Komunism va-Sarmayadari* (Third Path Between Capitalism and Communism), and S. Abdul Reza Hejazi's *Sistim-i Iqtisadi-i Islam* (The Islamic Economic System). Most of these were normally under government ban until the 1978 revolution.

Nonetheless the basic principles provided a valid basis at least for an ethical social criticism of state policies under Mohammad Reza Shah. All transactions — as in laissez-faire capitalism — are calculated as contracts between willing and knowledgeable partners. Unlike the situation in laissez-faire capitalism, however, property does not ultimately belong to individuals but to God or the community: individual rights are protected as usufruct rights. The taxation system is intended to redistribute to the public domain and to the poor what is not being used and what, through inevitable inequalities, builds up in the hands of the fortunate. Manuals of commercial morality like the *Makasib* of Shaykh Mortaza Ansari or the commercial sections of the various *Risalat Tawidih al-Masa'il* (Explanatory Text on Problems [of Religion]) are concerned with ensuring the conditions of knowledge and volition: for instance, children may not buy and sell but may only be agents of competent adults; goods may be returned if the buyer finds he bought them above the fair price or if the seller is uncertain of the price and finds he sold for too little. Of these rules, the rules concerning usury are most central and problematic. In Europe, both Christians and Jews eventually came to terms with the biblical injunctions against usury by differentiating between unjust return on money (usury) and just return (interest), thereby bringing the law into harmony with commercial practice and commonsense economic morality. In Islam also this distinction is argued, but it has not yet gained universal acceptance. Indeed the majority opinion in Qum was that all interest is usury. The result is the use of *hiyal-i shar'i* or *kulah-i shar'i* (lawful deceits), *qard-i hasana* (loans of goodness) or *mihrabani* (kindness), and *mukhatira* (contracts) — ways of calculating interest as if it were something else.[13]

There are problems with these principles. The relation between individual rights and the good of the community is but vaguely regulated by personal morality and litigation. This vagueness is recognized by al-Ghazali's metaphor that the bazaar is an arena of jihad, an internal holy war to maintain one's morality when there is temptation to take unfair advantage. Ibn Khaldun similarly spoke of the role of merchant as an occupation taken up as a service to the community but not for its own sake (*fard kifaya*). Another formulation is that the bazaar should be regulated under *hisba* (the religious obligation to avoid evil), and at times there were officials, *muhtasib*, who helped maintain order, set prices, and collect taxes. Second, the theory of ownership — that all may appropriate from nature what they can use — involves a premise of nonscarcity of resources and also perhaps small-scale organization. Given industrial organization, do workers have a free choice to strike a contract on wages? How does one calculate the value of labor in an economy in which, unlike an agro-mercantile economy, one cannot ignore labor as a commodity? Or how would one organize such an economy if one insisted that labor is not to be calculated as a commodity but that private property rights still be respected? Third, can khums, *zakat*, and the other taxes of Islam be applied in a modern economy? Until 1978 this was only an academic question, but one which, for instance, de Zayas (1960) in Syria had tried to work out. Finally there is the debate over usury, or rather over the interpretation of the Qur'anic word *riba*.

From the legal history of the word and its use in the early traditions, it seems clear that the prohibition of riba was intended to counter excessive interest rates and especially debt enslavement that resulted from doubling the principle if a debtor asked for an extension of time for repayment. It was also intended to make explicit equalities and inequalities of exchange and to reduce the uncertainties of speculation, such as in buying pregnant animals or crops that were not yet ripe. In time all interest payments came to be considered riba. The practical arena for debate in 1975 centered on the Islamic banks. These had been set up in many Iranian towns by merchants and ulama as a kind of charity operation: money was contributed and then lent out for small needs such as wedding expenses, opening a shop, and so on; maximum loans were usually 2,000-2,500 tomans ($375) for fifteen months. The borrower paid back the same amount he borrowed. Theoretically this is but one of the two forms of transaction an Islamic bank may engage in, what Shirazi (1393/1973) calls "charity loans," the other being business loans on a *mudariba* basis, that is, as a partnership in which the bank supplies capital for a share of the returns of the venture, whether profits or losses.

As long as Islamic banks were really only for charity loans, they existed on the philanthropy of the rich who did not expect their money back and whose further contributions kept the purchasing power of the bank's capital from deteriorating over time.

PERSONAL MORALITY

The linchpin in both the Islamic political and economic theory ultimately is faith and the morality it inspires: without the volition of all Muslims the edifice of justice collapses. Attention focuses on this especially in the rawdas of the month of Ramadan. The fast itself is meant to be a rededication to Islam, a slight discomfort and rearrangement of routine in order to be more continually conscious of moral commitment. Ramadan is also the month of 'Ali's martyrdom, and he is the focus of many rawdas.

The following rawda was given by Hashem-Iraqi on 8 Ramadan 1395/1975 in the Masjid Husaynabad of Qum:

Khutba (invocation)
Aya (Quranic verse): O believers, prescribed for you is the fast, even as it was prescribed for those that were before you—haply you be God fearing [Sureh Baqare: 177].
Du'a (prayer): That God help us avoid sin.
Salawat (blessings upon the family of the Prophet)
The subject we were discussing yesterday was *ghaybat* (talking behind someone's back). Some friends suggested . . . I should expand my commentary . . . I am also asked why I always give hadith and not *qissa* (stories). If I tell stories, people go to sleep. (Voice: No we won't.) Muslims may go to sleep; all things Muslims do is worship; sleep also is worship. I want to tell a story; now don't go to sleep . . . [He tells the story of a Jew who asks the Prophet the reasons for the Ramadan fast and the seven answers of the latter.]
A Muslim who fasts but after breaking his fast speaks ill of his fellow Muslim does as if he were eating the corpse of his fellow Muslim. Ghaybat is the food of the dogs of hell . . . *ghaybat-i kafir* (speaking ill of an unbeliever) is unimportant, and even *ghaybat-i Musalman ghayr-i mu'min* (speaking ill of Muslims who are not believers), who are not Shi'a, is unimportant. If you slander them it is too bad, but no matter. God does not accord them honor. Sure, non-Shi'a Muslims are clean according to the law (*fiqh*): we can marry with them. But in meaning (*az lihaz-i ma'na*) there is no difference between them and unbelievers. Whoever does not love 'Ali counts equally with an unbeliever. It is only through politics that one says they are Muslims . . . [Ghaybat is forbidden to both speaker and listener. Telling lies is worse. If what you say about a third party is obviously true—if he drinks openly or is openly an eater of usury, a *nuzul-khor*—then commenting on it is permissible.]
Abdu'l-Salt Harawi [servant of Imam Reza] tells the riwayat that God or the Prophet gave Imam Reza the five commands: the first thing you see in

the morning, eat it; the second thing you see, hide it under the soil; the third thing, accept it; the fourth thing, do not disappoint it; the fifth thing, run away from it.

The first thing Imam Reza saw was a large mountain. How shall I eat a mountain? Still God would not order me to do something I cannot do, so let me go a bit closer. The closer he came, the smaller it got, until it was only a bite and a tasty one at that. The second thing he saw was a golden bowl; this he buried. The third thing was a small bird, which an eagle was chasing. He caught the bird. The eagle complained: I am a hunter and I've exerted a lot of energy. So Imam Reza gave him something to replace the bird. The fifth thing was a stinking corpse, from which he ran away. Yes, there is a riwayat of Jarain that a back-biter and a liar's mouth give off a bad smell such that even the angels are irritated. All the people on Judgment Day are irritated . . .

The next night God sent a message: Do you know what all this was about? The dead body from which you ran was ghaybat: whenever you see a corpse eater, do not let him continue . . . The mountain that got smaller was anger (*ghadab*): You should swallow anger and joke it away from others; anger allows us to do all kinds of evil . . . The golden bowl: when you serve someone, hide it from others [poem of Sa'di]; if you do something for others, people will gradually learn of it, you don't have to blow your own horn. The bird was a good advisor: whenever you get good advice, grab it and pay attention. If someone is saying something good and you are not dozing, send a *salawat*. (Audience: Salawat.) Don't let it in one ear and out the other . . . Some of you take it in your ear and hold it, but when you leave the mosque you shake your head and pull your ear and it all falls out . . .

[He tells what a person he would be had he listened to all the good advice he had ever received; he jokes about his age, with audience response; and he relates a story about giving money to beggars even if most beggars are illegitimate. He ends with the *guriz* (the turning to Karbala), a story of Husain giving to a beggar, and finally with a rawda proper (versified version of Karbala intended to draw tears).]

Ghaybat and the idle tongue inveighed against in this rawda are part of a series of sins having to do with honor and reputation, sex roles, the family, and ultimately the harmony of society. One center of concern today is the challenge to male and female behavior patterns presented by the issue of women's liberation. In the rawdas, women are enjoined to be modest, to dress modestly, and not to be *zabandar* (literally, "having a tongue," flirtatious, exhibitionist). Men are enjoined to keep both their gaze and their tongue chaste and to respect the honor of other men (the virtue of ghayrat, conceived as a kind of male strength). There are several forms of honor protected by the religious code (*bab-i diyasat*), including the honor of men which can be lost through the misbehavior of their women (*namus*). But honor can be jeopardized from attacks on reputation and status as well as on the bodily or sexual integrity of the family.[14] It can be imperiled by the tongue as well as by actions such as adultery or murder. Hence the frequent cautionings in rawdas that charges of adultery require direct witnesses; else they are punishable slander.

The ulama have formulated a defense of the Islamic position on women against the pressures of the Pahlavi government and middle class women to follow Kemal Ataturk and the West; see, for example, Motahhari (1353 Sh./1974), Nuri (1343 Sh./1965), Tabatabai (1338 Sh./1960), Voshnui (1392/1972).[15] They begin by attacking the basis for the emancipation movement as rooted in the peculiar experiences of Europe and as destructive of social and psychological harmony. The industrial revolution in Europe caused the atomization of social relations, the breakdown of family and village cooperation, migration to the cities and increased sexual opportunities there, and consequently less need to marry. World War I followed, causing an oversupply of women and forcing widows and unmarried women to work and work for low pay. The ulama argue that Iranian women did not undergo these experiences and that demands for liberation are misplaced imitation of the West, even an imperialist trick of the West to sell European cosmetics and other sex-linked goods (Shariati n.d.: 26).

More important than that the proposed reorganization of male-female relations is being pursued for the wrong reasons is that regulation of sexual passion and morality is felt to be essential lest love, family, and psychological equilibrium be destroyed. The argument ranges from the primal power of passion to the aesthetics of love. Women and men, in the great poet Maulana Rumi's image, are like water and fire; if there is no separation the water extinguishes the fire (Motaheri 1353 Sh./1974). Open display of female beauty leads men to mental illness through desiring more than they are allowed or able to have, and through the alleged ill effects of masturbation, aggravated by the availability of explicit films, books, and magazines (Makarem 1350 Sh./1972). Free sex is empty sex, destroying both love and marriage as a family bond: where sex is limited to husband and wife, marriage is the arena of sexual freedom; where sex is not so limited, marriage becomes a restriction, a prison (Motaheri 1353 Sh./1974). Love is a volatile force which causes as much misery as joy; the misery is tragic or evil depending on how voluntary the affliction. Ibn al-Qayyim (fourteenth century A.D.) likened love to alcohol: the intoxication is involuntary, for it is the effect of alcohol on the body, but taking the first drink is voluntary (cited by Giffen 1971). The intoxication of love leads to the overpowering of the rational soul (*'aql*) by baser nature (*nafs*); the ensuing madness can lead to sins of incest, murder, suicide, and the enslavement of the self to another rather than only to God (*islam*). Veiling is a natural device of the female, not only for modesty but in the sexual game of the chased-chaser, spider-fly. Where in the West is love? Where in the modern West are to be found truly great love stories such as those of Layla and Majnun or Khusraw and Shirin?

Third, the ulama argue, Islam raised the status of women from that of chattel to that of full persons with legal rights: women may work, demand wages, get inheritance, control property, choose their spouses, initiate divorce. And they point to legal disabilities of women in the West. A Muslim woman is required to be modest, but she is not technically required to cover her face or hands; therefore she may engage in any activity and go any place a man may, but only up to the point of disturbing society by arousing desires.

Women are not — in the male ulama apologia — equal to men. They are after all biologically different: they bear children, they menstruate, they are more emotional. If they are more emotional, then society is better off if government, war, and justice are left to men. In household management the philosophy of Islam, says Tabatabai (1338 Sh./1960: 25): is that one should keep management in the hands of the partner with more reason and spending in the hands of the partner with more emotion. For the consent necessary for a good marriage, both men and women must be able to choose their spouses and initiate divorce, but to give fully equal divorce rights to emotional women would only drive up the divorce rates, an antisocial result. It is good for women to study, and there are learned women who have taught men as well as women, but technically — say the male mujtahids — a woman may not become a mujtahid. Why? To be a religious leader and model for others to follow, one must not be incapacitated religiously, intellectually, or biologically. And, to quote the famous sermon of the first Imam, 'Ali,[16]

> [Women] are deficient in faith, deficient in shares, and deficient in intelligence. As regards the deficiency in their faith, it is their abstention from prayers and fasting during their menstrual period. As regards deficiency in their intelligence, it is because the evidence of two women is equal to that of one man. As for the deficiency of their shares, that is because of their share in inheritance being half of men. So beware of the evils of women. Be on your guard even from those of them who are reportedly good. Do not obey them even in good things so that they may not attract you to evils. (Qibla 1972: 116-117)

All the apologia avoid the fact that Iranian society is changing. Perhaps it is not changing exactly as Europe did, but a transformation from a patrimonial-agricultural society to an industrial-technocratic one is going on. In an agricultural society it is plausible to argue that men and women have different but equal roles which conform to the Islamic morality revealed in 'Ali's sermon. When the sale of labor becomes the basis of income and personal valuation, it becomes increasingly difficult to justify differential access to work and pay on the basis of sex. But, the apologists would argue, Islam does not do this: there is no reason for a woman not to work and not to get equal pay as long as she deports herself with modesty. Indeed, say some of the religious young women, why all the hullabaloo about veiling: why should wearing a veil prevent one from going to the university or driving a car?

There are two sources of confusion. First, the Pahlavi state was not as flexible as it might have been. It pressed for unveiling and gave little support to young women who tried to work out solutions of modern Islamic life styles. This was particularly the case in education, where conservative parents frequently would take their daughters out of school after the sixth grade because the girls were forbidden to veil in school and because they would be taught by men as well as women. Some semireligious schools were established in a number of cities, where girls could veil and were taught only by female teachers. But there was concern that these schools, like all other private schools, gradually would be absorbed by the state system.[17]

Second, the ulama were in practice much more conservative than their mildly liberal statements implied. There was no real reason, for instance, that women should not be mujtahids if they were sufficiently learned. Yet the *Risala-i Tawdih al-Masa'il* of all the current maraji'-i taqlid insisted that one may only be a *muqalllid* (follower) of a mujtahid who is male (see Shariatmadari 1353 Sh./1975: 9; Khoi 1391/1971: 2). An interesting case in point was a woman in Isfahan, Banu Amin, author of a respected tafsir.

Informally she was called a mujtahid and she herself claimed the title and claimed to have an *ijaza* (license) from Ayatullah Marashi-Najafi, among others. Upon reflection, however, most ulama said that technically she could not be a mujtahid,[18] and they would cite the litany of female inferiorities starting with those in the sermon of 'Ali just quoted. Yahya Nuri, a professor at the Theological Faculty of the University of Tehran, even cited the nineteenth-century argument that women statistically have smaller brains hence less reason; and he gives a series of hadiths supporting the thesis that because women are emotional, justice, war and government should be left to men (1343 Sh./1965: 268-270). Particularly interesting in the Banu Amin case is that although she claims the title of mujtahid, she does agree that women are more emotional and therefore should not have fully equal rights of divorce (A. Betteridge, personal communication).

A more curious arena of personal morality is that of music and even, according to some, poetry. Why are they forbidden (*haram*)? This prohibition is particularly curious in a society that prides itself on its music and poetry. The prohibition is traced to several Qur'anic verses (Hajj: 30; Luqman: 6; Furqan: 72; Asrar: 39) and their explanation in several hadith (see 'Alam al-Huda 1352/1977). The key terms are *laghw* (idle tongue) and *ghina'* (song, pointless noise): one should not have an idle tongue; songs arouse the emotions and thus, in one tradition attributed to the Prophet, are a preliminary to adultery.[19] The question then arises whether the call to prayer, rawdas, the chant of the Qur'an, and nawha (praises to God) are not music. To this the answer is the Qur'anic verse "Read the Qur'an prettily (*tartil*)" and the hadith "He is not my follower who does not read the Qur'an with *taghanni*," where *taghanni* is said to be a form of *ghina* (richness) not *ghina'* (song). Clearly the concern parallels that of reason in matters of law: just as one is not free to issue any opinion (*fatwa*) as one is in philosophy, so there is a distinction between music that is disciplined and subordinated to intellectual and spiritual control and music for the sake of emotional expression.

REFORMING UTOPIA?

The charges that the ulama have fallen behind the times and that their training system and their mode of interpreting Islam need reform are not new charges. Khomeyni, responding to Kasravi in 1943, established some criteria for the acceptability of reformers:

> There are good and bad in every occupation. The ruhani do need reform but it cannot be done by someone illiterate like Reza Khan, who does not even know whether ruhani is spelled with ط or ح [a *he havvaz* or a *he hotti*]. All his attempts have been bad. He turned the Sepah Salar Mosque into the Danishkada-i Ma'qul va Manqul to train ruhanis for parliament, but he had them mix with unveiled women and they turned out badly . . . Conditions for a reformer: a ruhani himself who knows the course of study; belief that ruhani are needed and religion is needed; pure intention and not pursuing self-aggrandizement; wisdom and influence; that is, being one of the first-rank ulama. (pp. 202-203)

In 1962 a group of Qum graduates and others met to discuss the need for reform after the death of Ayatullah Borujerdi. They subsequently published a volume of essays: *Bahht-i darbara-i marja'iyyat va ruhaniyyat* (1341/1962). They argued for the establishment of some stronger form of collective leadership and for a strengthening of the historical understanding of hadith and ijtihad, subjects in which Borujerdi had had great interest. They demanded the modern mujtahids be conversant with contemporary problems (see especially Bazargan 1341/1962: 112) and that specialization and division of labor, as Shaykh Abdol-Karim Haeri-Yazdi had earlier suggested, was a most reasonable way of helping them attain the necessary familiarity.

Borujerdi had called for a further codification and annotation of the hadith literature collected in Shaykh al-Hurr al-'Amili's *Wasa'il al-shi'a* (Methodology of Shi'ism). 'Amili had separated correct hadith from questionable ones; the further annotation was completed by Borujerdi's

students as *Tahdhib al-wasa'il* (Refinement of the Methodology). Borujerdi himself had constructed a table of generations of rawis (relators of
the traditions), counting himself among the thirty-sixth generation, as a
way of codifying the chains of transmission. This presumably could lead
to a better appreciation of the development of the religious sciences,
against the charge that the ulama treated religion as totally ahistorical.
The Qum graduates also gave some attention to the budgetary and curriculum problems of Qum (see chapter 3).

In 1959-1962 a group of ulama, including many of those later
represented in the *Marja'iyyat va Ruhaniyyat* volume, began to collect
some of their speeches in a journal called *Guftar-i Mah* (Monthly
Speeches). The speeches so collected were ones that reflected upon the
need to redefine Shi'ite positions vis-à-vis the contemporary world. An
outgrowth was the establishment in northeastern Tehran of the Husayniyya Irshad, a mosque and modern teaching facility that served as a
forum for working out modern Shi'ite views. Around the same time, or
subsequently, other institutions were being founded such as the journal
Maktab-i Islam and the school, Dar al-Tabligh, of Shariatmadari in
Qum; the Kanun-i Bahth Wa Intiqad-i Dini (Center for Religious Discussion and Criticism) of Abtahi and Hasheminezhad in Mashhad; and later
a Husayniyya Irshad in Shiraz under Mahallati, which was aborted when
the Pahlavi government began to exert pressure on the original group in
Tehran. The discussions generated debate quite widely among religious
folk, and a number of lay preachers as well as ruhani became prominent
leaders: professors Mehdi Bazargan (thermodynamics), Ali Shariati
(history), Morteza Motahhari (theology); and ruhani S. Mahmud
Taleghani, S. Mortaza Jazayeri.

Of these, Dr. Shariati emerged as the cynosure of attention. Fired
from the University of Mashhad for his Islamic activities, he moved to
Tehran and organized classes in the Husayniyya Irshad, billing them as
working sessions toward an Islamic sociology. Trained at the Sorbonne,
his intellectual terms of reference and use of examples are French—thus
his use, already cited, of Algeria and Madagascar rather than Vietnam to
point to the moral failings of liberal democracy.[20] Both the challenge to
create an Islamic sociology and the claim that he embodied through his
training a direct dialogue with the latest thinkers of the West provided
Shariati with a vast audience, particularly among the religious youth in
the secular educational system, but also in the madrasas.

In perhaps his most popular work, *Ummat wa Imamat* (Community
and Leadership) (1351/1972), Shariati does three important things:

(1) He calls for rethinking the Islamic message. He states the need in
three ways. One needs to think about Islam in sociological terms rather
than metaphysical terms. Islam has become like medieval Catholicism,
negative toward life and full of alien beliefs; it needs a Protestant refor-

mation. The methods of the old akhunds are no longer suitable; methods are needed for new generations that can and will insist on thinking for themselves.

(2) He attempts to introduce critical methods. He does a rough content analysis of the Qur'an to demonstrate that the Qur'an is primarily concerned with social rules rather than with details of worship.[21] He does a linguistic-phenomenological analysis of key Islamic terms contrasting them with Western concepts. For instance, in discussing the contrast between politics and *siyasat* he tries to show that the Islamic terms for community (*ummat, imamat,* from *amm* "decision to go") are dynamic in a sense unlike all other terms for community: "nation," or those of common birth; "class," or those of one life style; "society" (*ijtima', jami'a*), or those of one set; "race," or those of one body form; "tribe" (*ta'ifa, qabila*) or those who circumambulate (*tawaf*) around one center or have one goal (*qibla*), such as a common pasture—all these Shariati dismisses as static. The Imam or leader in Shi'ism is both a model to other men and a leader; he is not a hero created by the fantasies of men in their need to identify with a powerful figure.

(3) He makes a preliminary political statement about the fundamental opposition between Islam and the backward countries on the one side and bourgeois democratic capitalism on the other. There is the assertion that social reform is impossible in a democratic context and thus the standard Shi'ite observation that Islam is not something created by popular election but is a set of divine directives for a just society. There is also the warning that Western models and exhortations are in the service of subordinating Islam and other third-world countries to the needs of Western capitalism. Here the mechanisms of underconsumption and of alienation and assimilation are introduced, together with the analysis of women's liberation as a form of colonial domination by the West.

These should be fundamental intellectual breakthroughs for modernist Shi'ite thought: the emphasis on new responses for changing conditions rather than the deadening insistence that Islam is timeless, ahistorical, and changeless; the possibility of comparative phenomenology which could allow an appreciation of other people's points of view rather than the traditional blinders "we are right, they are wrong"; and the possibility of an analytic understanding of historical forces such as capitalist imperialism. Further, one should remember that Shariati claimed only to be one Muslim trying to think things through, with all the implied possibilities for error and need for help from others. Indeed, according to the ulama, when Shariati first began, he made a large number of blatant mistakes (see table 5.1). For example, in the first version of *Islamshenasi* (Islamic Studies) he tried to illustrate Islam's progressive democratic spirit by citing two Qur'anic verses which he said referred to the election of the caliphs. The rejection of the election of the caliphs is a cardinal doctrine of Shi'ism, and so Shariati raised a furor.[22] Since then he has adjusted his formulations in accord with traditional Shi'ism[23] and reevaluated his democratic liberalism.

The same sort of corrective process was not available regarding his use of Western ideas as the ulama provide for his Shi'ism. So what should have been fundamental intellectual breakthroughs were vitiated by what was perhaps a necessity imposed by his audience to insist on the Islamic monopoly over truth and in so doing to misrepresent non-Islamic thought. He failed, in other words, to provide the bridge between Islam and the basically secular thought not only of the West but also of the Persian ruling elite. By falsifying the outside world, he reinforced isolation and increased the possibilities for political demagoguery rather than knowledgeable self-reliance.

For instance, it was unfortunate, but not surprising, that Shariati should not rise above the popular theory of a Jewish conspiracy controlling Western capitalism. In describing how liberal democracy is made a mockery by behind-the-scenes maneuvering, he asked rhetorically why American presidents were so friendly to the *Jahudha-yi khar-pul* (Jews who have so much money they need a donkey to move it). There was less reason to contrast Buddhism as worship of leaders who serve as brokers to escape the world with Islam as worship of God, with leaders as only guides (1350 Sh./1972: 78). What would be so humiliating to Islam about recognizing that for Buddhists the Buddha is an exemplary model as the Imams are for Shi'ites or that there are Muslims and Buddhists who worship these extraordinary human figures? Again, why must Camus be described as saying that since morality is an empty form of talk, one should enjoy oneself until death (p. 90), ignoring the onerous but positive philosophy that makes man the sole moral agent and creator of meaning, particularly when this could be either contrasted to Islam's advantage or incorporated in an Islamic framework of individual responsibility? Again and finally—though there are other examples—had Shariati never read Marx or was it deliberate falsification when he said he could not forgive Marx and the socialists for their lack of concern about the third world and for only worrying about getting the European lower classes a share in the profits of raping the third world?

To the uncharitable reader, Shariati displays a cavalier attitude toward facts and consistent explanations. To the charitable reader, he is in a process of working out acceptable formulations. Thus the notion of third-world assimilé as an emptied blind imitator clearly intrigues and bothers him, perhaps because (as a former friend of his caustically commented) he was a prime potential example. The assimilés clearly cannot provide leadership to their own countrymen, for they have become alienated and tools of the West. As in the past with prophets, so today, moral and intellectual leaders arise not from the nobles or priests, not from the

Table 5.1 Shariati's mistakes in dogma, according to "Husayni" and Makarem (1350/1971)

SHARIATI'S VERSION	NATURE OF MISTAKE
In *Islamshenasi* (Islamic Studies): Shariati relates the riwayat of the houses that opened directly into the mosque. The Prophet ordered all the doors sealed, except that of Abu Bakr.	False riwayat. This version is related by 'Ikrima, a known liar, who also interpreted the Qur'anic verse about the giving of a ring during prayers as referring to Abu Bakr instead of 'Ali. The riwayat about the mosque is related in twelve other versions in Sunni texts, all saying the unsealed door belonged to 'Ali.
At the end of his life Muhammad was too sick to lead prayers, so Abu Bakr did. Muhammad improved and came to the mosque, but refused to lead prayers, praying beside Abu Bakr instead.	Weak hadith. This hadith has been related a number of times and there are ten points of contradiction in the versions.
Election of the caliphs shows the majority-rule spirit of Islam: the notion of ijma'.	Ignorance of the meaning of ijma', which is unanimity and accordance with the meaning of the Qur'an, not mere majority. Election of the caliphs was neither democratic nor in accordance with Islam.
In *Che Bayad Kard* (What must be done?): Music is an Islamic art	The Qur'anic verse on *laghw* (pointless noise) is the justification for the prohibition of music.
In *Sima-yi Muhammad* (The Glory of Muhammad): Zoroaster, Buddha, Confucius, Lao-tze were prophets.	None of these had a divine religion.

In *Tashayyu' 'Alavi va Tashayyu' Safavi* ('Alid Shi'ism and Safavid Shi'ism):
Think how powerful Islam would appear in history if Muslims disregarded all the internal divisions; all the Sunni heroes, like Saladin, would be also Shi'ite heroes.

The Safavids rewrote history, joining the daughter of the last Sassanian king in marriage to Imam Husayn so that Persians could claim the Imams as Iranian.

In *Abu Dharr*:
'Ali would swear allegiance to Abu Bakr.

Saladin was an enemy of Shi'ism: he made 'Ashura a holiday, burned Shi'ite books, and killed Shi'ites. Think of all the Shi'ites killed by Sunnis, the fatwa of Shaykh Nuh Hanafi declaring Shi'ites to be kafir so the Ottomans could kill ten thousand Shi'ites.

Shaykh Mufid related this five hundred years before the Safavids.

'Ali never swore allegience to Abu Bakr while Fatima was alive. Fatima gave public khutba (sermons) on the illegitimacy of the caliphate election.

assimilé, but from the ordinary folk, from the masses. His examples are not totally convincing—Leopold Senghor, Aimé Caesire, Frantz Fanon—all French-educated, elite, thinking people, but not exactly men from the masses who use their religion tenaciously (*taasub*) to shield their people against cultural imperialism. Indeed Shariati admits his failure to convince Fanon of the usefulness of Islam in this regard. Whereas in *Farhang wa Ideoloji* (Culture and Ideology, 1350/1971) Shariati says all the prophets arose from the people, in *Are, Inchunin Bud, Baradar* (Yes, This Is How It Was, Brother, 1391/1971) he admits that all except Muhammad and his successor 'Ali were bought off by or were themselves of the ruling class, as were the ruhani of Islam. That Muhammad is the champion of the working class makes an interesting slogan, though of doubtful historical validity, just as is his claim (disputed by the ulama) that the Safavids completely remolded Shi'ism.

Despite all reservations, Shariati's call for reevaluation, self-reliance, and relevance was popular, and during the revolution it proved to be a powerful reference frame for ideological mobilization in which Khomeyni could be seen as the leader arising from the masses, without thereby abdicating to clerical rule:

> We need a leader like ['Ali] now. Our ruhani are as if they were in a *dakhma* (platform for exposing corpses) only concerned with worship. A new slavery had come under the name of freedom. Education, culture, sexual freedom, consumption, are the slogans. But they have taken from us purpose and responsibility. We are like a water jug: pretty but empty and taking in whatever is given us. We debate idiotically that this group does namaz with folded arms while that group does it with arms open; that this one uses a muhr and that one does not. (1351/1972)

Ritual Drama and Popular Shi'ism

On the eve of 'Ashura (the tenth of Muharram) the city of Yazd throbs with activity—lantern lights, chanting, preparations—as did the camp of Imam Husayn on the desert battlefield thirteen centuries ago. The great shrine, Imamzada Ja'far, its recently mirrored interior (a gift of the merchant Hajj Mohammad-Ali Rohanian) glittering and reflecting light, is packed with people sitting, praying, weeping, and invoking divine aid. At each of the two town squares, Maydan-i Shah and Mir Chak Mak, there is a black-draped and mirrored *naql* (a huge, tear-shaped, wooden structure, requiring a hundred men to lift it, representing the coffin of Husayn). Groups of black-shirted young men (dastas) light candles there and chant simple lines:

Shab-i 'Ashurast,	It is the eve of Ashura,
Karbala ghawghast,	Karbala is in commotion,
Karbala che jur shin-ast,	How sandy is Karbala,
Shab-i akhir shab-ast	It is the final evening.

In the square by the shrine Shahzadeh Fazel other dastas, in parallel lines facing each other, beat their backs with chains or beat their chests with open palms and chant. From all "seventeen" neighborhoods, they parade through a tent decorated with printed cloth from Isfahan,[24] keeping up a steady rhythm of flagellation and chanting. Many of these dastas proceed to the house of Herati, the first great factory owner of Yazd, where they perform and are given financial contributions. Near another square, in the house of Golshan, and along Iranshahr street, *ash-i Imam Husayn* (a thick stew in the name of the martyr of Karbala) is brewed in huge cauldrons. In the Akbarabad neighborhood a sufra (feast with freshly slaughtered sheep and rice) is given. In Bagh-e-Safa—a large forum on the edge of town—a huge rawda is held for women only. Smaller rawdas are held in various neighborhood mosques. In the Husayniyya 'Arabha (the forum for refugees from Iraq), the pitch of flagellation by the dastas reaches such an emotional level that women are excluded, because the men strip themselves to the waist to beat themselves.[25]

The naql is supposed to be carried at noon on Ashura, marking the three-fold desecration committed by the army of Yazid under Shimr and Ibn Sa'd: they shed the blood of the Imam, they shed his blood during the time for Friday noon prayer, they shed blood during the holy month of Moharram when fighting is supposed to be suspended. In 1936 Reza Shah outlawed the carrying of the naql in the city, the ceremony continues in three large villages outside Yazd, accompanied by parades of floats representing the events of Karbala (see appendix for lists of floats). As in town, activities build to a climax during the first ten days of Muharram. Each evening there are rawdas in the several neighborhood mosques, consisting of a series of speeches lasting from ten minutes to half an hour each. At mid-evening lines of dastas form; beating their backs and chests in rhythm with their chanting, they lead the local assemblies to the central Congregational Mosque of the village, where more rawdas are read by more important preachers brought from as far as Tehran, punctuated from time to time by processions of dastas. On 'Ashura (the tenth), the day Imam Husayn was martyred, crowds gather from Yazd city and surrounding areas to watch the dastas, the floats, and finally at noon the carrying of the naql to the chant of "Husayn, Husayn." Some men may still cut themselves on the forehead, although this is illegal.

Meanwhile in town on 'Ashura Day, the Barkhordar Mosque (endowed by the industrialist of that name) becomes the focal center to which all dasta groups come. On the edge of the town, in the Arestan graveyard, processions of people collect to march with standards and carry two small naqls to their villages. Given the ulama's hostility to Sufism, one of the interesting dasta groups is that of Posht-e-Bagh Neighborhood, which is led by a darvish singing to the accompaniment of a flute:

Baz divana shodam	I've become ecstatic
Zanjir ku!	Where are the chains?
Man Husaynullaham	I'm God's own Husayn
Takfir ku!	Call me kafir [if you will]!

On the third day after Ashura, the Mulla Ismail Mosque, behind the
bazaar, becomes the focal center for the dasta groups. This is the day
that the Bani Asad found the headless body of Husayn and buried it. A
special shovel-and-pick dasta, carrying mats and headless bodies, often
with a mourning lion putting straw on its head, chants: "The Bani Asad
have come to bury Husayn."

In 1932 Reza Shah outlawed the performance of passion plays (*shabih*
and *ta'ziya*) but in the villages of Yazd (and elsewhere in Iran) they are
still produced with greater or lesser elaborateness. Where they are most
elaborate, each night there is a play corresponding to the events of that
day thirteen centuries ago (see appendix). Although the following
description was written of events observed in India in the last century, it
gives a flavor of the passion of Ashura:

> The thronging visitors at first cover the whole area of the enclosure,
> laughing and talking like a crowd at a fair . . . a signal is given . . . muffled
> beating of a drum in slow time, the measured beats becoming faster and
> more faint, until step by step the people . . . are hushed . . . a moullah
> enters the pulpit and intones a sort of "argument" or prelude . . . "O ye
> Faithful, give ear! and open your hearts to the wrongs and sufferings of His
> Highness the Imam Ali, the vice regent of the Prophet, and let your eyes
> flow with tears" . . . For a while he proceeds amid the deep silence of the
> eager audience, but as he goes on, they will be observed to be swaying to
> and fro, and all together; at first almost imperceptibly, but gradually with a
> motion that becomes more and more marked. Suddenly a stifled sob is
> heard, or a cry, followed by more and more sobbing and crying and rapidly
> the swaying to and fro becomes a violent agitation of the whole assembly,
> which rises in a mass, every one smiting his breast with an open hand, and
> raising the wild rhythmical wail of "Ya Ali! ai Hasan! ai Hussein! ai Hasan!
> ai Hussein! Hussein Shah!" As the wailing gathers force, and threatens to
> become ungovernable, a chorus of mourners, which has formed almost
> without observation on the arena, begins chanting, in regular Gregorian
> music, a metrical version of the story, which calls back the audience from
> themselves and imperceptibly at last soothes and quiets them again. At the
> same time the celebrants come forward, and take up the "properties"
> before the *tabut*, and one represents Hussein, another al-Abbas, his
> brother. (Pelly 1879:1, xix)

This annual ritual drama in fact lasts the entire year. The Shi'ite calendar invests the entire year with meaning in terms of Karbala-related
stories. This is clearest in the month of Ramadan, which in contrast with
the Sunni calendar has become a memorial for 'Ali, with preliminaries in

the preceding month (Sha'ban) and intensification of activity during the last ten days, the days of *i'tikaf* (retreat into prayer), ending with the great feast of 'Id-i Fitr; all of these moments are invested with special Shi'ite meaning. The fifteenth of Sha'ban is the night on which the names of the living are written on the leaves of the tree of life, and the leaves that fall are those who will die in the coming year; but in Shi'ite Iran, the fifteenth of Sha'ban is also the birthday of the twelfth Imam. The days of i'tikaf, the last ten days of Ramadan, are dedicated to the memory of 'Ali and celebration for the gift of revelation of the Qur'an.

This process of systematizing and focusing attention on the parables of 'Ali and Husayn can be seen elsewhere as well. Other aspects of Islamic history are not necessarily denied, but emphasis is selective. The focus is on positive family relationships when discussing the family of the Prophet, the five pure souls (Muhammad, Fatima, 'Ali, Husayn and Hasan). During rawdas and ta'ziya, tears are most easily brought by referring to parents seeing their children martyred, to orphaned children crying for their parents, and to siblings caring for one another. Antagonistic family relationships are played down or left unexplored, with the exception of the mother-in-law problem in the Disobedient Son passion play collected by Lewis Pelly, although even here the Shi'ite explanations stress harmony.[26] Such family antagonisms as are recognized are external to the Prophet's family and are treated more as defects in character and faith than structural problems of the family. Thus 'A'isha, the vivacious young wife of the Prophet and daughter of Abu Bakr, carries on a feud with 'Ali for a variety of fairly obvious reasons;[27] but in Shi'ite homelitics this conflict is reduced to admonitions about the proper place of women. To Western observers, much of the feuding over the caliphate seems to be of a piece with the kinship relations between Abu Bakr, 'Umar (both fathers-in-law of the Prophet), 'Uthman (son-in-law of the Prophet, also from a clan whose leadership of the Quraysh was surplanted by the Prophet's grandfather), and 'Ali (son-in-law and cousin of the Prophet). Even Shimr, an archvillain without redeeming features, is maternally related to 'Abbas, the loyal half-brother of Husayn.

If one compares the story of Joseph in the Bible with the same story in the Qur'an and as it is elaborated in the passion plays, one sees this process at work. In the Bible, family antagonisms are open and complicated: Joseph creates difficulties by favoring one son; the story is already grounded in a legacy of intrigue by Jacob and his mother in getting the birthright from Isaac; Joseph's brothers clearly wrestle with ambivalent feelings: jealousy and hatred of Joseph, yet guilt and desire merely to get him out of the way, plus love of but annoyance at their father. In the Qur'an and the passion plays, this is all simplified: only Joseph's second dream occurs and it is interpreted by Jacob; the dream is a significant one — a message from God — hence the jealousy of the brothers is a defect in faith and lack of submission to the will of God; Joseph is very much aware of the jealousy of his brothers and has to be repeatedly assured by them of his safety before he agrees to accompany them; Jacob has to be cajoled to let Joseph go; there is foreknowledge on the part of both Joseph and Jacob, a sense of sacrifice being demanded like that demanded of Abraham and Ishmael, and an explicit reassurance by Gabriel that the sacrifice and suffering demanded of them is nothing compared with what will be demanded of the family of the Prophet at Karbala; the failure in faith and duty of the brothers is underlined in their refusal to give Joseph water, as Shimr would refuse water to the family of Husayn at Karbala. In the passion plays the parallel is taken one step further: the martyrs of Karbala, especially Husayn, refer to themselves as Josephs whose coats/bodies are rent by wild wolves and besplattered with blood, but who will themselves go on to be viziers in the next world, able to intercede for their people. Although it is worked out somewhat differently, it is interesting that in the Jewish rabbinic tradition, too, willingness to be sacrificed and suffer as a sign of obedience to God becomes the interpretation of the Joseph story.[28]

These comparisons of codification — Sunni, Shi'a, biblical, qur'anic, rabbinic — provide an initial access to the processes of keeping religion meaningful. There is a dynamic of rationalization — explaining the stories ethically and systematizing them. Indeed a major claim of Islam over the Judaeo-Christian tradition is that the Bible is full of contradictions and of allegations of sin against the messengers and upholders of God's law, indicating (to the Muslim) falsification of the divine book. But that is only step one. Step two is the provision in Islam of the proper version without the contradictions. On the other hand, rationalization has a limited claim on the mind; after a point, what once were complex multifaceted stories illuminating reality in a variety of ways become lifeless formulas of dogma and ultimately decay into obsolescence. This is the charge of the white-collar reformers (and their allies among the ulama) such as Ali Shariati and Engineer Bazargan, and, in the same tradition earlier, Zeynol-Abedin Rahnema, the author of what was in the 1930s considered an audacious and impertinent, nigh blasphemous, biography of the Prophet (treating the story as one would any popular biography).

The sources of creativity and maintenance of vitality require two dimensions of investigation: historical and ethnographic. Ethnographically, one can make only two points through evocative description and citing of native opinions. First, one source of vitality is the embodiment of the stories in popular drama and ritual: the events of Muharram and Ramadan; the weekly meetings (*hay'at madhhabi*) to practice *madh* and *nawha* (songs of praise), prayers (like the beautiful

du'a Komeil), chants to be used by dastas, Qur'an reading and the activities of the gymnasiums (*zurkhana*). This can be elaborated
sociologically in terms of who participates and who provides patronage
funds; but to get a sense of the importance of this sociological information one needs a historical-comparative perspective.

Second, ethnographic analysis can suggest how the Karbala story, for
instance, pulls together in a universal way anxieties and sufferings on
several dimensions and attempts to present acceptable solutions. To
create a sense of universality, certain images and metaphors are stressed
to connect the entire history of the world to Karbala. Thus Adam steps
down upon the plain of Karbala and cuts his toe, losing some blood; he is
told that this is a foreshadowing of the blood of martyrdom his descendants will suffer here. The heat and thirst suffered at Karbala by the
family of Husayn are compared to the heat and thirst on Judgment Day
and paralleled by Abraham's ordeal by fire. The willingness of Abraham
to sacrifice Ishmael parallels the sacrifice of Muhammad's son Ibrahim,
the self-sacrifice of 'Ali, and the martyrdom of Husayn. Through such
identifications and the foreknowledge that prophets are assumed to have
(stemming in part from their creation before all other creation—the doctrines of the light of Muhammad and the luminous virgin birth of Husayn to Fatima), one can go back and forth between stories. In the version of the seizure of the caliphate by Abu Bakr collected by Pelly (1879)
'Ali foretells to Fatima what will befall the family, using a technique of
pairing the indignities and pain he and Fatima will suffer with those of
Husayn at Karbala:

Two necks will be pierced by arrows: 'Ali's neck is only so threatened by
'Umar; Husayn's neck will be pierced.
Two heads will droop in chains: 'Ali is dragged before Abu Bakr by
'Umar; Zayn-al 'Abidin is dragged to Damascus before Yazid.
Two sides will be hurt: Fatima, when 'Umar forces the door against her,
falls down; Husayn, when his side is pierced by a dagger, will roll in
agony from side to side.
Two arms will be broken by flogging: Fatima's by 'Umar's whip; Zay-
nab's by Shimr.
Two hands will be cut: both belonging to 'Abbas.
Two marriages will be funerals: Fatima's wedding at which seventy-two
camels were slain; Qasim's at which seventy-two people were slain.

Death, suffering, political injustice, poverty, kinship emotions, honor
and group identity, need for expiation—all these strings are plucked.
Death is a welcome escape from a world of tribulation, if one is good and
a partisan of Husayn. Being a partisan of Husayn means not only
witnessing but active work, which holds the promise, as a Christian could
put it, of creating the Kingdom of God on Earth and by attempting that,

even in failure, of achieving personal redemption. The crying and dasta flagellation represent both the expiation of the sins of the Kufans (all Shi'ite sinners) who sold out Husayn and a continuous funeral for the martyr of Karbala, who was not given a proper burial, and for his ideals which were never implemented. The perseverance of his family without food and water and the similar perseverance of his parents under similar circumstances are models for the believers and badges of their moral identity. For Yazid to drag Zaynab off to Damascus uncovered and disheveled is an attack on the honor of the Prophet's family, but one that is defeated by Zaynab's heroic steadfastness and leadership. As the sufferings of the various characters of the family are related, people say they recall the trials and sufferings of their own beloved relatives and friends.

It would be of interest to be able to trace the ebbs and flows in the usage of the Karbala story in different historical periods so as to estimate the effects of royal and local elite patronage as contrasted with effects of ulama or popular elaboration. Unfortunately, the available historiography is only sketchily suggestive. There are claims that the mourning for Husayn runs very deep in Persian culture, going back to a pre-Islamic mourning for the hero Siavush. In Abbasid times, the poet Sudayf read *marthiyas* (dirges) about Husayn to the Caliph Saffah, which so worked up the caliph that he had Umayyad bodies cut up into little pieces and ate lunch over them (Javahir-Kalam: 1335/1956:20). Singing the virtues of 'Ali (*manaqib-khwani*) was a Shi'a propaganda technique in Buyid times, and the Buyids also supported ta'ziya. In the Seljuq period, *manaqib-khwani* on the part of Shi'ites was countered by Sunni *fada'il-khwans* who extolled Abu Bakr and 'Umar at the expense of Shi'ites. The passion plays apparently began to flower in the seventeenth century under the Safavids, and were supported by the Qajars who built a royal tekke (stage) for their performance in Tehran. Fath-'Ali Shah had his personal rawda-khwan, Mulla 'Abbas Gharqi, who read rawdas on Friday eve. There are a number of famous rawda-khwans in the Nasiruddin Shah period, and stories of competition among them. In one such story, when Hajj Mulla Aqa came out of the Tekke Hajj Mulla 'Arab in Tehran, he found that his rival had stolen his horse so that he could not proceed to his next engagement. He therefore began to sing the Rawda Dhu'l-Jinah (the horse of Husayn) in the street, and all the people poured out of the tekke leaving the rival alone inside; the rival found another horse to send Mulla Aqa on his way. The Pahlavi dynasty was hostile to these activities, although in the early years of his reign, Mohammad Reza Shah gave financial support to a number of the twenty named *hay'at-i 'azadari* (mourning groups) of Qum.

It is clear that over the past centuries royal and local elite (like the merchant-industrial elite mentioned for Yazd: Herati, Ruhanian, Barkhorda) patronage has been involved in ta'ziya or 'azadari (mourning ceremonies), though to varying extents; but one can only speculate that one effect may have been a kind of sublimation of discontents in a nonpolitical direction. During the 1940s and early 1950s Herati was painted by the Tudeh party as an archenemy of the people, a Mercedes-driving capitalist exploiter; cartoons showed him dropping his workers into a meat grinder to squeeze out their lifeblood. It would be of interest to know whether dastas paraded to his house during Muharram in those days as they did as late as 1975. Obversely, the emotional power of 'azadari is revealed not only in tales such as that of Caliph Saffah but in the fact that many "religious" riots that can be explained as expressions of fairly concrete economic, social, and political discontents, were touched off in the two months of intense 'azadari, Muharram and Ramadan (see Fischer 1973: appendix 1).

Some of this dual potential can be illustrated in the now dying celebration of the death of 'Umar. Effigies were constructed of 'Umar with wood, straw, cloth, donkey turds, firecrackers; neighborhoods would compete to make more impressive effigies, and obscene verses would be composed (see Fischer 1973: 302-304). The effigies would eventually be burned, and in towns with Sunni inhabitants, such as those along the Gulf, this often led to fighting. The ulama, however, often tried to turn the date into a moral lesson, saying in their preaching that burning 'Umar in effigy was not right, for "You people may be worse than 'Umar: you lie, you fornicate, you sin as he never did; 'Umar at times was just and good, his main sin was merely that he wanted to be caliph so badly he ignored the divine right of 'Ali (*haqq-i 'Ali zir-i pa kard*)." A popular rawda for the day is constructed around the hadith that he whom God loves must wait longest for an answer to a prayer: when an evil person raises his head in supplication, the angels ask God to give him what he wants that he may put his head down again, whereas when a good person raises his head in supplication, the angels wish to gaze upon it. There is then a guriz (turning) to a rawda of Fatima, wherein it is told that when 'Umar struck her by opening the door into her side, she cursed him, but it took eighteen years for him to die.

Much of the 'azadari activity is organized by the various *hay'at-i madhhabi* (religious circles), often led by bazaar merchants or organized around neighborhood mosques. One interesting minor development of the Shi'ite drama during the 1970s was the addition of legends surrounding the figure of Ayatullah Khomeyni. It is said that when he was first invited to join the Qum hawza, he did a simple divination (*istikhara*) with the Qur'an and it indicated that he would die in Qum, sign enough that he should move there. Khomeyni's followers took this as evidence that although exiled to Iraq, he would return to Qum, for he was fated to die there; and indeed he did return in 1979. This waiting for the return of the marja'-i taqlid led to elaborations of similarities between "Imam" Kho-

meyni and the awaited twelfth Imam, who will usher in an era of justice
before the final judgment.

The social context of the ulama can be stated in terms of religious style
and in terms of class linkages; putting the two together, one can indicate
a shift over time in the social position of the ulama. They represent a
style of discourse that contrasts with that of the religious upper class
(which is more individualistic, internalized, privatized) and with that of
popular religion (which is more communal, activity oriented, less intellectual). The rawda, however, is a key form that articulates the
scholastic learning of the ulama with the popular belief; the rawda is, as
Khomeyni defined it (1363/1943: 173), an assembly for moral lessons or
lessons for living. Even there, however, interpretation of belief is not a
pure ulama prerogative but occurs in a social dialectic, informed in part
by the dramaturgic ordering of the Karbala story.

A case in point is rapprochement with Sunnis. In many rawdas, defining Sunnis as not true Muslims has been standard rhetoric. Indeed some
preachers have built reputations on being able to successfully debate
Sunni and other alien religious leaders: S. Mohammad Soltan-ol-Vaezin
(d. 1971) and Mohammad-Ali Ansari are two contemporary examples.
Even if the festival of 'Umar's death has been in decline in recent years,
cursing 'Umar's name has not. Of the three illegitimate caliphs, he is
singled out because he finessed Abu Bakr's election, he threatened 'Ali
and Fatima, and it is popularly believed that under his leadership Iran
was invaded by the Arabs. The cursing of 'Umar is connected to the activity of scholarly ulama who collect hadith from Sunni sources
demonstrating 'Ali's claim. The greatest of these collections is Shaykh
'Abd al-Husayn Amini Tabrizi's *al-Qadir* (The Almighty). The group
around Ayatullah Marshi-Najafi, called Lajna-i Ihqaq al-Haqq (named
after the great work *Ihqaq al-Haqq* by Marashi's ancestor Qadi Shushtari
(d. A.D. 1610), has continued this work.

It is true that at various times the maraji'-i taqlid have voiced
ecumenical feelings toward Sunnis, most formally expressed through
Borujerdi's ability to get the Rector of al-Azhar in Cairo, Shaykh
Shaltut, to admit Shi'ism into the curriculum as a valid *madhhab* or
school of Islam, a remarkable one-way agreement. In general, one feels
the occasional ecumenical advances to be that part of the philosophy of
taqiyya (dissimulation) which demands that one not stress ritualistic differences when there are common goals, but that one continue
nonetheless to argue out in a friendly way the underlying differences.
Hence the ulama's negative reaction to Ali Shariati's suggestion that one
consider Sunni and Shi'ite history together as one glorious drama (see
Table 5.1 for some of Shariati's mistakes in dogma); hence also Shariatmadari's explanation at the opening of the Dar al-Tabligh that one ra-

tionale for the school was the need to send missionaries to non-Shi'ite Muslim communities; and the concern by the ulama over the Pahlavi government's attempts to alter the basic Shi'ite credo in the religious texts for secular schools in a way that would reduce the antagonism to Sunnis.[29]

If the rawda served to articulate the learning of the ulama with popular belief, the efforts of modernizers such as Shariati served a similar function in articulating the discourse of the ulama with that of the modern middle and upper classes. By focusing on this articulation and its difficulties one can see an emerging shift in the relative political strengths of the class constituencies of religious spokesmen, from landowners in the 1950s and the bazaar bourgeoisie in the 1960s to the modern middle classes in the 1970s. One can argue that at least until 1978, the ulama's claims that Islam had rules for all aspects of life was but an expressive, generalized stance providing few positive alternative programs to those of the government. The ulama saw themselves as guardians of social morality, as social critics, not as planners. Nonetheless, on occasion the ulama took specific stands — for instance, against land reform in the early 1960s on the grounds that it would hurt small landowners (Milani), religious endowments (Behbahani), or the bazaar through competition of the proposed cooperative societies (Khomeyni). In his study of the 1963 opposition to the White Revolution, Ahmad Ashraf (1971) divides the ulama into spokesmen for the landowners and spokesmen for the bazaar bourgeoisie. In the former group he lists Borujerdi, Behbahani, Khonsari, Tonkaboni, and Amoli; in the latter, Khomeyni, Milani, and Shariatmadari. The second group, Ashraf argues, "never attacked the government on the issue of land reform" but only on the dictatorial methods of the shah; he cites in support the call in the "clandestine tract" of the Council of United Muslims: "The estates and wealth of the majority of the ruling class have been acquired through illegitimate means. Thus after vigorous investigation their wealth should be confiscated and the shares of public factories should not be transferred to the landowners [as compensation for land reform]."

The complaints against dictatorship, the feelings against forced changes in male-female relationships, the slogans of right to private property and right to earn an honest living in trade, all transcended particular land- or bazaar-linked interests. The middle class's desire for political participation and a stable commercial environment not subject to capricious shifts in policy and bribery requirements found expression through these same complaints voiced by the ulama. And if today Khomeyni still seems to represent an older terminology and constellation of interests, other leaders such as Shariatmadari and Taleghani seem to speak out more clearly for interests of the bazaar bourgeoisie, the modern commercial class, and the white collar professionals. These latter groups have their own spokesmen, both secular and religious: Mehdi Bazargan, the late Ali Shariati, and a large group of younger men, as well as the secular National Front. It was largely in this ideological space of the new and old middle classes that the revolution of 1977-1979 would be fought.

6

The Revolutionary Movement
of 1977-1979

Revolutions are not made. They come. A revolution is as
natural a growth as an oak. It comes out of the past. Its foundations are laid back in history.

—Wendell Phillips, American abolitionist

*O*N JANUARY 16, 1979, the shah, Mohammad Reza Pahlavi, was
forced from throne and country for the second time. He left behind a government headed by an opponent, Dr. Shapur Bakhtiar, much as in 1953 he had fled the country leaving Dr. Mohammad
Mosaddegh in charge. On February 1, Ayatullah Sayyid Ruhollah
Musavi Khomeyni triumphantly returned to Iran after sixteen years of
exile, vowing to institute an Islamic republic. An Islamic republic would
be modeled on the just government of the third Imam, 'Ali, not on the inappropriately named and self-styled "Islamic" governments of contemporary Libya, Pakistan, or Saudi Arabia. The Islamic model of government in the absence of a divine Imam involved consultation to establish
what is just, not a military or monarchical dictatorship. On February 11,
the government of Dr. Bakhtiar collapsed. Ayatullah Khomeyni's
premier-designate, Engineer Mehdi Bazargan, moved into the official
chambers of government and appointed a seven-man cabinet. On
February 16, the former commander of the secret police, SAVAK,
General Nematollah Naseri, was executed by a revolutionary court under
Ayatullah Khomeyni, together with three other top generals who had
served the shah. Recognition of the new government came from Pakistan
and the Soviet Union, then from others, including the United States and
Morocco.[1]

The social drama of 1977-1979 had been rehearsed many times, and it
resonated with many associations of the past. It was a completion of the
1906-1911 Constitutional Revolution; throughout the year, the revolutionaries had invoked the constitution, which had been set aside in all but
name by the Pahlavi regime. It was a fulfillment of the Mosaddegh inter-

1979 revolutionary poster done in classical Persian miniature style, portraying Ayatullah Sayyid Ruhullah Musavi Khomeyni in the role of a Moses victorious over the evil pharaoh, Mohammad Reza Shah Pahlavi (with broken crown and sword, hanging on to the coattails of imperialism: an Uncle Sam with American, British, and Israeli insignia). The verses say (upper right): "We said: Fear not! Lo, thou art the higher" (Qur'an 20:68); "Go thou unto Pharaoh! Lo, he hath transgressed" (Qur'an 20:24); "He [God] said: Cast it down, O Moses! So he cast it down, and, lo, it was a serpent, gliding" (Qur'an 20:19-20). The single line below reads: "There is a Moses for every Pharaoh" (not a Qur'anic line). To the left the verses read: "In that day their excuses will not profit those who did injustice" (Qur'an 30:57); "Theirs is the curse and theirs the ill abode" (Qur'an 13:25). A hell of tortures is portrayed in the upper left.

regnum of 1952-53, which had nationalized oil in an attempt to establish an Iranian sense of independence and self-direction. Both Dr. Bakhtiar and Engineer Bazargan had served with Mosaddegh; the leadership of the National Front, which had backed Mosaddegh, was incorporated in the Bazargan cabinet.[2] It was also a vindication of the 1963 popular insurrection against the shah's White Revolution, a fifteenth of Khordad writ large; Khomeyni had become a major symbol of opposition to the shah in 1963, and his vindication became the rallying point of the revolution. Finally, it was the ultimate passion play of the Karbala paradigm, shifting from a passive witnessing of weeping for Husayn and waiting for the twelfth Imam to an active witnessing of fighting and working for the overthrow of tyranny. For years in rawdas the shah had been identified with the archtyrant Yazid, whereas Khomeyni was seen to uphold the ideals of Husayn. In 1978, during Muharram, the religious leadership called for marches instead of the traditional mourning processions. As the passion of the year increased, more and more people called Khomeyni "Imam Khomeyni"; and the religious dates of the year became staging times for major demonstrations.

The crucial fourteen months of 1977-1979 can be described as a social drama[3] or as a successful passion play. But these fourteen months were also a transformative event. Shi'ite preaching had been honed into a highly effective technique for maintaining a high level of consciousness about the injustice of the Pahlavi regime and for coordinating demonstrations. The Karbala paradigm helped unite disparate interest groups into a mass movement against an entrenched tyranny. But once the tyranny was removed, a new rhetorical discourse was required. For that, as Bazargan and Khomeyni both pointed out, one had to shift to the earlier portions of the paradigm of the family of the Prophet and to the principles of social justice associated with the name 'Ali. This new discourse had been pioneered fifteen years earlier by Mehdi Bazargan, the other contributors to *Bahth-i darbara-i Marja'iyyat wa Ruhaniyyat* (Study of Religious Leadership and the Clergy) (Tabatabai et al. 1341 Sh./1962), the late Dr. Ali Shariati (d. 1977), and the others associated with the Husayniyya Irshad. It was particularly Shariati who managed to instill an enthusiasm among the youth of Iran for an Islamic ideological revolution and liberation. The *Bahth-i darbara-i Marja'iyyat wa Ruhaniyyat* effort had been largely a call for reforming the clergy, for throwing off the scholasticism and stagnation of the past, and for modern interpretations of Islam that would be directly relevant to the political and social problems of society.

Shariati's call had little to do with the clergy. It was a call for Muslims to think for themselves, to rediscover true Islam. The idiom was one of rejecting thirteen centuries of corrupted Islam and returning to the original purity of an Islam of social justice. An important part of the effort was taking key theological and traditional terms, and giving them modern, ethical, and socially progressive interpretations. There was an intense rejection of referring to anything that had happened in the past as being representative or illustrative of Islam (except for the social justice of 'Ali and the universalism of Muhammad). A sectarian fervor accompanied the new discourse, making its partisans divide people into friends and opponents. It was, in sum, a call for a new discourse in the sense that Foucault has nicely formulated: "We must conceive discourse as a violence that we do to things, or, at all events, as a practice we impose upon them" (1972: 229).

With the revolution of 1979, this call for a new discourse suddenly achieved a credibility and coherence it could not achieve previously: that is, a compellingness derived from power. The revolutionaries furthermore claimed that the revolution itself was a purifying event for the participants. There are several senses in which this might be true. According to the old Soviet and Israeli theory, the praxis of revolution creates the new man. According to the Fanon theory, colonized peoples can throw off their mentality of inferiority only through a violent self-liberating act. But whatever truth either of those theories might contain, a third, and indubitable, truth is that political victory requires a spelling out in political and institutional terms of what previously could be left in vague philosophical and moral language.

What the new discourse of the Islamic republic will look like remains to be worked out. All that can be said at the beginning of the process is that Ayatullah Khomeyni, a conservative, midwifed what is, one hopes, the bourgeois revolution begun in 1905 and attempted again in 1952; and that Dr. Ali Shariati midwifed a new revolutionary discourse, which, like Moses, he was not allowed to live to experience.

The Social Drama: Political Liberation

Prologue

For a century, religiously phrased protest has been a regular feature of the relation between the Iranian state and its citizenry. The political articulateness of these protests has varied. Among the more articulate have been movements such as the Constitutional Revolution and the National Front activity of the 1940s in which Islamic protest was allied with secular reform movements that included members of the religious minorities. Among the less articulate protests have been riots against the minorities seen as symbols of foreign exploitation and attacks on Islam, such as the riots around the turn of the century and the 1955-56 riots against Bahais. The movement of 1977 to 1979 was one of the articulate examples, but one that, because of the political repression of the 1970s, was fought entirely in the Islamic idiom. What produced the Islamic form of the revolution was not Islamic revivalism so much as repression of other modes of political discourse.

This assertion can perhaps be substantiated to some extent by reviewing in summary fashion the Islamic phrasing in protest movements over the past century.[4] At the turn of the century protests against financial indebtedness to the British and Russians and against economic concessions to foreigners often took the form of riots against religious minorities who were seen as clients and agents of the European powers.[5] Often staged during Ramadan (a month of rededication to Islam) and Muharram (a month of contemplating the vulnerability of Islam and the need to aid Husayn as the Kufans had not), these riots were frequently directed by the ulama as a way of demonstrating their power against the state. Such demonstrations were conceded to stem from frustration.

When their letters and telegrams to the shah itemizing their discontents — spread of Bahaism, increasing numbers of Europeans in the administration, contracting of foreign loans, flight of gold from Iran — got through and received some response, the ulama were capable of counseling patience. Thus, a message to the ulama and Muslims of Iran from four of the leading mujtahids of the day counseled that foreigners were to be protected, that suppression of liquor and of Bahaism were to be left to the government. But when their letters were ignored, they were quite capable of inciting riots, making threats — "We will remove the present dog [shah] and put another dog in his place," said Mujtahid Sharabiani in 1903[6] — and using fatwas of impurity and excommunication. In 1891-92 tobacco was declared unclean, forcing a cancelation of the tobacco concession to a British firm. In 1903 tariffs were declared unclean because they included a duty on wine and spirits instead of outlawing them, and a writ of excommunication was prepared against the prime minister. Committees of ulama condemned Bahais to death for heresy against Islam, and in the case of the great massacre of Bahais in Yazd in 1903, there was a public ritual of performing executions in the several major public spaces of the city. In the 1920s, Muslims recruited by the British to help suppress rebellion in Iraq were declared to be kuffars, to be unclean, and not to be accorded Muslim burial.

Under Reza Shah in the 1930s, the old Qajar economy was reorganized into a self-reliant and nationalistic system; thus the direct connection between foreign domination and local minorities was lost, and the form of protests no longer used the minorities as hostages. There was a determination not to contract foreign loans, mercantile capital was no longer allowed to freely go abroad, merchants were forced to invest in state monopolies, and taxes were experimented with to generate income for the state. Consequently both the problems of the country and the form of popular protest were different from those in the preceding period. Taxes became increasingly regressive, and the printing press was increasingly resorted to.[7]

Part of Reza Shah's modernizing nationalism was a secularist attack on traditional dress and on the ulama, symbols of Islamic backwardness. In 1935-36 a campaign was launched to have people adopt European dress. These issues and problems—the tax burden, the tightening of the dictatorship, the dress code, and the attacks on Islam—elicited the protests culminating in the Mashhad riot of 1935. In this case the rawda was used at the direction of Ayatullah Qummi to provoke people to express protest and to provoke the government into an inappropriate and outrageous response. The police were seen as invading a religious meeting; the order to shoot inside the sacred shrine was seen as an extraordinary violation and exposure of an irreligious regime. The Karbala roles of the victimized Muslims and the tyrannical king were confirmed, and the people chanted, "Husayn, save us from this shah."

The legacy of these two sets of riots carry on into the present. The issue of the dress code has been reduced to a minor but symbolically potent theme in the struggle over the place of women in Iranian society. In 1977, women who attempted to register for class at the University of Tehran wearing a chador were refused; the issue of the right of hijab (modesty) became rekindled, with many women who otherwise would not wear chadors, turning up in them. The right to choose was at issue, so during 1978 the chador at universities became a symbol of protest against dictatorship in general. Women at the University of Isfahan were even reported to put the chador on to demonstrate at the University but to take it off when going out onto the streets to champion women's liberation.

More insidious is the legacy of attacking minorities, which carried on into the 1970s as a kind of daily petty terror. As late as 1970 in the town of Yazd public water fountains were reserved for Muslims only, barbers refused to serve non-Muslims, public baths had separate facilities for non-Muslims, glasses in which tea was served to non-Muslims had to be washed with special thoroughness, and many Muslims would refuse to accept tea from non-Muslims. Petty desecrations of graveyards and shrines of non-Muslims were also normal adolescent behavior. Such terrorism makes it hard for non-Muslims to be enthusiastic about political protest in Islamic idiom, however much the political protest may be justified. This is particularly the case when the *Risalas* (explanatory texts on problems of religion) of the Shi'ite mujtahids insist that the touch of a non-Muslim is najis (an impurity). Theologically, all this restriction means is that a Muslim must wash before praying. But at times of irritation and conflict, it is turned into a rule of social exclusion. Of all the minorities, Bahais are the most vulnerable, partly because they are still considered by Muslims to be heretical schismatics rather than followers of a separate religion and partly because the idiom of Bahaism is so close to that of Islam that it denies the normal construction of significance that Muslims place on their idiom. It was this fact that allowed Bahaism in its earlier more aggressive form, Babism, to appeal to so many Muslims, spread so rapidly, and hence become such a perceived threat.

In 1955 and 1956 the inarticulate antiminority form of riot broke out against Bahais. The context was the economic difficulties in the aftermath of the collapse of the Mosaddegh government, the roundup of Mosaddegh supporters, especially on the left, and the effort to buy off right-wing Islamic opposition represented by Ayatullah Kashani and the Fida'iyyan-e Islam, a political assassination group. The preacher Shaykh Mohammad Taghi Falsafi was allowed to use the radio during Ramadan to whip up hysteria about a Bahai threat to take over the country. The military governor of Tehran, Teimur Bakhtiar, participated with Falsafi in destroying the tilework on the Bahai temple in Tehran; and Prime Minister Alam told parliament that Bahai activities would be outlawed in Iran. Mrs. Teimurtash told the United Nations on behalf of the Iranian delegation that there were no Bahais in Iran. Ayatullah Borujerdi gave his blessings, meanwhile, to Falsafi's activities. Eventually, when the government reestablished control, it protected rights of all citizens equally while maintaining the fiction that Bahais did not exist.[8] A Muslim organization shadowed people to Bahai meetings and kept lists of suspected Bahais; whether or not religious leaders such as Ayatullah Mahallati approved of such activities, they knew about them and did nothing to discourage them. It is therefore not surprising that a number of anti-Bahai incidents occurred in 1978 and 1979.

Once Mohammad Reza Shah secured his rule in the 1950s the form of protest remained relatively stable, consisting of university student demonstrations, occasional strikes, and preachers using the rawda form. The 1963 demonstrations against the imposition of the White Revolution during the suspension of parliament came after three years of economic depression with high levels of unemployment and low levels of investment, and after election rigging had become so blatant that even the shah had to acknowledge it and annul the elections of 1960. In 1961 students and the National Front demanded annulment of the 1961 elections on the same grounds as in 1960, teachers struck for higher pay, Ayatullahs Behbahani and Borujerdi opposed land reform, and a National Front demonstration to commemorate Mosaddegh's accession to power in 1952 was met with tanks and troops. In 1962 there were student demonstrations and the army invaded the University of Tehran, causing the chancellor, Dr. Ahmad Farhad, to issue a celebrated letter of resignation citing the unheard of "cruelty, sadism, atrocity, and vandalism" visited by the troops upon the students. A roundup of opposition figures followed. In November 1962 the ulama launched a concerted set of protests against the Local Council Election Bill because of its enfranchisement of women and failure to mention the Qur'an. There were demonstrations on the eve of the referendum of the White Revolution and again on Nawruz (March 21) in Tabriz, Qum, Tehran, Shiraz, and Mashhad; hundreds died in Tabriz and Qum, and the Qum theological schools were invaded by the army. In April came further demonstrations. Fighting broke out against the tribes in Fars. Arsanjani, the author of the land reform program, resigned because not enough money was forthcoming to provide support for farmers through cooperatives.

The morning after 'Ashura, on June 5, Khomeyni was arrested in Qum. By mid-morning massive demonstrations were in progress in Qum, Tehran, Varamin, Shiraz, and Mashhad. They went on for three days. Thousands were massacred by the army, an event symbolized in popular memory with the image of thousands of black-shirted marchers enroute from Qum to Tehran being strafed by air force planes. Afterward, opposition leaders were rounded up, two hundred and fifty in the last four months of 1963, and the arrests continued for the next two years, especially in 1965 after the assassination of Prime Minister Mansur and the attempt on the shah's life (Zonis 1971a: 75).

Throughout the late sixties and the seventies protests continued sporadically. They were primarily directed against the tightening political system, with economic complaints being more scattered until the mid-seventies. From 1974 to 1977 there were some twenty-five major factory strikes, but they were quickly resolved by arresting the leaders and forcing the owners to meet the economic demands. Less controllable was the smoldering hostility to government meddling in all areas of organized life, and especially the intimidation by SAVAK. Reports of torture began to appear in the international press with consistency from 1965 on.

In March 1970, university students protested bus fare increases as a hardship on the poor; they attacked a hundred buses; five students were killed, five hundred injured, and a thousand arrested, of whom thirty to eighty were jailed for an extended period. In May there was a protest against the selling of Iran to foreigners on the occasion of a conference of thirty-five American executives in Tehran and a United States Commerce Department industrial exposition. Speakers S. Mohammad Reza Saidi and Tehran Polytechnic student, Nikdaudi, were arrested and tortured to death (Algar 1972: 250-252). Demonstrations were held in Qum. The government banned memorial services, but they were held nonetheless in the mosque where Saidi had been imam. S. Mahmud Taleghani and Dr. Abbas Sheybani were arrested for attending. In June, Mohsen Hakim, the marja'-i taqlid in Iraq, died. The shah pointedly sent letters of condolence to Ayatullahs Shariatmadari and Khonsari, but not to Khomeyni. Shariatmadari acknowledged the letter, and was rewarded by demonstrations at his house. Forty-eight ulama of Qum sent a letter of condolence to Khomeyni, for which many were exiled from

Qum by the government. In December university students demonstrated with the slogan, "Long Live Khomeyni."

During the month of the hajj (January-February) 1971, Khomeyni sent a message to Iranian pilgrims to stay away from the shah's planned celebrations of 2,500 years of continuous monarchy: "Anyone who organizes or participates in these festivals is a traitor to Islam and the Iranian nation" (Algar 1972: 253). Guerrilla activities followed: bank raids, attacks on police posts, explosions, and attempts to kidnap first Prince Shahram, a nephew of the shah, and then the American ambassador, Douglas MacArthur.[9] Before the 2,500-year celebrations, some six hundred to a thousand people were taken into protective custody; travel permits were required of anyone going near the celebration area.

In 1972 and 1973 three United States colonels, an Iranian brigadier-general, an Iranian gendarmerie sergeant, and an Iranian translator for the United States Embassy were assassinated. In 1975, a preacher, Ghaffari, was tortured to death in prison, and the largest anniversary commemorations of 1963 in the entire twelve years were held in Qum, protesting the introduction of a one-party state, the Rastakhiz party. In 1976 an Isfahan mujtahid, S. Abul Hasan Shamsabadi, was assassinated and death threats were made against three other ulama (S. Mohammad Reza Shafti, Faghih-Emami, and S. Hoseyn Ghaderi); the motives and identification of the perpetrators remain unclear, some blaming SAVAK, the government blaming followers of Khomeyni (Mujahidin guerrillas?) in an attempt to radicalize protest. In August 1977 Tehran slum dwellers protested in large numbers against eviction notices and the leveling of their accommodations; a number of people were killed. A series of arson incidents swept Tehran factories in the late summer. In September there was an attempt on the life of Princess Ashraf.

The August deaths of the slum dwellers is counted by some as the start of what grew in 1977 into an almost classic form of revolution, albeit in a structurally neocolonial society. The revolution, in its early stages at least, followed the classic pattern, outlined by Crane Brinton (1952), of the English, French, American, and Russian revolutions: a society with a rising prosperity was hit by recession (in this case engineered to counter inflation), and a government in trouble tried to make exactions not only on the lower classes but on the leading sectors of society, so that even those persons who should have supported the government turned against it, giving added weight to the moral ideological force which denied the government legitimacy and succeeded in demoralizing it. The case against the government was intensified by nationalist and anticolonialist strains. Not only was the government unresponsive to its citizenry, made possible by its financial independence of its citizenry through the oil revenues. But anger at its unresponsiveness was exacerbated by a military and police build-up intended to maintain the stability of oil production for the industrial world. As the various sectors of society increasingly felt their interests to take second priority to those of the industrial world, pressure against the government grew. As the government came to rely increasingly on foreigners both for labor and for technical advice, one group after another in society was alienated and embittered. The voice of the opposition became that of Islam; the demand, the removal of the shah and the reordering of national priorities.

The Breach: Muharram 1977

Cheerleader:	Naft ki burd?	Who took our oil?
Crowd:	Amrika!	America.
Cheerleader:	Gaz ki burd?	Who took our gas?
Crowd:	Shuravi!	Russia.
Cheerleader:	Pul ki burd?	Who took our money?
Crowd:	Pahlavi!	Pahlavi.

Refrain:

Marg bar in silsila-yi Pahlavi!	Death to this Pahlavi dynasty!
Marg bar in silsila-yi Pahlavi!	Death to this Pahlavi dynasty!

Chant:	Tup, tank, musalsal,	Cannon, tank, machine gun,
	Digar asar nadare.	They have no more effect.
Chant:	Shah khar shoda,	The shah is an ass.
	Bayad be zanjir keshida!	He must be chained.

('Ashura march, led by Ayatullah Mahallati, Shiraz, 1978).

The causes of the revolution, and its timing, were economic and political; the form of the revolution, and its pacing, owed much to the tradition of religious protest.[10]

The economic causes stem from the oil price increases in 1973: many of the older structural problems in the economy were exacerbated and new ones were created.[11] The increased revenues led to reckless spending, the tripling and quadrupling of urban wages, especially in construction, which drew rural migrants, and a very high rate of inflation. Had the spending been more careful, many of the negative results could have been avoided: the squeeze on the salaried classes from inflation; the market disincentives to farmers; the high labor costs that made building a factory in Iran as expensive as in Japan, without any of the benefits of a disciplined, quality-conscious workmanship; the importation rather than local training of semiskilled and skilled labor, leading to native resentment; and the expansion of bribery at the top of society to gain licenses for protected economic ventures. Three of these problems may serve to illustrate the deep sources of discontent.

(1) Agricultural policy. Agriculture, long a problem sector of the economy, was further dislocated in the 1970s. Instead of raising producer prices and supplying credit to stimulate production, food was imported on a massive scale and sold at subsidized prices. Money was channeled away from small producers and toward large new mechanized

projects dependent on large irrigation dams, with many peasants being literally squeezed off the land to make way for the agrobusinesses and state farm corporations.[12]

(2) Labor recruitment. Three hundred thousand foreigners were imported in semiskilled, skilled, and even unskilled capacities. Afghan laborers took jobs Iranians no longer wanted. But instead of hiring, training, and providing credit to Iranian truckers, for instance, Korean truck drivers were imported to handle government business from the port of Khorramshahr, a sizable commission on the deal accruing to the labor recruiter and the royal patron. Among the professional classes, more important than resentment against foreigners taking jobs was the widespread resentment at the misuse of their talents: being shunted into meaningless bureaucratic jobs, being forced to accept the existence of corruption, being denied a sense of contributing to policy formulation.

(3) Financing. Commitments for major projects quickly outpaced incoming oil revenues. Within two years of the 1973 oil price rise Iran began borrowing on the international market. By 1977, oil revenues had leveled off and the only way to keep employment levels up while trying to counter inflation would have been to siphon money away from the enormous military expenditures, a strategy that was not attempted. The anti-inflation policies of the Amuzegar government during 1977-78, introduced to relieve the salaried classes, led to widespread unemployment, especially in the construction industry.

At the same time as the economic picture was worsening, the political organization of the state between 1972 and 1977 had first been tightened and then in 1977 somewhat loosened. SAVAK activities seemed to intensify after 1972, and in 1975 there was the abortive and widely resented attempt to create a one-party totalitarian state through the Rastakhiz party.[13] The political organization of the economy also became an issue in two important areas, causing intensification of anti-shah feeling. First, the bazaar was singled out as a scapegoat for the inflation and a major price-regulation campaign was directed against it (see chapter 4). Second, the climate for private entrepreneurs was made more uncertain with the promulgation of laws adjusting the share of capital that foreigners could hold and the profits they could take out, and requiring major companies to sell public shares to workers or to a state holding company if there should not be enough private investors.[14] As a result, many businessmen began to strip their companies of assets and transfer money abroad. Although the share divestment program was billed as a profit-sharing initiative on behalf of the workers, there was continued refusal to allow labor to organize and negotiate on its own behalf: paternalism but not participation.

All of these issues provided the clergy with a receptive audience and fertile moral platforms. Their own material interests — the systematic removal from their control of education, administration of justice, notary responsibility, administration of religious endowments — were less important than their role as spokesmen for the interests of more important sectors of society, and than their articulation of the general protest against the secret police tyranny and the massive corruption.

In 1977, perhaps at the urging of President Carter and the American Congress's statements in support of human rights, the regime slightly loosened political controls. The intent and sincerity of the Iranian and American governments were ambiguous, but the opposition in Iran made the most of the opportunity. Open letters critical of the regime were addressed to the shah, Minister of Court Hoveyda, and other officials. In May, 53 lawyers sent a telegram protesting the decision to degrade the Supreme Court to the status of an ordinary court and asking that the legal profession be consulted before making major constitutional changes. In July, 64 lawyers signed a manifesto reaffirming the earlier telegram and adding demands for the independence of the judiciary, free elections, and freedom of speech. This was followed by a letter signed by 141 lawyers announcing the formation of an Association of Jurists to monitor the law.

There was some indirect response to these internal pressures and to the international initiatives: in April a military trial was held in public, and it was announced that future military trials would be conducted according to a new code. In June it was announced that civilian dissidents would henceforth be tried by civil courts rather than military courts, as before. But in September, when a letter signed by 54 judges and supported by 110 retired judges reaffirmed the previous missives of the lawyers, SAVAK intervened, forcing Judge Khan Seresht of Zanjan to resign and threatening others with dismissal if they did not sign a recantation. No more open military trials were held; the regulations for how they were to be conducted were never published.

An initiative similar to that of the lawyers was undertaken by first the Iranian Writers Association, then the bazaar guilds, and finally the remnants of political parties that had been forced underground. In June, 40 writers asked that their association be officially recognized, that they be allowed to publish a journal, and that they be allowed to hold meetings; they also objected to censorship. There was no response, so the demands were repeated in a letter in July with 98 members signing. In July, the bazaar guilds issued a complaint that the Rastakhiz party was strangling them. In August, a Writers Committee for the Defense of Prisoners was formed. During the summer, dissident political groups emerged in public: the National Front, the Tudeh party, and the two guerrilla groups, the Islamic Mujahidin and the marxist Fida'iyyan. In October the Writers' Association held ten days of poetry reading commemorating the death of the writer Jalal Al-i Ahmad, who died under mysterious circumstances and whose works had been periodically banned.

In November 1977, the shadow boxing began to turn into a real duel. On November 3, Khomeyni's son died mysteriously; funeral ceremonies were held all over Iran; police clashed with mourners in the Tehran bazaar. On November 13, the shah left for his twelfth visit to the United States. Students in the United States mobilized for a major demonstration. The Iranian government countered by mounting a pro-shah demonstration in Washington. Troops being trained in the United States were flown to Washington to demonstrate in civilian clothing. Armenian and Assyrian civic associations were recruited to fly members to Washington from Chicago and Los Angeles, each participant being given a hundred-dollar bill. Some four thousand anti-shah and fifteen hundred pro-shah demonstrators gathered around the White House on November 15. A twenty-one gun salute greeted the shah, touching off a clash between pro- and anti-shah demonstrators. Tear gas wafted across the White House lawn, causing shah and president to wipe away tears during their speeches. More demonstrations followed, the next day. Meanwhile, in Tehran the Writers' Association sponsored a second poetry reading with the poet Said Sultanpour on November 15 and 16, and a third poetry reading on November 25. On both occasions police arrested participants for chanting anti-shah slogans, leading to protest marches on the following days, in which there were further clashes between students and police, and a number of deaths. Abiding by the June law allowing civilian trials for civilian dissidents, the students were able to obtain lawyers from the Association of Jurists; all were released or given light sentences.

Harassment of dissidents continued, however. SAVAK began to put pressure on the members of the Writers Association to drop their demands. The names of lawyers who had signed the open letters of the last months were black-listed in a government circular. Dissidents were described in the press as "hooligans" and "supporters of international terrorism." The Rastakhiz party newspaper warned that government patience with dissent was running out. Dissident meetings were broken up. Various individuals were harrassed over the next few months: In December, Dariush Foruhar, a lawyer, leader of the Iran Nationalist Party and a leader of the National Front, was beaten. In January, Homa Pakdaman, a professor, was arrested for signing a petition for free speech, released, and then beaten up. In April, bombs were exploded at the homes of Rahmatollah Moghaddam (majlis representative from Maragheh), Mehdi Bazargan (leader of the Iran Liberation Movement), and Hajj Mahmud Manian (an activist bazaar merchant). In June, Abdul Lahiji (lawyer, leading figure in the Committee for the Defense of Freedom and Human Rights) was beaten and a bomb exploded outside his office.

The month of Muharram fell in December 1977 and January 1978.

The international, internal political, and religious threads began to interweave. The government banned any commemoration of the fortieth-day memorial of the death of Ayatullah Khomeyni's son. Khomeyni made no pronouncement on his son's death but renewed his call for the overthrow of the shah and the reinstitution of the 1905 constitution. President Carter paid the shah a visit at New Year's and praised him effusively. The Iranian government then responded to Khomeyni with an extraordinary bit of miscalculation and overconfidence: a newspaper article was printed ridiculing him as a medieval reactionary.

The scene was set. The end of Muharram coincided with civil holidays introduced by the Pahlavis to supplement, if not supersede, the religious cycle of holidays and to celebrate their own accomplishments. The twenty-seventh of Muharram (Islamic calendar) fell on 17 Dey (civil calendar), the date commemorating Reza Shah's liberation of women (7 January); celebrations were planned by the government's Women's Organization. Counterdemonstrations were held in Qum and Mashhad. On January 8, the Rastakhiz party organized larger demonstrations, especially in Tabriz, with women carrying slogans saying, "We do not wish to return to medieval times." The next day, the twenty-ninth of Muharram (January 9) coincided with 19 Dey, the anniversary of the shah's land reform. In Qum there was a sit-in to protest the government propaganda against Khomeyni and a reading of twelve demands: implementation of the constitution; separation of executive, legislative, and judicial powers; abolition of the bureau of censorship; freedom of speech; freedom for political prisoners; freedom for citizens to form religious associations; dissolution of the Rastakhiz party; reopening of Tehran University, closed because of the poetry readings; an end to police violence against students; state assistance to farmers; reopening of the Faydiyya madrasa, closed since 1975; and return of Ayatullah Khomeyni (Abrahamian 1978). This was followed by a march of four thousand students; police opened fire killing ten to seventy, and injuring many more.[15] Incensed, the leading marja'-i taqlid of Qum, Ayatullah Shariatmadari, declared the shah's government non-Islamic, called for a moratorium on communal prayers, and threatened a funeral march to carry the corpses to the Niavaran Palace.

The revolution was on. By mid-summer, all sectors of society had joined in: the students, intellectuals, and bazaaris who began things; the construction workers hurt by the economic slowdown; the factory workers incensed by embezzlement of pension funds and demanding higher wages (and later the right to unionize); the civil service, which had suffered a three-year wage freeze under soaring inflation; the urban slum dwellers, many of whom had been squeezed off the land; the bazaaris who had been the object of the punitive price campaigns; and finally the oil workers. Shariatmadari's statement was electrifying because he had finally broken the tacit agreement of maraji'-i taqlid within Iran to avoid public political pronouncements. In 1975, much to the chagrin of the students of Qum, he had remained silent when troops invaded the theological schools, cracking heads and arresting four hundred for shouting blessings upon Khomeyni and curses upon the shah.

There was a brief calm while the actors considered what had happened. Then the measured pace of the revolution began. On January 10, United Nations Secretary General Kurt Waldheim arrived in Tehran. The Writers' Association and the newly formed Iranian Committee for the Defense of Liberty and Human Rights sought meetings with him and sent him open letters citing violations of human rights. On January 13, 120 ulama backed up Shariatmadari's pronouncement by signing a protest of the Qum events and declaring a moratorium on public prayer in the mosques. Traditional death memorials are held on the third, seventh, and fortieth days. February 18 was the fortieth of the Qum martyrs, and the ulama called for a day of mourning, of peaceful strikes, and worship. There was, instead, violence and death. Twice more following this fortieth there were violent fortieths.

The main violence on February 18 was in Tabriz, sparked by the shooting of a young worker by the police and the locking of the public out of the congregational mosque. For 36 hours demonstrators took over the city, selectively attacking 73 banks, liquor stores, sexually explicit billboards on movie houses, any businesses that had not observed the strike call, offices of the Rastakhiz party, and anything displaying the blue-and-emerald emblem of the 2,500-year anniversary of continuous monarchy. The government responded with tanks and infantry: at least 9 (perhaps 100) were killed, 125 to 300 wounded, 700 arrested. The shah responded by dismissing the governor-general, publicly reprimanding and shaking up the Tabriz SAVAK, and sending a general to meet with a delegation of ten religious leaders in Tehran. Infantry troops remained on the streets of Tabriz until March 3; the damage done by the riot was repaired with amazing rapidity.

The next major event was the fortieth of Tabriz: March 30. But all was not quiet during the interim. Some two hundred political prisoners in Tehran's Qasr prison began a month-long hunger strike, protesting the conditions in the prison and demanding civilian retrials under the June law. The government at first denied that a hunger strike was occurring or that it involved so many people. However, the Iranian Committee for the Defense of Freedom and Human Rights publicized it and sent telegrams to the government in support of the strikers. The police responded by entering the prison and beating the fasters (March 15).

A day of mourning was called for March 30. There was violence this time in some fifty-five cities, including Tehran, Babol, Isfahan, Kashan, Qum, Yazd, and Jahrom. The government attributed it to "foreign-inspired" mobs. In Yazd a militant rawda by Rashed Yazdi demanding justice for Tabriz provoked a police attack in which 2 to 120 died. The tape of the speech circulated widely.

The next fortieth was May 8-9: there were disturbances in some thirty-four towns. On May 10 in Qum, a funeral was followed by a ten-hour demonstration. The demonstration was quelled after sunset by shutting off the town's electricity and firing upon the demonstrators. At least nine people died. The police invaded Ayatullah Shariatmadari's house and killed two ulama there, allegedly when they refused to shout "Javid shah" (long live the shah). The government made a public apology. On May 11, there was a major clash in Tehran: speeches were held in the congregational mosque of the bazaar; the police surrounded the mosque, tear-gassing the demonstrators when they emerged and then firing upon them. Many were killed, injured, and arrested. Dissidents claimed that through the cycle of the three fortieth days some 250 had died, 600 were injured, and 3,000 arrested. Khomeyni denounced the shah and "his family of looters . . . whose hands are sunk up to the elbows in the blood of innocents." He made a plea for the army to overthrow the tyrannical dynasty. It was not in the power of the students to overthrow the government, he indicated; more powerful forces were required.

RAMADAN AND BLACK FRIDAY 1978

So far the demonstrations, though the most serious since 1963, were still mainly in the mold of demonstrations of past years. By March Khomeyni was calling for the assassination of the shah, but his May pronouncements advised caution to his followers: the enemy was strong and the task required the army not simply street demonstrations. Shariatmadari began to counsel that strikes be conducted by staying at home rather than in street demonstrations, which would give the shah's forces the opportunity to kill. On June 17, Shariatmadari called for a peaceful general strike in Qum, and it was peaceful. By July there were indications that the demonstrations were beginning to involve wider and wider sections of society. Accounts of factory strikes began to circulate: 2000 workers in Tabriz demanded better wages, restoration of their New Year's bonuses, which had been withheld, and better housing; 600 sanitation workers in Abadan went on strike for higher wages; 1,500 textile workers in Behshahr struck for free union elections. On July 25, mourners in a funeral for a well-known religious figure chanted anti-shah slogans and were attacked by the police: 40 died.

Ramadan began on August 5. From the ninth to the seventeenth of August there were continual demonstrations, especially in Shiraz and Isfahan. In Shiraz the annual Festival of Arts was opposed and canceled: there had been lewd plays on a main street the previous year as part of the Festival, and, in general, for years there had been conflict between local sensibilities and the patrons of the avant-garde from Tehran and abroad. Not only the Shiraz Festival of Arts, but the entire series of international festivals scheduled for various cities (Isfahan, Hamadan, Tus) was canceled. In both Isfahan and Shiraz there were deaths, many injuries, and arrests. In Isfahan demonstrators even briefly returned the gunfire of the police. Local religious leaders were arrested in Isfahan on August 17 after eighteen hours of rioting and demonstrating.

On August 19th, timed to coincide with the twenty-fifth anniversary of the restoration of the monarchy in 1953, a stunning tragedy was perpetrated in Abadan: over four hundred people were burned alive in the Rex Movie Theater. The government tried to blame the dissidents: it was the sixth theater to be burned during Ramadan; two modern restaurants catering to the elite and foreigners had been burned in Shiraz and Tehran, the latter causing a death and forty injuries; clearly this was a reaction to modernization. Ten people were arrested, and confessions were extracted from five of them. The people, however, blamed SAVAK: the film had been an Iranian one with some social commentary, not a foreign one nor a sex-oriented one; the theater was in a working-class district, not catering to foreigners; the fire department was noticeably slow to respond and the equipment would not function when it did arrive; meanwhile the police prevented citizen rescue attempts. A third possibility placed in the general speculation was that the fire had been set, and the doors locked, by Palestinian trained guerrillas in an attempt to radicalize the revolution.

Over ten thousand people came to the funeral. Police and municipal officials were forced to leave the cemetery, and threats were made against the police chief's life should he ever set foot again in Abadan. Mourners chanted, "Death to the shah! Burn him! End the fifty years of Pahlavi tyranny! Soldiers, you are guiltless; the shah is the villain." On the seventh-day memorial, mourners streamed out of the Behbehanian Mosque, smashing windows of banks and government buildings, for the third straight night of violence. Ayatullah Kazem Dehdashti called for the shah's removal. There were student demonstrations in Washington, Los Angeles, and the Hague.

August 22 marked the beginning of the most important final ten days of Ramadan: normally one would spend the nights of the nineteenth, twenty-first, twenty-third, and twenty-seventh of Ramadan in the mosque reading the Qur'an through in commemoration of the day of its revelation. The first of these dates coincided with the Abadan funeral, the third with the resignation of the Amuzegar government (August 27), and the fourth (August 31) with the fortieth of the deaths in Mashhad on July 22. The fortieth in Mashhad began with thousands gathering at the house of Ayatullah S. Abdollah Shirazi; the gathering was moved to a more spacious venue, where a speech was delivered by S. Mohammad-

Taghi Hashemi-Nezhad (an important religious writer and leader for many years). A peaceful march followed, but afterward there were confrontations with the police in side streets: several people were killed. This final weekend of Ramadan saw disturbances in some fourteen cities: fifty to a hundred died.

After Prime Minister Amuzegar resigned, Jafar Sharif-Emami was made interim prime minister and was given a mandate to make concessions to the religious opposition. This was seen as, and proved to be, a superficial attempt at symbolic appeasement. Sharif-Imami ordered the closing of gambling casinos, the abolition of the Ministry of Women's Affairs, the creation of a Ministry of Religious Affairs, the approval of forming open political parties, and the lifting of censorship. Symbols of the Pahlavi ideology, which had played up Iran's pre-Islamic heritage, were dismantled: the newly introduced calendar, which counted from Cyrus the Great instead of from Muhammad or the arrival of Islam in Iran, was abolished; the long-entrenched minister of culture (a brother-in-law of the shah) and the director of the National Iranian Radio and Television (a cousin of the queen as well as a director of state ideology via the mass media) were removed. Sharif-Emami pandered to the allegation that the shah relied excessively on Bahais: the shah's personal physician and three other generals were dismissed; the general in charge of Iran Air was killed and Bahai employees of the airline were dismissed. He announced that seventy officers were to be dismissed and public officials were to be to be tried for their roles in the riots of the past months. The exit tax for Iranians traveling abroad, which had been raised the previous year without parliamentary approval, was lowered. But nothing was done about basic government policy: both the finance minister and the war minister were retained.

Shariatmadari gave the new government three months to prove it could meet the criteria of an Islamic just government; if it could not, civil disobedience would resume. The government was not to have three months.

Ramadan ended with a magnificent celebration ('Id-i Fitr): masses prayed in the streets and handed out flowers to the soldiers. In Tehran a small march interestingly revealed the widening and shifting public opinion. The marchers began in middle-class Tehran, chanting the slogan "Istiqhlal, azadi, hukumat-i Islami" (Independence, freedom, Islamic government); as they proceeded south into working-class neighborhoods, the marchers grew more confident; and as they crossed Shah Reza Street, some of them began chanting "Marg bar shah" (death to the shah). An old woman onlooker grew frightened and cried, "Nagid! Nagid! Mikushanetun!" (Don't say it, don't say it, they'll kill you!), and ran away; but when she saw that soldiers in the vicinity were not reacting, she grew calmer and returned. Other minor demonstrations continued until September 6, when the government announced a ban on demonstrations. The following day, an enormous peaceful parade of between a hundred thousand and half a million people marched down the hill from middle-class Tehran to the Parliament building, carrying pictures of Khomeyni and banners calling for his return, for an Islamic government, and for the end of Pahlavi rule. Symbolically, it marked a shift in the spatial center of the opposition from the bazaar and university to include middle-class territory.

This was the euphoric lull before the great storm of Black Friday, September 8. Although neither the religious leaders nor the National Front had called for a second march, several thousand people began to gather in Jaleh Square to repeat the message of the day before. Meanwhile at six o'clock that morning the government had declared martial law for twelve major cities, and troops were sent to disperse the crowd in Jaleh Square. Accounts of what happened differ over details and motives: what is clear is that hundreds or even thousands were killed. Whether or not the government intended to get rid of many troublemakers or, more likely, to perform an act of terror that would intimidate the people and end the growing public dissent remains unclear. Eyewitnesses relate that at eight o'clock the students, upon being told to disperse, sat down, facing Parliament and baring their chests to the soldiers. The troops fired, first over the heads of the demonstrators and then at them. A few witnesses claim there was provocation, that men standing behind women and children fired at the soldiers. One soldier, it is said, shot his commanding officer and then himself rather than obey the command to fire at the demonstrators. The massacre was followed by a rampage of the mob, stoning banks and post offices, building bonfires and barricades in the streets to slow the movement of tanks, which began to crisscross through town firing at people. Guerrillas carried out two actions: they killed a sentry at the barracks of the riot police, and they threw explosives at a bus leaving an air force base carrying British technicians.

Immediate reactions included a government crackdown, a publicized telephone call from President Carter affirming support for the shah, a demonstration in Qum which was met by police fire, the resignation in protest of four Pan-Iran party members from parliament (resignations took fifteen days to go into effect, and several withdrew the resignation first), the blowing up of the pipeline carrying natural gas to the Soviet Union, and factory worker strikes in nine cities. The government crackdown included reimposition of censorship, detention of opposition leaders (Bazargan, Matin-Daftari, Rahmatollah Moghaddam, Yahya Nuri, Rouhani in Qum), and symbolic assertions that it could respond to opposition demands that corruption be curbed. These latter consisted of a royal decree that henceforth no member of the royal family should have a role in the government and that Princess Ashraf would no longer control the foundation bearing her name, the resignation of the minister of court and former Prime Minister Hoveyda, and the arrest of eight officials on charges of corruption. Former chief of the Atomic Energy Organization, Akbar Etemad, was charged with embezzlement and mismanagement. Former Minister of Health Shoja'oddin Sheykholeslami and two deputies were charged with fraud, covering up the 1977 outbreak of cholera, payments of $6,500 to London prostitutes, taking commissions on sales to the ministry, purchasing overpriced and unneeded computers by the ministry, purchasing substandard ambulances, and selling narcotics confiscated by the government back to the black market.

There was almost a cosmic quality to the symbolism when on September 16 a major earthquake struck the area around Tabas, killing some 26,000 people. The queen went to the stricken area and was bitterly rebuked by villagers: "Why do you come to look at us? Grab a shovel and help us bury our dead." Dissidents claimed that the religious organization was much more effective in relief work than the army and Red Lion and Sun (the Iranian Red Cross).

The next month saw a hardening of the divisions. Ayatullah Khomeyni was forced to leave Iraq and after being refused entry to Kuwait flew to Paris (October 6). The French government, after repeatedly checking with the shah, who voiced no objection, allowed Khomeyni to establish residence in the village of Pontchartrain, 25 miles outside Paris. Strikes intensified all over Iran and became a determined vehicle of forcing the government to its knees. Demonstrations, of course, continued. On October 1 strikes and demonstrations protested Iraqi harrassment of Khomeyni. His expulsion from Iraq prompted three days of demonstrations all over Iran. Taxi drivers, Iran Air, government ministries, postal employees, railroad employees, government hospital employees went on strike, both for economic and social benefits and in support of Khomeyni. On September 12, Tehran's military governor, General Gholam-Ali Oveysi, sent censors into the two leading newspaper offices; four thousand employees walked out. Three days later, Prime Minister Sharif-Emami signed a charter guaranteeing free press. By then strikes were rampant in many cities: bus drivers in Kirmanshah, cement factory workers in Behbahan, tobacco factory workers in Gorgan, the Atomic Energy Organization in Bushire, teachers, bank employees, even employees of the Tehran Hilton. On October 18, oil workers went on strike. Between the bank employees and the oil workers the economy was under critical seige.

The government was gradually forced to take two serious steps: to cancel major nuclear and military purchases in order to meet wage demands of the strikers, and to send troops into the oil fields. On October 10, the government announced downward revisions of the $40 billion budget and the $20 billion to be spent on nuclear power plants and the canceling of orders for 70 Grumman F14 planes and 140 General Dynamics F16 planes, in order to pay the wage increases granted to telecommunication and state bank employees (100 percent increases, granted October 1 after a brief strike) and to government ministry employees (25 percent increases), and to make other settlements. Other measures were also tried. Amnesties were announced on October 2 and 19. On the Shah's fifty-ninth birthday (October 28) 1,126 prisoners were released leaving, it was claimed, only 600 still in jail. More allegedly corrupt officials were arrested. The former head of SAVAK, General Nematollah Naseri, was charged in a military tribunal for ordering illegal imprisonments and torture. The shah made a speech to parliament (October 7) in which he stated that liberalization of the political system would continue.

SAVAK, however, allegedly organized violent attacks to intimidate dissidents, notably an attack on a mosque in Kirman, in which women were stripped to the waist, and an attack in Hamadan on a girls' school, involving the raping of three girls. Major demonstrations were organized to protest both these events, and to mark the fortieth of the Jaleh Square massacre (October 17 and 18). The latter also saw two more guerrilla actions: pipe bombs were tossed into a Bell Helicopter bus in Isfahan causing three injuries; and three days later the houses of two West German technicians were attacked in Bushire. Demonstrations occurred throughout the month, all over the country, and constantly increasing in size.

Political negotiations finally were initiated; their negative results underscored the seriousness of the revolution. Ayatullah Shariatmadari had been consulted on the installation of the Sharif-Emami government and had been willing to allow it to take office: he neither supported nor condemned it in public. The amnesties announced in October were said to include Ayatullah Khomeyni, who was now free to return to Iran; but he said he would not return as long as the shah was on the throne. In parliament, Sharif-Emami survived three votes of confidence, but debates remained lively and four cabinet ministers resigned. Eventually negotiations were initiated between the government and the leader of the National Front, Karim Sanjabi. Sanjabi flew to Paris on October 25 to consult with Ayatullah Khomeyni. Mehdi Bazargan and Ardeshir Zahedi, the shah's ambassador to Washington and a close confidant during the last weeks, also flew to Paris. On November 4 Sanjabi announced that he agreed with Khomeyni that no compromise with the shah was possible and returned to Tehran.

Too many people had been killed, too many promises had been broken by the shah, too little trust was possible. Any compromise, Khomeyni (probably correctly) feared, might well lead to a restoration of the shah's power and an abandonment of all that had been so dearly won over the past months. After all, the shah had not yet yielded anything significant in terms of real power or structural change.

MILITARY RULE AND MUHARRAM 1978

For weeks Ayatullah Shariatmadari had warned people to stick to strikes and not give the enemy any excuse to impose a military government. In November the excuse was given.

At the University of Tehran, students gathered on November 4 and pulled down the statue of the shah at the front gates. A soldier, in a gesture of solidarity, gave his rifle to one of the students. The soldier's sergeant opened fire with a machine gun, killing the soldier and thirty to sixty others. The next day, November 5, the bazaar closed and students gathered at the university to pray for the dead; then the students took to the streets, selectively attacking banks, tourist hotels, American and British airline offices, liquor stores, cinemas, and part of the British Embassy. The riot was again interesting for its symbolic form: the object of attack was property not persons (people were cleared out of the British Embassy before two rooms were torched); symbols of the state and its international support were attacked (banks, international businesses) but not other shops, except those that sold things specifically objectionable in Islam (liquor, sexually immodest films). The army did not interfere, leaving many to infer that the day's events had been provoked in order to provide the excuse for a military government. As if more excuse were needed, reports circulated of mutiny in the garrison near the Tehran airport, and of garrisons in Isfahan, Hamadan, and Babol giving guns to civilian dissidents.

Sharif-Emani resigned. A military cabinet of six plus four civilians took over. Later the cabinet was more than half civilian, but it remained headed by a commander of the Imperial Guard, General Gholam-Ali Azhari, as the prime minister, and the military governor of Tehran, General Oveysi, as minister of labor, charged with getting the oil workers back to work. The oil strike had reduced production from 6 million barrels a day to 1.1 million barrels. November 11 was 'Id-i Qurban, the day of sacrifice in the month of the hajj, a ceremonial occasion on which the Islamic diplomatic corps paid its respects to the shah: he appeared quite demoralized. That morning, just before a scheduled news conference, Karim Sanjabi was arrested, together with Dariush Foruhar; oddly, the text of their statement was left behind: it called for no compromise with the "illegal monarchy" and demanded a referendum on an Islamic republic. The new government ordered the oil workers back to work, offering them 22-percent pay raises and higher housing allowances but refusing to respond to political demands. Strike leaders were arrested; other strikers were threatened with dismissal and eviction from their housing. Sixty percent of the oil workers did return to work and production slowly began to rise, reaching near normal levels by the end of the month, only to drop again thereafter. The army painted over anti-shah wall graffiti, covering the walls with new slogans: "Long live the shah, The people are ingrates." The anticorruption campaign was continued: former SAVAK chief Naseri and former governor of Khorasan, Valian, were arrested (November 7); Navard steel mill board members and other alleged racketeers were sought. The newspapers reviewed scandals in the construction and management of the plush Kish Island resort and the Asian Games of 1974; speculation was rife about Sharif-Emami's past role in administering the Pahlavi Foundation, a source and haven for much alleged corruption.

The opposition called a general strike to protest the arrests of Sanjabi and Foruhar (November 12). On November 14, demonstrations in the Tehran bazaar drew army fire. There were three days of disturbances in the oil cities of Ahwaz, Abadan, and Khorramshahr. The bazaar remained closed for sixteen days, until November 20, when a three-day opening allowed reprovisioning; then it closed again. Demands that foreign technicians leave the country began to escalate; some companies began to order dependents out. On November 11, an oil company helicopter was stoned by villagers, and the car of an oil drilling company president, Cameron, was stoned. On November 14, the car of George Links, the managing director of the Oil Services Company, was bombed, injuring the Iranian driver. Bell Helicopter employees were warned to stay away from work. Individuals were threatened by telephone and written notes, windows were stoned, and a few bombs were left at apartment buildings housing foreigners in Tehran and Isfahan (though once again targeting was selective).

On November 19, the traditional anniversary of the naming of 'Ali as the successor to the Prophet, the queen made a gesture to the opposition by going to Najaf in Iraq to visit the Imam's tomb and to ask Ayatullah Khoi to make a conciliatory statement; he refused. Indeed the queen was blamed for having destroyed Khoi's reputation by simply appearing at his house and forcing him to be hospitable to a royal family seen as evil, disgraced, and an enemy of Islam. Two days earlier had been Armed Forces Day, and for the first time the shah had failed to review the troops. On November 19, 210 prisoners were released; 267 more were released on November 23. Demonstrations continued, and on November 21 in Mashhad, troops chased demonstrators into the sacred shrine and opened fire there. A major general strike was called in protest for Sunday, November 26. Some million and a half people marched in Mashhad and some two hundred thousand in Qum; the troops withdrew from those two cities, leaving them to the demonstrators. There were also smaller demonstrations in Tehran, Gorgan, Kangavar, and Isfahan. The following day, a list of people who had taken large sums of money out of the country was circulated by striking Central Bank workers; it implicated many members of the current and past governments. On November 29, there were a number of wildcat oil strikes, and oil production began a steady downward trend.

Muharram began on December 2. For weeks people had speculated that 'Ashura would break the military government or would provoke a bloody massacre by the army. The government announced seizures of arms caches in Mashhad, Tabriz, and Tehran, and a ban on 'Ashura demonstrations. Ayatullah Khomeyni issued letters saying that torrents of blood might be spilled on 'Ashura, but blood would triumph over the sword; that good Muslims must be prepared to die to defeat the enemy of the people; that good Muslims in the army should desert if ordered to fire on their brothers; that the oil fields should be blown up if the army intervened. Ayatullah Shariatmadari responded to the government ban by saying that no one needed permission to take part in religious celebrations. In Tehran the bazaar was plastered with cartoons of the shah as Pharoah lording it over a man representing the Iranian people with a whip marked "Made in U.S.A." Banners proclaimed, "Every day is 'Ashura and everywhere is Karbala."

Muharram began with an explosion. For three consecutive nights, men in white shrouds signifying their willingness to be martyred went into the streets in defiance of the curfew. Others went onto the rooftops to chant anti-shah slogans. The BBC claimed that some seven hundred persons died in the first days. On December 4, marxist guerrillas attacked a police station, the homes of three American advisors were firebombed, and the oil workers went on strike. General Azhari called a press conference on December 5, in which he tried to present a strong front, threatening a 48-hour curfew for 'Ashura, claiming that less than 5 percent of the population was involved in the revolution, calling Khomeyni "a tool of the enemies of this country"; but he also conceded that he would allow 'Ashura marches if the opposition promised they would be controlled. Sanjabi and Foruhar were released from prison the following day. Promises were made to release 472 prisoners on International Human Rights Day (which incidentally fell on the eve of 'Ashura). There were some attempts to negotiate with opposition figures about a post-'Ashura government: there were said to be meetings and contacts between the shah, his ambassador Zahedi, and former prime minister Dr. Ali Amini, Ayatullah Shariatmadari, and others. What was achieved was at least a compromise for the marches on 'Ashura. In an attempt to discourage mass marches and meetings, the government issued warnings that communist guerrillas planned to throw bombs and grenades into crowds and that women guerrillas were concealing weapons under their chadors.

On Friday, December 8, some six thousand people gathered at the Behesht-e-Zahra cemetery south of Tehran chanting, "Death to the shah, Peace unto Khomeyni." Plans were announced for a massive march on Sunday, the ninth of Muharram to be led by Ayatullah Mahmud Taleghani (released from a four-year prison term on November 12) and Karim Sanjabi (released after twenty-six days in jail on December 6). General Azhari announced the lifting of the ban on the marches, the relaxing of curfew hours, and the stationing of troops well away from the line of march. Meanwhile in Isfahan, after mosque services, the army disrupted a march of twenty thousand people, leading to attacks on five banks, a movie house, several office buildings, the headquarters of the Grumman Company, and an apartment building in which five American technicians lived. Some two thousand Americans fled the country on December 8 and 9, before the scheduled closing of the airport for three days.

Tasu'a (Muharram ninth, the eve of 'Ashura) saw a massive six-hour peaceful march in Tehran by three hundred thousand to a million and a half people, led by the sixty-eight-year-old Taleghani. Forty abreast, the marchers converged along various major routes to the Shahyad Monument, built with money extorted from merchants for the 2,500-year celebrations. Similar peaceful demonstrations were held in Tabriz, Qum, Isfahan, and Mashhad. One major incident of violence was reported from Hamadan: a rebel soldier shot the governor-general.

'Ashura (Muharram tenth) saw an even larger march: eight hours and some two million people in Tehran. March marshalls tried to stop people from shouting "Death to the shah," but soon gave up. (The agreement for Tasu'a had been that no motorcycles or trucks would be used, for fear they might carry explosives, and that chants would be limited to sixty, none of which would directly attack the shah.) A goat was sacrificed by some mullas along the line of march. Green flags (Islam), red ones (martyrdom), and black ones (Shi'ism) were interspersed with banners reading in English and Persian, "We will kill Iran's dictator," "We will destroy Yankee power in Iran." Groups of women chanted, "Azhari, do you still think it is done with tapes?" (General Azhari had complained that the rooftop chanting was partly prerecorded and that the tapes contained sounds of firing to make it seem the army was more bloodthirsty than it was.) Other chants included "Arms for the people," "Hang this American king." In Isfahan there were two marches in the morning; in the afternoon statues of the shah were pulled down, pictures of Khomeyni put in their place, a Saderat bank was set afire, two movie houses and a restaurant were attacked, and SAVAK headquarters was attacked. In Dezful a soldier shot his officer; in Tehran three Imperial Guardsmen killed twelve officers and injured fifty men at their Lavizan base.

For three days after 'Ashura, the army tried to organize pro-shah demonstrations in various cities, sometimes using violent intimidation to get people to join these demonstrations. In Isfahan, troops first swept through the city on December 12, firing into the air, and then brought in truckloads of villagers to demonstrate for the shah. The soldiers tore down pro-Khomeyni posters, put up banners of the national colors (green, white, and red), and painted over anti-shah graffiti. They stopped motorists, forcing them to place pictures of the shah on their windshields and shout "Javid shah" (long live the shah). A man and his wife were shot for refusing. They smashed the windshields of motorists displaying pictures of Khomeyni or with their lights on (a pro-Khomeyni sign). In Najafabad troops attacked a hospital and set fire to a mosque. In Isfahan troops gunned down a line of people waiting to give blood at Soraya Hospital. At least forty were killed in the two towns.

In Shiraz, Bahai houses in the neighborhood of Sa'di's tomb were attacked. Accounts of the attack on Bahais are confused, Muslims claiming that Bahais were involved in the army-organized pro-shah violence against the revolutionaries, Bahais hotly denying the charge. One account suggests that the house of a certain arrogant Bahai officer was attacked by Muslims who wished to get even, that he opened fire, and that they returned fire, after which they went on a rampage. Other accounts say Bahais who had been repeatedly threatened had been stockpiling weapons for self-defense; when the attack came, they went up on their roofs to return the fire, but by so doing tragically identified their houses. Forty Bahais and Muslims are said to have been killed and hundreds of houses and shops attacked in three nights of violence.

In Mashhad, club-wielding civilians and troops invaded three hospitals where doctors and nurses had expressed prorevolutionary feelings. Khomeyni in Paris commented on the violence in some fifty-five cities, saying that the shah was mentally disturbed and could be expected to commit more atrocities before he was removed. A rumor circulated that the shah had vowed to turn Iran to ashes before he would leave the throne. Former prime minister Amini called for the shah's abdication or at least his leaving the country under a regency council. Sanjabi met with the shah. A general strike was called for Monday, December 18. Meanwhile General Azhari banned street demonstrations, threatened to dismiss civil service employees who did not return to work, and ordered the arrest of oil strike leaders. On Monday, ten thousand people gathered in the Behesht-e Zahra cemetery to mourn those who had died.

The efforts of the government to get the oil strikers back to work or to provide some hope of transition to a civilian government gradually broke down. Clashes between the army and civilians turned increasingly brutal. In the oil fields, strike leaders were arrested and other strikers dismissed on December 17. Oil production temporarily increased. But on December 23, the Mujahidin guerrillas assassinated the American acting director of the oil industry's management firm and an Iranian production superintendent.[16] Notes were sent to workers telling them to resign or face death. These actions had the desired effect of stiffening the strike. Within three days, three thousand workers had resigned and many more had walked off the job. Minor terrorist acts against foreign military and technical advisors increased in the form of fire-bombing of cars and homes, notes warning them to leave the country, and attacks on the United States Embassy.

On December 21, Gholam-Hoseyn Saddiqi, a member of the National Front, was asked to form a civilian government. Cynics saw this as a maneuver to avoid dealing with the leadership of the National Front and therefore doomed to fail. It did fail, whether for that reason or because, according to other accounts, Khomeyni's message of support was sabotaged.[17]

On December 29, a similar gambit would be tried with Dr. Shapur Bakhtiar, another member of the National Front. This effort eventually would succeed. Bakhtiar was to become the great unloved hero who provided the means to get the shah out of the country without provoking a military coup; the middle class failed to rally to him because they could not afford to break with the Khomeyni-led momentum, but also because Bakhtiar was perceived to be using the threat of a coup long after he should have declared a referendum to abolish the monarchy.

In the meantime, violence in the streets turned brutal, first in Mashhad, then Tehran, and then Qazvin. Part of the context was the takeover of more and more institutions by workers, leaving the army increasingly isolated as a defender of the government. Part of the context was the buildup to a Day of Mourning called by Khomeyni for December 30, the anniversary, according to the Islamic calendar, of the killings in Qum.

In Mashhad, doctors had taken over the Sixth of Bahman Hospital, named after the anniversary of the shah's White Revolution, and renamed it Seventeenth of Sharivar Hospital, after the date of the Black Friday massacre in Jaleh Square. The ministry of justice and the provincial administration were taken over. Three sets of incidents in the last week of December illustrate the way young men were willing to be martyred as vanguards when backed by crowds, the way physicians turned against the army and the reaction this elicited, the way Islam was potent politically rather than ritually, and the way a frustrated army itself rampaged.

On December 23, a few soldiers tore up pictures of Khomeyni being sold outside the house of Ayatullah Shirazi. A scuffle ensued and a dozen people were killed. Crowds descended upon the soldiers. They began to retreat, firing at the ground in front of the crowd to keep it back. Young men willing to be martyred formed a vanguard, with the rest of the crowd some yards behind. The soldiers fired, again at the ground, and again retreated. The young men halted, then followed. Eventually the soldiers were rushed and their officer was killed. The following day tens of thousands marched to protest the killings by the soldiers.

On December 27, the day after the Mashhad jail had been burned from the inside,[18] a group of royalist toughs[19] were allowed entry to the Shah Reza Hospital, now renamed by the physicians Imam Reza Hospital. After incidents in Tehran, Isfahan, Shiraz, and Mashhad, demonstrating that the army granted hospitals no privileged sanctuary status, the doctors had announced that military personnel would not be treated in the hospital under the military insurance scheme but only as private individuals.[20] Soldiers guarding the hospital let in the toughs, who proceeded to the children's ward, tearing off bandages and generally roughing up patients and intimidating the staff. After word had been passed to a large march farther up the street, a group of young men approached the hospital chanting, "Javid shah" (long live the shah) and were allowed entry by the guards. They chased the royalist toughs out. Realizing their mistake, the guards opened fire to provide cover for the escaping toughs, riddling the hospital with bullets. Eighteen were shot and two died. Enraged, the demonstrators happened upon a retired colonel in his car; they dragged him out and demanded he shout, "Marg bar shah" (death to the shah). He refused, repeating "Javid shah," as they beat him, then blinded him, and finally killed him. The mass of demonstrators, which had been proceeding along the street, now arrived and the hospital was made the site of a rally. Afterward people dispersed, although it was prayer time and some of the mullas tried to get everyone to stay for prayers: it was clearly Islam as a political vehicle not Islam as a ritual system that was bringing people together.

On December 30, a jeep with a colonel and a truckload of soldiers drove up to the great anniversary Day of Mourning march. They jumped out, declared themselves on the side of the revolution, and began changing into civilian clothing. They were chased by several tanks, which crushed a number of people while the soldiers aboard fired at the mutineers. The crowd reacted by going on a rampage. They attacked the Pepsi Cola Company, the Army Cooperative Stores (the staging site for pro-shah demonstrators), a woman's prison (inmates were freed), American and British libraries, and two police stations; and they lynched three members of SAVAK. The following day there was more violence: the troops had been primed by viewing corpses of soldiers on the parade ground. When demonstrators attacked an army compound, the troops reacted and hundreds were killed.

Meanwhile, in Tehran on December 27 there was a major shooting of civilians by the army. The preceding day a professor participating in a sit-in at the Ministry of Science and High Education had been shot. His body was taken to Pahlavi Hospital (called now Khomeyni Hospital by demonstrators). On the twenty-seventh, a march of largely middle-class people—unveiled women, men in coats and ties—proceeded to the hospital to take the professor's body for burial. The march was stopped by two tanks and a dozen elite rangers, who tried to disperse the march with tear gas, but the marchers regrouped and sat down in front of the tanks. The ranger colonel consulted with martial law authorities and gained permission for the march, and for the rangers to escort the body, by one account as far as 24 Esfand Square, by another account south from 24 Esfand Square but not going past the University of Tehran. The ranger colonel marched with the funeral in the front row. Troops awaited the march at the Square and stationed on rooftops. As the marchers approached, the waiting troops opened fire, to the consternation of the ranger escort, whose colonel was killed in the first rounds. The shooting went on for hours. Enraged youths dipped their hands in the blood of their comrades to alert the public, and march marshalls stopped cars, begging for blood donations.

In Qazvin, a similar firing on a funeral the next day turned even uglier. On December 27, three men in a demonstration had been shot, and on December 28, 120 were shot when troops fired on a funeral. The crowd attacked banks, liquor stores, and other shops. On New Years' day the troops themselves went on a rampage.

In both Qazvin and Mashhad, reporters interviewing the military commanders found them extremely upset about attacks on particular officers by the crowds. In Mashhad the commander had gruesome photos of mutilated officers; in one case he had even received a gift of intestines packed in a plastic bag with a note "executed by the people's court." In Qazvin the commander, Brigadier General Nematollah Motamedi, was arrested by his own men after the return of Khomeyni and was one of the first eight to be executed by the new government. Similar retribution was to be visited upon the military governors of Isfahan and Tehran and upon General Manuchehr Khosrowdad, who had led the troops into the theological schools of Qum in 1963.

VICTORY 1979 AND ITS PROBLEMS

The year 1979 began with the hope that Bakhtiar would succeed in easing the shah out of the country and the fear that this would trigger a military coup. The economy was at a standstill. Gasoline and kerosene were running out. Garbage collection and bus services in Tehran were suspended. Barricades and bonfires were being built daily in the streets to hamper troop movements. The military prime minister, General Azhari, had resigned on December 31 in the aftermath of two days of severe violence in twelve cities as the army appeared to be losing discipline and control.

The new civilian prime minister designate was given preliminary approval by parliament on January 3. Among his first acts were the lifting of censorship on the print media and the easing of curfew hours. The first newspapers since military rule had begun appeared on January 7. Meanwhile, Engineer Mehdi Bazargan went to the oil fields with messages from Khomeyni asking workers to produce oil for domestic needs. The workers had to be persuaded: at first they booed Bazargan, but by January 5 an agreement had been worked out. General Oveysi, the much hated military governor of Tehran and minister of labor in the military government, fled the country. The United States backed the Bakhtiar effort and sent Air Force General Huyser to Tehran to help persuade the Iranian army not to stage a coup. Most Iranians were convinced he was there to organize a coup if it was not too late.

Meanwhile, the various factions of the revolution began display activities to jockey for position in the post-shah era. The National Front called a national Day of Mourning for January 7 to mark the anniversary of the Qum killings according to the Iranian civil calendar. Khomeyni called a separate Day of Mourning for the following day. Bakhtiar announced support for both Days of Mourning and banned music from the radio for the two days. He also lifted martial law in Shiraz. The demonstrations were largely peaceful, with scattered disturbances in Tabriz, Hamadan, and Qarchak.[21] Forty thousand marched in Qazvin, half a million in Isfahan, tens of thousands gathered at the Behesht-e-Zahra cemetery in south Tehran, and five hundred more gathered in front of Ayatullah Taleghani's house, with chests bared, daring the army to shoot. Khomeyni and Sanjabi separately condemned the Bakhtiar government, but Ayatullahs Shariatmadari and Shirazi pointedly did not join in the condemnation. On January 13, a Regency Council was named to take the place of the shah, so he could "go on vacation." Khomeyni countered with an announcement that he had a ten-member provisional Islamic Revolutionary Council.[22] January 14 was a day of euphoria: crowds put flowers in the guns of soldiers, and soldiers displayed pictures of Khomeyni on their vehicles. On January 15, parliament accepted Bakhtiar's cabinet. On January 16, the shah left the country.

There was jubilation in the streets. Soldiers and civilians embraced. Anti-American slogans were in evidence—"After the shah, now the Americans," and "Yankees go home, the shah is dead"—but Americans on the streets were treated with friendliness. Pictures of the shah were cut out of banknotes. And the perennial dog metaphor was brought to life: a canine trotted about the streets with a sign affixed to its back reading, "My brother-traitor has just escaped; please arrest and punish him." Even the cosmos responded with an earthquake 21 minutes after the shah left.[23]

The final step of easing the Bakhtiar government out proved relatively easy. It was also a period of increased factional display. Khomeyni insisted that because Bakhtiar had been nominated by the shah, his government was illegitimate. Bakhtiar's only chance for long-term success would have been to abolish the monarchy, but he did not have the time. Part of Bakhtiar's function was to reassure and restrain the army. Moreover, the army was the only threat Bakhtiar had against Khomeyni's simply setting up an alternative government. The army leadership was presumed to be royalist.

January 19 was Arba'in, the fortieth of Husayn's death, and Khomeyni called for a massive march against Bakhtiar. Sanjabi and the National Front leadership did not participate. Over a million people marched in Tehran, half a million in Mashhad, two hundred thousand in Qum. Few banners, however, showed hostility to Bakhtiar. Two days later, leftists called a march: ten thousand marched to Aryamehr Technical University, with hostile hecklers following. Included in the march were socialists, marxists, communists, and factory workers who said they would not support an appeal from Khomeyni to go back to work unless they were allowed to organize unions. Marxist newspapers warned Khomeyni not to try to monopolize the revolution, saying that the people would resist any attempt to use Islam as a pretext for imposing a single-party system.[24] Islamic students demonstrated at the Kayhan Newspaper offices against leftist editorial biases and were invited in by the staff. Two days later the Imperial Guard put on a drill display of pro-shah fighting readiness for foreign newsmen at their Lavizan Base parade grounds. Meanwhile, however, there were reports of air force and army defections in favor of Khomeyni.[25]

Negotiations proceeded between the army, Bakhtiar, Bazargan, and Khomeyni. Khomeyni announced his intention of returning to Iran for Friday prayers on the sixth of Bahman (January 26), the anniversary of the shah's White Revolution, and for the anniversary of the Prophet Mohammad's death (January 27). Bakhtiar closed the airports. There were huge demonstrations of a hundred thousand on Friday and half a million on Saturday, with slogans "Death to Bakhtiar" and "Neither shah nor Shahpur" (a pun: Shah-pur means "son of the shah"). On Friday there were several clashes, with twenty deaths near the university. On Saturday, troops were kept away. The whole cycle of violence threatened to break out anew. A compromise was reached: Bakhtiar would fly to Paris, resign, and Khomeyni would appoint him to set up electoral machinery for a new government. At the last minute, Khomeyni's aides convinced him to change his mind. Bakhtiar reopened the airports. On January 31, there was a massive display of troops in Tehran, to warn Khomeyni supporters. On February 1, Khomeyni returned to a welcoming crowd of some two million people.

Negotiations went on. Bakhtiar retreated from his previous assertions that he would arrest any provisional government appointed by Khomeyni. Such a government could act as a shadow government only. Khomeyni thereupon named Bazargan as his prime minister designate. Khomeyni in turn retreated from his assertion that the referendum abolishing the monarchy had already passed in the streets and that he would present a new constitution. The 1905 constitution could provide a framework for transition. The military now began to negotiate with Khomeyni directly. Bakhtiar began introducing bills in parliament to fulfill the demands of the revolution: a bill to abolish SAVAK, a bill to establish jury trials for former corrupt officials, a bill to withdraw from CENTO; he continued the cancelation of expensive military contracts begun under the shah. Small demonstrations in support of Bakhtiar now began to be held. Bazargan told a rally on February 9 at the University of Tehran that strikes should continue until Bakhtiar resigned but that credit should be given Bakhtiar for freeing the press, easing the curfew, lifting bans on demonstrations, and freeing political prisoners.

On Friday night, February 9, and Saturday, February 10, the marxist and Islamic guerrilla groups, concerned by the notion of compromise with the shah's army, forced the issue by attacking two military bases.[26] On Sunday, the army withdrew its defense of the Bakhtiar government, declaring its neutrality in the political struggle. Bakhtiar went underground. Bazargan moved into the prime minister's offices.

The struggle to construct a new political system had begun. On the religious side the charismatic authority of Khomeyni and the conflict between middle-class, scholarly, and folk interpretations of Islam would become immediate issues. Khomeyni had allowed his followers to call him "Imam" Khomeyni. Newspapers and intellectuals now began to object that at most he was a Nayib al-Imam (aide of the Imam), hardly a messiah. In the fervor of the revolutionary struggle, even middle-class educated people voiced the interpretation that Khomeyni was the marja'-i taqlid of the era and therefore whatever he said to do must be done without question. Ayatullah Shariatmadari quietly reminded people on several occasions that Khomeyni was merely one of the learned men of Islam. The frequent tactical use Khomeyni had made of terms like *haram* and *jihad* also caused concern. Bakhtiar responded to Khomeyni's threats of jihad if he should not resign by pointing out that jihads were to be called only against non-Muslims, not against Muslim brothers. Khomeyni's labeling marches by leftists or other activities as haram or didd-i shar' (against the Islamic law) raised eyebrows and fears of authoritarianism. Most of all, the exercise of power by a secretive committee around Khomeyni without informing the Bazargan government angered leftists, intellectuals, and Bazargan himself, who on March 1 threatened to resign.

One of the contradictions of the religious revolutionary movement had begun to be played out. During the past year university students had denied any contradiction between their two heroes, Khomeyni and Ali Shariati, between the granting of special authority to a marja'-i taqlid and denying such special authority but insisting instead that Muslims should democratically think for themselves. Indeed by the end of February the Islamic guerrilla organization, the Mujahidin, had become allied with the marxist Fida'iyyin against Khomeyni and his more authoritarian aides.

One interpretation of this contradiction from the point of view of a liberal Shariati supporter, is that an ideological revolution was part of the ferment and disruption of the past year. The interpretation is constructed partially from the logic of Shariati's writings but primarily from the defences of the revolution offered by Muslim students in the United States in the days immediately following the installation of the Bazargan government.

Ideological Revolution

Two important ideological shifts occurred in the course of the revolution. First, it became practical to stress that the Karbala paradigm is not a passive weeping for Husayn but rather an active fighting for Husayn's ideals, and it is not merely a personal and individual commitment but a social one. Second, after the removal of the shah there was a shift from Husayn as the symbol of protest against tyranny to 'Ali as the symbol of constructive government and Muhammad as the symbol of universalism.

KARBALA IN THE ACTIVE MOOD

The insistence that the Karbala metaphor should trigger action rather than weeping is an old one. It served as a standard admonition in rawdas, especially during Ramadan, the month of commemorating 'Ali. It served as an objection of the more scholarly and the more middle-class Shi'ites to the lower-class folk religion and to the akhunds who catered to them. And it served as a slogan of the modernists such as Dr. Ali Shariati against the dry religion of the ulama. During the revolutionary year, the most striking illustration of the active interpretation of Karbala was the suspension of traditional mourning processions during Muharram and especially on 'Ashura: political marches were substituted.

Ayatullah Khomeyni's first speech upon returning to Iran was also illustrative. He spoke in the Behesht-e-Zahra Cemetery in South Tehran, where the Tehran martyrs of the revolution were buried. He spoke in Lot number 17, to commemorate the seventeenth of Shahrivar (Black Friday). He began:

> For the children who lost their fathers [of whom he was one], for the parents who lost their children [of whom he was one], I feel very sad. I cannot stand it. I cannot stand it . . . The shah destroyed everything and built big and beautiful cemeteries for us . . . Is it human rights [O American President, who kept talking about human rights and issuing statements of unconditional support for the shah] to say that when we want to name a government we get a cemetery full of people?

What magnificent possibilities for a rawda. But Khomeyni used none of the rhetorical cues for weeping, and no one wept. The form was totally different: it was a speech not a rawda. People listened intently and applauded once, when he said the revolution would continue until the Bakhtiar government was replaced by an Islamic one.

Partisans and participants claimed that the revolution was a purifying process. They meant that a catharsis and exposure of the shah's lies had been performed, that the spilling of blood had produced an indelible commitment, and that false interpretations of Islam by the ulama and the state had been laid to rest. A great deal was said during the revolution about disgracing the shah and his government (*rusva'i kishidan*): each time the shah or the government experienced a setback, it was commented on as a disgrace and exposure. It was self-reassurance that the shah was not invincible, that assertion of civil rights was not hopeless. A beautiful minor illustration of this growing confidence is the story of the little old woman on 'Id-i Fitr who reacted in terror to the chant "Death to the shah" but then returned to watch the demonstration when she saw that the soldiers were not going to shoot.

The theme of martyrdom was of course central to the revolution. Husayn is the martyr par excellence. His martyrdom, in the passive version of Karbala, provided an intercessor for ordinary mortals at the last judgment. In a more active interpretation, his martyrdom is the model for others to emulate: through struggle on the side of good one achieves heaven without need of any intercessor. Since martyrs are said to go to heaven, one need not mourn their deaths as one does those of ordinary people. The symbolism of martyrdom was thus omnipresent. Demonstrators wore white shrouds to symbolize their willingness to die. Wall graffiti proclaimed that those who died did the work of Husayn, those who fought did the work of Zaynab (she kept the survivors of Karbala together and maintained the message of Husayn until the fourth Imam had recovered and could assume the political leadership), and those who did not fight did the work of Yazid. Young men willing to die formed lines at the front of the demonstrations between the soldiers and the people. Banners at rallies included pictures of the latest male and female martyrs. Stories were collected of soldiers who aided the revolution and died for it, such as the soldier who shot his officer in Jaleh Square on Black Friday and the soldier who was killed for giving his weapon to the students in the November 4-5 events leading to military rule. Two of the most treasured stories were set in Tabriz and Hamadan.

In Tabriz, it is said, an officer asked three hundred men how many of them were willing to shoot to kill if so ordered. About half the soldiers stepped forward. He then asked how many of these would shoot their own relatives. Perhaps a hundred stepped forward. Finally he asked how many would shoot their own parents, and sixty stepped forward. He then shot the sixty and himself.

In Hamadan on 'Ashura, it is said, twenty-two-year-old conscript Mohsen Mobashsher Kashani was on guard duty at a meeting of the governor-general, the local SAVAK chief, the local military law administrator, the chief of police, and three other officials. The governor-general told Kashani that they were about to interview a mulla, and instructed him that at a specified time he should enter the room and shoot the mulla. The soldier slipped out to a phone and warned the mulla to come ten minutes late to the meeting. At the assigned time, when the mulla was originally supposed to be in the meeting, Kashani burst into the room and opened fire, killing the governor-general and wounding several of the others. He was shot in turn. His father in Mashhad refused to come to Hamadan to claim the body and pay the bond of 15,000 tomans ($2000) required by the government as insurance that other members of the family would not become involved in revolutionary activity. (People commonly believed the ransom was a gruesome fee to pay for the bullets used by the government.) Instead, some ten thousand people escorted the body to an airplane to be flown to Mashhad. When the father met the body, he was told not to cry, for a martyr (*fida'i*) goes to heaven.

Most important, especially for the future, was the sense that the revolution was laying to rest the false interpretations of Islam of the past and that the interpretations pioneered by Shariati would provide the framework for a creative, open, progressive, and just society. In the past the state and many of the ulama had misused Islam for their own purposes: the justification of second-class status for minorities on the grounds of ritual impurity (*najis*), the stress on divisions between Shi'ites and Sunnis, the justification of excluding women from the vote and from participation in public affairs, the allegation that land reform had been opposed because of the sacredness of private property in Islam or because of the material interests of the ulama—all were condemned. Instead, it was argued, the true Muslim was one who contained in himself faith (*imam*), self-purification (*taqwa*), and practicality (*'amal-i salih*). The true Islamic society was one in which there was an organic relation between the community (*ummat*) and the leadership (*imamat*), in which social cohesion reflected divine unity; hypocrites (*munafiqin*), especially materialists who used Islam as an opportunistic cover, were to be rejected. In this sense the Muslim guerrilla group, the Mujahidin-i Khalq, were a vanguard: they had already purified themselves several years earlier by purging marxists who had tried to infiltrate. They called themselves holy warriors (*mujahidin*), ones who struggle in the path of justice. Although they had split from Mehdi Bazargan's Movement for the Liberation of Iran over the use of force, which Bazargan rejected, in February 1979 they played a vanguard role in bringing Bazargan to power by helping precipitate, through armed struggle, the final fall of the Bakhtiar government. It was Iran, the revolutionaries felt, that would show the Islamic world the proper path to a just society.

Governing in the Mold of 'Ali and Muhammad

The rapid inflation of religious titles after the revolution so that almost every senior mulla was called Ayatullah or Hojjat al-Islam was a benign overenthusiasm. But underneath this rhetorical euphoria lay the more important relation between mullas and political authority. Although for the National Front the revolution was almost complete and what remained was to allow the professionals and bourgeoisie to take control of the institutions of government, for Khomeyni the revolution would not be complete if essentially the same policies of the past were continued. For him the revolution was not merely a political or an economic one, but a moral one changing the tone and value orientation of the government and of social behavior.

Khomeyni did not have a Leninist revolutionary party with a disciplined cadre, nor did he have a clear program. He could only use his charisma, the rhetoric of a clarified Islam, occasionally the dogmatic style allowed old men, and tactics of intimidation to negotiate and pressure the various elements in society toward his vision of an Islamic moral society. It was to be expected that the dual sovereignty of a nominal government headed by Bazargan and an informally constituted series of revolutionary councils, largely manned and coordinated by mullas and backed by irregular revolutionary militia, would continue for some time in an uneasy, unstable, and tense relation to each other. The Bazargan government and the middle class, feeling insufficiently strong to confront or break with Khomeyni, awaited the decay of his charisma and the Islamic fervor as economic and administrative problems piled up. The Khomeyni forces, lacking clear organization or program, often relied on terror tactics adopted from the shah. The very name Revolutionary Committee was motivated by the Committee Prison, the most feared of the interrogation and torture centers under the shah: that the name was deliberate was made clear by the announcement that the headquarters of the Revolutionary Committee would be in the old Committee Prison. The names of the members as well as their deliberations remained secret. It was announced that a new secret police with a slightly modified acronym had been set up: SAVAMI. There was a running feud with the press over the acceptability of political criticism and over the management of the news.[27] There were crises over whether Khomeyni had the right to countermand administrative decisions of the Bazargan cabinet.[28] It became clear that Khomeyni had the authority to override the policies of the Bazargan government on such matters as summary executions and ethnic minorities. He did not, however, have the power to dismiss completely the political demands of the revolution for constitutional processes.

It is not suprising that for some time after the revolution the symbols and rhetoric of a clarified Islam should remain a potent tool in Khomeyni's hands, at least as long as he used them flexibly and strategically. *Hijab* (female modesty), justice, *jihad* for rural reconstruction, and unity (*tawhid*) are all examples of redefining terms in an attempt to renegotiate the rules of society.

Ramadan 1979 (July-August), for instance, was used by Khomeyni as a symbolic tool against the Kurdish resistance to his unilateral decisions, against the criticism by the press and by Bazargan, and against the boycotts of the elections for an assembly to pass on his draft constitution by the National Front, the National Democratic Front of Matin-Daftari, Ayatullah Shariatmadari's Muslim People's Party, and leftists. He called for unity, redefining tawhid (unity of God in all his manifestations) so it not only included, but specifically denoted, national political unity and solidarity with all Muslims in the world. He called for the reinstitution of the khutba after Friday communal prayers and urged that everyone attend Friday prayers. As Ayatullah Taleghani explained in his khutba on the first Friday of Ramadan (July 27), which Bazargan attended, Shi'ites had more or less suspended the use of the khutba because the political leadership of the community had fallen into the hands of the *taqout* (oppressors, corrupters). The Friday assembly originally was intended by Muhammad for both worship and politics. Now that the taqout had been overthrown and replaced by a just and equitable imamate, the khutba should be reinstituted. Khomeyni asked that the preachers use the khutba to stress the need for unity within Iran and among all Muslims, both Shi'a and Sunni. He declared the last Friday of Ramadan, Jerusalem Day, in solidarity with the Muslim Arab struggle to recapture that city.

Although it is too early to tell how the new discourse of Shi'ism in Iran will develop, four issues dealt with in chapter 5 can be reexamined in a preliminary way: politics, Islamic economics, the status of women, and the position of minorities.

Politics. From the beginning the revolutionaries stressed constitutionalism and the moral role of the ulama. As the movement gathered force, the call shifted from reinstating the 1905 constitution to underscoring more pointedly the illegality of the Pahlavi monarchy and its activities under the constitution, and finally to the need to reconstruct the political system. The 1905 constitution contained a provision for supervision over legislation by a council of five mujtahids. Ayatullah Khomeyni proposed that he continue to exercise an analogous function for the new Islamic republic, but he would not participate directly in the new government and the provisional government that he would name would not contain any ulama. Ulama would have the right to run for parliament as individuals. The process of transition was to be a referendum on the monarchy, a constitutional convention to amend or rewrite the constitution and free elections.

An important part of the demand for constitutionalism was for reform of the judicial system to allow open trials, defense of the accused, and the protection of due process. A third promise of the revolution was political pluralism, decentralization, and increased regional and local autonomy. All three of these liberal goals — most clearly articulated by the National Front, given full support by Ayatullah Shariatmadari and apparently only tactical support by Ayatullah Khomeyni — rested uneasily alongside the conservative interpretation of Islam articulated by Khomeyni. This conservative vision denigrated democracy as mindless popularity contests, and contrasted the infallible wisdom of divine law. It valued swift and final justice over the celebration of due process, which allows escape to the guilty on technicalities. And it insisted on submission (islam), community (ummat), and correct actions expressed by a unified leadership (imamat), over any demands for autonomy or pluralism.

Thus, in December and January, Khomeyni claimed that the referendum on the monarchy had essentially passed in the streets and that his advisors would present a constitution for the people's approval. This, together with his failure to consult with his allies in the National Front, with Mehdi Bazargan, or with Ayatullah Shariatmadari, throughout the course of the revolution, caused considerable fear of authoritarian tendencies. When the Bazargan government was installed, Khomeyni retained a Revolutionary Committee, which in short order executed eight generals and then a traffic warden accused of setting the Abadan Rex Cinema fire (a charge few found credible), and another unknown man accused of being a torture expert. There were neither public trials nor consultation with the new government. Protest was heard from all sides: from Prime Minister Bazargan, from Ayatullah Qummi in Mashhad, from the International Commission of Jurists, from leftists. But Revolutionary Committee member Ayatullah Mohammad Reza Mahdavi-Kani replied that the executions would continue, for "we must purify;

we have to renew." The furor grew as people were executed for sexual offenses as well as crimes under the shah. Bazargan made a major speech on March 14 (by which time sixty-eight people had been executed), denouncing the executions as "irreligious, inhuman, and a disgrace to the country and revolution." Ayatullah Taleghani disassociated himself from the executions.

On March 15, former prime minister Hoveyda's trial began. Khomeyni bowed to the outcry against the summary executions and halted the trial until a code of procedure could be established. The code he produced allowed him to appoint prosecutors, obligated sentences to be carried out within twenty-four hours, and denied the need to provide criminals with lawyers. Hoveyda's trial resumed, and he was executed on April 7. Trials became slightly more public: witnesses were called against the accused, and the accused was allowed to speak in his own defense (though Hoveyda was denied his request to prepare a full statement of defense). In early May, Khomeyni announced that executions were to be limited to persons proven to have killed people, or issued orders for killing, or committed torture resulting in death. But executions continued for sexual deviance, pornography, prostitution, political dissent (in the case of the Kurds), and even for contact with Israel (in the case of a prominent Jewish businessman). By the end of August 1979 over five hundred people had been executed. Ayatullah Sadegh Khalkhali ran for election to the constitutional convention proudly claiming to be personally responsible for condemning two hundred to death (the electorate rejected him).

At issue was the authority of the Bazargan government, revolutionary retribution (spokesmen justified the executions by pointing out that many more people had died in other revolutions), and judicial rights and procedures. One of Khomeyni's first directives upon return to Iran was to the Minister of Justice that decisions should be swift and final and there should be no appeal processes in either civil or criminal cases. He repeated a number of times that criminals had no right to lawyers. In part, he was reacting to the interested slowness in the Pahlavi regime's administration of justice which allowed graft. In part, the executions were motivated by a fear that the military officers and secret police personnel might promote a coup. And certainly there was indignation as stories of torture under the shah were publicized. But Khomeyni's lack of concern for deliberation, his blindness to the possibility of error, and his simple faith in swift justice were not reassuring.

Other areas in which Khomeyni was able to override the wishes of the Bazargan government were, first of all, the exercise of power through the loosely coordinated, or even uncoordinated, activities of the Revolutionary Committee and the numerous local revolutionary committees which began to spring up, instead of through the public government; second, the reliance on the irregular revolutionary militias instead of reconstructing the army and absorbing the irregulars into it[29]; and third, negotiation with the ethnic minorities. Although Ayatullah Taleghani on behalf of the government had repeatedly expressed willingness to negotiate the demands of these minorities, and although the Bazargan government was opposed to the use of force to decide these issues, Ayatullah Khomeyni refused to consider the demands legitimate and insisted on defining their expression as treason against the state to be crushed militarily.

Even in the progress toward a constitution Khomeyni bucked the demands of the other factions of the revolution. A basic promise of the revolution had been political pluralism and local autonomy. A leitmotif of the year had been the separation of identity of the different allied factions. By spring 1978, Marxist demonstrations had been distinguished from those of the bazaar and of Islamic partisans. The need for the National Front to ally itself with Khomeyni was underlined by Khomeyni's ability to veto any compromise negotiations between the shah and Sanjabi and by the failure of Sadeghi and even of Bakhtiar to shake that National Front stance. But in January 1979, when victory was almost assured, the National Front and Khomeyni called separate marches to protest against the Bakhtiar government. Earlier, in the fall, the oil workers pointedly refused to obey commands from Khomeyni and had to be cajoled by Bazargan. About the same time factory workers said they would not return to work merely on the demand of Khomeyni unless their political demands for free unions were agreed to. So, when Khomeyni returned to Iran and his Revolutionary Committee began to exercise power, the left warned that no single faction should be allowed to monopolize the revolution. This stand was given support by various groups protesting the arbitrary appointment of bosses without consultation with the workers: the National Iranian Radio and Television workers objected to the appointment of Khomeyni aide Ghotbzadeh as their chief; workers in the oil fields demanded a say in management decisions; objections were voiced to a number of police and military appointments; workers in various factories and organizations formed their own management committees.

There was considerable pressure on Khomeyni to accede to a referendum, and it was held on March 30. Ayatullah Shariatmadari, the National Front, and the leftists, however, all protested the manner in which it was formulated. One had only a choice of voting for an as yet undefined Islamic republic (with a green ballot, the color of Islam), or against (with a red ballot, the color of Yazid). Kurds, Turkomen, and numerous others announced a boycott of the referendum. To counter a possible low turnout, the voting age was lowered from eighteen to sixteen to enfranchise the youths who had helped man the street demonstrations. On April 1, Khomeyni declared an Islamic Republic and the first day of a government of God.

The next step was to provide a new constitution. Shariatmadari, the National Front, and leftists demanded a constitutional convention. Khomeyni and his aides preferred to publish a constitution themselves. After repeated postponements, a draft was leaked to the press at the end of May, looking very much like the 1905 constitution.[30] On August 3, an election was held for a seventy-three-member Assembly of Experts to approve or amend the draft before putting it to a general referendum. This election was boycotted by Shariatmadari, the National Front, and the National Democratic Front on the grounds that the criteria for candidacy were restrictive (of 417 candidates, 383 were mullas), that there was not enough time to campaign, and that political meetings were harassed and disrupted by Khomeyni followers. The opening of the Assembly on August 19 was overshadowed by demonstrations against new restrictions on the press promulgated by the Ministry of National Guidance, and by the use of the army to drive Kurdish dissidents from the major towns of Kurdistan.

The Assembly of Experts (*majlis khabrigan*) redrafted the constitution, placing all aspects of government under clerical guidance. In the preamble the failure of the constitutional movement of 1905 and the nationalist movement of 1952-53 were attributed to a lack of proper Islamic philosophy. The new movement was dated, coincidentally with Khomeyni's political career, from 1963. The marja-i taqlid or nayib ul-Imam of the moment—initially Khomeyni—was empowered to preside over the selection of the president of the republic, to dismiss him in concert with the supreme court or the parliament, to appoint the supreme judiciary, to act as supreme commander of the armed forces, to declare war and peace, and to appoint six clerics to a twelve-member Council of Guardians which could veto parliamentary legislation deemed contrary to Islam and which would select the successor or council of successors to Khomeyni. Exactly how the various checks and balances between the nayib ul-Imam, the legislative, executive, and judicial organs of government, the Council of Guardians, and the Assembly of Experts (which could be convened to change the constitution or remove the nayib ul-Imam or council of leadership should they become incapacitated) would work remained unclear.

Objections to this form of instituting the wilayat-i faqih were voiced in vain by members of the Assembly of Experts such as Ayatullah Naser Makarem and the Azarbaijani lawyer Rahmatullah Moghaddam-Maragheh (one of four civilians in the Assembly); by members of the government such as Prime Minister Bazargan and Azatullah Sahabi (also a member of Bazargan's Movement for the Liberation of Iran); and by Ayatullah Shariatmadari. Shariatmadari insisted that because the notion of wilayat-i faqih was ambiguous and disputed in Islamic jurisprudence—some interpreting it as merely moral guidance, or even more narrowly as financial guardianship for children and for the mentally incompetent; others, like Khomeyni, interpreting it as political activism — it should not be incorporated into a constitution. He was among those who argued that institutionalization of the wilayat-i faqih contradicted the constitutional article vesting sovereignty in the people.

On the anniversary of the Black Friday massacre at Jaleh Square, Ayatullah Taleghani, who had received the largest number of votes in the elections for the Assembly of Experts but had been outmaneuvered for its presidency by Ayatullahs Montazari and Beheshti (the latter, head of Khomeyni's Islamic Republican Party), spoke at the Behesht-e Zarah cemetery, warning Iranians to avoid despotism masquerading as religion. It was against Islam, he reminded his listeners, to deprive people of the right to criticize, to protest, and to express grievances. A few days later, on September 9, he died. He had long argued in behalf of democratic local councils; to honor his memory — or to avoid protests in his name — local councils were hurriedly organized a month after his death in provincial towns.

Behind Taleghani's warnings lay not only the struggle over the constitution but also clerical demands to purge the oil fields, the civil service, and the army. The irregular militias or revolutionary guard (*pasdaran*) were gradually organized under Ayatullah Lahouti and under Minister of Defense Mustafa Chamran, a Berkeley-educated activist who had spent time in Lebanon and was considered to be a leader of the so-called Amal group that had participated in Shi'ite struggles in Lebanon. Revolutionary guards were scrutinized by members of Khomeyni's Islamic Republican Party before being recruited; eventually, in December 1979, Lahouti resigned, charging that the guards were becoming an arm of the Party. Ayatullah Khomeyni's son-in-law, Shahabuddin Eshraqi, led a campaign against Hasan Nazih, the human rights activist lawyer and ally of Bazargan who had been made head of the national oil company. The campaign began in early June, with charges by Revolutionary Council members Mohammad Beheshti and Mohammad Mofatteh that Nazih had criticized Khomeyni and therefore should be removed. One benevolent theory had it that Nazih was maneuvering to run for President of the new republic as the candidate of Shariatmadari's Moslem People's Republican Party, and that Khomeyni contenders wished to see him sidelined. By September 28 Nazih had been removed by order of Khomeyni and forced underground. He was charged with refusing to purge the labor force, refusing to remove major pay differentials between white- and blue-collar workers, and giving financial support to newspapers critical of the regime. Nazih responded with detailed refutations of the charges; he demanded a public investigation by a panel including Khomeyni and Bazargan. The prosecution quietly dropped the case, and Ahmad Khomeyni, the Ayatullah's son, telephoned Mrs. Nazih with expressions of sympathy.

The campaign against Nazih was but one of a series of struggles that attempted to silence moderate, critical, or independent voices. In April, Ayatullah Taleghani had gone underground for three days after two of his sons and a daughter-in-law were arrested. The Mujahidin declared their willingness to fight at his direction, but he met with Khomeyni and drew back from any challenge. His critical voice was essentially silenced or muted until the final week of his life. At the same time, in mid-April, Sanjabi resigned as Foreign Minister in an attempt by the Bazargan government to dramatize its protest against interference by the Revolutionary Council. Council member Ibrahim Yazdi replaced him. Hedayatullah Matin-Daftari was driven underground in the summer. Bazargan attempted to disprove criticism that the government was insufficiently revolutionary by nationalizing a number of banks, companies, and industries in early summer; toward the end of July he announced the gradual merging of the secret Revolutionary Council with the public government. But by September, Mohammad Beheshti, who had become the de facto head of the Assembly of Experts, and Abol Hasan Bani-Sadr were again calling for Bazargan's ouster, complaining among other things that he refused to purge the civil service.

What was occurring during the course of 1979 was quite clearly a second phase of the revolution, fitting very nicely Crane Brinton's *Anatomy of Revolution*: the collapse of the *ancien regime* is followed by a period of dual sovereignty, with a public government and a secret power structure; a terror in which over six hundred executions occurred; and a series of crises in which moderates were increasingly neutralized. Bazargan's resignation, along with that of Foreign Minister Yazdi, ending the period of dual sovereignty, came on November 6th in the drama surrounding Muharram 1979 (see Epilogue).

Economics. Just as there were fears about the ambiguity of the nature of an Islamic constitutional government (*mashruta*, "constitution," from *shart*, "condition," implying conditioned by the Qur'an), so too there was considerable speculation about what Islam would mean for the economy. Ayatullah Shariatmadari tried to allay fears in January 1979 by saying that not all interest was usury, that the future government would need international technical help, and that international banks with their interest rates would be welcome. But Abol-Hasan Bani-Sadr, an economist who seemed to be close to Khomeyni, issued an economic program that called for abolishing all interest, nationalizing banks, canceling all international debts owed by Iran, establishing workers' committees to run all public enterprises (such as the oil industry, the banks, and the media), lowering oil production and raising oil prices, and introducing high taxes on imported industrial goods to stimulate domestic industry. Another major set of demands, much discussed in broad nonspecific terms and incorporated into the platform of the National Democratic Front, called for redistribution of wealth and a new land reform.

The call to abolish interest received much attention in the Islamic world. Kuwait in particular moved to establish modern banking facilities on a significant scale which avoided interest calculations and operated on a profit- and risk-sharing basis. The calls for worker participation in management had been present among various groups in the revolution since the summer of 1978. University professors threw out their administrators and elected their own deans and department chairmen. After the revolution, secret committees were established in some of the universities, and these conducted the hiring and firing procedures. Workers in the oil fields demanded a say in production and export strategies. In January 1979 various workers' committees were set up in the news agencies, at the airport, and at other places.

Perhaps the most interesting expression of Islamic economics during the revolution were the cooperative organizations set up to support the strikes, to feed the poor, and to organize relief. This first became evident on a large scale perhaps at the time of the Tabas earthquake. Relief was organized by Ayatullah Shirazi in Mashhad, and television coverage played up the contrast between the inefficiency of the government relief and the efficiency of the religious network. The piece de resistance was the television coverage of the peasant who turned to the queen and told her not to come merely to look at their suffering but to grab a shovel and do something useful. In Tehran, merchants and the religious network organized to subsidize food and to support people who had no income either because they were impoverished or because they were on strike. Most important, the critical oil strike was supported by donations throughout the country, with professionally printed receipts being given to donors. Granted that the revolutionary enthusiasm helped maintain these networks, nonetheless cooperation was demonstrated to be a viable organizational tool. So much for the ideology of the shah that the people had to have everything done for them. Once again the shah was exposed.

Economic issues after the revolution took second place to political reorganization. Oil production was initiated, but while revenues came in, there was little ability to infuse the money into the domestic economy. Production levels were lowered to roughly three million barrels per day as compared with nearly six million barrels before the revolution, but as world oil prices continued to rise, Iranian government receipts did not suffer. In addition, Iran expanded the number of customers from about ten to about forty companies. Banks, insurance, and a number of industrial enterprises were nationalized in June and July. In December, Bani-Sadr, now Finance Minister, announced the amalgamation of banks into eight national banks, seven divided functionally (housing, mining, agriculture, and so on) and a provincial bank, divided according to province and incorporating the former Bank Sadarat, the most aggressive commercial bank with a wide network of local branches. These Islamic banks, it was announced, would no longer charge interest on loans, but only a fixed 4 percent fee. Wages were raised for workers and lowered for management. Credits were provided for farmers. But the revolutionary economic policy remained unclear.

Peasants and sedentary tribal farmers in Fars, in Turkoman country near Gorgan, in Shahsavan country near Ardebil, in villages near Tehran, and in Kurdistan thought the revolution meant a new land redistribution; they seized lands they thought had been taken from them unjustly and resisted landlords who attempted to recover their property. The ulama protested. Khomeyni told the Turkomen that irrigated lands previously owned by a number of the shah's generals should now belong to the community at large (bait-ul-mal). Shariatmadari issued a similar fatwa against the Shahsavand seizure of the Dasht-e Moghan irrigation project. Ayatullah Dastgheeb issued similar opinions in the Shiraz area. The Ministry of Agriculture announced that the Dez Irrigation Project in Khuzistan would be sold to private persons rather than restored to the thousands of families evicted from the land. On the other hand, when the **Mujahidin interpreted the Qur'anic verses on the spoils of war (Sura Anfahl) as support for public or collective property in pursuit of a** classless society (*jama'i tawhidi*) and said that this should apply to mines, forests, and other national resources as well as to land seized from the shah's retainers, they were condemned as marxists illegitimately manipulating Islamic terminology. Mines and forests belong to the discoverer, as long as he pays Islamic taxes.

A basic problem in the industrial sector and the cities was that of getting people back to work. Revolutionary committees were set up to aid management in a number of firms, and many of those who had jobs considered their lot improved, despite high inflation, low productivity, and shortages. A new spirit of proletarian — or ascetic Islamic — austerity reigned in some of the largest firms, where managers received salaries considerably smaller than those of their predecessors, occupied smaller offices, and replaced fancy hand-woven carpets with machine-made floor coverings in emulation of Khomeyni's simple life style. But many did not have jobs. On April 11 the unemployed demonstrated in Isfahan, Abadan, and Tehran. In Tehran, failing to gain satisfaction from the Ministry of Labor, a thousand people marched to the home of Ayatullah Taleghani. During the summer of 1979 Khomeyni called for a jihad for rural reconstruction, asking urban dwellers to go into the villages and volunteer help to the peasants. When those who did so — either following the jihad or simply returning to aid their families' seasonal labor need — returned in the fall, they again swelled the ranks of the unemployed. On October 1 and 2, 1,500 demonstrated, chanting "death to this fascist regime" and "death to the Islamic republic." On November 12 there was a major demonstration of some thousand people at the Ministry of Labor.

Women. That women participated in all aspects of the revolution is evidence that it was a genuine social movement; it is not necessarily evidence that their position would be improved after the revolution. In Algeria women were full partners in a revolution whose ideology was explicit equality of the sexes; yet afterward women were again reduced to a traditional role. The religious leadership of the Iranian revolution stressed the liberal interpretation cited in chapter 5: women are not prevented from participating fully in the public sphere: they can vote and hold any office; but they should not be used as sex objects divorced from conjugal and family obligations as ways of selling and packaging the commerce of the West, which is a form of sexual exploitation and neocolonial domination. Occasionally there were reactionary statements: in the open parliamentary days of early September 1978 a member from Minab, Heydarzadeh, joined what he thought was the religious bandwagon by proposing a law revoking the gains women had made under the Family Protection Laws, only to find himself roundly abused by women members. In order to allay the fears of otherwise sympathetic progressives, Khomeyni appointed a female physician as one of a committee of five to represent him in Washington in January 1979. She appeared on American television to speak for the revolution, her hair covered with a modernistic headcloth. But upon his return to Iran, one of Khomeyni's first instructions to the new Minister of Justice was to review the Family Protection Law and strike out what was against Islam. He then caused an uproar by saying that women must not work "naked" in the government ministries, widely interpreted as an order that women work in chadors, and indeed there were cases of revolutionary militia turning women away from their offices until they came in chadors.

On March 8, International Women's Day, some ten thousand women marched from the University of Tehran to the prime minister's office; three thousand went by bus to Qum. Heard during the march were cries of "Down with Khomeyni," "Down with this dictatorship." Khomeyni retreated, saying that he had meant only that it was a personal duty of devout Muslim women to wear the veil, not an order to be enforced by the state. The veil, he said, was to be honored as the flag of the revolution, but anyone insulting women in the name of the revolution should be punished. On March 10, a second march was held to the ministry of justice. Although protected by male friends, this time there were ugly clashes with foul-mouthed, knife- and broken-bottle-wielding men. At issue in the marches was not only women's rights, but also the values of democracy the middle class had fought for during the revolution. People were protesting Khomeyni's insistence that the referendum on the Islamic republic be a yes/no vote, without any chance to indicate support for a secular republic or other form of government than one under his guidance. They were supported in this by Ayatullah Shariatmadari.

Although anti-Khomeyni sentiment was building, marches were abruptly canceled on the grounds that the revolution was too fragile to be split. The women's issue gradually sank into the background, and on the birthday of Fatima, the daughter of the Prophet — May 17 — declared Iranian Women's Day, a march of some ten thousand veiled women was held, with men segregated, but with some veiled women carrying rifles.

Khomeyni suggested bans on coeducation, on music, on the practice of males and females swimming together or mingling in public gatherings such as political marches. All these remained open to negotiation. Marches were segregated, but women continued to be seen without veils, although progressive activists wore headcloths, and the ban on music was ignored.

Minorities.   Because the 1905 constitution had made second-class citizens of non-Ja'fari Shi'ites (in the sense that they could not become cabinet ministers or judges) and because it contained provisions confining freedom of press and education to things that were not harmful in Islam, there was a good deal of concern over what a more fully Islamic interpretation of the constitution might bring. Minorities had participated in the National Front movement of the 1940s and felt considerable solidarity with the political and social goals of the revolution, but they were uneasy about fighting for those goals in Islamic rather than secular terms. During the winter of 1978, handbills and wall graffiti calling for the death of Zoroastrians, Jews, Assyrians, and Armenians evoked fearful memories of the religious riots of the turn of the century.

The position of Bahais remained a concern throughout. Sadarat bank branches were regular targets of demonstrators on the grounds that the bank was Bahai controlled; there was the riot after 'Ashura in Shiraz; Khomeyni repeatedly refused to acknowledge any rights of Bahais, although he said Jews and Christians would be protected. The double slander on American television by Dr. Mansur Farhang, a defender of the revolution, that hostility to Bahais was understandable because they had been recruited in great numbers into SAVAK and had been trained in Israel did not help. On July 12, 1979, the Bahai temple in Tehran and other Bahai property were seized, and the temple was given to Alama Nuri to turn into an Islamic institute. In September the house of the Bab in Shiraz, a major Bahai shrine, was destroyed. Graveyards in Yazd and other towns were desecrated, corpses exhumed and burned. A total of sixteen shrines and historical sites were confiscated or destroyed, graveyards in at least nine towns were bulldozed or desecrated, and homes in over a score of villages were burned or looted.

And yet the revolution was remarkably protective of minorities. Jews were extremely nervous because of Khomeyni's anti-Zionist rhetoric and Israel's participation in the creation of SAVAK was constantly played up and given as the main reason oil to Israel would be cut off, whereas

Israeli development aid in the Qazvin plain, the poultry industry, and elsewhere was never mentioned. Five to ten thousand of the eighty thousand Iranian Jews left the country during the turmoil, many hoping to return. Of the majority who stayed, a few were active in the movement. The November 5 riot in Tehran which swept down Shah Reza and Ferdowsi streets, destroying Armenian liquor stores, passed by the solid row of Jewish carpet shops, leaving them untouched.

Jews worried again when Ayatullah Khomeyni and Ayatullah Taleghani both repeated the absurd demagoguery that Iranian soldiers would not shoot their Muslim brothers and that it had been Israeli soldiers who had fired on the crowd at Jaleh Square. A Jewish delegation went to Qum to present a contribution to the movement to Ayatullah Shariatmadari. Another delegation was received in Paris by Ayatullah Khomeyni. Both ayatullahs said Jews would be protected. During the bloody riots a Jewish hospital in Tehran became a center of blood donations and transfusions for the wounded. When Khomeyni returned to Iran, a Jewish delegation was present to welcome him. After the Bazargan government was installed, four Jewish leaders in Tehran held a news conference in which they announced solidarity with the revolution, that they expected but would overlook minor incidents of discrimination, that they were cutting all ties to international Jewish organizations, and that they felt themselves to be first and foremost Iranians. This same group, eventually calling itself the Society of Intellectual Jews, held a memorial service after the assassination of Professor — and since the revolution, Ayatullah — Mortaza Motahhari, a leader of the Revolutionary Committee, and expressed again solidarity with the revolution.

Nonetheless, on May 9, 1979, in an extraordinary warning to the Jewish community, the prominant businessman and Jewish community leader Habib Elghanian, was executed by a revolutionary court. The crime was "contact with Israel and Zionism." One of the rumors floated among New York's Iranian students was that he had been killed in revenge for Motahhari's assassination, because only an Israeli agent could have killed such a central figure in the revolution — this despite the fact that Motahhari's death was claimed by the Forghan guerrilla group, and despite the fact that a Jewish delegation which had visited Khomeyni after Motaheri's assassination had been promised again that Jews were protected. Two months later a Jewish businessman was killed in Isfahan by an anonymous assassin allegedly in retaliation for Israeli raids on Lebanon.

Christians too were promised protection by Khomeyni. At the time of the November 5 riot, the Armenian bishop issued a statement that the destruction of Armenian liquor stores was anti-liquor, not anti-Armenian. During 'Ashura a Christian contingent marched chanting:

| *Din-i ma masihi'st* | Our religion is Christianity, |
| *Rahbar-i ma Khumeyni'st* | Our leader is Khomeyni. |

At Khomeyni's request, electricity blackouts were suspended at Christmas and New Year's so that Christians could celebrate. For the Armenian Christmas in January, the Armenian archbishop announced that public festivities would be suspended in solidarity with the revolution. A priest in Shiraz was slain early in the revolution, and in October 1979 there was an attempt on the life of Anglican Bishop Hasan Dehghani-Tafti (a convert many years ago from Islam). Shaykhi leader, Abdul Reza Ibrahimi, was assassinated in Kirman in December 1979. Shaykhis are a sect within Twelver Shi'ite Islam which has common nineteenth-century roots with Babism and Bahaism.

Ismailis (members of a non-Twelver but Shi'ite branch of Islam), like Jews, were anxious: the leadership in Mashhad involved itself in the movement, but Ismaili villagers, like many Muslim villagers, remained faithful to a king who had protected them against the excesses of the mullas or remained simply bewildered by the events. Zoroastrians also were frightened and anxious. Shortly after the installation of the Bazargan government, some guerrillas walked into the main Tehran fire temple, removed the portrait of the Prophet Zoroaster, and replaced it with one of Khomeyni. That, commented an old Zoroastrian woman, was going too far. Sunni minorities also expressed doubts, and in their case the issue was also compounded by ethnic and linguistic issues.

Despite much speculation during 1978 about the potential for the ethnic minorities to attempt to break away from the central government, ethnic divisions did not become an actual political issue until the spring of 1979, when the Kurds, the Turkomans, the Arabs of Khuzistan, and the Baluch began to assert their linguistic differences and make administrative demands. And once again the religious boundary proved critical. Kurdish Sunnis armed themselves during the course of the revolution and, while supporting its goals, demanded autonomous status within an Iranian federation. They worried that Khomeyni always spoke of Iran as a Shi'ite state, never acknowledging that there were Sunnis as well; and they spoke bitterly of past humiliations when they had gone to Tehran or to other Shi'ite parts of Iran and were caught, for instance, performing the namaz differently. But there was more to their demands than this. The Pahlavis, in the interest of national integration, had discouraged the use of Turkish, Arabic, and Baluchi in the schools and as a medium of literary production. For similar reasons, the Pahlavis had also systematically throughout Iran appointed governors, heads of bureaucratic offices, and military personnel to serve in areas where they had no local ties. In spring 1979, first the Kurds, then the Turkomans, Arabs, and Baluch, demanded a reversal of these policies. They wanted the right to teach and use their own language, to appoint their own civil and military officials, and to have a larger say over regional development plans. This became one of the first major struggles for Khomeyni, who, like the Pahlavis, preferred a unitary state over any form of federation.

Interestingly, the Azerbaijanis — previously the most vocal of the opponents of the Pahlavis' linguistic policy — were not visibly involved. In part the explanation for their relative silence may be that they were represented in the revolution by Bazargan (although his Turkish language skills are minimal), Taleghani (although his home village has its own distinctive dialect and is on the linguistic border between Turkish and Persian speakers), and Shariatmadari. None of these exercised central power, but all three clearly were jockeying for position. In part the explanation may also be that they are Shi'ite, and not Sunni as are the Kurds, Turkomans, and Baluch. Karim Sanjabi, a Kurd, was nationally important but he is not only an upper-class Tehrani, far removed from the concerns of Kurdish villagers, he also is a Shi'ite.

From the movement's point of view, minorities ought to have no fears. The model is 'Ali. 'Ali dealt justly with minorities. He rebuked 'Umar for adjudicating a case against a Jew just because the other party was a Muslim, and he rebuked 'Umar for being discourteous to a Jew in court, even though the Jew's case was weak. A few of the revolutionaries point out that Jews experienced a period of intellectual glory in Muslim Spain and were better off there than under Christianity. The case might be stronger if they could also claim that minorities were better off under Islam than under the secular modern West. That is a challenge for the revolution to live up to.

A New Era

Four times previously — in 1873, 1891, 1905-1911, and 1952 — religious and liberal-reformist groups had joined in alliance and forced a major government policy reversal or a major change in the form of government. Four times, as soon as the immediate objective was achieved the alliance unraveled. The question in 1979 is not only whether the alliance can hold but, more important, whether a liberal civil order can be established. Two of the previous efforts — 1906 and 1952 — can be seen as attempts at a bourgeois revolution, with intellectual leadership coming largely from secular liberals. In the 1978 effort religious leaders — especially Ayatullah Ruhollah Musavi Khomeyni, but also Ayatullahs Mohammad-Kazem Shariatmadari and Mahmud Taleghani and Engineer Mehdi Bazargan — played the key roles. This was not a regressive atavism of religious fundamentalism; nor was there any failure of liberal imagination. Rather, it is argued, Islam could play a unifying political role because the monarchical dictatorship of the 1930s-1940s and the 1960s-1970s had suppressed all other forms of political debate and organization. A variety of divergent interests therefore expressed themselves through the Islamic idiom. The question now is not only whether the use of the Islamic idiom will decay but whether the progressive promise of Islam can be fulfilled.

If 1979 proves to be a turning point for Iranian Shi'ism, a "translation" of Shi'ism will be involved. Over the past decades Shi'ism has been crafted into a powerful moral platform for criticizing the diseases of the Pahlavi regime: the intimidation by the secret police, the massive corruption at the top of society, the destruction of agriculture, the punitive price-regulation campaigns against the bazaar, the misuses of the talents of the middle class, the subordination of Iranian development to outside imperialist interests, and the separation of the monarchy from accountability and responsiveness to its own people. Today Shi'ite leaders have the opportunity to translate their moral opposition and social criticism into a framework for modern politics. Issues such as the nature of politics and economics, the position of women, and the rights of religious, linguistic, and cultural minorities take on new relevance. It has been well said that the Western revolutionary tradition stresses individual freedom, sometimes at the expense of economic justice, that the Eastern (Communist) revolutionary tradition stresses economic justice at the expense of freedom, and that the Shi'ite promise is one of combining freedom and justice. We wish the Iranian people well in their attempt to reach for that promise.

Epilogue: Muharram 1400/1979

To American eyes, everything that goes on in Iran is a bit strange. It appears to be like an Oz with minarets where the only hope for not being devoured or otherwise zeroed out by the wicked ayatollah of the west is to be saved by the good ayatollah of the east.

—Nicholas von Hoffman, 25 December 1979

*M*UHARRAM 1400/1979 perhaps should have been a celebration of deliverance from the shah and shifting to an active mood of construction rather than protest. Instead, the shah's entry into the United States for medical treatment virtually on the eve of Muharram, as the crisis over the constitutional referendum was building, reactivated the Karbala paradigm and touched off a symbolic protest drama involving the entire world through diplomacy, economics, and the media. The coincidental seizure of the Kaaba in Mecca by armed Saudi fundamentalists on the first day of the new Islamic century was incorporated into the Iranian drama: Khomeyni used it in his repeated assertion that the Iranian revolution was not a nationalist one, but an Islamic one, which respected neither the political boundaries drawn by Western colonialism in an attempt to divide the Islamic world nor the tyrannical puppet regimes imposed on long-suffering Muslims. The drama ended the period of dual sovereignty and inaugurated a bid by young Islamic leftist militants to negotiate with the Revolutionary Council and with Khomeyni for a greater voice in policy-making. Using world preoccupation with the Iranian crisis as a cover, the Soviet Union invaded Afghanistan, thereby raising the geopolitical stakes in Iran.[1]

The Muharram Drama

On October 22, 1979, the deposed shah was flown from his refuge in Mexico to New York City for treatment of gallstones, a blocked bile duct, jaundice, and lymphoma cancer.[2] Both the U.S. State Department and the Iranian government had repeatedly warned against allowing the shah to enter the United States; former Secretary of State Henry Kissinger and David Rockefeller, however, argued that the country should

232

offer refuge to a man who had been a loyal friend. The Carter administration cited medical humanitarianism, ignoring the issue of moral honor invoked by Kissinger and the moral indictment by the revolutionaries that entry of the shah was harboring a criminal of the order of an Adolph Eichmann (a puppet of others, in this case, American and Western imperialists). The Carter administration was naive and once again demonstrated insensitivity to the rhythm of the revolutionary process (the crisis over the constitution), its symbolic structure (the approach of Muharram), and the depth of Iranian paranoia about the intentions of the United States (the suspicion that the shah was not ill; that a counter-revolutionary restoration was being plotted by the financial and political directors of Western imperialism; and that foreign press coverage of internal domestic problems was part of a strategy to destabilize the nascent Islamic republic). For Iranians the admission of the shah was a symbolic insult similar to Carter's much publicized praise of the shah, in Tehran, on the eve of the revolution (January 1978) and telephoned support at the time of the Jaleh Square massacre. Khomeyni would drive the symbolism home in a speech on the eve of Muharram. On previous Muharrams, he thundered, Iranians had faced only the offspring of the mother of corruption (the shah); this Muharram they faced the mother of corruption herself (the United States).

The symbolism was used to mobilize support for the Khomeyni forces in the constitutional referendum. Objections to the new constitution were being voiced from various quarters. And there were other signs of discontent: the October and November demonstrations of the unemployed; clashes in Bandar Enzeli and Rasht on October 16 and 17 between fishermen and revolutionary guards over the revocation of rights to fish caviar in favor of a government monopoly, leaving ten to thirteen dead and forty to fifty injured; clashes in Baluchistan, Kurdistan, and Khuzistan (where in one early October week alone nine bombs exploded leaving thirteen dead and many injured); the shooting of two students by revolutionary guards in Tabriz during a demonstration at a vocational school demanding upgraded diplomas; the breaking up with chains and clubs by pro-Khomeyni toughs (or possibly by Islamic leftists) of a teachers' rally addressed by Ehsan Shariati, son of Dr. Ali Shariati. Shariati had been complaining about irresponsible clerics. Khomeyni's speeches at the beginning of November were filled with injunctions to "break the pens and tongues" of those who worked for the American imperialists. The middle class was beset with arbitrary attachments of bank accounts, seizure of "unutilized land" by the Bonyad-e Mostasafin (Foundation of the Poor), and regulations that couples could own only one thousand square meters of urban Tehran land or two thousand square meters in provincial cities.

November 4, 1979, was Students' Day, the anniversary of the slayings at the University of Tehran. Shortly after noon prayers, several hundred students and activists seized the United States Embassy, taking hostage sixty-three Americans (plus several others who were soon released). They demanded that the shah be returned to Iran to stand trial. In New York City several Iranians chained themselves to the Statue of Liberty with the same demand.

On November 6 Khomeyni accepted the resignations of Prime Minister Bazargan and Foreign Minister Yazdi, ending dual sovereignty. The Revolutionary Council was ordered to take over. Bazargan and Yazdi had met briefly with American National Security Advisor Brzezinski in Algiers, which was held against them, as were their objections to the seizing of the hostages and passive reaction to the shah's entering the United States. But Bazargan was thanked by Khomeyni for his service and was not excluded from the Revolutionary Council, and Yazdi was later appointed emissary to Baluchistan. In Khorassan, meanwhile, Governor Ahmadzadeh resigned, citing interference by the clergy in government affairs. Ahmadzadeh—like Bazargan, a senior figure who had supported Mosaddegh in the 1950s and a religious man—had repeatedly criticized Bazargan for yielding too easily to the demands of Khomeyni and other clerics.

The first goal of the student activists was successful: removing the moderates ("reformists," to them) from the center of power, forcing the political struggle to move faster (to keep the revolution "on course"). A struggle ensued over how best to utilize the hostages. The seizure of the embassy and hostages, creating international furor, proved to be a spectacular ploy. Foreign journalists, especially the television media, were welcomed back to Tehran to film daily demonstrations outside the embassy. At midday the students inside would come to the front gate and toss carnations and tulips (symbols of martyrdom) back and forth to the demonstrators. Demonstrators were bussed in from industrial plants and occasionally from military units. Although when Fida'i leftists marched in support of the seizure they were heckled as American provocateurs, the captors of the embassy seemed to be Islamic leftists: they called themselves *khat-i Imam* (adherents of the "line of the Imam"), a leftist phrasing which also fit their dress (headcloths, as opposed to chadors, for the women, and full beards, as opposed to close cropped beards, for some of the men). When asked by journalists if they would release the hostages if Khomeyni ordered them to do so, they replied not that they would follow the Imam, but rather, "You do not know the Imam; he would never order us to do such a thing."

Khomeyni's approval of the seizure of the hostages and his delegation of revolutionary guards to the embassy may have been an attempt to control the outcome. For Khomeyni and for Ayatullah Beheshti, the head of Khomeyni's Islamic Republican Party, the seizure of the hostages initially must have seemed a godsend to silence criticism of the new constitution and to smooth passage of the referendum on it, scheduled just after 'Ashura to capitalize on the heightened religious feelings of Muharram. Indeed, Khomeyni reveled in the confrontation with the United States, pointing to continuing imperialist oppression when that country blocked Iran's request for a UN Security Council hearing on its case against the shah. With the approach of Muharram, any military action by the United States would reinforce its role as Yazid in the Karbala symbolism, and Khomeyni repeatedly warned that Iranians were united in their willingness to be martyred. Thirteen female and black hostages were released two days before the start of Muharram at Khomeyni's request, in a further attempt to draw attention to the various forms of oppression associated with the American system of government.[3]

At dawn prayers on Muharram 1, several hundred armed Saudi fundamentalists seized the Kaaba in Mecca and attempted to proclaim their leader as the Mahdi, the messiah. Khomeyni immediately denounced the sacrilege of Islam's central shrine as the work of the Americans. Within hours, angry Pakistanis besieged and burned the American Embassy in Islamabad; those inside narrowly escaped after six hours, casting doubt on the concern of the Pakistani authorities for them. Anti-American demonstrations followed in Turkey, India, Pakistan, Bangla Desh, and Libya. The secretary of the Pakistani student union, leader of a fundamentalist group that had just won student elections, apologized for the loss of two American lives in Islamabad, though not for the attack on the embassy, and charged that the Jewish lobby in the United States was involved in the seizure of the Kaaba.[4] Iran declared a military alert against American retaliation, and Foreign Minister Abol-Hasan Bani-Sadr announced at Friday prayers, November 23 (Muharram 3), that his country would not honor international debts accrued illegally under the shah's regime.[5]

The demand for the return of the shah to stand trial was a popular one in Iran. As Bani-Sadr noted on November 11, a Nuremberg-style trial was needed to renew the dignity of the Iranian people and to raise morale for reconstruction. The holding of hostages was not so universally popular; Bani-Sadr himself attempted to mediate, suggesting that if the shah's money were returned to Iran, if there were an international investigation of the shah's regime, if the United States would acknowledge its role in the tyranny of the shah, perhaps the activists at the embassy would release their hostages.[6] All these compromises were rejected by the activists, as were subsequent suggestions by Sadegh Qotbzadeh, who replaced Bani-Sadr as Foreign Minister after 'Ashura. Khomeyni advisors were divided on the hostage issue. Bani-Sadr wished to attend a UN Security Council meeting requested by the United States so that he could present Iran's case for the return of the shah and prevent that forum from concentrating solely on the issue of the breach of international law in the taking of hostages. But he lost an argument in Qum with Khomeyni's grandson, Sayyid Husayn. Bani-Sadr argued that the seizure of hostages was against international law and Islamic tradition; that it would allow the United States to mobilize world opinion, including that of other Islamic countries, against Iran; and that it diverted attention from Iran's real economic and social problems. Sayyid Husayn responded that the seizure of hostages was a blow against imperialism that would unite the third world behind Iran, and that it would mobilize support within Iran behind Khomeyni, quieting criticism. Qotbzadeh sided with Sayyid Husayn. Khomeyni denounced the Security Council as being controlled by the United States.[7]

Meanwhile, American public outrage at the violation of diplomatic immunity and seizure of the hostages and at American impotence to secure their quick release was expressed by the refusal of transport workers to service Iranian aircraft or Iran-bound ships, by demonstrations, by the burning of Iranian flags, by hostility toward individual Iranians, and by a flurry of sarcastic cartoons in the press.[8] Statements condemning the seizure were made by the Pope, Egyptian President Sadat, European and Arab League foreign ministers, the United Nations Security Council, and the World Court. Iranians countered with charges of illegalities committed by the CIA in helping restore the shah to his throne in 1953 and by international firms through bribery and collusion with the shah's regime and of the illegalities of the shah's regime itself. The call for Iranian students in the United States to reregister with immigration officials, which would have led to the deportation of those whose papers were not in order, may have helped inflame the American public, though other actions were taken to channel and contain popular indignation. An end to the import of Iranian oil was a popular symbolic gesture countering any suggestion that economic blackmail by Iran could work, as was a freeze of Iranian assets in American banks in response to Iranian threats to withdraw funds and create havoc in the banking system.[9] Further economic and military threats were hinted at.[10] Iran attempted to use these reactions as proof of imperialist malevolence, resorting at times to unabashed false and demagogic rhetoric — for home consumption as much as to confound the Americans.[11]

Despite all the symbolic mobilization, the constitutional referendum did not do well. Those who voted passed it overwhelmingly; but Kurdistan, much of Khuzistan, Baluchistan, many of Tehran's middle class, and most importantly much of Azerbaijan refused to vote. On the eve of the referendum Ayatullah Shariatmadari, the association of human rights lawyers, the Mujahidin, the Feda'yyin, and the Kurds called for postponement. Bani-Sadr, Bazargan, Ayatullah Bahonar (of the Revolutionary Council), and Ayatullah Marashi-Najafi appeared on television urging people to vote for the referendum; the Tudeh Party also lent its support. Shariatmadari's statement that there was a serious conflict between the article of the constitution vesting sovereignty in the people and the articles on *wilayat-i faqih* was sufficient to keep many of his followers from the polls. In a crude attempt to circumvent the impact of his statement, an edited version was shown on television. The original statement began that the constitution was Islamically acceptable, except for the contradiction between the two articles on sovereignty and wilayat-i faqih which would have to be altered. But only the first clause was broadcast. Some Tabrizis were misled and did vote; when they found out what Shariatmadari had actually said, they demanded their ballots back and burned some ballot boxes.

Demonstrations and fighting broke out on December 5. In Qum, Shariatmadari's house was attacked by Khomeyni supporters who shouted that those who had not voted had no right to criticize; a guard was killed. In Tabriz, Shariatmadari supporters seized the radio station, called for the ouster of Qotbzadeh as director of the national radio and television network, and chased the pro-Khomeyni governor from his office. On December 7, Shariatmadari and Khomeyni met and agreed that Shariatmadari was to be consulted on changes in the constitution and on all matters dealing with Azerbaijan. A joint committee was to be sent to mediate the tempers in Tabriz by the Revolutionary Council and by Shariatmadari. Shariatmadari's appointees included Hasan Nazih, Azerbaijani lawyer and former head of the national oil company who had been driven underground in September, and Rahmatullah Moghaddam-Maragheh, Azerbaijani lawyer and representative to the Assembly of Experts. The joint committee never materialized; Nazih went back underground; and Moghaddam-Maragheh was soon driven from his Tabriz offices. The struggle in Tabriz continued: planes carrying revolutionary guards were denied permission to land by Shariatmadari forces; Khomeyni forces regained the radio station and ransacked the offices of Moghaddam-Maragheh. Khomeyni militants in Qum and Tehran demanded that Shariatmadari disband his Muslim People's Republican Party, charging that it was divisive. Shariatmadari, with quiet sarcasm, replied that he did not need to disband the party; the Khomeyni government would do it soon enough, and would then disband all other parties as well. Kurdish leader Shaykh Ezzedin Husayn sent Shariatmadari a message of support. In Baluchistan the governor was taken hostage and fighting broke out: Baluchis charged the governor, an outsider, was staffing local offices with his cronies. Far more important, the Baluchi religious leader Mowlavi Abdul-Aziz Mollazadeh accused the revolutionary guards of molesting women during their house-by-house search to disarm the Baluch; guns so seized, it was charged, were being given to local Shi'ites. Khomeyni charged that the troubles in Tabriz were

American-inspired. Shariatmadari responded sharply that to connect all events to American imperialism would not solve any problems, that he could not guarantee peace in Tabriz when agents of the Islamic republic caused death and injury without reason, that civil war could ensue if the sensibilities of the Azerbaijanis were threatened or played with, and that Khomeyni was at fault for having broken the December 7 agreement. At Friday prayers, December 28, Shariatmadari commented acidly to some three hundred followers: "Under the shah I was not free to speak and they came to my house and killed a student. Under this government, I am still not free to speak and they come to my house and kill a guard." Shariatmadari followers in Tabriz the night before had taken nine revolutionary guards hostage, in a kind of mirror image of the American Embassy hostage situation, with supporters demanding release of two hundred persons arrested by the revolutionary guards in the previous weeks and shouting slogans attacking Khomeyni, Qotbzadeh, the Khomeyni-appointed governor, and the Khomeyni religious represen-tative.[12] Shariatmadari, demonstrating that his leadership was different from Khomeyni's, ordered the release of the hostages. The Khomeyni regime subsequently executed eleven members of Shariatmadari's party in retaliation for this resistance.

The bread-and-circus game into which the Khomeyni regime in part had been maneuvered by the activists at the American Embassy began to wear on the Revolutionary Council, as the activists began to charge, first, Amir Abbas Entezam (a former Bazargan deputy minister, then Ambassador to Sweden), then Bazargan's Movement for the Liberation of Iran, and then Jamshid Iranpur (allegedly a member of the Revolu-tionary Council) with collusion with the United States. The activists had threatened to try the hostages as spies if the shah were moved from the U.S. to another country. When the shah did leave for Panama, and when the U.S. managed to get the UN Security Council to entertain discussions on economic sanctions against Iran, the Revolutionary Council at-tempted to divert the threat of spy trials into symbolic trials of the United States — after which the hostages would be released. Such trials were vaguely scheduled for the period following elections for the president of the new republic to be held on January 25, 1980. Ibrahim Yazdi, however, revived the arguments of Sayyid Husayn Khomeyni for con-tinuing use of a show:

> In order to rally the masses, this kind of thing should continue. If this cam-paign against the Americans ends just by a trial of these Americans and their deportation, it will be a disaster. It has to go further. We have to divert this to the reconstruction of the country. When the masses are com-pletely mobilized against the Americans, it is easier to tell them to go to the fields and do this and that.[13]

But the Revolutionary Council began to move away from this use of the hostages and support of the activists in an attempt to consolidate control.

Revolutionary Processes and Youth

While the circus media symbolism was of increasing importance on all sides as a critical technique of domestic political persuasion and to a lesser extent of international dialogue, bread issues were also slowly being pursued.[14] Two major social processes were taking place: a revolutionary process, and, perhaps even more important, a demographic explosion which unleashed both popular culture and the young generation as massive social forces for the coming decade. Each of these can only be pointed out, for they are just beginning.

Although we can describe the Iranian revolution in the general stages outlined by Crane Brinton, it is still premature to characterize in Weberian fashion how the revolution might function to create a stronger state with greater mass mobilization, participation, or loyalty.[15] Is the promise of a bourgeois revolution, or at least a liberal political structure, still viable, awaiting only the ebb of religious fervor as economic conditions deteriorate or as a political arena is organized? So asserts Shapur Bakhtiar in Paris, and so did Hedayatullah Matin-Daftari until forced underground. Or have the opportunities been squandered?[16] So worry Mehdi Bazargan and Ayatullah Shariatmadari. Is the promise of a social revolution—a new land reform, a new social contract for industrial workers, a redistribution of wealth—still on the agenda? Will the terror (nearly seven hundred executed; executions still occurring in December 1979, though at a slower pace, and with review of sentences rather than immediate implementation) be taken in stride or will it increase and cause a reaction moving the revolution sharply to the right or left? Bakhtiar warns that the Tudeh strategy is to support Khomeyni until he collapses and then seize control. Are the clergy playing the role of the traditional petty bourgeoisie (guild craftsmen, rich peasants) of the German 1848 revolution: by breaking with the liberal bourgeoisie, inviting a counter-revolution? So hopes Princess Azadeh Shafiq, daughter of the shah's twin sister, Ashraf, who—also, like Bakhtiar, in Paris—speaks of a royalist restoration under a younger generation, or at least a military coup.[17] Will the clergy reconstitute the shah's state with a secret police (SAVAMA), a military constructed from the revolutionary guards and the purged military, public foundations such as the Bonyad-e Mustafasin (the former Pahlavi Foundation), a controlled media, a controlled legislature, and oil revenues? Will the clerical leadership survive politically discrediting charges of opportunism and physical assassination?[18] Or will the Soviet invasion of Afghanistan (December 1979) provide the groundwork for either a defensive military coup or a greater sense of urgency in consolidating a new government?[19]

A major factor in determining the long-term outcome may well be the youth of the population. Over half the population of Iran is under seventeen. Those who compose the revolutionary rank-and-file are young men in their teens and twenties. The leadership of the revolution was the old generation, men in their seventies, who had struggled already in the heady days of the forties and fifties: Bazargan, Khomeyni, Shariatmadari, Sanjabi, Bakhtiar. Relatively few middle-aged men in their fifties or forties were prominent in their own right: Motahhari and Montazari and, to a lesser extent, Makarem and Qoddusi (who became first head of the revolutionary committee in Qum, and then the chief revolutionary public prosecutor). Others came to prominence as functionaries of Khomeyni: Rafsinjani (who was Khomeyni's first spokesman when he returned to Tehran), Yazdi, Qotbzadeh, Bahonar, Beheshti, Mofatteh (the last three were students of Motahhari; Motahhari and Montazari were students of Khomeyni). The youth of the group that seized the United States Embassy — and their relation to the two older generations — is not unrepresentative of the structure of the revolution, and perhaps a vision of the future. Respectful of the senior generation, they have relatively little time for the middle generation, which was largely cowed by the Pahlavi regime, and seem only to tolerate the functionaries of the Khomeyni regime — Qotbzadeh, Yazdi, Beheshti, Rafsinjani — according them little independent authority.

Eli Kedourie some years ago made a shrewd, if bitter, observation:

> The young are those who possess the techniques of Europe which Middle Eastern society, so they insist, must adopt or perish. Therefore, they know better than their fathers, and they have the key to political salvation. The passion and presumption of youth, their rooted belief in their ancestors' ignorance and folly, their inexperience and clumsiness in the exercise of power combine to deprive them of that decorum and gravitas which impressed observers about Moslem ruling classes of past centuries, and which served to put a check on the full expression of greed and cruelty.[20]

For Iran the stress on lack of restraint — at least so far — is misplaced; the recognition of the changing of a generational guard, however, is correct. The revolutionary youth of Iran are introducing a new populist-religious idiom.

Writing of a similar and older situation in Turkey, Allen Dubetsky points out that as demographic explosion led to an inundation of the cities by peasants, a new urban social class emerged: religious yet enamoured of technology, acknowledging their ignorance yet feeling morally superior to Europe, and derisive of religious fanaticism, ridiculing rural preachers but supportive of university trained religious leaders.[21] It is a similar "class" which carries the revolution in Iran: religious but cynical about the clergy. Politics in Turkey became more unruly as it became democratized, and as rural and religious traditions became honored on the national stage. Similarly in Iran the call is for a more popular cultural code in the national arena, for religious discourse and morality, but not necessarily for the discourse of the clergy or for scholastic puritanism. The idiom of clarifying Islam continues to dominate the revolutionary debate and political process in Iran.

Continuing Conversations

I began this book on a personal note as well as one self-reflective about the ethnographic and anthropological endeavor. I would like to end the same way. When I went to Iran I did not know how to translate the Trinity into a philosophical discourse on God's attributes. Upon my return I found Wolfson's clue. While in Qum, I found it difficult to talk to students about the linguistic form of their discourse, and I charged them with a limited mental framework stemming from not being conversant with such philosophers as Wittgenstein, Dilthey, or Walter Benjamin, though recognizing their concern with rhetoric and logic. Something prevented them from giving any non-Islamic writer a fair reading, not to mention a charitable one. The task they set themselves was rarely understanding, but usually only finding the errors of non-Muslims.

Long after I returned to the United States and struggled with the problems of getting Americans to give a sympathetic hearing to Shi'ism and, as the events of 1977-1979 unfolded, to the voices of the Iranian revolution, I met Professor Mehdi Hairi-Yazdi. The younger son of the founder of the hawza-i ilmi in Qum, a student of Ayatullah Khomeyni, a faculty member of the Theological Faculty of the University of Tehran, a Ph.D. from the University of Toronto as well as the University of Tehran, here was a man who might be able to handle both traditions. His dissertation at Toronto was an attempt to translate the ontology and epistemology of the Persian mystical "illuminationist" tradition (Shihab al-Din Surawardi, Sadr al-Din Shirazi "Mulla Sadra") into the language of English analytic philosophy: Wittgenstein and Russell come as easily into this discourse as Plato, Avicenna, and St. Thomas Aquinas.[22] I had heard of him of course in 1975, as the man from among the ulama who would go to the West and broker what it had to offer, as well as be able to provide a well-grounded defense of Islamic philosophy to the West. With the deaths of Shariati, Taleghani, and Motahhari, the hope of serious brokering falls even more heavily on his shoulders, a task recognized by Ayatullah Khomeyni through repeated requests that he return to Iran and Qum. The request will be honored when the revolutionary fervor subsides sufficiently for students to return to classes. I wish the effort well.

One place for such brokering is in reevaluating the notion of Imam, pointing out to Westerners its philosophical ancestry in Plato's

philosopher-king as well as his dialectics of being and becoming as interpreted by the Islamic philosophers al-Farabi, Ibn Arabi, and Mulla
Sadra. Mulla Sadra particularly provided the account of the spiritual
development of a leader and his relation to the community which Khomeyni studied, taught, and then attempted to execute. This account
describes four journeys: from man to God, from God to God (moving
back and forth between considerations of God's attributes and His
essence, until their unity is apperceived), from God back to man, and
from man to man (instituting the divine law). The relation of God to man
and of leader to community is not the charisma of Weber (*à la* Shariati),
nor the love in Christology, nor the cause-and-effect of secular theorists
of power; rather it is one of divine emanation, both creative and il-
luminative (that is, not one of psychological or emotional feelings in-
duced in the community, but an illumination that reveals real relations of
the world). Whether or not Khomeyni feels he has achieved union with
God and carries that sense of unity in his current political role, he did
study Mullah Sadra with Rafi'i Qazvini and mysticism with Shaykh
Muhammad Ali Shahabadi; and he taught these subjects first to Mehdi
Hairi-Yazdi, and then to Motahhari and Montazeri, before calling a
halt — for unknown reasons — to the teaching of these subjects.

This history of the term Imam and Khomeyni's involvement in
speculative mysticism is of importance in evaluating Khomeyni's
psychology — one perhaps quite distinct from that of most ulama[23] — and
in providing future rapprochement with Shariati's interpretations (as well
as understanding why the clergy find Shariati's interpretations shallow or
philosophically ungrounded). But philosophies of emanation are not
unknown to Western medieval philosophy. It will be a task for Mehdi
Hairi-Yazdi and others to come to terms with post-medieval Western
thought — not only ontology, epistemology, logic, and language-
philosophy, a task already begun in Hairi-Yazdi's dissertation, but also
political and social theory — if they wish to engage in dialogue.

At the time of my meeting with Hairi-Yazdi, I lunched with several
members of the Iranian legation in Washington. Talk turned to Ali
Shariati; the consensus of my hosts was that he was unique and brilliant.
Mohammad Iqbal, Muhammad Abduh, and Jamal ud-Din al-Afghani,
leaders of Islamic modernism early in this century, were predecessors,
but until Shariati, they said, Iranians had had no access to this kind of
thought — a comment on the youth of the movement, who lacked personal experience of the 1890s or the 1920s or, most of them, even the
1950s, but also on the stagnation of Shi'ite thought and the role of censorship and intimidation under the Pahlavis. Writers such as Bazargan,
they admitted, had tried, but none had the depth and particularly the
literary power or aesthetic skill of Shariati, whose book on the *Hajj*
could be read again and again, with new insights gained each time.

I reread the *Hajj*, an almost lyrical interpretation of the meaning of the different parts of the pilgrimage to Mecca; it may be the Shariati equivalent to Khomeyni's mystical journey. It is the journey toward God, the merging of the individual with the community, and the return of a spiritually purposeful individual to ordinary life. The pilgrimage is an antidote to aimless individualism. One begins with proper intention (*niyyat*) to move from self-centeredness to Allah; from slavery to freedom; from racial, national, and class distinctions to equality; from alienation to consciousness. The white dress of the pilgrim is the dress of the hereafter, a spiritual resurrection.

One begins with the seven circumambulations around the Kaaba, where the individual loses himself in the community like, using the traditional metaphor, a drop in the ocean, or a flowing and whirling river:

> Approximately one hour ago, you were at the bank of the "river" standing, thinking of yourself, watching the people and not being one of them; you were a useless particle . . . But now you are flowing and moving. No longer are you stagnated nor putrefied. You are roaring, washing away the rocks, breaking the dams and finding your way to the gardens to grow heaven in the heart of the salty deserts. You irrigate the earth, the fields . . .[24]

Following the circumambulations, one runs seven times between the mountains of Safa and Marwa, like Hajar in search of water for her thirsty infant, Ishmael, purposefully, relying on one's own searching powers as well as on God. The niyyat, circumambulation (*tawaf*), and running between Safa and Marwa (*sa'y*) is the preparatory lesser pilgrimage (*umrah*). The hajj proper then begins. One goes to Arafat at high noon (representing the light of knowledge); at sunset one proceeds to Mashur-ul-Haram, where one selects seventy pebbles in preparation for the next day's jihad: it is a time of concentration, planning, and consciousness. At Mina the next day three idols are stoned, representing the three times Satan whispered to Abraham that it was only a bad dream, that God had not commanded him to sacrifice Ishmael. The Trinity is Shariati's key symbol of evil. He invests it, and the three idols which represent it, with various meanings: despotism or tyranny or Pharaoh or the wolf is the first face of Satan or of Cain, the first idol; the second is exploitation or capitalism or Croesus or the sly rat; the third is hypocrisy and false ideology or Balam or the fox. Cain introduced these vices by killing his brother, thereby turning equals into unequals, subordinating pastoralists to landowners, creating power relations of tyranny and exploitation. After the stoning of the Trinity, one sacrifices as a sign of temporary victory and continuing commitment. One must stay at Mina for three days to discuss the experience, exchange views with others from distant parts of the world, contemplate, and resolve. Only then does one return to the world, invested with a commitment and social purpose.

Shariati's imagery and language are attractive, as are his investment of ritual prescriptions with moral content and his juxtaposition of ancient mythic terms in order to reinvigorate their messages. At the same time, we can see why the ulama find it shallow and facile. The outsider must wonder why Shariati insists on the Trinity as the core symbol of evil. Granted it is a traditional target of attack; granted, too, that Christianity somehow symbolizes the West and so stands for imperialism, the modern object of attack; nonetheless to the modern world it seems a false barrier, an unnecessary hiding behind a traditional wall to the outside, a failure to confront the outside. Philosophy and sufism are rejected by Shariati with less elaboration but with equal firmness—they are at best incomplete approaches to truth, while Islam is complete and perfect.

My hosts at the Islamic Embassy of Iran had no trouble harmonizing Khomeyni and Shariati; their confidence in the revolution was infectious. I was tempted to pursue such harmonization myself: of Khomeyni the mystic and the philosopher (and the politician?), of Shariati, and perhaps even of the middle class Westernized sufis like S. Hussein Nasr.[25] But the ethnographic endeavor—unlike that of the philosopher or political activist—is not to harmonize other people's thought, but to inquire why people who seem to be saying similar things insist they are doing quite different things and why their followers may ignore the differences, to try to present the ranges of interpretation, the differences, the changes over time.

I am reminded of a wonderful exchange with Ayatullah Shariatmadari. He very patiently and good-humoredly allowed me to elicit his genealogy. When I was done, he asked, with a wry twinkle in his eyes, "Now about this science of anthropology, tell me: is it cooked or raw (*pokhta ya napokhta*)?" Returning his grin, I replied: "raw, not yet a science." Perhaps it is not a science at all, but a humanist attempt at dialogue and learning, both for myself and as an aid for others. The task on all sides remains to ascend to fuller levels of understanding, clarity, appreciation, and even truth.

Appendixes
Notes
Glossary
Bibliography
Index

Appendixes

1. Courses of Study

TRADITIONAL MADRASA COURSE OF STUDY

Level I.   Muqaddamat (Preliminaries)

(Items marked with asterisks are contained in *Jami' al-Muqaddamat.*)

'ILM-I SARF (etymology and derivation): *Amthal,* Sarf-i Mir,* Tasrif,* Sharh-i Tasrif**. *Sarf-i Sada*, and *'Arabi asan* have been added recently.

'ILM-I NAHW (syntax): *'Awamil Mulla Muhsin,* Hidaya,* Samadiyya,* Suyuti* (or *Alfiyyat* Ibn Malik, or properly, *al-Nahja al-Mardiyya*, i.e., the thousand verses on grammar by Ibn Malik with commentary by Jalaluddin Suyuti), and chapters 1 and 4 of *Mughni al-Labib* by Ibn Hisham.

BAYAN, MA'ANI, BADI' (rhetoric): *Jawahir al-Balagha* is the preferred text; *Mukhtasar al-Ma'ani* or *Mutawwal* (both commentaries on Qazvini by the Sunni Taftazani) are alternatives, the former and shorter version being more frequently read. *Kubra** of Mir Sayyid Sharif.

Level II.   Dhat (the subject proper)

MANTIQ (logic): *Hashiya*, the "notes" of Mulla 'Abdullah on Taftazani; or *al-Mantiq* by Shaykh Muzaffar (d. in the 1950s). *Sharh-i Manzuma* by Hadi Sabzavari is read occasionally (volume 1 is logic, so is read by those particularly interested in philosophy; volume 2 is gnosis or speculative mysticism: 'irfan).

USUL-I FIQH (principles of jurisprudence): *Ma'alim* of Shaykh Hasan ibn Zaynuddin, "Khatib al-Usuliyyin," (d. A.H. 1011) is read before or with volume 1 of the *Shari-i Lum'a* by his father. (*Ma'alim* superceded the *Sharh-i 'Amidi 'ala't-Tahdhib* of S. 'Amiduddin 'Abd al-Muttalib ibn Muhammad al-Araji al-Husayni, a commentary on the *Tahdib al-Usul* of his uncle Alama Hilli.) *Qawanin al-Usul* by Mirza Abu'l-Qasim Qummi (d. A.H. 1233) is fuller than *Ma'alim* and is read only in part, again with volume 1 of the Sharh-i *Lum'a*. *Rasa'il* of Shaykh Murtada Ansari (d. A.H. 1281) is read only in part; does not contain alfaz (exegesis of technical terms); *Rasa'il-i Jadid* is an abridged edition by Ali Meshkini, containing only those parts normally read. *Kifaya* of Shaykh Mulla Kazem Akhund-i Khurasani (d. A.H. 1329) is read together with *Rasa'el*; does contain alfaz. *Usul-i Fiqh-i Muzaffar* by Mohammad-Hoseyn Mozaffar was produced in the 1960s for the B.A. program in the modernized madrasas of Najaf to replace *Ma'alim* and *Qawanin*.

FIQH (law): *Sharh-i Lum'a* by Shaykh Zaynuddin ibn-'Ali al-Jubba'i al-'Amili, Shahid-i Thani" (martyred in A.H. 966); there is now a Persian pony (khod-amuzesh). *Shara'i' al-Islam* by Muhaqqiq al-Hilli, though not used as a text is read as background; about the same level as *Sharh al-Lum'a*; the commentary Jawahir is in 30 volumes; a Persian version has been published by the University of Tehran. *al-'Urwat al-Wuthqa* of Sayyid Kazim Yazdi (the forerunner of the various *Risala-i Tawdih al-Masa'il. Makasib* of Shaykh Murtada Ansari is read in its entirety over several years.

Level III.   Dars-i Kharij (no texts)

Dars-i fiqh includes taharat, salat, sawm, hajj, 'itq.

Dars-i usul includes alfaz, or exegesis of technical terms (for example, in applying the rule that a thief should not preach from a mimbar, who is a thief? once a thief, always a thief?).

Muqaddama-i wajib (necessary elements: for example, what makes a wudu' valid?)

One compiles a taqrirat (a "setting down," a report or compilation) on usul; if it is accepted, one is eligible for an ijaza-i ijtihadi, which is the permission to follow one's own reasoning skills, to be a mujtahid.

"Electives"

Akhlaq (moral philosophy)

Tafsir (commentary on the Qur'an)

Hikmat (philosophy): *Asfar* of Mulla Sadra, *Usul-i Falsafa* of 'Allama Mohammad-Hoseyn Tabatabai, *Masa'el-i Jadid-i Falsafa* of 'Allama Mohammad-Hoseyn Tabatabai.

MADRASA GOLPAYEGANI COURSE OF STUDY

Year 1 Sarf (etymology), insha (composition), imla (orthography), 'aqa'id (doctrines), hadith, akhlaq (morals), risala (law in abridged form)

Year 2 *Suyuti*, fiqh-i 'arabi, akhlaq, hifz-i Qur'an (memorizing the Qur'an), mantiq, 'aqa'id

Year 3 Tafsir, 'aqa'id, *Hashiya*, Ma'ani

Year 4 *Ma'alim*, tafsir, *Mukhtasar al-Ma'ani*

Year 5 Tafsir, English, akhlaq, *Qawanin*, *Lum'a-i Jadid* (from the chapter on hajj), 'aqa'id, *Lum'a* part one

MADRASA HAQQANI (MUNTAZARIYYA) COURSE OF STUDY

1. Fiqh and usul
2. Akhlaq
3. Persian literature: spelling, composition, reading, vocabulary, grammar
4. Arabic literature: etymology, syntax, rhetoric, vocabulary
5. Languages: English, spoken Arabic
6. Mathematics
7. Logic and Philosophy
8. Qur'an: introduction, memorization, history, commentary, reading
9. Science: physics, chemistry, nature
10. Hadith: history of hadith, evaluating the transmitters of hadith (diraya, rijal)
11. 'Ulum-i Insani (humanities): khodshenasi and khodsazi (morals), psychology, sociology, Islamic economics, geography, and history.
12. Religion: doctrines, history of religions, peoples, and beliefs.

FACULTY OF THEOLOGY AND ISLAMIC STUDIES, UNIVERSITY OF TEHRAN

In 1975 there were twenty-seven faculty members. Twenty-one of these held Ph.D. degrees. Six faculty members, of whom three held Ph.D. degrees, dressed in religious garb. Place of education was as follows:

University of Teheran		United States and Canada	4
Faculty of Theology	12	France and Switzerland	3
Faculty of Literature	2	England	1
Cairo	2	Turkey	1
Beirut	1	Qum	4

The faculty offered five degreee programs: a general B.A., plus both M.A. and Ph.D. degrees in Religions and Speculative Mysticism ('irfan), Islamic Philosophy, Islamic Law, and Arabic Culture. English and French were taught from *The Encyclopedia of Islam* (as well as the text *Success with English*). Of note perhaps is the general absence of concern with early Islamic philosophy and with the Andalusian and North African philosophers. There is an emphasis on post-Avicenna philosophy of the eastern Islamic world, particularly the blending of philosophy and mysticism from the twelfth century on. The most advanced classes are reserved for the philosophical tradition of Mulla Sadra and its continuity to the present. The absence of serious concern with European philosophy is also evident; to rectify this, one faculty member, Yazdi-Ha'iri, was given leave to study extensively in the United States. (He is the younger son of Shaykh Abdol Karim Yazdi-Ha'iri.) The absence of non-Shi'ite *kalam* is also evident.

Arabic Culture. The program was essentially literature and history, including as a text C. Brockelman's *History of Arabic Literature.*

Religions and Speculative Mysticism ('irfan). Twenty-five courses are listed. The texts include:

Bleeker, C. J., and G. Widengren, ed. *Historia religionum.*
Durant, W. *History of the orient.*
The Encyclopedia of Islam.
Massignon, L. Selection of articles.
Nicholson, R. A. *The mystics of Islam.* (in Arabic translation).
Baqillani. *At-tamhid.*
Dorabi, Mohammad. *Latifa.*
Hedayat, Mirza Golkan. *Riyad al-'arifin.*
al-Hilli ibn al-Mutahhar. *Anwar al-malakut fi sharh yaghut.*
Ibn 'Arabi. *Tarjuman al-ashwaq.*
Kashi, 'Abd al-Razzaq. *Istilahat al-sufiyya.*
Mufid, Shaykh. *Al-ikhtisas.*
Nawbakhti. *Firaq al-shi'a.*
Pour-e Davoud. Selection of articles.
Razi. *Mirsad al-'ibad.*
Shabistari. *Gulshan-i Raz.*
Tabarsi. *Ihtijaj.*
al-Ta'arruf, li-madhhab ahl al-tasawwuf.

Islamic Philosophy. Eighteen courses are listed. Attention is given to Aristotle, Kindi, Farabi, the Ikhwan al-Safa, Ibn Sina, Mir Damad, Mulla Sadra, Hakim Nuri, Zanawzani, Qumsha'i, Sabzavari, and Suhravardi. A course in the history of Western philosophy lists under texts "Russell et al." In the M.A. program particular attention is given to the Peripatetics (a four-term course) for which the text is Ibn Sina's *Isharat va tambihat,* to Mulla Sadra (a four-term course), for which the text is Sabzivari's *Sharh-i manzuma,* and logic (a three-term course) for which the text is the *Jawhar al-Nadid.* In the Ph.D. program particular attention is given in three-term courses to theology (for which the text is the *Tajrid al-i'tiqad*), to the Peripatetics (for which the text is *The theologia of Avicenna's shifa'*), to Illuminationism (for which the text is Suhravardi's *Hikmat al-ishraq*), and to Mulla Sadra's *Asfar.*

Islamic Law. Twenty-five courses are listed. There are offerings in Shafi and Hanafi law as well as Ja'fari Shi'ite law. The text for Shafi commercial law is the *Sharh-i Minhaj* of Qadi Zakariya Sawi. The text for a course in rules of conduct and law found in the Qur'an is the *Kanz al-'irfan* of Banu Amin Isfahani. Otherwise the texts are familiar from the traditional madrasa course of study: the *Sharh-i Lum'a*; the *Amali,* the *Rasa'il,* and the *Makasib* of Shaykh Murtada Ansari; the *Usul al-fiqh,* the *Qavanin* of Muzaffar; the *Kifaya* of Akhund Mulla Kazim Khurasani; the *al-Kafi* of Kolayni; and the *al-Wafi* by Fayd of Kashan.

DAR AL-TABLIGH CLASS SCHEDULE, 1974-75

DAY	10:30-11:30	11:30-12:30	3:30-4:30	4:30-5:30	5:30-6:30
Sat.	—	Fiqh (Shariatmadari)	Psychology Tajwid (Qur'an reading)	English Tajwid	English Writing
Sun.	Tafsir	'Aqa'id (beliefs about God)	—	Philosophy	English
Mon.	Baresi-i khutab (research for sermons)	'Aqa'id (beliefs about prophecy)	Psychology	English Mathematics	English
Tues.	Tafsir	'Aqa'id (beliefs about the Imams)	Tafsir	Philosophy Mathematics	English Health
Wed.	Morals	Fiqh (Shariatmadari)	Mathematics	Khutba (sermon practice) Mathematics	Khutba (sermon practice)
Thurs.	History of Islam[a]	Khutba (sermon practice)[b]	—	Health	Health

Note: A course in sociology was also offered by Ayati, who is French trained and normally resides in France. He returned to Iran for two years (1974 and 1975). His course was late nineteenth- and early-twentieth-century sociology. It contained no content about Islam or Iran.

[a] Scheduled for 8:00-9:00.
[b] Scheduled for 9:00-10:00.

2. Maraji'-i Taqlid since the Twelfth Imam
(Names numbered 1 through 61 are taken from Asaf-Aqa, 1384/1964.)

NAYIB-I KHASS (SPECIAL ASSISTANTS NOMINATED BY THE TWELFTH IMAM,
260/872-329/939)

a. 'Uthman ibn Sa'id
b. Muhammad ibn 'Uthman (son of 'Uthman ibn Sa'id)
c. Abu'l-Qasim Husayn ibn Ruh (Nawbakhti)
d. 'Ali ibn Muhammad Thimmari (d. 329/939).

NAYIB-I 'AMM (GENERAL AIDES TO THE IMAM), OR MARAJI'- TAQLID

1. Kulayni (Abu Ja'far Muhammad) ibn Ya'qub ibn Ishaq Razi (d. 328/939, buried in Baghdad), author of *al-Kafi*, the greatest Shi'ite collection of hadith
2. Shaykh al-Saduq Muhammad ibn 'Ali ibn Babawayh (d. 381/991), buried in Rey)
3. Shaykh-i Mufid (Abu 'Abdullah) Muhammad ibn Nu'man (d. 413/1022, buried in Kazimayn)
4. S. Murtada ibn Abu'l-Qasim ibn 'Ali ibn Husayn ibn Musa (d. 436/1044, buried in Kazimayn); brother of Sharif al-Radi, collector of the *Nahj al-Balagha*
5. Abu'l-Fath Muhammad ibn 'Ali ibn 'Uthman Karachaki (d. 449/1057), author of *Kanz al-Fawa'id*
6. Shaykh al-Ta'ifa Abu Ja'far Muhammad ibn Hasan ibn 'Ali Tusi (d. 460/1067, buried in Najaf), founder of the Hawza-i 'Ilmi Najaf
7. Shaykh Muhammad (son of Shaykh al-Ta'ifa Tusi) (d. 494/1100)
8. Shaykh Abu Ja'far Muhammad ibn Abu'l-Qasim 'Ali ibn Muhammad al-'Amili al-Tabari (d. 514/1120), author of *Bisharat al-Mustafa*
9. Shaykh-i Tabarsi (Abu 'Ali Fadl) ibn Hasan ibn Fadl (d. 548/1153, buried in Mashhad)
10. Ibn Zoreh Halabi (Abu'l-Makarim Hamza) ibn 'Ali (d. 585/1189, buried in Aleppo)
11. Ibn Shahrashub (Shaykh Rashiduddin Abu Ja'far Muhammad ibn 'Ali) (d. 588/1192, buried in Aleppo), author of *Ma'alim al-'Ulama* and *Manaqib*
12. Ibn Idris Hilli (Shaykh Muhammad ibn Ahmad) (d. 598/1201)
13. Abu'l-Fadl Shadhan ibn Jibra'il Qumi (d. 618/1221)
14. Najibuddin Abu Ibrahim Muhammad ibn Ja'far ibn Abu'l-Baqir Hibatullah ibn Ni'ma Hilli (d. 645/1247, buried in Najaf)
15. Najmuddin Ja'far (called ibn Ni'ma) ibn Muhammad ibn Ja'far (son of No. 14)
16. Ibn Ta'us al-Hasani al-Husayni (Radiuddin Abu'l-Qasim 'Ali ibn Musa ibn Ja'far) (d. 664/1265), collected the sayings of the fourth Imam in *Sahifa-i Sajjadiyya*
17. Khwaja Nasiruddin Tusi (prime minister of Hulagu Khan)
18. Muhaqqiq-i Hilli (Shaykh Ja'far ibn Hasan ibn Yahya ibn Sa'id) (d. 676/1277, buried in Hilla)

19. 'Allama Hilli (Shaykh Jamaluddin Abu Mansur Hasan ibn Yusuf ibn Mutah-har) (d. 726/1325, buried in Najaf), converted Sultan Muhammad-Khuda-banda

20. "Nasiruddin Kashani" 'Ali ibn Muhammad al-Baghdadi al-Hilli (d. 755/1354, buried in Najaf)

21. Abu Talib Muhammad ibn Hasan ibn Yusuf ibn Mutahhar

22. Ibn Ma'uya (Tajuddin Abu 'Abdullah Muhammad ibn Qasim ibn Husayn) (d. 766/1364, buried in Najaf)

23. Shahid-i Awwal (Abu 'Abdullah Muhammad ibn Jamaluddin al-'Amili (d. 766/1374), author of *Lum'a*

24. Abu'l-Hasan Zaynuddin 'Ali ibn Kazim al-Ha'iri (d. 820/1417)

25. Shaykh Abu 'Abdullah al-Mighdad ibn 'Abdullah ibn Muhammad ibn Hu-sayn (d. 826/1422, buried in Baghdad), author of *Kanz al-'Irfan*

26. Abu'l-'Iyash Ahmad ibn Muhammad ibn Fahd (d. 841/1437, buried in Kar-bala)

27. Shaykh Shamsuddin Muhammad, ibn Makki al-Amili al-Shami (d. 860/1455)

28. Shaykh Nuruddin 'Ali ibn 'Abd al-'Ali al-'Amili (Muhaqqiq Karaki) (d. 937/1529)

29. Shahid-i Thani (Shaykh Zaynuddin ibn Nuruddin 'Ali ibn Ahmad), author of *Sharh al-Lum'a* (killed 966/1558)

30. Ahmad ibn Muhammad Ardabili (d. 933/1526, buried in Najaf)

31. Muhammad 'Ali ibn Muhammad al-Balaghi (d. 1000/1591, buried in Kar-bala)

32. Jamaluddin Abu Mansur al-Hasan ibn Shahid-i Thani (d. 1011/1602, buried in Jubba')

33. Shaykh Baha'i (Muhammad ibn Husayn ibn 'Abd al-Samad al-Jubba'i al-'Amili al-Horasi) (d. 1031/1621, buried in Mashhad)

34. Majlisi Awwal (Muhammad Taqi ibn Maqsud 'Ali) (d. 1070/1659)

35. Mulla Muhammad Salih Mazandarani (d. 1080/1669)

36. Mulla Husayn ibn Jamaluddin Muhammad ibn Husayn Khwansari (d. 1098/1686, buried in Isfahan)

37. Majlisi Thani (Muhammad-Baqir ibn Muhammad-Taqi ibn Maqsud-'Ali) (d. 1111/1699, buried in Isfahan)

38. Muhammad ibn Hasan (Muhammad Isfahani Fadil Hindi) (d. 1137/1724, buried in Isfahan), author of *Kashf al-Lisan*

39. Shaykh Ahmad Jazayiri al-Najafi (d. 1150/1737, buried in Najaf)

40. Aqa Jamaluddin ibn Muhammad-Husayn ibn Muhammad-Rida Mazandar-ani Khajui (d. 1155/1742, buried in Khonsar)

41. Mulla Isma'il ibn Muhammad-Husayn ibn Muhammad-Rida Mazandarani Khajui (d. 1173/1759, buried in Isfahan)

42. Vahid Behbahani (Muhammad-Baqir) (d. 1208/1793, buried in Karbala)

43. Bahr al-'Ulum (Sayyid Muhammad-Mahdi) (d. 1212/1797, buried in Najaf)

44. Shaykh Ja'far ibn Shaykh Khidr al-Janagi an-Najafi Kashf al-Qeta (d. 1223/1813, buried in Najaf)

45. Mirza Qumi (Mulla Abu'l-Qasim ibn Muhammad-Hasan Jilani Qumi) (d. 1231/1815, buried in Qum), author of *Qawanin*

46. Mulla Ahmad ibn Mulla Mahdi Naraqi (d. 1244/1828)
47. Shaykh Muhammad-Hasan al-Najafi (d. 1266/1849, buried in Najaf), author of *Jawahir al-Kalam*
48. Shaykh Murtada Ansari (Mulla Murtada ibn Muhammad-Amir) (d. 1281/1864, buried in Najaf), author of *Rasa'il* and *Makasib*
49. Sayyid Muhammad-Mahdi al-Qazvini (d. 1300/1882, buried in Najaf)
50. Mulla Muhammad ibn Muhammad-Baqir al-Irvani (d. 1306/1888, buried in Najaf)
51. Mujaddid Shirazi (Mirza Hasan) (d. 1312/1894, buried in Najaf), of Tobacco Protest fame
52. Shaykh Muhammad-Hasan ibn Mulla 'Abdullah Mamaqani (d. 1313/1895, buried in Najaf)
53. Shaykh Mirza Husayn ibn Mirza Khalil Tihrani (d. 1326/1908, buried in Najaf)
54. Akhund-i Khurasani (Shaykh Muhammad-Kazim) (d. 1329/1911, buried in Najaf), author of *Kifayat al-Usul*
55. Sayyid Muhammad-Kazim Yazdi (d. 1337/1918, buried in Najaf), author of *'Urwat al-Wuthqa*
56. Mirza Muhammad-Taqi Shirazi (d. 1339/1920, buried in Karbala), leader of the Iraqi opposition to the British
57. Shaykh Fathullah "Shaykh al-Shari'a" Isfahani (d. 1339/1920, buried in Najaf)
58. Shaykh 'Abdullah ibn Shaykh Muhammad-Hasan Mamaqani (d. 1351/1932, buried in Najaf)
59. Shaykh Mirza Husayn Na'ini (d. 1355/1936, buried in Najaf)
60. Shaykh Aqa Diya'uddin al-'Iraqi (d. 1365/1945, buried in Najaf)
61. Sayyid Abu'l-Hasan Isfahani (d. 1365/1945, buried in Najaf)
62. Hajj Husayn Qummi (d. 1365/1945)
63. Ayatullah Husayn Borujerdi (d. 1381/1961)
64. Sayyid Muhsin Hakim (d. 1390/1970).

3. Qum Statistical Profile
POPULATION

	1956	1966	1975
City of Qum	96,499	134,292	–
Males		68,908	
Females		65,384	
Households		28,424	
Metropolitan area	160,981	177,862	220,100
Males		92,685	
Females		85,177	

(Data from National Census of Population and Housing 1956, 1966; Qasemi-Nejad 1975.)

OCCUPATIONAL STRUCTURE, 1966

NUMBER OF WORKERS

	CITY	METROPOLITAN AREA
Agriculture	2,374	8,060
Mining	112	884
Construction	4,664	5,984
Manufacturing	15,842	21,682
Utilities	460	483
Commerce	5,847	6,646
Transportation, storage, communications	2,582	2,819
Services	5,837	6,700
Unclassified	284	460

(Data from Qasemi-Nejad 1975.)

INDUSTRY, 1975

Carpet looms (rough estimate)	25,000
Sohan (a sweet) makers	157
Textile mills (10)[a]	1,100
Shoe factories (6)	150
Cartons, nylon bags (3)	400
Heaters, gas oxygen, brushes (3)	70
Mines (8): 10-90 km. from Qum	620
Brick kilns (204)	1,000
Plaster (14)	140
Stone cutting (4)	50
Flour mills (4), ice (2)	43

SERVICES, 1975

Telephones	4,000
Taxis	260
Private cars	1,225
Libraries	15
Newspapers	2
Printing houses	7
Public baths: for men	112
for women	66
Butchers: sheep/goat	128
beef	37
Bread bakers	165
Hotels, guesthouses	85
rooms	2,000
Hospitals	7
Clinics	18
Nursing home	1

[a.] Excluding administrators. (Data from Qum Office of Labor, 1975.) The largest unit had 600 workers. Three new mills were under construction, one of which planned a work force of 3,000. A large mill (350-500 workers) established in 1935 was closed in 1958.

(Data from Qasemi-Nejad 1975.)

SCHOOLS, 1975

	TOTAL STUDENTS	MALE	FEMALE
Nursery	108	62	46
Literacy Center			
Children	1,272	74	1,198
Adults	1,046	489	557
Elementary school			
Government	24,934	15,822	9,112
Private	8,372	6,574	1,798
Junior (Rahnemah) school			
Government	7,969	6,065	1,904
Private	2,501	2,033	468
High school			
Government	4,337	3,275	1,062
Private	557	537	40
Second cycle of high school			
Government: Science	2,305		
Mathematics	698		
Literature	284		
Private: Science	6,304		
Mathematics	212		
Vocational high school	650		
College	1,400		

(Data from Office of Education, Qum.)

4. Chronology of Religious and State Administrations

Religious	State
1861 Death of Shaykh Mortaza Ansari	
1892 Death of Mojaddid Shirazi	1898 First modern school in Qum: Fatimiyya, opened by Rushtiyya
	1905 Constitutional Revolution
1909 Death of Akhund-i Khurasani	1915 Education Office opens in Qum
1916 Ayatullah Fayd begins reconstructing the Hawza-i 'Ilmi Qum	
1920 Ayatullah Shaykh Abdul-Karim Haeri-Yazdi assumes leadership of the Hawza-i 'Ilmi Qum	
1921 Ruhani forced out of Iraq for several months and come to Qum	
	1924 Reza Khan dissuaded by the ulama from declaring a republic
1925 Hajj Nurollah Isfahani calls for ousting of the dictator Reza Shah	1925 Reza Khan becomes shah

1928 Begin clearing the graveyard
near Masjid-i Imam and cutting
motorable roads through Qum

1933 Flood: Haeri-Yazdi organizes rehousing in Mobarakabad

1935 Death of Haeri-Yazdi. Triumvirate (Hojjat, Sadr, Khonsari)
assumes leadership of Hawza

1935 Push to unveil women and outlaw emotional Shi'ite rites
(rawda, flagellation, etc.); first
major textile mill opened in
Qum

1936 Conflict between Ayatullah
Bafqi and the royal ladies

1936 Fatima Hospital opened in Qum

1937 Major push on road building
1938 Attempt to administer exams to
the talaba

1941 Wine riot in Qum

1941 Abdication of Reza Shah; accession of Mohammad Reza Shah

1943 Khonsari leads namaz istisqa
(prayer for times of peril)
1944 Ayatullah Hoseyn Borujerdi assumes leadership of the hawza
1945 Kasravi assassinated by the
Fida'iyyan-i Islam

1949 Assassination attempt on shah
1951-52 Dr. Mohammad Mosaddegh
becomes prime minister
1952 Talaba demonstrate against the
Tudeh Party

1952 Ostad Meshkat sent as temporary mutawalli of the Qum Shrine

1955 Talaba close hawza in demonstration against the Bahais;
hay'at-i madhhabi (religious
meeting groups) still get support
from the shah

1955 New market opened; bazaar repairs; city notables (mu'tami-
din-i mahall) elected

1956 Borujerdi makes Pepsi Cola
makruh

1956 Work on flood walls begun;
Nikui Hospital opened; Bakh-
tiari becomes head of SAVAK;
Iraqi army invades Najaf madrasas

1957 Borujerdi and King Saud exchange gifts

1957 Police outlaw ta'ziya in Qum;
strike at Risbaf Factory; Bank
Sadarat opens
1958 Prime Minister Eqbal introduces
new ambassador to Iraq to Ayatullah Borujerdi

1959 First issue of *Maktab-i Islam*;
Hakim issues fatwa against joining Communist Party

1961 Borujerdi dies, triumvirate
(Marashi, Shariatmadari, Golpayegani) assumes leadership of
hawza

1962 *Bahth-i Darbara-i Marja'iyyat*   1962 Local Council Election Bill;
va Ruhaniyyat (Study of Islamic   plan to enfranchise women
Leadership and Clergy)

1963 Demonstrations against White   1963 White Revolution
Revolution; occupation of Qum
by security forces; arrest of
Khomeyni

1964 Journal *Goftar-i Mah* (forerun-
runner of Husayniyya Irshad)

                                              1965 Mohammad Mehran takes over
                                              the Shrine in Qum from Mes-
                                              bah-Towliyat

1966 Dar Rah-i Haqq opens

                                              1968 Abdul-Wahhab Eqbal takes over
                                              the Shrine; ghubar-rubi cere-
                                              mony introduced (counting
                                              donations); new darih unveiled
                                              by the Queen

                                              1971 First cinema opens in Qum

1975 Demonstration against the Ras-   1975 Cinema burns down
takhiz party

1978 January: students shot by
police, who invade Shariatmadari's house, helping to ignite the
revolution

1979 Khomeyni returns   1979 Pahlavi dynasty deposed; Is-
                                              lamic republic declared.

5. Budget of the Shrine of Fatima, Hadrat-i Ma'suma, in Qum

The Shrine's financial records were subject to some tampering (see chapter 4). A discrepancy, for instance, will be noted between the figure for the total income in 1973 and the detailed breakdown of sources of income. In 1970 and 1971 similar discrepancies of roughly 3 million rials were simply listed as a separate category of "additional income" (*mu'tamina*). If we assume, however that there is some rough validity to the accounts, it is interesting to note that in 1973, of a total of 36 million rials income, 26 million rials were generated in the shrine itself (half by pilgrims and a third in funeral fees); only 10 million rials were rents from en-dowed lands. That is, the shrine was generating two and a half times the income of its property. This is presumably an entirely different relationship from that in the income of the great shrine of Imam Reza in Mashhad.

Total budgets, 1965-1975, in rials

Year	Income	Expenditures	Year	Income	Expenditures
1965	8,592,213	7,418,147	1971	33,796,704	—
1966	15,034,368	14,097,576	1972	36,017,780	20,847,000
1967	16,843,373	16,411,891	1973	40,174,176	—
1968	22,523,000	20,308,649	1974	104,750,185	29,979,648
1969	35,065,810	27,221,316	1975	78,416,277	—
1970	44,698,136	37,468,583			

Income sources, 1973, in rials

Shrine
Coins tossed into the darih or bier enclosure	12,000,000
Shoe check	3,300,000
Candles	700,000
Sale of electricity for mausoleums	100,000
Funerary fees	7,500,000
Museum	1,100,000
Miscellaneous (loans, auction)	1,690,000
Subtotal	26,390,000

Property (rents)
Shops (220), fruit and vegetable market	2,544,214
Urban land plots (360), hotels (2), flour mill (1)	3,301,572
Rural land and water	4,732,921
Subtotal	10,578,707

Expenditures, 1972 and 1974, in rials	1972	1974
Shrine		
Salaries and bonuses (73 caretakers, 43 clerks)	7,540,200	11,393,548
Official acts, travel, hospitality	1,668,000	750,800
Cigarettes and tea	90,000	100,000
Candles and candle caretakers	220,000	240,000
Ceremonials and memorials	200,000	200,000
Utilities, uniforms, and insurance	2,730,000	3,618,900
Books for the Library	50,000	120,000
Publication of a history of the shrine	1,000,000	—
Philanthropy		
Aid to students and pilgrims	1,900,000	2,303,600
Religious works	320,000	360,000
Hospitals and medication	1,604,800	820,800
Orphanage and children's center	420,000	560,000
Literacy classes	120,000	12,000
Bangladesh flood victims, African starvation victims	—	200,000
Miscellaneous	2,984,000	9,300,000
Total	20,847,000	29,979,648

6. Karbala
THE DRAMA OF KARBALA
Act One. Foreshadowings

1. Abraham's trial by fire. The angel Gabriel made the flames cool and Abraham through his steadfast faith emerged from the fire unburnt.
2. Abraham's sacrifice of Ishmael. This is the archetype of all sacrifice and a key symbol of submission to God.
3. Jacob's tears at the separation from Joseph. What is stressed here is that this suffering is nothing compared with that of the family of the Prophet.
4. The death of Muhammad's son, Ibrahim. Muhammad is asked to choose between Ibrahim and his grandson Husayn. He chooses Husayn to live, since Ibrahim's mother is already dead whereas Husayn's is not (a principle of least suffering). Ibrahim becomes the ransom for Husayn as Husayn will be for all Shi'ites.
5. The disobedient son. Muhammad is told by Gabriel that Muslim sinners, like other sinners, will go to hell. A man cries out from hell. His mother had cursed him for preferring his wife. One after another of the family of the Prophet attempt to intercede; only finally with Gabriel's threat that she had better relent for Husayn's plea does the mother release the son from hell.
6. The death of Muhammad and the usurpation of the caliphate. While 'Ali, 'Abbas, Zubayr, Salman, Abu Dharr, Miqdad, and Ammar were burying Muhammad, Abu Bakr and 'Umar hold the Thaqifa election for the caliphate. 'Umar comes to force 'Ali to swear allegiance to Abu Bakr by banging the door of the house against Fatima, burning the door, and dragging 'Ali before Abu Bakr.
7. The death of Fatima. She reviews her treasures—the tooth of the Prophet knocked out in the Battle of Uhud, the ring of Solomon which will provide moisture to the martyrs of Karbala, and the blood of Husayn with which she will help intercede for Shi'ites on Judgment Day.
8. The martyrdom of 'Ali. 'Ali is invited to dinner by his daughter Kulthum. He sleeps and dreams, calling out to Muhammad to relieve him of the hardships of the world. Zaynab, his daughter, begs him not to go to the mosque, and geese attempt to block his path, but he says it is foreordained and his duty. Gabriel tells the angels that 'Ali has gone to the prayer niche to offer his obedience. Ibn Muljam mortally wounds 'Ali. 'Ali says that if he dies, Ibn Muljam is to be similarly slain with only one blow, but until then he is to be treated well and his family is not to be molested.
9. The martyrdom of Hasan. Hasan's drinking water is poisoned (a reversal of the thirst of Karbala) by his wife at the order of Mu'awiya, who thereby doubly breaks his agreement to return the caliphate to Hasan at his death.

Act Two. Karbala

10. The martyrdom of Muslim and his two sons. Muslim, the cousin of Husayn, transmits to Husayn a plea for him to come to Kufa and help Hani and Shahri throw out the governor of Yazid. The plot is discovered and Muslim's arrest is ordered. Muslim prepares to fight. He asks for water and is given some by a pious woman, Tawah, but when he tries to drink it, it turns to blood; he then drops a tooth into the second cup and it too turns into blood. Muslim is

defeated and executed. His sons are arrested; allowed to escape by the jailer, Ibn Zayd, they are caught and killed by Harith, who collects a reward.

11. Husayn leaves Medina for Kufa. He is intercepted by Hur and camps on the plain of Karbala. 'Umar ibn Sa'd and Shimr come from Kufa to make sure Hur makes Husayn submit. Husayn releases his followers.

12. Martyrdom of Hur, Abis, and Shawdhab. Hur and his brother defect to Husayn and are martyred in battle. Abis releases his slave Shawdhab but the latter decides to stay and aid in the battle for Husayn. Abis answers the taunts of Ibn Sa'd that Yazid may have territory and money to disperse but Husayn has paradise. Ibn Sa'd challenges him to fight without armor; he does and is killed.

13. Martyrdom of 'Ali-Akbar. 'Ali-Akbar compares himself to Ishmael. Zaynab compares him to Joseph. He fights and dies.

14. Marriage and death of Qasim. Qasim is married to Husayn's daughter on the field of battle to fulfill a promise Husayn made to Hasan when Hasan was on his deathbed.

15. Martyrdom of 'Abbas. Sakina, the youngest daughter of Husayn, cries for water. The Euphrates is cut off by Ibn Sa'd's army. 'Abbas makes it to the river to fill a lambskin. He does not drink, for it is not right to drink first before the children. He is intercepted on his way back to camp and his hand is cut off; he catches the waterskin with his other hand. That hand too is cut off, so he catches the skin in his teeth. The skin is pierced, so the water runs out; and 'Abbas is slain.

16. Martyrdom of Hashim, cousin and son-in-law of Ibn Sa'd. He defects to Husayn and is killed.

17. Martyrdom of Husayn. His infant son is killed in his arms by Harmala. Sinan pierces Husayn's side with a spear. He reaches the river but does not drink for he thinks of his sister Zaynab being taken prisoner and his daughter Sakina in the hands of the soldiers. He fights and dies. His head is cut off to be taken to Yazid. His body is trampled into a formless mass of blood, mud, and bone. He refers to himself as Joseph: his cloak has been torn and bloodied by wolves while he is off to become a vizier in paradise.

Act Three. Aftermath

18. The flight of Shahbanu. The wife of Husayn and daughter of the Persian king, Yazdegird III, flees to Rey in Persia on Husayn's horse, Zuljaneh. Her brother, who has set out with an army to prevent her from falling into Syrian hands, meets her and marches on to confront Shimr and Ibn Sa'd and demand the women of Husayn. Ibn Sa'd refuses to yield the women, except for Shahbanu's daughter, the widowed bride of Qasim.

19. The trek to Damascus. Zaynab takes charge, for the only unslaughtered male of the family, Zayn al-'Abidin, is seriously wounded. He would have been killed but that the army of Shimr had thought him dead.

20. Conversion of the European ambassador in Damascus. Yazid entertains the ambassador with a display of the prisoners and heads of the martyrs. The head of Husayn recites the Qur'an; Yazid hits it with a stick. The ambassador protests and speaks in defense of Husayn, whom he had met in Medina. He is killed.

21. Death of Ruqayya, daughter of Husayn. The girls of the Prophet's family are mocked by the girls of Damascus. The daughter of Yazid feels some shame and agrees to Ruqayya's entreaty to bring her Husayn's head. Ruqayya asks the head to allow her to join him in heaven. Other accounts have her dying on the trek to Damascus.
22. Zaynab's sermon in Damascus. Zaynab delivers a sermon at Friday prayer which shames the followers of Yazid.
23. Zayn al-'Abidin's sermon in Kufa. In a moment of regret Yazid allows the captives to leave Damascus. Zayn al-'Abidin gives a sermon that destroys Yazid's credibility among his followers.
24. Resurrection. Gabriel tells Israfel to blow the trumpets to rouse the dead. Jacob complains of the heat and pleads to be saved no matter what happens to Joseph; Joseph says the same about Jacob. Abraham says the same about Ishmael, and Ishmael about Abraham. Only Muhammad and 'Ali are concerned about the suffering of others and try to find a mode of intercession; they call the other members of the family to help. Gabriel says that intercession will be allowed to the prophet who suffered the most. There is a comparison and it is clear that Husayn is the one.

'ASHURA FLOATS
Floats in Zarch-e Yazd, 1970

1. Shimr (the general of Yazid), dressed in red, tying up and leading away the two young sons of Muslim, dressed in green.
2. A flock of black-clad children running after a black-cloaked man with a white headcloth, all clapping their hands to their heads in grief, chanting and running, kneeling and running on. They converge around a tent which first turns black (from a fire lighted inside) and then bursts into flame, representing the burning of the tents of Husayn by the soldiers of Yazid.
3. Dasta groups of young men.
4. Decorated camels and horses carrying Yazid, Ibn Sa'd, Shimr, and the bloodied corpse of Husayn.
5. A man in white, representing the Christian who tried to intervene with Yazid on behalf of Husayn, holding the head of Husayn and alternately polishing it with a rag and clapping his hand to his thigh and mouth in a gesture of disbelieving grief. He comes around a second time with binoculars looking off to see Husayn and with a camera which he points at the crowd (the European par excellence). He comes around a third time with two heads in a pan.
6. A man dressed in green with a cup trying to get water ('Abbas).
7. A float with only a large pan of water, signifying the thirst of Husayn and his family and the inhumanity of Yazid in not allowing them to quench their thirst.
8. Husayn's bloodied corpse, with live pigeons feeding on him and a lion mourning.
9. A dasta of men in white blood-stained dress and bloodied faces, clapping their hands to their heads.

Floats in Dareh-e Yazd, 1960s

1. Husayn in the bazaar of Damascus with his infant son 'Ali-Asghar.
2. The bridal chamber of Qasim and Fatima, son of Hasan and daughter of Husayn. The latter is played by a boy in a chadur veil.
3. The bread oven of the wife of Kholi, a supporter of Yazid, who one night saw a light in her oven and found the luminous head of Husayn. She wipes the head with a handkerchief and cries out the poem: "O head, who are you? Where did you come from?"
4. The white-clothed Christian monk Rahib-i Nasrani begs a man standing before him with a head on a stake to be allowed to see the head; but is refused until he gives the man a bribe. He too mourns with a poem: "O head who are you? What nice features you have."
5. A lion and a corpse.
6. Harith, dressed in red, whipping the children of Muslim, dressed in green.
7. The cradle of 'Ali-Asghar and his nurse, who sings:

Ay Asghar-i bishir-i man,	O Asghar without milk, my dear,
Ay tifli bitaqsir-i man,	O child without fault, my dear,
Aram-i janam lai lai,	My dear peaceful one,
Shirinzabanam lai lai.	My sweet-tongued one.

8. The court of Yazid: Yazid in red, a bowl before him with Husayn's head in it, a stick in his mouth with which he beats the head, a servant beside him pouring him wine, and other red-clad aides. Yazid sings the first line of the *Divan* of Hafiz:

Alaya ayyuha 'l-saqi,	O wine pourer, arise and
adir ka'san va-navilha.	Pass 'round the cup.

9. The daughter of Yazid: A boy dressed in gold and drinking wine, seated on a horse and surrounded by many retainers:
10. Harmala, the man who killed the baby 'Ali-Asghar, as an archer dressed in red, shooting arrows in all directions, with soldiers, trumpeters, and drummers around him.

Notes

1. Culture, History, and Politics

1. Michele de Angelis has drawn my attention to the fact that the formula "two things are divided and make three, three . . . five . . ." also is a venerable one, used in early Islamic disputations on God's power of efficient causality, which resides in his being and cannot be said to be divisible lest God's unity and omnipotence be denied. The argument can be found, among other places, in Kulayni's *al-Kafi*, Ibn Babuya's *Tawhid*, and Tabarsi's *Ihtijaj*.

2. For a superb introduction to this tradition, see Hans-Georg Gadamer's *Truth and Method* (New York: Seabury, 1975); also Rudolf A. Makkreel, *Dilthey: Philosopher of the Human Sciences* (Princeton, N.J.: Princeton University Press, 1975). In recent years the French have appropriated the tradition, especially Maurice Merleau-Ponty, Jean-Paul Sartre, Paul Ricoeur, Jacques Lacan, and Michel Foucault. American anthropologists received the tradition initially, somewhat bowdlerized, from the students of Franz Boas and from Talcott Parsons, then more accurately from G. H. Mead, later Clifford Geertz, and now through the French philosophers. Two recent surveys of social science use of the tradition may be found in A. Giddens, *New Rules of Sociological Method* (New York: Basic Books, 1976), and Z. Bauman, *Hermeneutics and Social Science* (London: Heinemann, 1978); see also Fischer (1977b).

3. These definitions and their uses will be familiar to readers of the so-called Chicago school of symbolic anthropology, particularly the work of David M. Schneider, Clifford Geertz, and Victor Turner.

4. Akhavi (1980), Algar (1969, 1972), Binder (1966), Browne (1910, 1918), Ferdows (1967), Fischer (1973), Garoussian (1974), Ha'iri (1973), Kasravi (1951), Keddie (1966a,b, 1972), Lambton (1962, 1964, 1965), Thaiss (1973).

5. Lambton (1964), Algar (1969), Keddie (1969).

6. According to Shi'ites, political and religious leadership of the community of Muslims was supposed to pass from the Prophet Muhammad to his son-in-law

and cousin, 'Ali, and thence through 'Ali's male descendants. There were twelve of these successors, called Imams.

7. Amr bi ma'ruf va nahy az munkar.

8. According to Sunnis, political and religious leadership of the community of Muslims properly passed from the Prophet Muhammad to elected successors: Abu Bakr, 'Umar, 'Uthman, and then 'Ali. Sunni and Shi'ite groups differed in their later notions of caliphate and imamate, but both tended to recognize the principle that bad government is preferable to no government. See Gibb (1962) and Lambton (1962).

9. It is sometimes claimed that there is a Persian pre-Islamic tradition of unity of church and state, stemming from the Sassanian dynasty, which remains influential, and which both Safavid and Qajar dynasties in slightly different ways drew upon in trying to legitimize their authority as divinely blessed. It is at least interesting, given those who claim Shi'ism doctrinally denies legitimacy to any temporal ruler, that Shi'ite theologians often granted legitimacy to governments as Muhammad-Baqir Majlisi (d. 1700) did for the Safavids and as Mirza Muhammad-Husayn Na'ini did for Reza Shah in 1925.

10. The term "thick description" is appropriated from the philosopher Gilbert Ryle by Clifford Geertz (1973) in a sophisticated but disturbing major statement on the potentials of ethnography. While on the one hand Geertz increases the sophistication of his handling of signification and cultural communication over his earlier notions of a system of symbols, on the other hand he turns away from the larger historical and sociological contexts which save thick description from triviality. It is unsatisfactory to plead division of labor with other social scientists when what is at issue in both the description of, and the theoretical accounting for, culture is the historical and structural (tropic) dimensions of the forms being explored.

11. I do not mean to sound overly complacent. Fundamentalism in the United States is enjoying a minor upsurge and the most positivist of scientists admit that science goes but so far, beyond which metaphysical notions are unavoidable. But the rhetoric of discussion is ecumenical and nonparochial, as the fundamentalist religious rhetorics of a century ago were not. This is largely due to political accommodation and what Robert Bellah calls the institution of "civil religion" (1967). Jewish, Protestant, and Catholic theologians and leaders are able to speak to each other in the neutral metalanguage of systematic theology, that is, in a language reflecting upon the language of religion (see The Royal Institute of Philosophy, 1969). In Iran such a disinterested mode of discourse is not yet normally available.

12. For descriptions of the Persian political system under the Pahlavis, see Abrahamian (1969), Ashraf (1971), Banani (1961), Bayne (1965, 1968), Bill (1972), Binder (1962), Cottam (1964), Sarraf (1972), and Zonis (1971a).

13. For analyses of the structural problems of the educational system, see Zonis (1971b), and Eicher, Lewis, Morton, and Zonis (1976).

2. Rise and Decline of the Madrasa

1. The Sunni version will be given later for contrast. For the Shi'ite version, see, for instance, the *Najh al-Balagha* (collected sermons, letters, and sayings of 'Ali), of which there are several editions in English translation; Allamah Mohammad-Hoseyn Tabataba'i (1975), Pooya (1972), and Lassy (1916).

2. On the evolution of the body of hadith literature, see especially the classic study by Goldziher (1971); also Schacht (1950), Rahman (1965), Abbott (1957-67), Sezgin (1967), Van Ess (1975).

3. "Truly the likeness of Jesus, in God's sight, is as Adam's . . . The truth is of God . . . and whoso disputes with thee . . . say, 'Come now let us call our sons and your sons, our wives and your wives, our selves and your selves, then let us humbly pray and so lay God's curses upon the ones who lie.' " According to the hadith, Muhammad had with him his grandsons Hasan and Husayn ("our sons"), Fatima ("our wives"), and 'Ali ("ourselves"). Thus Muhammad's family again is affirmed as the paradigmatic carrier of Islam.

4. At least one source of ill will stemmed from A.H. 6, when 'A'isha accompanied Muhammad on his way back from an expedition against the Banu Mustaliq. At a rest stop, 'A'isha withdrew to do her ablutions. When she returned to her litter she noticed she had left her Yemeni shell necklace behind. Leaving the curtains of her litter closed, she went to fetch the necklace. Meanwhile Muhammad gave the signal to move out, the litter was placed on the camel, and the camel train moved on. 'A'isha, finding she had been left behind, sat to await someone to come for her. A soldier, Safwan ibn al-Mu'attal, happened by and brought her to the camp. Allegations were raised against her chastity. 'Ali advised Muhammad to repudiate her on the grounds that one should not allow suspicions to be raised against one's integrity. Muhammad then had a revelation (Sura 24:10) that exculpated 'A'isha: no charge of adultery is valid unless there are four witnesses.

5. 'Amr ibn Abu Da'ud was a pagan champion in the Battle of the Moat (A.H. 5) who challenged any Muslim to individual combat. 'Ali, then sixteen, took the challenge. 'Ali was on foot, 'Amr was mounted. One version says that 'Ali appealed to 'Amr's sense of honor: "Now, look, I am a child and you are a grown man; is it right that I should be on foot while you are mounted?" And 'Amr dismounted and even killed his mount. Another version has it that 'Ali tricked 'Amr by pointing to his saddle straps and saying they were coming undone; 'Amr looked, and as he did, 'Ali knocked him from the horse. In the ensuing battle 'Amr split 'Ali's skull. 'Ali retired to Muhammad's side. The latter put some spittle on the wound and bound it up with his own turban. 'Ali then returned to the fight and pinned 'Amr to the ground. As he was about to take off 'Amr's head, 'Amr spit in his face. 'Ali became angry and left 'Amr lying there disabled. When 'Ali returned later, 'Amr cried, "Why did you not finish me off the first time?" 'Ali replied, "That time you spit in my face and I became angry. Had I killed you then, it would have been to revenge my own anger rather than for the honor of Islam. So I arose to cool my anger." 'Ali then cut off the head and brought it to Muhammad. 'Amr is supposed to have begged for his life; 'Ali refused unless 'Amr became Muslim, which 'Amr refused. 'Amr also begged 'Ali not to strip and dishonor his body; to this 'Ali agreed. 'Amr's sister, who came to mourn him, decided that for this latter reason there was no need to demand revenge or mourn too deeply.

6. In explicit contrast to 'Ali's behavior. At the Battle of Siffin, Mu'awiya had cut 'Ali off from the Euphrates and denied him water. 'Ali broke through to the river but allowed Mu'awiyya's forces access to water. Just because others are inhuman is no excuse for a Muslim to be inhuman.

7. For an excellent description of the rise of Islam, from which the following

is adapted, see Hodgson (1974:I, 146-230). I do not mean to imply that Sunni views and those of Western historians are necessarily the same; for the present purpose, however, the two can be conflated to draw an initial background contrast for Shi'ism. The procedures and analytic style of traditional Sunni ulama would look different, but that is another subject.

8. A Jewish woman is said to have given Muhammad poison, but the Egyptian version points out that Muhammad did not die until ten years after the alleged poisoning. In both Sunni and Shi'ite versions Muhammad is told by Gabriel that he can request God to extend his life, but Muhammad shows himself a true Muslim and says that he is ready at God's call.

9. Gibb and Kramers (1961: 469).

10. Young boys and poor people may put on chadurs and knock on doors calling out: *dust ya 'Ali dust* (friend, O 'Ali's friend). They are given sweets or money. It is also a time for practical jokes: a rich man may put on a chadur and go to a relative's house; the latter, recognizing him, might go up on the roof and throw water on him. Solicitation may be in rhyme:

In khana cheqadr qashang-e	How beautiful is this house
Hamash sharbat-o qand-e;	All of sugar and sweet drink;
Imam Husayn daresh nabande.	May Imam Husayn not close the door

If the owner replies with insults, the solicitor may reply in kind:

Nish kash takht-e pus(t),	Go eat the skin of an animal,
Bikhur guh-i khurus.	Eat rooster shit.

If the owner does not reply, one may try:

Ya arda bi tasam kun,	Either put arde (a sweet from Ardekan) in my bowl,
Ya bikush-o khalasam kun.	Or kill me and let me be.

Also on this night young unmarried girls may sit in the alleys sewing and begging for "twenty-seventh-night money" (*pul-i shab-i bist-o-haftum*).

11. For Sunnis *tavalla* and *tabarra* refer merely to Allah, but for Shi'ites this inevitably and explicitly involves the Imams. The Pahlavi government attempted to remove these two terms from school books in the hopes of reducing animosity toward Sunnis. The gesture was taken ill by the ulama.

12. For accounts of the nur doctrine, see Lassy (1916), E. G. Browne (1924: IV, 394-395), and Asghar (1963).

13. Mawlana Hajji Mulla Muhammad-Salih al-Burqani, author of *Makhzan al-Buka*, a major work of *ta'ziya* (mourning dirges about Karbala). The passage is translated in Asghar (1963: 96) from page 26 of the *Hakhzan*.

14. The Qur'anic version of the biblical Abraham-Isaac story is about Abraham and Ishmael.

15. There are suggestions that the Muharram ceremonies may derive from older Persian traditions of mourning the hero Siavush.

16. Bulliet (1972) traces such shifts in the town of Nishapur.

17. For the Qajar period and the transition from the Safavid period, see Algar (1969).

18. On the Tobacco Protest see Keddie (1966), Lambton (1965); on the Constitutional Revolution see Browne (1910) and Kasravi (1330 Sh./1952).

19. Eickelman (1978), Quchani (1351 Sh./1972), Kasravi (1323 Sh./1944), S. Hussein Nasr's various writings, and those of Fazlur Rahman.

20. Compare Karl Jaspers's notion of an Axial Age, Robert Bellah's category of archaic religion, Marshall McLuhan's notions of linear and postlinear communication, and Jack Goody's writings on literacy.

21. Modern Zoroastrians have enthusiastically taken up modern education. At issue here are the education of priests and the nature and use of the scriptural canon. See Fischer (1973) and Boyce (1977).

22. Among the contemporary Iranian experiments is a Free University with televised course work and computer terminals in small towns, modeled on the British Open University.

23. On China see especially Ping-ti Ho (1971) and J. Needham (1956); on Buddhist sanga colleges, see Tambiah (1977).

24. In Iraq in the third century A.D., for instance, the Sassanian court appointed an exilarch as the political leader, and he in turn appointed tax collectors and market supervisors. These latter were usually rabbis, or rather scholars (*rav*). When one of these latter, Rav, refused to enforce the exilarch Mar Uqba's decree on market prices, he was jailed until he yielded (Neusner 1968: 438-459). The exact nature of the dispute is not preserved, but one theory suggests that the exilarch froze prices in a period of scarcity, and Rav, disputing the danger of scarcity, acted according to the rules against price fixing.

25. Ringer (1969: 39).

26. Ministry of Science and Higher Education (1973a, b); Zonis (1971b); Eicher, Lewis, Morton, and Zonis (1976).

27. But see the citations of teachers who refused to allow their students to take notes in Ahmed (1968: 92). The dispute is similar to that in ancient Greece between the Sophists and Aristotle, the former believing in the spoken word, the latter in the written. The ideology of oral instruction is still strong and invoked as a proof of the genuineness of the Qur'an: so many memorizers of the same text are a guarantee, it is said, against tampering. But in fact Islam was almost immediately, if not from the start, heir to a literate civilization.

28. *Al-rihla* is the term for these educational travels. As Ahmed (1968) correctly notes, a biographical dictionary such as the one he analyzed contains among its conventional entries the date when a person went to his first class and an account of the *rihlas* in search of teachers or manuscripts.

29. The synagogue service is composed of reading the scripture plus prayers and poetical pieces to be sung (*piyyut*, from Greek *poetes*; Arabic *hizana*, hence sung by a *hazan* or cantor). It is incumbent upon every adult male to participate. A Muslim can get away with being able to perform the namaz prayer and to listen to preachers; but the Talmud has the requirement, "Everyone is obliged to say something new in his prayer everyday," a derivation from Ps. 98:1 ("Sing unto the Lord a new song"). The biblical verse, "You shall study [Torah] day and night" (Josh. 1:8) was early on incorporated into the daily prayer. The Talmud says that God will accuse even the poor man who fails to study, and when a poor man protests that he has a family to support, God will reply that Rabbi Akiba too was poor and had a wife and child, but finally God will concede that few men have

wives like Rachel (who separated from Akiba to work and help make ends meet). (This is an opinion of the school of Hillel, which achieved dominance. The opposite school of Shammai opinion was that God gave the Torah to a people to whom he had also given manna so they had no need to work; thus only the leisure class — priests and patricians — should be allowed to study.) Even the legal definition of a town (as opposed to a village) in Jewish law revolves around scholars: it is a place that can support at least ten *batlanim*, those who do not work but study or serve the community (Goitein 1971: II, 159, 197; Finkelstein 1975: 80-81). There are many injunctions to study in the Qur'an and hadith as well, but the liturgy and minimum duties of a Muslim, I would suggest, are less; and this had an effect in the small face-to-face communities of premodern times.

30. The following sketch depends mainly upon Drazin (1940), Gamoran (1925), Goitein (1971), Menes (1960), and Steinsaltz (1976). For a discussion of the obscurities and arguments about the organization of the community under the second Temple, especially of the sanhedrin, see Mantel (1961).

31. Following the anthropological principle of respecting the sensibilities of the people being studied, the Christian calendar dates in this section will be marked C.E. (common era) and B.C.E. (before the common era) rather than A.D. (anno Domini) and B.C. (before Christ).

32. On the dispute as to when the titles *nasi* and *ab bet din* were introduced, see Mantel (1961).

33. The number seventy comes from the seventy elders who assisted Moses: Exod. 19:7, Num. 11:16-17, Deut. 27:1.

34. The dispute between the Sadducees and the Pharisees is much more complicated than this. In certain respects, the Sadducees are more appropriately called the conservative traditionalists: it is they who insisted on the prerogatives of the priests and Levites and who denied legitimacy to the sanhedrin because it was composed of laymen instead of priests and Levites as required by Deut. 17:9. This labeling problem occurs repeatedly in Islamic history as well: a sense of creating traditions and extending them provides the dynamic corpus of Islamic and Jewish law (though ideologically the insistence on a chain of transmitters of an interpretation or tradition denies that there is change). Those who argue against these traditions in the name of scripture alone (the Sadducees, the Akhbaris in later Shi'ite history, and the Ahl-e Sunnat in earlier Islamic history) in fact have to create their own system of interpretations. The situation is dynamic: Sadducee or literalist positions can be both conservative (pro-priestly perogatives, pro-patrician rule) and liberal (pro-Hellenistic behavior). The Pharisee position also has conservative and progressive tendencies, identified usually with the school of Shammai and the school of Hillel, respectively. That the Pharisees were introducing changes is indisputable: Lev. 13:1 says that a priest should decide whether a leper is clean or unclean; by the time of Hillel, the decision was being made by a scholar who then told a priest to pronounce the words "clean" or "unclean" (Mantel 1961: 99).

35. In medieval times *tannaim* came to mean literally "repeaters," those whose expertise was simply to know the text and its proper cantilation. Often, as in the Muslim community, such people were blind.

36. A famous story is told about Hillel to illustrate. He came from a wealthy Babylonian family to study in poverty in Jerusalem. He supported himself and his

family by cutting wood. One day he did not have the money to enter the academy, yet despite a snowstorm he climbed up to a window or skylight so he could listen. He was found at the end of the session half frozen.

37. Roman rhetors taught sitting while their students stood (Deansley 1961: 59). Presumably, however, the justification was different.

38. The word *smicha* originally referred to consecrating the sacrifice by the laying on of hands (Mantel 1961: 2). Ordination gave one the right to adjudicate cases involving fines (*kenas*) and the right to define the traditional law ("put fences around the Law") by means of penalty-bearing injunctions to do or not do something (*gezerot*) and of institutions to ensure better observance of the spirit of the Torah (*taqqanot*). An example of the latter is the *ketubah* (marriage contract) introduced by Simeon ben Shetah to modify the biblical *mohar* (compare Islamic *mahr*) from a bridewealth payment to a payment should the husband die or divorce, the object being to encourage marriage and discourage divorce. (On the Islamic and Jewish marriage payments, see Fischer 1973.) Scholars living outside Palestine were denied this ordination (smicha): hence to this day the title in Iran and Iraq is rav rather than rabbi. This prohibition meant that scholars outside Palestine could not constitute themselves into a legislative court on legal questions, imposing fines or introducing *gezerot* and *taqqanot*. However, communities can impose fines and rulings upon themselves, either through some voting procedure or through elected rabbis. The technical smicha in this sense lasted until the eleventh or twelfth century. The smicha of Eastern Europe was an academic degree given by a yeshiva but without any force of authority unless a community accepted the rabbi; and it is in this same sense of rule by consent of the ruled that the yeshivas of Babylonia (Sura and Nehardea) were able to decide communal and religious issues (Mantel 1961: 214-221). Goitein translates *taqqanot* simply as "statutes" introduced either by the scholars or by the community, and notes that there is a principle that the agreement of men is the same as the will of God (vox populi vox dei), that congregations were called "holy communities" (Hebrew *ha-kahal ha-kadosh*; Arabic *al-jamaa al-muqaddasa*) after Exod. 19: 6 ("a kingdom of priests and a holy nation"), and that after God, authority rests in the congregation, according to the Talmud. Compare the Muslim *'ijma'* (consensus), based on the hadith "My community will never be unanimous in disobedience to God."

39. *Yeshiva*, means, literally, a place where people sit together. *Haver* is a comrade and in medieval times came to mean doctor of law as opposed to merely a scholar (*talmid*). The term *havurot ha-sedeq* (righteous corporation) was often used for the yeshiva of Palestine.

40. Jewish law requires at least three men to be convened as a court, for "none may judge alone but God." Goitein notes that although a single man might be appointed judge in the manner of the Muslim *qadi*, decisions in the Geniza records always bear at least three signatures.

41. The office of patriarch in Palestine was abolished in the early fifth century by Byzantium; *patriarch* was the Latin term for the nasi of the sanhedrin and yeshiva. On the medieval evolution of the titles nasi and nagid, see Goitein (1971: II, 17-39).

42. Ezekiel, the Minor Prophets, Daniel, Esther, Ezra, Nehemiah, and the Chronicles were added.

43. In the entry ceremony for a five-year-old starting the heder the child is questioned, while standing on a table, by a second child. (The following description is from a memoir cited in Gamoran 1925: 80-81.):

"What is your name child?"
"I am no longer a child but a young man who has begun the study of Humosh in a propitious hour."
"What is Humosh?"
"Humosh is five."
"What five? Five cakes for a cent?"
"No, the five books of the Torah that God gave Moses."
"And what book will you study?"
"I will study Leviticus which deals with sacrifice."
"Why do you want to study about sacrifices?"
"Because sacrifices are clean and I am a clean Jewish child. Let therefore the clean come and busy themselves with the clean."
"And why is the 'Alef' in the word 'Wayikra' small" [The letter alef is printed small in the Pentateuch in the word 'wayikra".]
"Because I am a small boy and I will study the Torah. Alef means 'to study' and the Torah cannot exist except for him who is humble in the study of it and not falsely proud."
"If so, why are you proud?"
"God forbid, I am not."
"Then why do you stand upon the table?"
"I will take your advice and get down."

44. Girls were also taught, but irregularly, since they had no active role in the synagogue. In Eastern Europe, girls were admitted to some heder, but generally they were taught not the Pentateuch but a Yiddish adaptation (first published in 1600), the *Ze'enah Ureenah*, which includes much folklore and many legends (Gamoran 1925; Menes 1960: 384). In the Talmud there are two opinions on educating women: Rabbi Eliezer of the school of Shammai opined that girls (like the poor and undistinguished of ancestry) ought not to be taught the Oral Law or Mishnah and Talmud; Ben Azzai of the school of Hillel opined to the contrary (Drazin 1940: 127). This is in keeping with the Shammaite desire to restrict learning and the Hillite desire to democratize it.

45. *Bimeh* is Greek for a movable podium. The fixed podium was called by the Latin-Coptic-Syriac term *anbol*. In twelfth century Christian countries, the Arabic term *minbar* was used (Goitein 1971: II, 146).

46. For instance, one teaching has to do with adding or dropping a letter on a person's name according to his deeds: "Now Jethro, priest of Midian, Moses' father-in-law, heard . . . (Exod. 18:1). Originally they called him merely Jether, as it is said, 'And Moses went and returned to Jether his father-in-law' (Exod. 4:18). After he had performed good deeds they added one more letter to his name so that he was called Jethro. You find this also in the case of Abraham, whom they originally called merely Abram. [Sarah and Joshua are two more examples.] And there are others from whose names they took off one letter [Ephron, Jonadab]" (Drazin 1940: 97).

47. The image of students sitting around long tables is associated with

preparatory work. For good descriptions see Menes (1960); Gamoran (1925); and the autobiographical novel by Grade (1976).

48. Until 1013, when al-Hakim ended the practice and instituted a series of discriminatory measures including the destruction of synagogues and forcible conversions (Goitein 1971: II, 57, 300, 12).

49. Goitein 1971: II, 207; based on French emigrés to the Levant after 1200.

50. The Ashkenazi, says Menes (1960: 377-379), were more secure in faith and more concerned with rites. Hence Rabbi Jacob b. Asher begins his *Arba'a Turin* with the procedures upon rising in the morning: what must a Jew do? The Sephardim, on the other hand, were more secure in the world. Hence Maimonides begins his *Mishna Torah* with the existence of God: what must a Jew know?

51. The full quotation includes fourteen stages from age five to marriage at eighteen and death at one hundred (Ulich 1968: 15).

52. The following account relies mainly upon Little (1922), Marrou (1948), Smalley (1964), and Rashdall (1895).

53. Charlemagne had a palace school that trained future bishops and abbots under Alcuin, but he also ordered that every monastery and cathedral have a school open to lay as well as religious students.

54. The word *university* merely meant a community of people or a legal corporation, and usually referred to the guilds of masters or students. The academic institution in the abstract was called a *studium*.

55. Bologna's development was slightly different. In Italy the classical system of education had not quite disappeared and the revival of interest in Roman law gave rise to the studium at Bologna. More important, the students there formed particularly strong guilds and subjugated the masters to their will, paying them and making them take oaths to the guilds. The masters of course retained the right to admit men to their own ranks. Other universities followed the pattern of Bologna and Paris, more or less. Students were often divided not only by faculty but by nation. In Prague, the first of the Germanic universities (founded only in the fourteenth century), there was a good deal of violent competition between the Germans and the Czechs. Hastings Rashdall's (1895) account of the constitutional developments of the medieval universities is still the most complete.

56. In fact, he attracted the largest crowds not while at Notre Dame but while at St. Genevieve.

57. The seven liberal arts, originally what a free Roman should know, were divided into two parts: the trivium consisted of grammar, logic, and rhetoric; the quadrivium was music, arithmetic, geometry, and astronomy. Grammar tended to be studied from Priscian, Donatus, and some of the classics; rhetoric, from Cicero and some elements of Roman law; and logic, from Aristotle's *De Interpretatione* and *Categories*, both in Latin translations by Boethius. From 1141, other treatises of Aristotelian logic became known (the *Prior Analytics*, *Topics*, *Sophistical Arguments*). A translation of Porphyry's *Isagoge* was also used. The trivium was universally taught as preparation for further study; the quadrivium often was not taught at all.

58. In Iran, when I complained on occasion that I could not follow the intricacies of this or that preacher, someone invariably would say, "Never mind, it is not important; we have heard it so often we never listen, we only come to drink tea and smoke cigarettes."

59. This does not refer to the training itself. A 1976 study of University of Tehran medical students revealed study habits that are not likely to produce creative scientists. Only half the students said they sometimes used the library; most learned by rote, often by walking alone and reading aloud to themselves; only half regularly attended lectures, saying they were useless (Ziai et al. 1976).

3. Madrasa: Style and Substance

1. Approximate reconstruction from memory by Mehdi Abedi each day after the sessions of October 20-26, 1975. The Borujerdi Mosque is attached to the Shrine precincts. As a non-Muslim, my presence was a source of discomfort, but Mehdi as a Muslim could attend freely. I went to this mosque only in the company of a mulla or for important events such as the annual death memorial for Ayatullah Borujerdi, when my presence was favorably acknowledged, in part as a pro-'ulama, anti-Pahlavi gesture. The ambiguity about a non-Muslim's presence has to do with Shi'ite notions of pollution: a non-Muslim's touch makes one impure for prayer. Technically this means only that before praying one must be sure to perform the proper ablution; buildings do not become impure. The Borujerdi mosque is not inside the shrine precincts but adjacent to it. No one objected when I entered the shrine with a mulla. But somehow the notion of a non-Muslim in a particularly sacred space was viewed as inappropriate. There was no problem in entering any of the other mosques or teaching spaces of Qum.

2. Other localities have slightly different variants of the story behind the saying.

3. Recounted, among other places, in the biography of Borujerdi by his son-in-law, S. Mohammad-Husayn Alavi Tabataba'i (1341 Sh./1962).

4. Summarized from tapes of the sessions as well as the handouts.

5. Fozelat: 12; Baqareh: 117; Al-e Emran: 47; Mariam: 35; Mozamel: 20; Yasin: 39.

6. Modaser: 38; Tur: 21; Najan: 39; Rad: 11; Anfahl: 35.

7. Ayatullah Muhammad-Hasan Shirazi, known for his vigorous defense of the faith as *al-Mujaddid* (the renewer of the faith), led the fight against the granting by the Persian government of a monopoly on tobacco to an English company. He declared the smoking of tobacco to be worse than fighting the messiah. Other mujtahids quickly followed suit. During the troubles over the Bahais in the 1950s, Ayatullah Borujerdi issued the opinion (*fatwa*) making Pepsi Cola makruh, because the franchise is held by a company owned by the Bahai entrepreneur Sabet. Again others followed suit, and Shariatmadari reaffirms the fatwa, even in the new issue of his *Risala*.

8. Part of the folklore about the Sirat Bridge stems from the Chinvat Bridge of Zoroastrian legend. After death the soul of a good man finds the bridge broad, and on the other side a fair woman greets him. She is a representation of his good deeds. The evil man in contrast finds that the bridge narrows to a razor's edge, and he falls down into a series of hells with the reflection of his deeds, an old hag, to accompany him. Such imagery was elaborated by Muslim authors in various ways, but among Shi'ite theologians, perhaps the fullest exposition is in the *Haqq al-Haqin* of the leading Safavid mujtahid, Muhammad-Baqir Majlisi (number 37 in the list of *maraji'-i taqlid* in the appendix).

9. Although banned, the books would pop out of all sorts of hiding places upon request. They could not be bought legally. The students felt that if they could say that their purpose in having them was to write attacks upon them, they would have an easier time if they were caught. One precaution was to keep the books widely dispersed among a group of friends so that no cache of books could be found in the room of any one person.

10. The figure for Qum is a minimum, taken from the registers of students who receive stipends; there could be as many as another thousand unregistered students. The Mashhad and Tabriz figures come from the Office of Endowments, checked roughly in the Mashhad case with estimates of a student, madrasa by madrasa. The Isfahan figure is a pure estimate by a madrasa teacher. The Shiraz figure is a fairly good estimate gained by going to each madrasa. The Yazd figure is an estimate by members of the madrasa system.

11. Taleghani and Jazayeri claim it is one to two hundred years old; Motahhari points out that it was only with Mujaddid Shirazi that funds were centralized to any significant degree; others cite Vahid-e Behbahani in his almost single-handed victory over the Akhbaris as the start of the tradition; still others cite Shaykh Mortaza Ansari.

12. The linkages shown in figure 3.2 are approximate, having been compiled from several incomplete sources, including genealogies of Ayatullah Mar'ashi, Adamiyyat (1337 Sh./1959: IV; 373), Razi (1352 Sh./1974 V), and Tehrani (1386/1966).

13. There was some student agitation over the issue; in confidential memos the police agencies were advised to stand by.

14. Similarly the members of the religious side of the Lajevardi and Kashani families claim to maintain no contact with their respective illustrious industrial and agro-industrial relatives.

15. British Public Records Office, file number FO 416/94, 1936.

16. On May 7, 1956, the army seized the Bahai Temple in Tehran; pictures are extant of the military governor of Tehran, General Teimur Bakhtiar, together with Falsafi, picks in hand, stripping the dome of its beautiful tiles. On May 17, the minister of interior, Asadullah Alam, appeared before the Majlis to answer charges that the government was not doing enough to root out Bahaism, and assured them that the 700,000 Bahais in 500 communities would not be allowed to create political intrigue. Falsafi and others were charging that the Bahais were fomenting a conspiracy to take over the government in the spring of 1956 and that Bahaism should therefore be banned and Bahais be dismissed from government jobs and have their property sequestered (*New York Times*, July 10, 1956, and July 17, 1956, p. 3; [Tehran] *Kayhan* 17 Mordad 1334/1956, p. 7).

4. Qum: Arena of Conflict

1. He represented 'Ali after the Battle of Siffin and was tricked into disavowing 'Ali. Mu'awiya's representative said, "In order to settle these conflicting claims to leadership of the community let us start afresh: each of us will disavow our leader's claim and we will then reason the issue out; you go first."

2. Early Muslims are divided into concentric circles: the Prophet, his companions, and then those who learned from the companions, or the *tabi'in*.

3. Ahmad ibn Ishaq Ash'ari, Vakil-i Vaqf-i Qum for Imam 'Askari.

4. Ustad Meshkat was sent as mutawalli in 1331/1952, but the Mesbah-Towliyat family was not firmly removed until 1965 when Mehran came and reorganized the shrine administration.

5. Cinema and television have been opposed on the grounds that they show immoral sex and violence. The first cinema built in Qum opened only in 1970, in the new town across the river from the shrine where in 1975 at least one place even sold Pepsi Cola. The first film shown was *Khana-i Khuda* ("The House of God"), a film of the hajj; but the second was called *Hot Passion*. The cinema burned down in 1975. (It remains unclear whether arson was involved.) Some religious leaders, recognizing the power of cinema, have urged that an alternative, religious cinema be created rather than futilely attempting to ban all cinema, but nothing has been done. Television has moved into Qum homes without much fanfare. It is alleged by cynics that Borujerdi, while opposing television publicly, had a set himself. (He died in 1961, long before television was available.)

6. *Muhr* are small rectangles of packed clay from Mecca or Karbala which are placed on the ground by Shi'ites when they pray; the forehead touches this remembrance of sacred turf during the prostration.

7. The allegation comes from one of the injured parties to the case and has not been cross-checked; however, the cultural logic, even should the case prove to be more complex, fits into the pattern.

8. According to current regulations, the mutawalli has a right to 10 percent and the overseer to 5 percent, except in the case of hospitals and schools, when the amounts are 3 percent and 2 percent (Mustaufi-Rajali 1351 Sh./1973: 97).

9. Allegations of misuse of endowments go both ways. In 1957-58 Timsar Akhavi, then minister of agriculture, gave a piece of land for a mosque or school to one of the maraji', who allegedly used it for something else. Presumably the Timsar failed to make out a formal deed, or the case would be litigable.

10. Admittedly this is not very reassuring in a judicial system where bribery and favor trading was allegedly widespread. Bribery worked on various levels, including payment to clerks in the Endowments Office to destroy items in the files. Although time, money, and the nature of bureaucratic procedures seemed to be on the government's side, the government did not always get its way.

11. The figure 170 is given by Eslami in a speech reprinted in Langerudi 1348 Sh./1970: 17-26.

12. The Goods and Services Price Control Act was administered by the Board of Trade, which established permissible profit margins and fined those caught exceeding them.

13. Similarly for the Sahami Hospital: money was willed by Saham-ud-Dowleh to be overseen by Haeri-Yazdi and Motamen-ul-Mulk, Moshir-od-Dowleh; when the supporting endowment was lost during the post-1963 land reforms, Ayatullah Shariatmadari got control of the building and raised funds for refurbishing it. The Nikui Hospital, started with a third of the inheritance left by Masud Nikui, was turned over to and expanded by the Imperial Organization for Social Services.

14. The following excerpts are freely translated from Khomeyni (1363/1943: 190-214). Khomeyni was responding to *Asrar Hezar Sol* (Secrets of a Thousand Years) by Shaykh Mehdi Painshahr, a disciple of Kasravi, and clearly is attacking the master instead of the relatively obscure disciple. He avoids Kasravi's name but

attacks his book *Shi'a-gari*. Lesser opponents like Shariat Sangelagi are mentioned by name and book title (p. 60) and dispensed with quickly.

15. The trampling of personal dignity by Endowment Office officials was often more crude and severe than the similar trampling described in welfare procedures of the 'ulama.

5. Discourse and Mimesis

1. Such as that to Mashhad on the death of the seventh Imam, described in chapter 4.

2. This healthy genre of self-mockery was maintained after the revolution. Two jokes about Khomeyni circulating in Shiraz in March 1979 responded to his fundamentalism and his charismatic hold over the popular imagination. Both depend for their full flavor on puns. In the first, Khomeyni is asked who his favorite female singer is. He says Haideh, an enormously fat woman. Asked why, he says, *Ba regime mokhalef bud* (she opposed the regime). The joke depends first on the depreciation of Khomeyni as allying himself with anyone who opposed the shah, regardless of what else he might represent (popular singing of Haideh's variety is makruh in Islam, if not actually haram; it is somewhat scandalous for an ayatullah to interest himself in female singers, and doubly funny to pick one with ambiguous sexual attraction, being on the fine line between grossness and desirable – in the Middle East – female corpulence). Second, the joke depends on a pun on "regime," the French-borrowed term for a government and the French-derived word for a diet.

The second joke has to do with a rooster, a dog, and an ass, who come to Khomeyni in Qum to seek exit visas out of the new Islamic republic. (After the revolution no males above eighteen were allowed to leave until their records were checked.) Khomeyni asks why they wish to leave. The rooster says that now so many people call the people to prayer in the mornings that his skills are redundant. The dog says that he used to be an alley dog, stopping and terrifying people in the streets at night; now there are so many armed Islamic militiamen and boys stopping people every hundred yards and firing at them for the least misunderstanding or misstep, there is nothing for him to do either. Finally the ass says his job has been usurped by Khomeyni himself. (The words *khar* in Persian and *ass* in English have similar metaphorical implications.)

3. There is a sahih hadith of Imam Ja'far al-Sadiq that faith (iman) consists of professing by tongue, believing with conviction, and acting according to Islamic principles (al-Tamimi 1974: 4). To be *'adil* technically means not to have committed any of the major sins, such as adultery, gambling, drinking, or displeasing a parent, and to attempt to avoid the minor sins, such as wearing gold if male, shaving, dressing like a non-Muslim, and so on).

4. Culture and Personality Circle tape.

5. The Ni'matullahi order in Qum includes older high school teachers, cloth merchants, retired government clerks, a barber, a zurkhana operator, and sons and womenfolk of such men. The two Ni'matullahi groups in Yazd include a similar spread.

6. Delivered in Yazd at the death memorials for Rasulian, an industrialist and philanthropist (Maneqebi 1971).

7. The world, he says, must conform to the shari'at, not vice versa.

8. What is valuable in religion is its distinctive features.

9. Khomeyni (1943: 110), for instance, lists the following mistakes for Abu Bakr: cutting off a thief's left hand instead of his right; mistakenly burning a man to death; not knowing the share a grandmother receives; excusing Khalil ibn Walid for the identical crime for which he executed Malek ibn-Noveid and then marrying the latter's widow. For 'Umar: stoning a pregnant woman; stoning a crazy woman; making a mistake in adjudicating a *mahr* (marriage payment) and being corrected by a woman behind a curtain; making things haram which are permitted in the Qur'an like temporary marriage and going on the hajj out of season; setting fire to the door of the family of the Prophet.

Allamah S. Muhammad Husayn Tabataba'i (1975: 40-60) lists the following mistakes under the first three caliphs: the secret election of Abu Bakr while 'Ali and the followers of the Prophet were burying the Prophet; the free use of ijtihad (interpretation) instead of sticking to the *shari'at* (laws); the cutting off of khums (religious tax monies) to sayyids; the ban on writing down the Qur'an and hadith. Specifically for 'Umar: the banning of out-of-season pilgrimage and temporary marriage; allowing triple divorce at one time; uneven distribution of public funds, leading to beginnings of class divisions. For Mu'awiyah: by breaking the agreement with Hasan to return the caliphate, introducing the separation of religion and politics. For Yazid ibn-Mu'awiyah: in his first year, the slaying of Husayn; in the second year, the massacre and looting of Medina; in the third year, the destroying and burning of the Kaaba.

10. He is present in the world and occasionally manifests himself to certain people.

11. When, because of the Russo-Japanese War, the price of sugar rose, the governor of Tehran tried to lower the price by fiat. A leading sugar merchant said the governor could have his current stock and he, the merchant, would go into other trade lines, but he could not guarantee the flow of sugar at those prices. He was bastinadoed; the bazaar closed in protest.

12. Despite his aid to Muzaffaruddin Shah, Nuri complained that in the shah's promise of an Islamic parliament the "Islamic" had gotten lost.

13. *Hiyal-i* or *Kulah-i shar'i* techniques tend to be of the form: I lend you $10 plus a match and you return to me the "equivalent" amount of $15. *Qard-i hasana* and *mihrabani* techniques tend to be of the form: I lend you $10, you return to me $10 and voluntarily add a gift of $5 as a token of appreciation. *Mukhatira* contracts, which incidentally were also important in medieval Europe and were called by their Arabic name (*mohatra*), are contracts to buy something at above market price on credit and immediately to resell it to the creditor for cash at the lower price.

14. Not only is reputation itself protected, but in the law of marriage a wife is entitled to support according to her status and a husband may prevent a wife from taking a job injurious to his status.

15. Further discussion of the issue of women in Islam and women's liberation in Iran can be found in Fischer (1978).

16. Delivered because 'A'isha (the widow of the Prophet) had taken to the battlefield against him.

17. Reza Shah first outlawed foreign-run schools in the 1930s. Then the state offered to pay part of the salaries of staff for private schools in return for

standardization of curriculum. In the 1970s the state declared education free to students who signed a statement that they would work for the state. Private schools were administratively also being turned into public schools.

18. Technically she can be a mujtahid for herself but not a source of imitation (*marja'-i taqlid*) for others. Hence the point becomes meaningless, since everyone follows himself to the level of his expertise. The question to be asked to keep the issue clear is how many female mujtahids can be named.

19. 'Alam al-Huda begins with a demonstration of the physiological ill effects of music: musicians die young, they go insane, they masturbate, they get syphilis; music causes neuroses.

20. A possible rationale is that Iran supported America's anticommunist rhetoric; because Shi'ism is anticommunist, this would have introduced a complication. Still, most of Shariati's audience would have been opposed to the American bombing of Vietnam, if casual opinion in Yazd in 1970 is representative, an opinion that became stronger as the United States withdrew in moral defeat.

21. Shariati is not the only one to use this technique on the Qur'an. Bazargan (1341/1962: 123) uses it and comes up with different results. Even Ibn Khaldun used it, in a sense, when he explained the preference of some early theologians for insisting that the Qur'an is free of anthropomorphism since there are many antianthropomorphic verses and few anthropomorphic ones.

22. According to Naser Makarem's review, Shariati confused the Prophet's use of councils for *foru'al-din* (mundane rules of religion) and God's decision in *usul-i din* (basics of religion) like selecting Imams; and further, he confuses ijma (consensus, unanimity, coincidence with the will of God and the opinion of the Imams) with democratic majority (1350: 76-78).

23. His father, a high school teacher in Mashhad, is a well-known wa'iz and author of a tafsir. The son must have absorbed something as a youth. Evidently in Paris he came under the influence of liberal, modernist Sunni interpretations of Islam.

24. *Qalam-kari*, as the print is called, used to be made in Yazd as well, but no more. There are said to be seventeen neighborhoods, but there are more named neighborhoods in actuality.

25. The element of male display in flagellation is recognized. A few years ago the police wanted to stop the slashing of the foreheads in a village near Tehran. Their successful strategy was to keep women away from the route of the male march. See also the description in M. Good (1976) of sex aggression in 'Ashura rites in Maragheh.

26. The sin dramatized is *'aq-i validayn* (displeasing a parent)—a major sin—which prevents one from going to heaven. In a popular version of the story used in Iran to discipline small children, the son killed his mother at the urgings of his Jewish wife. Salman Farsi passes a graveyard, notices a flame coming from the grave of the son, and calls up the son's tormented soul to learn the story. Muhammad and his family try to intercede with the mother, and eventually Husayn gets her to remove the curse.

27. Jealousy that the children of someone else ('Ali and Fatima) should be successors to the Prophet; dispute between her and 'Ali over the propriety of her having gone to fetch something alone and having thereby raised rumors of inchastity;

conflict between her and 'Ali over the amount of money from community funds to which she was entitled as a wife of a Prophet.

28. See Elie Wiesel (1976: 139-169) for an account of Joseph as a *tzaddik* (pious man). The theme of sacrifice is linked to the Abraham-Isaac story (the *akada*).

29. The Shi'a credo consists of five basic principles (*usul-i din*) and ten duties (*foru' al-din*). Of the five principles, three are common to all Muslims: tawhid or unity of God, *nubuwwa* or prophethood, and *ma'ad* or resurrection. The other two are special to the Shi'ite school (*madhhab*): imamat and *'adl* (the belief that God is just). The ten duties are: namaz, sawm (fast), khums, zakat, hajj, jihad, *amr bi ma'ruf* (encouraging good), *nahy az munkar* (dissuading people from evil), *tavalla* (loving the Imams and their followers), and *tabarra* (hating the enemies of the Imams). By the mid-seventies the government texts in *Ta'limat-i Dini* had dropped the last two.

6. The Revolutionary Movement of 1977-1979

1. First Egypt, then Morocco, gave refuge to the shah.

2. Bakhtiar displayed a portrait of Mossaddeqh at his first press conference; he had been a deputy minister of labor under Mossaddeqh. Bazargan had been a deputy minister of state for education, and managing director of the National Iranian Oil Company under Mossaddeqh. Karim Sanjabi, the leader of the National Front coalition in 1978, became Bazargan's foreign minister. Dariush Farohar, the deputy leader of the National Front in 1978, became Bazargan's minister of labor.

3. The notion of social drama has been elaborated at great length in the various works of anthropologist Victor Turner.

4. A more detailed review of these riots with a fuller analysis of their dynamics may be found in Fischer (1973: 407-456).

5. Jews suffered most in Shiraz, Tehran, and western Iran. Armenian villages were ransacked in Kurdistan. Occasionally even Europeans were threatened: missionaries in Isfahan, Belgian customs officials in Tabriz, merchants in Tehran. Of all, Bahais were the most vulnerable, being accused of heresy, a capital crime in Islam. Relations between the minorities and European powers were diplomatic protection and economic clientship. Many Ismailis and Zoroastrians were British citizens. Jewish philanthropic organizations were English- or French-based. Russians attempted to utilize and missionize the Armenians; the English Church Missionary Society and the American Presbyterian Mission made the same attempt on other Iranians. The British preferred to use Zoroastrians and Armenians as trade partners and as employees on the Indo-European Telegraph. In western Iran much trade was handled by Baghdadi Jews; in northern Iran Armenians were well placed; Zoroastrians were drawn to the Shiraz and Bandar Abbas routes. Reality, of course, was much more complicated than these connections suggest, but at times of frustration these connections became symbolically magnified in the minds of Muslims.

6. British Public Records Office, file FO 416/14, 1903: 176.

7. In 1928 a surtax was placed on tea and sugar; in the mid-thirties a road tax on motor vehicles was replaced with a tax on petrol and kerosene, and a tax on agricultural produce replaced the difficult-to-collect land taxes. Note circulation increased more than threefold between 1933 and 1937.

8. This required a number of dodges under the laws regarding marriage licenses, death certificates, job applications, and so on, none of which could be obtained by Bahais since they did not exist. On the other hand, it was charged by anti-Bahai Muslims that the legal fiction allowed Bahais to rise to ministerial posts from which recognized minorities were excluded. In other words, the compromise encouraged the theory of Bahai conspiracy at high levels in the government as well as elsewhere.

9. There were two guerrilla groups: Cherikha-yi Fida'i-yi Khalq (marxist); Mujahidin-i Islami or Mujahidin-i Khalq (Islamic). The latter took their name from the militias of the Constitutional Revolution, who called themselves *mujahidin* (holy warriors) and from the armed bands of Muhammad who robbed caravans to support the fledgling Islamic movement. For a review of the guerrillas operating in the 1960s and 1970s, see Halliday (1978).

10. Details of events during 1977-1979 are taken primarily from the reportage of *Christian Science Monitor* correspondants Tony Alloway and Geoffrey Godsell, *Washington Post* correspondents William Branigin and Jonathan Randall, *New York Times* correspondents Youssef Ibrahim, Eric Pace, and Nicholas Gage, *Manchester Guardian* correspondant Liz Thurgood, *Observer* correspondant Patrick Seale and various others who filed less frequent accounts. Information and corrections were also obtained from anthropologists in Iran at the time: Rafiq Keshavjee, Eric and Mary Hooglund, William Beeman, and Anne Betteridge.

11. On the economic and social conditions of the 1970s, see Abrahamian (1978), Graham (1978), Fischer (1977a), and McLachlan (1977).

12. See Goodell (1977), Fischer (1976), and Halliday (1978: ch. 5).

13. Abrahamian (1979) makes the interesting suggestion that this initiative was at the urging of two very different groups: former Tudeh members who were coopted by Asadullah Alam into the ministry of court (Mohammad Baheri, for example, who was to become minister of justice in 1978 in the Sharif-Emami cabinet); and political scientists who took to heart Samuel Huntington's writings on the utility of single parties for social mobilization. The language of the first Rastakhiz manifestos spoke of resolving the conflicts and contradictions of society through the party; Abrahamian detects debased Leninist rhetoric as the handiwork of the first group. The latter group, he suggests, forgot that to make a single-party system work, you need a sizable social base supporting the party.

14. Somewhat like the Egyptian program in 1956 of nationalizing industry by buying up former foreign-held shares, which private nationals do not buy through a state Economic Corporation.

15. Casualty figures vary enormously: low estimates are government figures, high ones are opposition figures.

16. The acting director was Texaco executive Paul Grimm, who ironically had protected strikers by refusing to supply their names to martial law authorities. He had taken over when managing director George Link went on leave after his car had been fire-bombed, November 14, in a foreshadowing of this guerrilla action. The Iranian slain was Malek Borujerdi.

17. According to this account, Khomeyni gave preliminary approval to the proposal and Sadeghi arranged a cabinet; but Khomeyni's letter of support was not allowed to leave Paris by Ebrahim Yazdi and other uncompromising aides. According to the other account, Sadeghi had no support because of a feud with

Sanjabi, who publicly denounced the attempt, as he would also denounce the Bakhtiar effort.

18. The fire, set on the evening of December 25, burned throughout the night. There was chaos inside, with reports of beatings, rapes, and killings. Tanks ringed the outside as smoke poured into the sky.

19. People from Quchan, in particular, were paid $15 per day to participate in pro-shah demonstrations. Others were army personnel or relatives of army personnel.

20. In Tehran, even before 'Ashura, a television cameraman had recorded a scene in which a soldier turned away a bloodmobile with the words "We try to kill these people and then you want to come and save them." The young women in the bloodmobile returned later in taxis with bottles of blood hidden in their chadurs. In Shiraz students running from the army sought refuge in Nemazee Hospital. The army pursued them into the hospital and even into an operating theater. The physicians consulted with the dean, Dr. Khosrow Nasr, who then resigned in protest. In Isfahan, on December 13, eleven persons were shot as they lined up at Soraya Hospital to donate blood; an hour later, troops came back with clubs to finish off those who had not learned. And in Mashhad, also on December 13, club-wielding pro-shah civilians and troops invaded three hospitals where doctors and nurses had staged pro-Khomeyni rallies.

21. Movie houses, shops, and libraries were burned in Tabriz. A policeman was shot in Hamadan. In Qarchak (eight miles south of Tehran) two Afghans were lynched for stealing; they had been reported to the police who had replied, "Go to your Khomeyni for law and order."

22. The names were never announced.

23. Some two hundred people were killed a hundred miles to the east of the September disaster area. The earthquake registered 6.7 to 7.5 on the Richter scale, but no reading was taken at Tehran University's Geophysics Institute because everyone was out celebrating the shah's departure.

24. The Tudeh party issued a statement in support of Khomeyni's Revolutionary Council initiative, stressing the continued need for unity. But the Marxist Fedayan put out a communique stressing the importance of ideological pluralism.

25. At Shahrokhi Air Base in Hamadan. There were also allegations that 160 to 190 men were shot for mutiny at a Tehran Air Base on January 27. In the first week of December, 7 to 20 Northrop F5 fighters had their wiring slashed in Tabriz.

26. Near midnight on February 9, the commander of an Imperial Guard detachment in the Dashtan Tapeh Air Base called for reinforcements to put down a demonstration by technicians who, after viewing Khomeyni on television, began antigovernment chanting. Guerrillas and armed civilians rushed to aid the technicians; others rushed to form a cordon around Ayatullah Khomeyni in case this was the beginning of the long-awaited and feared coup. The following day they attacked Eshratabad Air Base.

27. From the beginning after Khomeyni's return, there were conflicts between writers and printing staff over articles critical of the regime. By May newspapers were periodically closed for criticism of the regime or for reporting things other than what the government wished. Khomeyni called a boycott, for instance, of the paper *Ayandegan* on May 12, 1979, because it had reported the interview

given to *Le Monde* in which he had blamed the assassinations of General Qarani and Professor Motahhari on American agents, and for reporting that the Forghan guerrillas who claimed the assassinations were anticlerical followers of Shariati. Khomeyni wished to deny any factionalism within the revolution and to use the press to manipulate the news and disseminate different things domestically from what was disseminated abroad. Various press codes were promulgated making it a crime to criticize Khomeyni, restricting the freedom of the foreign press, and attempting to return the press to a propagandistic role. The Ministry of Information was renamed—as it had been under Reza Shah following the Italian fascist model—Ministry of National Guidance.

28. In June 1979, Defense Minister General Taqi Riahi dismissed the military police commander, General Seif Amir Rahimi, for opposing the government policy of not using troops against ethnic political dissidents, for publically opposing the use of foreign technical advisors, and for telling the press that military commanders were plotting against Khomeyni. Rahimi refused to resign, saying that only Khomeyni had authority to dismiss him, and displaying his own black-shirted military guards to the press. Khomeyni reinstated him, causing another cabinet crisis and trip to Qum by Bazargan.

Eleven days later the armed forces chief of staff, General Nasser Farbod, resigned because of interference by the secret Revolutionary Council.

29. There was much debate and ambivalence about how to deal with an army which had been a tool of repression. It was agreed that a purge was necessary: numerous officers were retired; 31 generals were executed by May. There was debate about integrating the army with the revolutionary militia so as to control the latter and purify the former. On March 27, the Chief of Staff, General Mohammad Vali Qarani, was dismissed for using a unit of the old elite Imperial Guard and gunship helicopters against the Kurds as the shah would have done, as well as for failing to submit to the authority of the Minister of Defense, Admiral Madani. For good measure he was accused of having participated in torture for the shah twenty-five years earlier before being dismissed by the shah for an anti-royalist plot. (A month later Qarani was assassinated.) Thereafter the army was used hesitantly, and there was considerable unease within the army about its being used to put down political dissent. Admiral Madani became Governor of Khuzistan and used troops in a bloody confrontation with Arab demonstrators in Khoramshahr at the end of May. Ayatullah Khomeyni ordered the army to crush the Kurds in August 1979, and a number of soldiers were executed for refusing orders.

30. Improvements included replacement of the council of five mujtaheds with veto power over legislation by an expanded council including three mujtaheds and a number of others so that the ulama did not have a veto power. There was a statement of the equality of men and women, and a provision for guaranteeing the cultural rights of linguistic minorities.

31. The cultivation and consumption of opium increased dramatically as did the black market export of heroin. Drug traffic became such a problem that at one point Khomeyni announced the reintroduction of the shah's death penalty for the sale of narcotics. Flogging was introduced on a sporadic basis by local revolutionary committees for drinking alcohol and for minor sexual misdemeanors.

7. Epilogue: Muharram 1400/1979

1. In April 1978 Nur Mohammad Taraki led a marxist coup against the government of Daoud Khan. The more pro-Soviet faction, headed by Babrak Karmal, soon forced out of power, was kept in reserve by the Soviets in Eastern Europe as rebellions arose all over Afghanistan against the drive to socialize the country. In September 1979 the Soviets attempted to engineer a coup against the strongman of the Taraki government, Hafizullah Amin. This backfired: Taraki was killed instead, and Amin emerged as the leader of the government. Conditions continued to deteriorate, and Soviet military missions began to prepare for invasion: in April 1979 several Soviet generals reconnoitered; in August, General Ivan G. Pavlovsky, commander of Soviet ground forces, brought a team of fifty officers for a two-month study. The Bagram airfield north of Kabul was secured in July by Soviet troops; troops, tanks, and artillery were airlifted there on December 8; the Salang Pass was secured on December 18; and an airlift of five thousand troops was executed on December 24-27, followed by the entry of some 70,000 ground forces. Amin was removed, Kabul and the provincial cities were secured, and Babrak Karmal was installed.

It is of note that the Russian ambassador to Tehran visited Khomeyni shortly before the invasion, presumably to assure him that the Soviet Union was opposed to the anti-Islamic stance of the Amin government, an assurance reiterated by Babrak Karmal.

2. The shah stayed at the New York Hospital-Cornell Medical Center until December 2, 1979, when he was moved to Lackland Air Force Base in Texas. Mexico had refused to receive him back; President Sadat of Egypt reiterated offers of asylum. On December 15 he moved to Panama.

3. Two women and one black remained in custody.

4. Subsequently Iranian accounts justified the attacks on the American Jewish lobby by citing the initial speculations by newsmen that the Kaaba had been seized by dissident Shi'ites from Saudi Arabia's Eastern Province. This, the Iranians claim, was a Zionist smear.

5. Iranian diplomats later quietly tried to reassure the international community that this was for domestic consumption only.

6. On November 28, 1979, Iran filed suit against the shah and his wife for $56 billion plus damages. Bani-Sadr made public a letter from former Attorney General Ramsey Clark to Ibrahim Yazdi, shortly before the latter's resignation as Foreign Minister, advising Iran to file such a suit. The suit was filed by Schack, Abourezk and O'Dwyer; former U.S. Senator Abourezk had been retained by Iran to advise on legal matters. Erich Diefenbacher was retained in Switzerland to file claims against the shah there.

7. When Senator Edward Kennedy made a campaign speech condemning the shah—a speech received favorably in Iran and unfavorably by Americans incensed by the hostage seizure—Mehdi Ha'iri-Yazdi, son of Shaykh Abdul-Karim Haeri-Yazdi, tried again to suggest to Khomeyni that Iran could insure that an American delegation to a UN-sponsored investigation might include persons sympathetic to the Iranian·cause; this too was rejected by Khomeyni. In the event, despite Iran's refusal to participate, Khomeyni was proved wrong. Security Council members, while unanimously condemning the seizure of hostages, expressed sympathy toward the revolutionary cause and Iran's legitimate grievances.

8. Among the best were Mike Peters' portrait of Khomeyni holding out a coffee cup, with the legend, "My coffee's cold: seize the Brazilian Embassy"; Donato's Thanksgiving Day (2 Muharram) cartoon of Khomeyni as the Statue of Liberty holding a tomahawk aloft in his right hand and cradling the White House in his other hand; McNelly's of the U.S. as a cow chewing her cud with Iranians thumbing their noses and waving a burning flag in the belief they were enraging an undisciplined bull. Among the most scurrilous was Szep's repeated bad pun of Khomeyni as a black "bird of prey," this time in worship on a prayer carpet with the wish, "Kill, Kill." On the 204th birthday of the Marine Corps, T-shirts were sold at the Quantico base in Virginia picturing a marine with drawn bayonet advancing on an Iranian cowering behind a pile of money and a barrel of oil; the legend read: "How much is the oil now?"

9. The initial effect of the oil boycott was to free more Iranian oil to be sold more lucratively on the spot market. It was pointed out that withdrawal of Iranian funds would have had only slight impact, whereas loss of confidence in the free movement of capital was potentially more serious. The American move ensured Iran's default on loans, countered by American and European banks' filing and obtaining court orders to attach Iranian holdings. Iran began to experience a commercial credit squeeze, but its oil revenues continued to buffer this inconvenience. Complaints were voiced by European and smaller American banks that Rockefeller and major American banks had attached the funds unfairly in breach of customary sharing of such action by all creditors.

10. The aircraft carrier *Kitty Hawk* was dispatched from Subic Bay in the Philippines to join the naval task force in the Indian Ocean. The United States tried to get the other industrial countries not to buy additional amounts of Iranian oil on the spot market. By the first week of 1980 the Security Council had agreed to consider economic sanctions.

11. For example, a picture labeled "Iranians being harassed" put on the Embassy wall was identified as being not a picture of a harassed Iranian, but of an American anti-Vietnam War demonstrator in San Francisco in the 1960s; Khomeyni's charge that American hands were involved in the seizure of the Kaaba in Mecca; allegations by Qotbzadeh that Christmas cards sent from America to the hostages contained bombs and razor blades.

12. In several cities religious leadership had a dual structure of a pro-Khomeyni leader and a more progressive or liberal leader allied with either Taleghani or Shariatmadari. In Shiraz, Ayatullah Mahallati was seen as following Taleghani; Ayatullah Dastgheeb followed Khomeyni. In Tabriz, Qazi Tabataba'i was Khomeyni's first representative; he fell into popular disfavor in the "days of armed struggle" when the military was disarmed following the Fida'yyin and Mujaheddin actions against the Tehran garrisons in February 1979. Tabrizis began seizing suspected or known SAVAK agents and bringing them to Qadi Tabataba'i. The military commander, Bidabadi, offered to jail them. The offer was accepted but it was soon discovered that they were being released from the jail. Bidabadi was recalled to Tehran and was executed. Ayatullah Madani was sent by Khomeyni to replace Qadi Tabataba'i. During the summer Tabataba'i went to Qum and was rehabilitated; he returned to Tabriz, but on Id-e Qurban, after prayers, he was shot and wounded. In December 1979 Ayatullah Madani became a focus of Tabrizi anger; the platform from which he led Friday prayers (the minbar?) was burned. Shariatmadari's representative in Tabriz was Aya-

tullah Hokmabadi. Shariatmadari was of course also represented by secular leaders like Moghaddam-Maragheh and youthful activists in his Moslem People's Republican Party.

13. Interview in *The Iranian*, quoted by *The Washington Post*, 12 December 1979.

14. Herblock was to pen a bitter cartoon on December 28, 1979, showing Secretary of State Cyrus Vance at a globe saying to President Carter, "Here's the strategy: we'll pray for the Afghans, burn candles for the Cambodians—and in Iran, we'll follow up our Christmas cards with a barrage of New Year cards." Carter had at one point suggested Americans work off their frustration by ringing church bells for the hostages. A massive popular campaign was organized to send Christmas cards to the hostages as well as messages to the Iranian government demanding the release of the hostages.

15. See Theda Skocpol, *States and Social Revolutions* (Cambridge: Cambridge University Press, 1979), for such an analysis, focusing on the experiences of France, Russia, and China.

16. Many Iran experts felt a sophisticated American foreign policy might have finessed the bourgeois revolution in the summer of 1978 by telling the shah that now was the time to step down in favor of a real constitutional monarchy or republic. A second, if slight, opportunity was squandered by Bakhtiar in not declaring an end to the monarchy or at least holding a referendum. Bazargan's own second thoughts (in an October 1979 interview with Oriana Fallaci) that the middle class did not stand up more forcefully against the clergy came much too late. Military hawks, in contrast, felt that the military should have crushed the revolution and maintained the shah.

17. Her brother, Prince Shariar Mustafa Shafiq, was assassinated in December 1979 in Paris.

18. Charges, for instance, that Ayatullah Beheshti had been conspicuously absent from anti-shah demonstrations when he resided in Germany; that Ayatullah Hashemi Rafsinjani was a corrupt opportunist as symbolized by his moving into former Minister of Court Assadullah Alam's house and by his wounding in a dispute over two million tomans worth of bribes to let people out of Iran; that Yazdi and Mansur Farhang—appointed to Iran's UN delegation—were American citizens; and so on.

The Forghan guerrilla group, claiming to be Shariati followers, took credit for the assassinations of Ayatullahs Motahhari (May Day 1979), Razi Shirazi (July 15, 1979), and Mohammad Mofateh (December 18, 1979), General Qarani (April 23, 1979), Mehdi Eraqi (once associated with the Fida'yyan of the 1950s, a religious right-wing assassination group), Haj Taghi Tarkhani (a Tehran merchant), and Hans Joachim Leib (a German manager for Merck Pharmaceuticals). The government claimed to have arrested most of the Foghan in January 1980.

19. Might, for example, General Fardust, once a childhood companion and classmate of the shah and head of the Imperial Inspectorate, now head of Khomeyni's secret police, change sides again? Or if not he, others like him.

20. Quoted by Flora Lewis, *New York Times*, December 29, 1979.

21. Allen Dubetsky, "A New Community in Istanbul, A Study of Primordial Ties, Work Organization, and Turkish Culture." Ph.D. dissertation, University

of Chicago, 1973. See also Serif Mardin, "Youth and Violence in Turkey," *Archives for European Sociology* 19 (1978): 229-254.

22. M. Y. Hairi. "A Treatise on Knowledge by Presence." Ph.D. dissertation, University of Toronto, 1979.

23. See Bruce Mazlish's attempt to sketch a psychological profile: "The Hidden Khomeini," *New York* 12, no. 50 (December 24, 1979): 49-54. He stresses Khomeyni's mysticism, his ethnic marginality (a Kashmiri grandfather), and the legend of his father's and son's deaths.

24. Pages 33 and 34 of the English translation by Somayyah and Yaser, published by the Free Islamic Literatures Incorporated, Bedford, Ohio, 1977.

25. See, for instance, the article by the Isfahan-based psychiatrist and former all-American football player, Jamshid A. H. Bakhtiar, "Crisis in Iran: A Birth of Consciousness," *Islamic Revolution* 1, no. 8 (November 1979): 20-25.

Glossary

ābrū: reputation, honor

ākhund: cleric; fr. *rawḍa-khwāndan* ("to read *rawḍa*"); once a term of respect, now the common word for those in religious garb, slightly depreciatory

ʿālim: one who is learned (pl. *ʿulamā*, but whereas ʿālim may be used of someone learned in secular subjects, ʿulamā refers only to the learned in religious subjects)

ʿallāma: title of respect for one who knows all the Islamic sciences; e.g., today the dean of philosophy in Qum, S. Moḥammad-Ḥoseyn Ṭabāṭabāʾī, is accorded the title ʿallāma

āqā: title of respect, both for an ordinary male and for a person of true authority (pl. *āqāyān*, usually refers to religious leaders)

ʿaqāʾid: beliefs, especially religious beliefs or doctrines as defined by *kalām* (dialectical theology)

āqāyān: plural of āqā; the leading members of the religious community, the *marājiʿ-i taqlīd* or *āyatullāhs*

āqāzāda: son of an āqā, often implies laziness

ʿaql: reason, intellect, intelligence

ʿatabāt: the holy shrine towns of southern Iraq: Karbala, Najaf, Kufa, Samarra

āya: verse of the Qurʾān

āyatullāh: "sign of God"; a leading *mujtahid*

āyatullāh al-ʿuẓmā: "greatest sign of God"; supreme *mujtahid*, title of respect for the leading mujtahid of the day

ʿazādārī: mourning; includes *taʿziya, rawḍa, shabīh, dasta-zani*

bāṭil: void, invalid

chādur: "tent"; Iranian veil for women

dars: lesson, class

dars-i khārij: "external class"; the third level of the madrasa system

dasta: group; groups of young men, usually in black shirts, who beat their chests with their hands, or their backs with chains, during religious processions (the activity is *sīna-zanī*, "beating the breast with the hands") du‘ā: prayer; the general term for expository prayer, as opposed to the stylized liturgical prayer, *namāz*

fāḍil: "industrious"; an upper level ṭālib or religious student

faqīh: expert in the law; from fiqh

fatwā: opinion, decision on religious matters

fiqh: religious law, jurisprudence, elucidation of the sharī‘at

ghaybat: concealment; the occultation of the twelfth Imām; slander, talking behind someone's back

ghayrat: the sense of shame or honor that prevents one from spoiling the honor of another man

ghusl: full ritual ablution

gurīz: "turning"; in a rawḍa the final turning to the story of Karbala

ḥadīth: a report of the saying or action of the Prophet, his companions, or the Imāms; the standard gloss is "tradition" of the Prophet, companions, or Imāms

ḥarām: religiously forbidden

ḥawza-i ‘ilmī: "reservoir of learning"; center of religious learning, composed usually of a group of madrasas

hay'at: group, gathering, meeting; approximately synonymous with majlis

ḥujjat al-islām: "proof of Islam"; originally a title of high respect, equivalent in e.g. Ghazālī's time to the contemporary āyatullāh, now devalued and used for any ākhund

‘ibādat: worship

ijāza: permission; document of permission to perform specified religious acts

ijmā‘: consensus of the Islamic community in regard to a legal decision

ijtihād: exercise of reason to interpret the intent of the law

imām: prayer leader, synonymous with the Persian term pīshnamāz

Imām: for Ja‘farī Shi‘ites one of the legitimate leaders of the Islamic community: one of the twelve successors to the Prophet descended from ‘Alī; in Arabic usage a marja‘-i taqlīd or learned man in Islamic sciences

imāmat: that form of leadership that the Imāms provide the Shi‘ite community

imāmzāda: "son of an Imām"; shrine dedicated to a descendant of an Imām

īmān: faith

‘irfān: speculative mysticism; gnosis

jihād: holy war, defense of the faith

kalām: dialectical theology; from the Arabic for "speech" because of the rhetorical and dialectical formulations used in defending Islamic belief, independent of philosophy

khānaqāh: Sufi lodge; Ismaili mosque

khums: "one fifth"; religious tax to support the poor descendants of the Prophet

khuṭba: sermon, usually delivered after the Friday noon prayer

majlis: meeting

makrūh: religiously discouraged but not forbidden

maktab: religious elementary school

marja‘-i taqlīd: supreme authority on the law (pl. *marāji‘-i taqlīd*)

mawqūfa: items that have been made *waqf*; endowed for specific purposes minbar: lecturn or podium; physically a set of stairs on top of which the preacher or teacher sits

minbarī: preacher, collective term for *wā'iẓ* and ākhund

mudarris: teacher

mujtahid: one who exercises *ijtihād*, or interpretive reason, to inquire into and clarify the intent of the law; one who has completed the course of jurisprudence and has written a *taqrīrāt*

mullā: obsolete term for ākhund; in the past it was a term of respect for one who was literate

mu'min: believer; one who has īmān or religious faith

muqallid: follower of a mujtahid

mutawallī: administrator of a *waqf*

nafs: soul, the animal soul of man as opposed to 'aql or reason

najis: ritually unclean

namāz: the ritual worship involving prostrations enjoined upon Muslims five times a day; properly called ṣalāt in Arabic

nāmūs: honor, women; that form of honor that a man can lose through the misbehavior of his women

naqīb: head of a local group of sayyids

naql: wooden bier used in Muḥarram ceremonies

nawḥa: songs of praise to God

niyyat: intention

pīshnamāz: prayer leader

qadamgāh: stopping place of a saint, shrine; literally, "footstep"

qarīb al-ijtihād: one who is almost a mujtahid

qibla: orientation for prayer toward the Kaaba in Mecca

rāwī: one who relates riwāyat

rawḍa: preachment, homiletic sermon; fr. the *Rawḍat al-shuhadā* (Garden of the Martyrs) of Husayn Wā'iẓ Kāshifī (d. 1504), a verse account of the tragedy at Karbala, used to frame sermons

rawḍa-khwān: preacher

rawḍa-khwāndan: to read a rawḍa

ribā': usury

riwāyat: stories of the Prophet and the Imāms; approximately synonymous with ḥadīth but usually more elaborate

rūḥ: spirit

rūḥānī: collective term for those who wear religious garb, clerics

sahm-i Imām: "portion of the Imām"; half of the khums which is often given to the marāji' for support of the rūḥānī and madrasa students

sanad: document

sayyid: descendant of the Prophet; entitled to wear a black or green turban (abbreviated when used as a title: S.)

shabīh: simulation; refers here to the passion plays of Muḥarram

shaykh: as now used, a rūḥānī who is not a sayyid, and who thus wears a white turban

sharī'at: the law of Islam

shathiyyāt: ecstatic sayings or exclamations of Sufis (pl. of *shath*)

sufra: table cloth, ritual feast

sunnat: normative practices or customs associated with the Prophet and Imāms, contained in the ḥadīth

ta'aṣṣub: tenacity in belief; pejoratively: fanaticism

tafsīr: exegesis of the Qur'ān

taklīf: duty, moral obligation (pl. *takālīf*)

ṭālib: religious student (pl. *ṭalaba*); abbreviated from *ṭālib 'ilm* "seeker after knowledge"

taqiyya: dissimulation

taqlīd: imitation, following one more learned than oneself

taṣawwuf: mysticism, the beliefs of the Sufis, as opposed to gnosticism (*'irfān*)

tawliya: trusteeship, office of the mutawallī

ta'ziya: mourning; used colloquially to mean *shabīh*, the passion plays of Muharram

thiqat al-islām: title for one who defends Islam rhetorically well, but is not particularly educated in Islam

thiqat al-muḥaddithīn: minbarī who recites only ḥadīth

'ulamā: religious leaders, *rūḥānī*

ummat: the religious community or followers of a Prophet

usūl: the "root" sources of legal authority and the principles for legal deduction of fiqh from those sources

wā'iz: lecturer, preacher

wājib: mandatory

waqf: pious endowment (pl. *awqāf*)

waswās: "doubt," concerning orthopraxis

wuḍū': the ablution that begins the namāz

ziyārat: pilgrimage, visit (to a sacred location)

zūrkhāna: "house of strength"; the traditional gymnasium

Bibliography

Persian and Arabic Sources

(Dates are given in the Persian Shamsi calendar, unless marked Q. to indicate the Qamari or Hijri calendar.)

RAWDAS (tape-recorded)

BAHLUL (SHAYKH MOHAMMAD TAQI WA'IZ SABZEVARI). On wine and gambling. 27 May 1975 (Vafat-i Fatima). In the Qum bazaar.

BORGA'I. On Fatima. 27 May 1975 (Vafat-i Fatima). In Tekke Marashi-Najafi, Qum.

FALSAFI, SHAYKH MOHAMMAD TAQI. On worship. n.d. In Masjid-i Sayyid, Isfahan.

_____. On the Iranians expelled from Iraq. n.d. In Masjid-i S. Azizullah, Tehran.

HASEHM-IRAQI. On backbiting and the idle tongue. 8 Ramadan 1395/1975. In Masjid-i Husaynabad, Qum.

HASHEM-NEJAD, S. ABDUL KARIM. On why Islamic countries have remained backwards. n.d.

KAFI, SHAYKH AHMAD. On vilayat. n.d. (Vafat-i Fatima). In Qum.

_____. On 'Ali. 19 Ramadan 1975. In Mahdiyeh, Tehran.

KHATAMI, S. MAHMUD. On uli'l-amr. 21 September 1975. For the Hay'at-i Karbala, Qum.

MANEQEBI, JAVAD. On 'Ali and worship. 1971. In Masjid-i Rasulian, Yazd.

MILANI, MOHAMMAD ALI. On Fatima and 'Ali. 1975. In Madrasa Milani, Mashhad.

SHARIATI, ALI. On shahadat. n.d. Ashura.

_____. On civilization and imitation. 22 Safar 1391 Q./1971.

BOOKS AND ARTICLES

ADAMIYYAT, MUHAMMAD-HUSAYN RUKNZADA. *Danishmandan va sukhansarayan-i Fars.* Tehran: Islamiyya and Khayyam, 1337/1959.

'ALAM AL-HUDA, S. MURTADA. *Saz va avaz.* Qum: Ustuvar, 1352/1977.

ASAF-AQA, S. AHMAD AL-HUSAYNI ASHKAVARI. *al-Imam al-Hakim.* Najaf: Dar al-Shifa, 1384Q/1964.

———. *al-Imam al-Sharudi al-Sayyid Mahmud al-Husayni.* Baghdad: Bayan, n.d.

ASTANA-I MUQADDAS-I QUM. *Guzarish-i 'amal-kard-i do-sala.* 1346/1967.

———. *Nashriyya.* 1348/1969.

———. *Rahnama-yi Qum.* 1354/1975.

BAZARGAN, MEHDI. "Intizarat-i mardum az maraji'." In Tabataba'i et al. 1341/1962.

BORUJERDI, HOSEYN [BURUJIRDI, HUSAYN], et al. *Risala-i tawdih al-masa'il.* Qum: 'Ilmiyya, n.d.

DAVANI, 'ALI. *Zindagani-i Ayatullah Burujirdi.* Qum: Hikmat, 1340/1961.

———. *Nahdat-i do maha-i ruhaniyan-i Iran.* Qum: Hikmat, 1341/1963.

FAGHIHI [FAQIHI], 'ALI-ASGHAR. *Tarikh-i madhhab-i Qum.* Qum: Hikmat, 1391/1971.

FALSAFI, SHAYKH MUHAMMAD-TAQI. *Buzurgsal va javan az nazar-i afkar va tamayulat.* Tehran: Ma'arif-i Islami, n.d.

GHAFFARI, 'ALI. "Islam va 'alamiyya-i huquq-i bashar." In *Guftar-i mah* 3 (1344/1965): 166-246.

HOMAYUNI, SADEGH [SADIQ HUMAYUNI]. *Ta'ziya va ta'ziya-khwani.* Tehran: Jashn-i Hunar, n.d.

"HUSAYNI." *Duktur che miguyad?* Mashhad: Tus, n.d.

IRAN, GOVERNMENT OF. *Guzarish-i mashruh-i Hawza-i sarshumari-i Qum.* Tehran: Ministry of the Interior, 1335/1956.

IRAN, GOVERNMENT OF. *National census of population and housing: Qum shahristan.* Tehran: Plan Organization, Iranian Statistical Center, 1345/1966.

ISLAMI, HAJJ SHAYKH 'ABBAS. "Tarh-i naw." In Langarudi 1348/1969.

JAVAHIR-KALAM, 'ALI. "Rawda-khwani va rawda-khwandaniha-yi mashhur-i Iran." *Khwandaniha,* 17, No. 2 (1335/1956): 20-21.

———. "Madrasa va talib." *Khwandaniha* 17, No. 3 (1335/1956a): 24-25.

———. "Bachcha-i maktab." *Khwandaniha* 17, No. 19 (1335/1956b): 27-29.

JAZAYIRI, S. MURTADA. "Taqlid-i 'alim ya sharayi'-i fatwa." In Tabataba'i et al. 1341/1962.

JAZAYIRI, S. MUSTAFA. *Gulistan-i payghambar: khanidan-i sadat-i mar'ashi-i Shushtar.* Najaf: Haydari, 1374/1954.

KASHMIRI, MIRZA MUHAMMAD-'ALI. *Nujum-i musamma fi tarajim-i 'ulama.* Qum: Bahthsiyyati, 1394/1974.

KASRAVI, AHMAD. *Khuda ba mast.* Tehran: Parcham, 1321/1942.

———. *Zindagani-i man.* Tehran: Parcham, 1323/1944.

———. *Shaykh Qurban az Najaf miayad.* Tehran: Paydar and Parcham, 1324/1945.

———. *'Atsa ba sabr che rabt darad?* Tehran: Parcham, 1324/1945.

———. *Shi'a-gari.* Tehran: Parcham, n.d.

———. *Tarikh-i Mashruta-i Iran.* Tehran: Amir Kabir, 1330/1952.

KHADA'ILI, MUHAMMAD. *Ahkam-i Qur'an.* Tehran: Javidan, 1353/1974.

KHO'I, S. ABU'L-QASIM. *Risala-i tawdih al-masa'il.* 1391/1971.

KHOMEYNI [KHUMAYNI], S. RUHULLAH MUSAVI. *Kashif-i asrar.* 1363Q/1943.

_____. *Hukumat-i Islami: Wilayat-i Faqih.* 1391Q/1971.

LANGARUDI, MUHAMMAD MUHAMMADI TAJ. *Guftar-i wa'iz.* 3 volumes. Tehran: Khidr, 1348/1970.

MAHALLATI, SHAYKH DHABIHULLAH. *Qidavat-i Hadrat-i 'Ali.* N.d.

MAKAREM, NASER [NASIR MAKARIM]. *Faylasufnama.* Tehran: Dar al-Kutub-i Islamiyya, 1333/1954.

_____. "Aya hukumat-i islami bar pa-yi shura ast?" *Maktab-i Islam* 13, No. 1 (1350/1972a): 76-78.

_____. *Mushkilat-i jinsi-i javanan.* Qum: Hikmat, 1350/1927b.

_____. *Dars-i 'aqa'id va madhahib.* Polycopy. Qum: Madrasa Imam Amir-ul-Mu'minin, 1354/1975.

MAR'ASHI, QADI NURULLAH. *Ihqaq al-Haqq.* Tehran: Islamiya, n.d.

MUDDARIS, MUHAMMAD 'ALI. *Rayhan al-adab.* Tabriz: Shafaq, n.d.

MUSTAWFI-RAJALI, MINUDUKHT. *Waqf dar Iran.* Tehran, 1351/1973.

MUTAHHARI, MURTADA. Introduction. In S. Muhammad-Husayn Tabataba'i, *Usul-i falsafa va ravish-i realizm.* Tehran: Akhundi, 1335/1956.

_____. "Islahat-i Ruh." *Maktab-i tashayyu'* 1 (1338/1959): 362-382.

_____. "Ijtihad dar Islam." In Tabataba'i et al. 1341/1962.

_____. "Mushkil-i asasi dar saziman-i ruhaniyyat." In Tabataba'i et al. 1341/1962.

_____. *Mazaya va khidmat-i marhum Ayatullah Burujirdi.* In Tabataba'i et al. 1341/1962.

_____. *Masalih-i hijab.* Tehran: Anjuman-i Islami-i Pizishkan, 1353/1974.

NAGAHANI, HUSAYN, AND MUHAMMAD NASIRI. *'Umr-i pur iftikhar.* Mashhad: Gutenberg, 1346/1967.

NASIR AL-SHAR'IYYA, SHAYKH MUHAMMAD-HUSAYN. *Tarikh-i Qum va zindagani-i Hadrat-i Ma'suma.* Qum: Dar al-Fikr, 1350/1971.

NURI, YAHYA. *Huquq-i zan dar islam va jahan.* Tehran: Farahani, 1343/1964.

QASIMNIZHAD. *Rahnuma-yi Qum.* Qum: Shahrdari, 1354/1975.

QUCHANI, AQA NAJAFI. *Siyahat-i sharq.* Mashhad: Tus, 1351/1972.

RAHIMI, AHMAD. *Paykar-i mardum.* Qum: 1954/1958.

_____. *Ganjina-i danishvaran.* Qum: Qum, 1339/1960.

RAHNUMA, JAVAD, et al. *Qum-ra bishnavid.* Qum: Qum, 1328/1949.

RAHNUMA, ZAYN AL-'ABIDIN. *Payambar.* English translation by L. Ellwell-Sutton. Tehran: Gulshan, 1964.

RA'IN, ISMA'IL. *Huquq-bigiran-i inglis dar Iran.* Tehran: Javidan, 1346/1967.

RAWDATI, SAYYID MUHAMMAD-'ALI. *Zindagani-i Hadrat-i Ayatullah Chaharsuqi.* Isfahan: Ha'ida, 1332/1953.

RAZI, SHAYKH MUHAMMAD. *Athar al-hujja.* Qum: Hikmat, 1332/1953.

_____. *Ganjina-i danishmandan.* 5 volumes. Qum: Piruz. 1352-1353/1973-1974.

_____. *Fasl-i az zindagi-i pishva-yi ruhani Hadrat-i Ayatullah Kashani.* N.d.

SADIQI-GULDAR, AHMAD. *Nama-i sargushada bi hawza-i 'ilmiyya-i Qum va Sanandaj.* 1353/1974.

SADR, MUHAMMAD-BAQIR. *Iqtisad-i ma.* Baghdad: 1381/1961.

SAHIB AL-ZAMANI, NASIR AL-DIN. *Dibacha-i bar rahbari.* Tehran: 'Ata'i, 1347/1968.

SAZMAN-I AWQAF. *Karnama-i hajj, 1352.* Tehran: Sazman-i Awqaf, 1343/1974.

SHARI'ATI, 'ALI. *Islamshinasi.* Mashhad: Tus, 1347/1968.

_____. *Hajj.* Tehran: Husayniyya-i Irshad, 1350/1971.

_____. *Intizar.* Tehran: Husayniyya-i Irshad, 1350/1971.

_____. *Farhang va ideolozhi.* Tehran: Husayniyya-i Irshad, 1350/1971.

_____. *Az kuja aghaz-kunim?* Tehran: Husayniyya-i Irshad, n.d.

_____. *Are, inchunin bud, baradar.* 1391Q/1971.

_____. *Ummat va imamat.* Tehran: Husayniyya-i Irshad, 1351/1971.

SHARI'ATMADARI, SAYYID MUHAMMAD-KAZIM. *Risala-i tawdih al-masa'il.* Qum: 1353/1974.

SHIRAZI, SAYYID MUHAMMAD. *Naqsh-i ruhaniyyat dar sarnivisht-i mardum.* Qum: Qur'an, 1351/1972.

SHIRAZI, SAYYID SADIQ. *Rah-i bi-su-yi bank-i islami.* Translated from the Arabic by 'Ali Kazimi. Qum: Mihr-Ustuvar, 1393Q/1973.

SHUSHTARI, QADI NURULLAH. *Majalis al-mu'minin.* Hajji Ibrahim Basimchi Tabrizi, n.d.

TABATABA'I, SAYYID HUSAYN MUDARRISI. *Qum dar qarn-i nuhum-i hijri.* Qum: Hikmat, 1350/1971.

TABATABA'I, SAYYID MUHAMMAD-HUSAYN. Zan dar islam. *Maktab-i Tashayyu',* 1338/1959.

_____. Ijtihad va taqlid dar islam va shi'a. In Tabataba'i et al. 1341/1962.

_____. Valayat va za'amat. In Tabataba'i et al. 1341/1962.

_____. *Qur'an dar islam.* Tehran: Islamiyya.

TABATABA'I, S. MUHAMMAD-HUSAYN, et al. *Bahth-i darbara marja'iyyat va ruhaniyyat.* Tehran: Intishar, 1341/1962.

TABATABA'I, SAYYID MUHAMMAD-HUSAYN ALAVI. *Khatirat-i zindagani-i Hadrat-i Ayatullah 'Uthman Aqa-yi Burujirdi.* Tehran: Intisharat va Ittihad, 1341/1962.

TALIQANI, SAYYID MAHMUD. Malikiyyat dar islam. *Guftar-i mah* 1 (1340/1961).

_____. Tamarkuz va 'adam-i tamarkuz-i marja'iyyat va fatva. In Tabataba'i et al. 1341/1962.

_____. *Islam va malikiyyat.* Tehran: Intishar, 1344/1965.

VUSHNU'I, SHAYKH QAVAM. *Hijab dar islam.* Qum: Hikmat, 1392/1972.

ZIAI, SAYYID REZA [RIDA DIYA'I]. *Ikhtilaf-i fatva az chist?* Qum: Mihr-Ustuvar, n.d.

ZANJANI, SAYYID ABU'L-FADL MUSAVI. Sharayit va vazayif-i marja'. In Tabataba'i et al. 1341/1962.

European Language Sources.

(For English translations both original date and date of translation are given.)

ABBOTT, NABIA. *Studies in Arabic literary papyri.* 2 vols. to date. University of Chicago Oriental Institute Publications, vols. 75, 76. Chicago: University of Chicago Press, 1957-1967.

ABRAHAMIAN, ERVAND. The social bases of Iranian politics: the Tudeh party, 1941-53. Ph.D. dissertation, Columbia University, 1969.

_____. Iran: the political challenge. *Middle East Research and Information Reports,* No. 69. 1979.

_____. Iran in Revolution: the opposition forces. *Middle East Research and Information Reports,* No. 75/76. 1979.

AHMED, MUNIR-UD-DIN. *Muslim education and the scholar's social status up to the fifth century Muslim Era (eleventh century Christian Era) in the light of Ta'rikh Baghdad.* Zurich: Der Islam Verlag, 1968.

AKHAVI, SHAHROUGH. *The relationship between religion and state in Iran under the Pahlavi dynasty.* Binghamton: State University of New York Press, 1980.

ALGAR, HAMID. *Religion and state in Iran, 1785-1906.* Berkeley: University of California Press, 1969.

_____. The oppositional role of the ulema in twentieth-century Iran. In N. R. Keddie, ed., *Scholars, saints and sufis.* Berkeley: University of California Press, 1972.

ARBERRY, A. J. *Revelation and reason in Islam.* London: George Allen and Unwin, 1957.

ARJOMAND, SAID AMIR. Religion, political action and legitimate domination in Shi'i Iran: 14th to 18th centuries A.D. Master's thesis, University of Chicago, 1976.

ASGHAR, JALAL. A historical study of the origins of the Persian passion plays. Ph.D. dissertation, University of Southern California, 1963.

ASHRAF, AHMAD. Iran: imperialism, class and modernization from above. Ph.D. dissertation, New School for Social Research, 1971.

AVI-YONAH, M. The facade of Herod's Temple. In J. Neusner, ed., *Religions in antiquity.* Leiden: E. J. Brill, 1968.

BANANI, AMIN. *The modernization of Iran, 1921-1941.* Palo Alto, Calif.: Stanford University Press, 1961.

BATESON, M. C., J. W. CLINTON, J. B. M. KASSARJIAN, H. SAFAVI, AND M. SORAYA. Safa-yi Batin: a study of the interrelations of a set of Iranian ideal character types. In L. C. Brown and N. Itzkowitz, eds., *Psychological dimensions of Near Eastern studies.* Princeton, N.J.: Darwin Press, 1977.

BAUSANI, A. Religion in the Seljuk period. Religion under the Mongols. In J. A. Boyle, ed., *The Cambridge history of Iran.* vol. 5. Cambridge, England: Cambridge Press, 1968.

BAYNE, E. A. Iran. In *Four ways of politics.* New York: American Universities Field Staff, 1965.

_____. *Persian kingship in transition.* New York: American Universities Field Staff, 1968.

BEEMAN, WILLIAM O. The meaning of stylistic variation in Iranian verbal interaction. Ph.D. dissertation, University of Chicago, 1976.

BELLAH, ROBERT. Civil Religion in America. In *Daedalus* 1967.

BILL, JAMES A. *The politics of Iran.* Columbus: Merrill, 1972.

_____. The patterns of elite politics in Iran. In G. Lenczowski, ed., *Political elites in the Middle East.* Washington, D.C.: American Enterprise Institute for Public Policy Research, 1975.

BINDER, LEONARD. *Iran: political development in a changing society.* Berkeley: University of California Press, 1962.

_____. The proofs of Islam: religion and politics in Iran. *Arabic and Islamic studies in honor of Hamilton A. R. Gibb.* Leiden: E. J. Brill, 1966.

BOURDIEU, PIERRE. *An outline of a theory of practice.* 1972. Cambridge, England: Cambridge University Press, 1977.

BOYCE, MARY. *A Persian stronghold of Zoroastrianism.* Oxford: Clarendon Press, 1977.

BRINTON, CRANE. *Anatomy of Revolution.* New York: Random House, 1938.

BROWNE, E. G. *The Persian revolution 1905-1909.* Cambridge, England: Cambridge University Press, 1910.

————. *A literary history of Persia.* 4 vols. London: T. F. Unwin, 1902-1924.

BULLIET, RICHARD. *The patricians of Nishapur.* Cambridge, Mass.: Harvard University Press, 1972.

COTTAM, RICHARD. *Nationalism in Iran.* Pittsburgh: University of Pittsburgh Press, 1964.

DEANSLEY, MARGARET. *The pre-conquest Church in England.* London: Black, 1961.

DERRIDA, JACQUES. *Of grammatology.* 1967. Translated by G. C. Spivak. Baltimore: The Johns Hopkins University Press, 1976.

DRAZIN, NATHAN. *History of Jewish education from 515 B.C.E. to 220 C.E.* Baltimore: The Johns Hopkins University Press, 1940.

EICHER, C., A. LEWIS, A. MORTON, AND M. ZONIS. *An analysis of U. S. - Iranian cooperation in higher education.* Washington, D.C.: American Council on Education, 1976.

EICKELMAN, DALE. The art of memory: Islamic education and its social reproduction. *Comparative Studies in Society and History* 20, no. 4 (1978):485-516.

ELIADE, MIRCEA. *The quest: history and meaning in religion.* Chicago: University of Chicago Press, 1969.

ELIASH, JOSEPH. The ithna'ashari juristic theory of political and legal authority. *Studia Islamica* 29 (1969):17-30.

FERDOWS, ADELE KAZEMI. Religion in Iranian nationalism: Fedayani Islam. Ph.D. dissertation, University of Indiana, 1967.

FISCHEL, HENRY A. Israel in Iran. In L. Finkelstein, ed., *The Jews.* New York: The Jewish Publication Society, 1960.

————. Studies in cynicism and the ancient Near East: the transformation of a chria. In J. Neusner, ed., *Religions in antiquity.* Leiden: E. J. Brill, 1968.

FISCHER, MICHAEL M. J. Zoroastrian Iran between myth and praxis. Ph.D. dissertation, University of Chicago, 1973.

————. Review of Eckhart Ehlers and Grace Goodell, *Traditionelle und moderne Formen der Landwirtschaft in Iran,* Marburger geographische Schriften vol. 64 (1975). *Iranian Studies* 9, no. 4 (1976):288-294.

————. Persian society: transition and strain. In H. Amirsadeghi and R. W. Ferrier, eds., *Twentieth century Iran.* London: Heinemann, 1977.

————. Interpretive anthropology. *Reviews in Anthropology* 4, no. 4 (1977b): 391-404.

————. On changing the concept and position of Persian women. In L. Beck and N. R. Keddie, eds., *Women in the Muslim World.* Cambridge, Mass.: Harvard University Press, 1978.

————. Protest and revolution in Iran. *Harvard International Review* 1, no. 2 (1979):1-6.

————. Iran and Islamic Justice. *Middle East Executive Reports.* January 1980.

————. Portrait of a Mulla: The Autobiography and Bildungsroman of Aqa Najafi Quchani. In press.

FOUCAULT, MICHEL. *Archeology of knowledge.* New York: Harper and Row, 1972.

GAMORAN, EMANUEL. *Changing conceptions in Jewish education.* New York: Macmillan, 1925.

GAROUSSIAN, VIDA. The ulama and secularization in contemporary Iran. Ph.D. dissertation, Southern Illinois University, 1974.

GEERTZ, CLIFFORD. *The interpretation of cultures.* New York: Basic Books, 1973.

GIBB, H. A. R. *Studies on the civilization of Islam.* Boston: Beacon Press, 1962.

_____, AND J. H. KRAMERS. *Shorter encyclopedia of Islam.* Leiden: E. J. Brill, 1961.

GIFFEN, LOIS A. *Theory of profane love among the Arabs.* New York: New York University Press, 1971.

GOITEIN, SHLOMO DOV. *A Mediterranean society.* Berkeley: University of California Press, 1971.

GOLDIN, JUDEH. The third chapter of 'Abot De-Rabbi Natan. *Harvard Theological Review* 58, no. 4 (1965): 365-386.

GOLDZIHER, IGNAZ. *Muslim Studies.* vol. 2. 1890. Translated by C. M. Barber and S. M. Stern. London: Allen and Unwin, 1971.

GOOD, MARY-JO DELVECCHIO. Social hierarchy and social change in a provincial Iranian town. Ph.D. dissertation, Harvard University, 1977.

GOODELL, GRACE. The elementary structures of political life. Ph.D. dissertation, Columbia University, 1977.

GRADE, CHAIM. *The yeshiva.* 1967. Translated by Curt Leviant. New York: Bobbs-Merrill, 1976.

GRAHAM, ROBERT. *Iran: the illusion of power.* London: Croom Helm, 1978.

HABERMAS, JURGEN. Communicative action. Lecture, Boston University Philosophy of Science Colloquium Series, December 1976.

HAILPERIN, HERMAN. *Rashi and the Christian scholars.* Pittsburgh: Pittsburgh University Press, 1963.

HA'IRI, ABDUL HADI. Shi'ism and constitutionalism: a study of the life and views of Mirza Muhammad Husayn Na'ini, a Shi'i mujtehed of Iran. Ph.D. dissertation, McGill University, 1973.

HALLIDAY, FRED. *Iran: dictatorship and development.* London: Penguin, 1979.

HALPERN, ISRAEL. The Jews in Eastern Europe. In L. Finkelstein, ed. *The Jews.* New York: The Jewish Publication Society, 1960.

HASKINS, CHARLES HOMER. *Studies in medieval culture.* New York: Frederick Ungar, 1929.

HO, PING-TI. *The ladder of success in imperial China.* New York: Columbia University Press, 1962.

HODGSON, MARSHALL. How did the early Shi'a become sectarian? *Journal of the American Oriental Society* 75, no. 1 (1955).

_____. *The venture of Islam.* Chicago: University of Chicago Press, 1974.

HOUSEGO, DAVID. A Survey of Iran. *The Economist.* 28 August 1976.

JAEGER, WERNER. *Paideia: the ideals of Greek culture.* Oxford: Oxford University Press, 1939.

KEDDIE, N. R. Religion and irreligion in early Iranian nationalism. *Comparative Studies in History and Society* 4, no. 3 (1962):265-295.

_____. Symbol and sincerity in Islam. *Studia Islamica* 19 (1963):27-64.

_____. *Religion and rebellion in Iran: the tobacco protest of 1891-1892.* London: Frank Cass, 1966a.

_____. The origins of the religious-radical alliance in Iran. *Past and Present* 34 (1966b): 70-80.

_____. The roots of the ulama's power in modern Iran. *Studia Islamica* 29 (1969): 31-53.

———. *Scholars, saints and sufis.* Berkeley: University of California Press, 1972.

LAMBTON, A. K. S. Secret societies and the Persian revolution of 1905-1906. *St. Anthony's Papers* 4 (1958):43-60.

———. Quis custodiet custodes: some reflections on the Persian theory of government. *Studia Islamica* 5 (1955):125-148; 6 (1956):125-146.

———. Justice in the medieval Persian theory of kingship. *Studia Islamica* 17 (1962):91-120.

———. A reconsideration of the position of the marja' taqlid and the religious institution. *Studia Islamica* 20 (1964):115-135.

———. The tobacco regie: prelude to revolution. *Studia Islamica* 22 (1965): 119-157; 23 (1965): 71-91.

———. Some new trends in Islamic political thought in late 18th and early 19th century Persia. *Studia Islamica* 39 (1974): 95-128.

LASSY, IVAR. *The Muharram mysteries among the Azarbaijan Turks of Caucasia.* Helsinfors: Lilius and Hertzberg, 1916.

LAURIE, S. S. *Studies in the history of educational opinion from the Renaissance.* 1903. Reprint, New York: Agustus M. Kelley, 1969.

LITTLE, A. G. Scholastic philosophy and universities. In Arthur Tilley, ed., *Medieval France.* New York: Harper and Row, 1922.

McKEON, RICHARD. The organization of sciences and the relations of cultures in the twelfth and thirteenth centuries. In J. E. Mardoch and E. D. Sylla, eds., *The cultural context of medieval learning.* Boston Studies in the Philosophy of Science 26, 1975.

McLACHLAN, KEITH S. The Iranian economy 1960-1976. In H. Amirsadeghi and R. W. Ferrier, eds., *Twentieth century Iran.* London: Heinemann, 1977.

MANTEL, HUGO. *Studies in the history of the sanhedrin.* Cambridge, Mass.: Harvard University Press, 1961.

MARROU, H. *A history of education in antiquity.* 1948. Reprint, London: Sheed and Ward, 1956.

MASSIGNON, LOUIS. *Salman Pak and the spiritual beginnings of Iranian Islam.* Translated by J. M. Unvala. Bombay, 1955.

MAZZAOUI, MICHEL. Shiism and the rise of the Safavids. Ph.D. dissertation, Princeton University, 1966.

MENES, ABRAHAM. Patterns of Jewish scholarship in eastern Europe. In L. Finklestein, ed., *The Jews.* New York: The Jewish Publication Society, 1960.

MILANI, S. MUHAMMAD REZA. *General Aspects of Prayer.* Abridgment of *Risala-i tawdih al-masa'il.* Translated by Abul Qassem Tahiri. Mimeographed. Mashhad, 1968.

MILLS, C. W. *Sociology and pragmatism: the higher learning in America.* New York: Oxford University Press, 1966.

MILLWARD, WILLIAM G. Aspects of modernism in Shi'a Islam. *Studia Islamica* 37 (1973):111-128.

MINISTRY OF SCIENCE AND HIGHER EDUCATION, IRAN. The system of higher education in Iran. Mimeographed. Tehran, 1973.

———. Statistics of higher education in Iran. Mimeographed. Tehran, 1973.

NAKOSTEEN, MEHDI. *History of Islamic origins of Western education, A.D. 800-1350.* Boulder: University of Colorado Press, 1964.

NASR, S. HOSEYN. *Three Muslim sages.* Cambridge, Mass.: Harvard University Press, 1964a.

_____. *An introduction to Islamic cosmological doctrines.* Cambridge, Mass.: Harvard University Press, 1964b.

_____. *Ideals and realities of Islam.* London: Allen and Unwin, 1966.

_____. *Islamic studies.* Beirut: Librairie du Liban, 1967a.

_____. The Sufi master as exemplified in Persian Sufi literature. In *Iran,* 1967b.

_____. Man in the universe: permanence amid apparent change. *Studies in comparative religion* 2, no. 4 (1968a): 35-40.

_____. Revelation, intellect and reason in the Qur'an. *Journal of the Regional Cultural Institute* 1, no. 3 (1968b): 60-64.

_____. *The encounter of man and nature.* London: Allen and Unwin, 1968c.

_____. *Science and civilization in Islam.* Cambridge, Mass.: Harvard University Press, 1968d.

_____. *Sufi essays.* Albany: State University of New York Press, 1972.

_____. Preface to S. Mohammad Hussein Tabataba'i, *Shiite Islam,* 1975a.

_____. *Islam and the plight of modern man.* New York: Longmans, Green, 1975b.

NEEDHAM, J. *Science and civilization in China.* vol. 2. Cambridge, England: Cambridge University Press, 1956.

NEUSNER, JACOB. Rabbis and community in third century Babylonia. In J. Neusner, ed., *Religions in antiquity.* Leiden: E. J. Brill, 1968.

_____. *A history of the Jews in Babylonia.* 5 vols. Leiden: E. J. Brill, 1965-1970.

PELLY, LEWIS. *The miracle plays of Hasan and Husain.* London: W. H. Alden, 1879.

PHILLIPS, JOHN. *The reformation of images: destruction of art in England, 1535-1660.* Berkeley: University of California Press, 1973.

POOYA, MEHDI. *Genuineness of the holy Quran in its text and its arrangement.* Karachi: Pakistan Herald Press, 1971.

_____. *Fundamentals of Islam.* Karachi: Pakistan Herald Press, 1972.

QIBLA, MUFTI JAFAR HUSAIN SAHIB. *Nahj ul-Balagha.* Karachi, 1972.

QURESHI, ANWAR IQBAL. *Islam and the theory of interest.* Lahore: Sh. Mohammad Ashraf, 1946.

RAHMAN, FAZLUR. Reba and interest. *Islamic Studies* 3, no. 1 (1964):1-43.

_____. *Islamic methodology in history.* Karachi: Central Institute of Islamic Research, 1965.

_____. Islam and the problem of economic justice. *Pakistan Economist,* 1974.

RAMSEY, IAN. Hell. In *Talk of God,* Royal Institute of Philosophy Lectures, vol. 2. New York: St. Martins, 1969.

RASHDALL, HASTINGS. *The universities of Europe in the middle ages.* Oxford: Oxford University Press, 1895.

RINGER, FRITZ. *The decline of the German mandarins: the German academic community 1890-1933.* Cambridge, Mass.: Harvard University Press, 1969.

RODERICK, G., AND STEPHENS, M. *Scientific and technical education in 19th century England.* New York: Barnes and Noble, 1972.

ROSENTHAL, FRANZ. The technique and approach of Muslim scholarship. *Analecta Orientalia,* vol. 24. Rome: Pontificium Institutum Biblicum, 1947.

ROYAL INSTITUTE OF PHILOSOPHY. *Talk of God.* London: Macmillan, 1969.

SARRAF, TAHMOORES. The effectiveness of patrimonial rule as a means to modernization: a study of contemporary Iran. Ph.D. dissertation, University of Washington, 1972.

SCHACHT, J. *Origins of Muhammadan jurisprudence.* Oxford: Oxford University Press, 1950.

SCHIMMEL, ANNEMARIE. *Mystical dimensions of Islam.* Chapel Hill: University of North Carolina Press, 1975.

SEZGIN, FUAD. *Geschichte des arabischen Schrifttums.* vol. 1: Qur'anwissenschaften, Hadit, Geschichte, Fiqh, Dogmatik, Mystik bis ca. 430 H. Leiden: E. J. Brill, 1967.

SHABAN, M. *The Abbasid revolution.* Cambridge, England: Cambridge University Press, 1970.

SHERIFF, A. H. *Music and its effects.* Mombassa, Kenya: Rodwell Press, 1974.

SMALLEY, BERYL. *The study of the Bible in the middle ages.* Notre Dame, Ind.: University of Notre Dame Press, 1964.

STAHMER, HAROLD. *Speak that I may see thee: the religious significance of language.* New York: Macmillan, 1968.

STEINSALTZ, ADIN. *The essential Talmud.* New York: Basic Books, 1976.

STROTHMAN, R. Shi'a. In H. A. R. Gibb and J. H. Kramers, eds., *Shorter Encyclopedia of Islam.* Ithaca, N.Y.: Cornell University Press, 1953.

TABATABA'I, S. MOHAMMAD HUSSEIN. *Shi'ite Islam.* Albany, N.Y.: State University of New York Press, 1975.

TAMBIAH, S. J. *World conqueror and world renouncer.* Cambridge, England: Cambridge University Press, 1976.

AL-TAMIMI, AL-QADI AL-NU'MAN B. MUHAMMAD. *The Book of Faith.* From the *Da'a'im al-Islam* (Pillars of Islam), c. 970 A.D. Translated by Asaf A. A. Fyzee. Bombay: Nachiketa Publications, 1974.

THAISS, GUSTAV. The drama of Husain. Ph.D. dissertation, University of Washington (St. Louis), 1973.

ULICH, ROBERT. *A history of religious education.* New York: New York University Press, 1968.

UNDERWOOD, JAMES. Hussein Nasr's Sermon. *Kayhan International,* 29 April 1970a.

————. Qum. Kayhan International, 16 May 1970b.

VAN ESS, JOSEPH. The beginnings of Islamic theology. In J. E. Mardoch and E. D. Sylla, eds., *The cultural context of medieval learning.* Boston Studies in the Philosophy of Science 26, 1975.

WENZEL, SIEGFRIED. Vices, virtues and popular preaching. In D. Randall, ed., *Medieval and Renaissance Studies.* Durham, N.C.: Duke University Press, 1976.

WILKINSON, RUPERT H. Education as the servant of government: Victorian public schools compared with Confucian education and the Chinese examination system. Master's thesis, Harvard University, 1961.

WOLFSON, HARRY A. *The philosophy of the kalam.* Cambridge, Mass.: Harvard University Press, 1976.

YUSUF, S. M. *Economic justice in Islam.* Lahore: Shaykh Mohammad Ashraf, 1971.

DE ZAYAS, FARISHTA G. *The law and philosophy of Zakat.* Damascus: Al-Jadidah Printing Press, 1960.

ZIA'I, M. et al. Medical education at Teheran University. *Pahlavi Medical Journal* 7, no. 4 (1976): 546-549.

ZONIS, MARVIN. *The political elite of Iran.* Princeton, N.J.: Princeton University Press, 1971a.

_____. Higher education and social change: problems and prospects in Iran. In E. Yar-Shater, ed., *Iran faces the seventies.* New York: Praeger, 1971b.

_____. The political elite of Iran: a second stratum? In F. Tachau, ed., *Political elites and political development in the Middle East.* New York: Schenkman, 1975.

Index

305